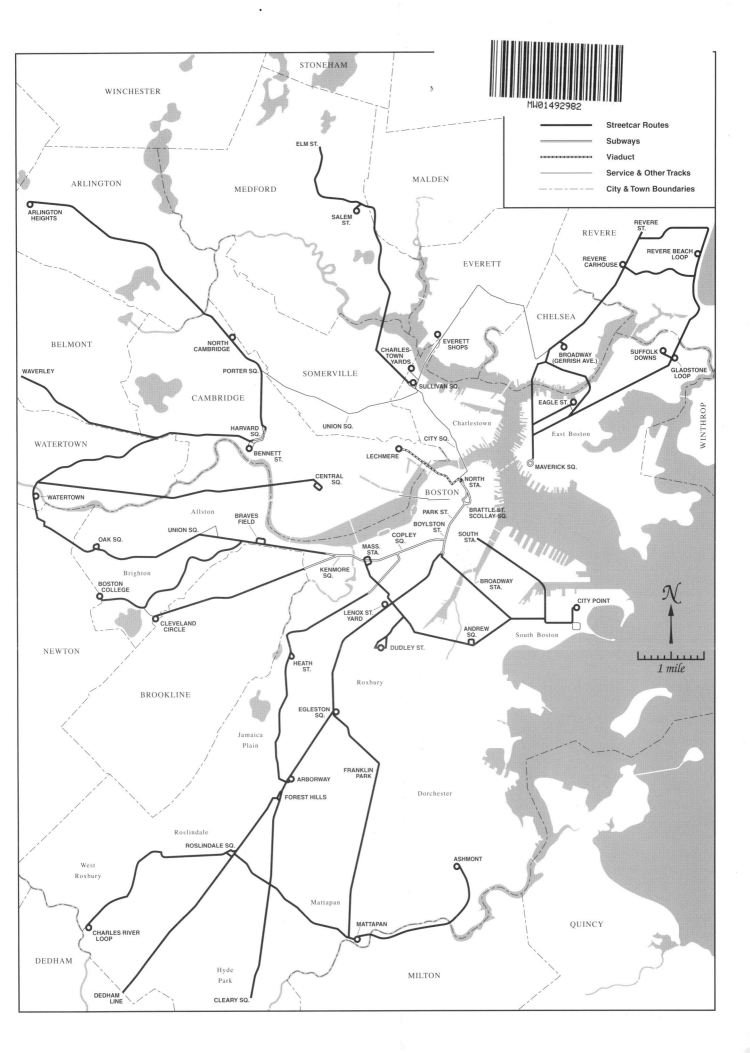

STONEHAM

WINCHESTER

ARLINGTON

MEDFORD

MALDEN

REVERE

REVERE ST.

REVERE BEACH LOOP

ELM ST.

SALEM ST.

EVERETT

CHELSEA

ARLINGTON HEIGHTS

BELMONT

NORTH CAMBRIDGE

SOMERVILLE

EVERETT SHOPS

REVERE CARHOUSE

BROADWAY (GERRISH AVE.)

SUFFOLK DOWNS

WAVERLEY

PORTER SQ.

CHARLES-TOWN YARDS

GLADSTONE LOOP

CAMBRIDGE

UNION SQ.

SULLIVAN SQ.

EAGLE ST.

WINTHROP

WATERTOWN

HARVARD SQ.

CITY SQ.

Charlestown

East Boston

BENNETT ST.

LECHMERE

MAVERICK SQ.

CENTRAL SQ.

NORTH STA.

Allston

BRAVES FIELD

BOSTON

BRATTLE ST. SCOLLAY SQ.

WATERTOWN

UNION SQ.

PARK ST.

OAK SQ.

KENMORE SQ.

BOYLSTON ST.

COPLEY SQ.

SOUTH STA.

Brighton

MASS. STA.

BOSTON COLLEGE

BROADWAY STA.

CITY POINT

CLEVELAND CIRCLE

LENOX ST. YARD

ANDREW SQ.

South Boston

NEWTON

HEATH ST.

DUDLEY ST.

N

BROOKLINE

Roxbury

Jamaica Plain

EGLESTON SQ.

1 mile

FRANKLIN PARK

ARBORWAY

Dorchester

FOREST HILLS

Roslindale

ROSLINDALE SQ.

ASHMONT

West Roxbury

Mattapan

CHARLES RIVER LOOP

MATTAPAN

QUINCY

DEDHAM

Hyde Park

DEDHAM LINE

CLEARY SQ.

MILTON

MW01492982

	Streetcar Routes
	Subways
	Viaduct
	Service & Other Tracks
	City & Town Boundaries

Streetcar Lines of the Hub

The 1940s
Heyday of Electric Transit in Boston

Afternoon rush hour riders enjoy a breezy trip on the Harvard Bridge across the Charles River late in the summer of 1949. Metropolitan Transit Authority 5572 is making its way from Massachusetts Station in the Back Bay to Harvard Square in Cambridge against the backdrop of a skyline that has since changed dramatically. The only recognizable commercial buildings today are the gilded top of the tower of The New England Mutual Life Insurance Company and the second of the three John Hancock Insurance Company buildings, Boston's first true skyscraper. Reconstruction of the bridge in November would bring streetcar service to an end on this line, and the trolleys would be no more.

Leon Onofri

Streetcar Lines
of the Hub

The 1940s
Heyday of Electric Transit in Boston

by
Bradley H. Clarke

Bulletin Number 23

Boston, Massachusetts
Boston Street Railway Association
2003

First Edition

Published by:

Boston Street Railway Association, Inc.
Post Office Box 181037
Boston, Massachusetts 02118-1037

Printed in the United States of America

Cartography by Charles Bahne

Layout and Design by Stephen P. Carlson

Printed by LPI Printing & Graphics, Inc.

ISBN 0-938315-05-6

Table of Contents

Routes

Eastern Mass. Routes

Foreword

The 1940s strongly challenged the Boston Elevated Railway Company[a]. Ridership, which had been slowly declining for a long time, began growing rapidly, and the El was suddenly confronted with legions of workers going to and from their wartime jobs. Providing reliable public transportation became very difficult as the war continued, with ridership steadily increasing in the face of gasoline, tire, and commodity rationing.

At the end of the conflict, many commuters returned to their cars. The Boston Elevated infrastructure, which was in good condition in 1940, was worn out by 1945. Reinvestment capital was needed to revitalize the system. The political will to spend the money was there, but the public wanted more control over the process. In 1947 the state-owned Metropolitan Transit Authority replaced the privately owned but publicly controlled Boston Elevated Railway.[b]

In 1940 the Boston Elevated operated 45.4 million revenue miles. Surface streetcars contributed 45 percent of this total, buses added 26 percent, trackless trolleys another 5 percent, and rapid transit lines a final 24 percent.[1] So, in 1940, the dominant transit mode in Boston was still the streetcar. And while approximately 60 streetcar lines in whole or in part, many of them money losers, had been converted from streetcar to bus or trackless trolley between 1922 and 1940, 52 heavy streetcar lines remained, and they would save the day.[c] During World War II and in 1946, the immediate postwar year, ridership would achieve levels never before attained and strain the capacity of the system. The viability of the trolley would be reaffirmed one last time—the 1940s would be the heyday of electric transit in Boston.

The focus of this book is the Metropolitan Boston streetcar system of the 1940s, including the streetcar operations of the Boston Elevated Railway, its successor, the Metropolitan Transit Authority, and the remaining rail operations of the Eastern Massachusetts Street Railway Company to Stoneham and Quincy.[d] An overview is also presented of the rail transit infrastructure and the people and policies that ran the system and made it change.

The contribution of the rapid transit lines, 24 percent of the 1940 revenue miles, was considerable yet lower in mileage than that accumulated by the streetcar lines. It is important to realize, however, that the streetcar lines were arranged system-wide to act as feeders to the rapid transit system. Car lines usually ran to rapid transit stations, and passengers transferred to rapid transit trains for the final leg of their trips into or through downtown Boston.

The rapid transit lines were the heart of the rail network of the Boston Elevated Railway. These routes included the Cambridge–Dorchester Line, which ran between Harvard Square and Ashmont; the Main Line Elevated between Everett and Forest Hills; and the East Boston Tunnel Line, which connected Maverick Square with Bowdoin Square. These heavy routes were built between 1900 and 1927 and essentially eliminated cross-town streetcar operations. The rapid transit lines have a rich and varied history, much of which has been documented in other publications. For this reason, references to the rapid transit lines in this book are incidental and are only included in the light of their effect on streetcar operations.

This book is not a history of streetcar rolling stock. Noted transit historian O.R. Cummings has fully documented Boston's pre-PCC streetcars, and I have made frequent references to his six-volume series, *Street Cars of Boston*, the definitive work on the subject. *PCC Cars of Boston*, by Edward A. Anderson, and *PCC From Coast to Coast*, by Fred W. Schneider III and Stephen P. Carlson, cover Boston PCC cars thoroughly. The reader is advised to consult these sources for detailed information.

---

[a] The terms "El," "Elevated," "Boston Elevated," "BERy," and "the railway," will be used interchangeably with "Boston Elevated Railway Company" throughout this book. The name "Boston Elevated" may seem to some readers a peculiar one for an operator of so many surface lines, but it is deeply rooted in Boston transit history. In 1897, the Boston Elevated Railway leased the West End Street Railway, which in turn had signed a twenty-year lease in 1896 for the use of the soon to be opened Tremont Street Subway. The Boston Elevated wanted to run its elevated main line through the Tremont Street Subway in the downtown area. However, leasing the West End also meant running the enormous network of surface lines that the West End operated. Thus, the Boston Elevated ended up with a surface streetcar network. The Boston Elevated, by virtue of its lease of the West End, was running streetcars well before its namesake elevated railway opened in 1901!

[b] The Metropolitan Transit Authority is also referred to in this book as the "MTA" and the "Authority."

[c] See Appendix 9, Weekday Streetcar Line Service Levels & Statistics, Selected Rating Dates, for a complete listing of these lines of the Boston Elevated. Four more lines of the Eastern Massachusetts Street Railway Company are covered in Appendix 9A.

---

[d] The company is also referred to in this book as the "Eastern Mass." and "EMSR."

I have not attempted to discuss bus or trackless trolley operations in detail. These topics are covered in those instances where a direct relationship existed with streetcar operations, such as a line conversion or supplementary service. I have covered trackless trolley operations in a prior work, *The Trackless Trolleys of Boston*.

The organization of the book is straightforward. Chapter 1 provides background and overview. It focuses on events that affected the entire system or large segments of it. The remaining chapters cover the surface streetcar network geographically. Starting with Chapter 2 on the South Boston lines, the chapter topics move clockwise around Boston Proper ending in East Boston. My intent is to discuss related lines and groups of lines and to provide the reader with a local base of reference.

Route descriptions of each streetcar line have been given throughout this book. A track map at the start of each chapter enhances these descriptions. Except where noted, both the route descriptions and the track maps present the system as it was in 1940. Subsequent changes are included in the written descriptions and in some cases where space permits, on the maps themselves as insets. The reader is advised to refer to the track maps when reading the route descriptions because the routes were often complex.

It is important to read the *Legend For All Maps* on Map 1 for a complete understanding of the symbols used on the maps. Municipal boundaries have been shown on the maps including district and neighborhood boundaries within the City of Boston. These boundaries are subject to interpretation and should be considered approximate. Allston, Back Bay, Jamaica Plain, Roslindale, Mattapan, and the South End are generally recognized Boston neighborhoods, while Boston Proper, Brighton, Charlestown, East Boston, Dorchester, Roxbury, South Boston, and West Roxbury are officially designated districts.

In addition, many carhouse, yard and loop descriptions have been supplemented with detailed diagrams placed nearby. Reviewing these diagrams in conjunction with reading the descriptions will clarify many complicated details. The end papers of this book contain maps of the active system tracks in 1940 and 1950. Comparison of these maps yields a good overview of the changes during the decade. Finally, Chapter 1 contains diagrams of the Night or Owl Service operated in 1940 and at the end of 1949, again providing useful comparative information.

I grew up in Arlington, Massachusetts, a Boston suburb, and by the early 1950s I had acquired a strong interest in the remaining streetcar lines in the Boston area. While making trips on the streetcar, bus, and trackless trolley lines of the M.T.A., a question often occurred to me when I saw a solitary line pole, a section of abandoned track, or a rail segment showing through the pavement: "What was here before?" This book answers the question. More importantly, though, the lines themselves are discussed in detail. An in-depth review of individual Boston streetcar lines has not previously been attempted; this analysis is the true purpose of this book.

To effectively document the history of street railways in Boston, I feel that there are three viable models. The first approach is to write an all-time history, covering the development of the entire system from horsecar to the Light Rail Vehicle (LRV) of today. A second technique is to cover the system by discussing individual geographical segments, such as South Boston, again from horsecar to LRV. A third way is to cover the entire system in a specific slice of time-an era.

I have selected the third method as the approach for this book. The decade of the 1940s is a period that many remember, or with which they would like to have had a greater familiarity. Furthermore, as a basis for a history of the surface streetcar lines of Boston, the 1940s are an ideal time to start. Much of the trackage operated at the maximum extent of the system remained in place, and locking in the available information on this period has produced a baseline for future efforts.

I have made every effort to ensure accuracy in this book. Much of the information has come from a historical database that I have assembled over the last forty years. Other sources are directly cited. Reader comments are always appreciated and should be forwarded to me in care of the Boston Street Railway Association.

Footnotes, using letters of the alphabet, are found throughout the book for information directly relevant to the text. Endnotes, which are numbered, are mainly used for reference citations or for items of interest, but which are usually of incidental importance.

The photographs used in this book come from a variety of sources. Except as otherwise noted, however, most of the photographs have come from the author's collection. A number of photographs were originally taken by the Boston Elevated Railway or by the MTA and are credited accordingly, regardless of the source of the particular print used. Other photos are credited to the photographer when known. This is not an easy task, since railfans have always conducted a trade in pictures, often, unfortunately, not noting the original source. Errors in attribution, therefore, may be present, and I offer in advance my sincere apologies where this is the case.

While all of the photographs featured in this book make substantial contributions to the historical record, among the most noteworthy are photos and collections from several Massachusetts fans that are now deceased. They were Charles A. Brown of Sutton, Norton D. "Skip" Clark of Newton, Charles A. Duncan of Danvers, Stanley M. Hauck of Quincy, Foster M. Palmer of Watertown, and Richard L. Wonson of Fall River. The photographs taken by these pioneers are credited to them, again, regardless of the source.

Charlie Brown, originally of Milton, Massachusetts, worked for the Baldwin Locomotive Works of Eddystone, Pennsylvania. He went on to work for Fairbanks-Morse. Charlie Brown took many high-quality photos of the Boston and Philadelphia transit systems over the years, and was one of the founders of the Seashore Trolley Museum.

Norton D. "Skip" Clark was an avid photographer of railroads and trolleys. He had a life-long interest in the Middlesex & Boston Street Railway, an extensive suburban system to the west and north of Boston. His collection of railroad and trolley photos from eastern Massachusetts, especially in and around Boston, was excellent. "Skip" made the local paper on April 2, 1950, when his hobby interests were featured in the *Boston Sunday Globe* Pictorial Section.

Charlie Duncan was a true visionary, recognizing before most fans of his time that the operation of streetcars on city streets would end before long. As a freight solicitor for the Texas Car Package Company, he traveled all over New England from the mid-1930s to the early 1950s shooting scenes that no one else recorded. His black and white and color photography of the Boston Elevated was probably the most extensive coverage ever attempted by anyone outside the company itself, providing a superb record for future historians and enthusiasts.

Stan Hauck was recognized for his extremely high-quality photography of the Boston Elevated and Eastern Mass. in the 1940s and 1950s. A friendly and generous individual, Stan is also well remembered in the railfan community as an avid trolley modeler.

Foster Palmer worked as a librarian at Harvard University starting in 1938. He is best known, however, for his superb photographs of electric railways worldwide, visiting more than 200 cities with trolleys in his lifetime. Much of his best work was in the Boston area, and many of the black and white and color photographs in this book are credited to him. In a number of instances the subject matter that he covered was available nowhere else.

Dick Wonson was an official of the United Electric Railway of Providence, Rhode Island and later its successors, the United Transit Company and the Rhode Island Public Transit Authority. Dick was a life-long and well-known trolley fan, particularly of the Eastern Mass. Street Railway.

A word on the use of color photographs in this book is also in order. When work began in 1994, the 1940s color images of Boston trolleys were generally deemed to be too challenging for publication. The initial illustrations planned were black and white, but in the nine years that have passed, photo enhancement software and printing techniques have undergone tremendous change, and I have included many color images previously felt to be unusable.

Special appreciation is in order to Robert A. Kennerly of Northboro, Massachusetts for providing a superb group of Boston Elevated and Eastern Massachusetts Street Railway slides taken by him in the 1940s and for making available color material from the estate of the late Foster M. Palmer.

While not known as a photographer, William Werner of Randolph, Massachusetts painted his pictures with words. Bill Werner was a former MBTA facilities superintendent who kept and published copious records of Boston area transit events for many years. His preserved transit chronologies were extremely useful in the preparation of this book.

I would especially like to thank Charles Bahne of Cambridge, Massachusetts, for his superb work in preparing the maps for this book, for his exhaustive proofreading, and for his sidebar, *The True Story of Charlie on the MTA*. Special thanks are also due to James P. Teed of Quincy for his extensive work on Appendices 9 and 9A, which are snapshots of route statistics, and for track change data throughout the system. This information was essential for the completion of this book.

In addition to the people mentioned above, I would like to thank Robert Willoughby Jones of Los Angeles, California; Richard L. Barber of East Greenwich, Rhode Island; O.R. Cummings and Michael C. Lennon, both of Manchester, New Hampshire; Arthur S. Ellis of Pittsburgh, Pennsylvania; David L. Klepper of New York City; and the Seashore Trolley Museum of Kennebunkport, Maine. Contributors from the Bay State included Edward A. Anderson of East Dennis; J. Leonard Bachelder of Merrimac; Jonathan Belcher of East Boston; Stephen P. Carlson of Saugus; Edward P. Collins of Milton; David J. Allen, John V. Cahill, Daniel R. Cohen, Jeffrey N. Sisson, and J. Leo Sullivan of Boston; Fr. Richard Driscoll of Tewksbury; Kevin T. Farrell of Billerica; Robert W. FitzGerald of Reading; Fred F. Freeman of Dorchester; James E. Gately of Walpole; William J. Grimes of Watertown; Thomas J. Humphrey of Newton; Professor Arthur Krim of Cambridge; the Massachusetts Bay Transportation Authority (MBTA); Paul M. Paulsen of Woburn; George M. Sanborn, Transportation Librarian, Massachusetts State Transportation Library; Elwyn "Al" Silloway of Franklin; Lester Stephenson, Jr. of North Reading; Anthony F. Tieuli of Revere; Eugene Victory of Salem; and George Zeiba of Quincy. Your contributions and those of the late Lawson K. Hill of Newton, Albert S. Jenness of Quincy, Leon Onofri of Boston, Walter L. Tyo of Bellingham, and Edward E. Wood of Scituate, all in Massachusetts, have made this book possible.

BRADLEY H. CLARKE
Boston, Massachusetts
October 6, 2003

Hail the conquering hero! World War II in Europe has ended, and General George Patton, returning home to Massachusetts, receives the accolades of his fellow citizens during a parade in his honor on Massachusetts Avenue in Cambridge. This scene is north of Harvard Square looking toward Porter Square. The public took advantage of the streetcar safety islands as reviewing stands, and it was reported that riders on the trolleys tried to reach out and touch the General as he swept by. Behind Patton's car are at least three Type 5 streetcars heading north toward Arlington Heights and North Cambridge. *Arthur Griffin*

Chapter 1

Historical Background and Overview

In 1940, the Boston Elevated Railway was still operating a large surface streetcar system. The trolleys would soon allow the company to handle record-setting wartime traffic after years of declining ridership. Despite the impressive contribution of the company to the war effort, however, new thinking about public transportation and new expectations about its role in the community would sweep the Boston El and much of its surface rail system away. By the end of the decade, the Metropolitan Transit Authority had replaced the El and was poised to replace most remaining streetcar lines, extend the rapid transit system, and profoundly change the way Bostonians used mass transit forever.

Trolley cars in Boston and nationwide were on their way out, but the pace of the change to rubber-tired transit vehicles in Boston was more thoughtful, more deliberate. Nationally, most transit operators realized that bus conversions offered immediate relief from the heavy expenses of fixed plant maintenance and yielded somewhat lower operating costs. The transit industry also knew that the buses of the time carried far fewer riders than the average streetcar. Often, therefore, the decision to change from rails to rubber was based on the condition of the overhead trolley wire, the track, and the streetcars themselves rather than on the vehicle operating cost savings that were possible with buses.

The Boston Elevated Railway knew that it could operate busy lines with buses. In 1938 the company had converted the Allston–Dudley car line to buses. This line was a high-ridership cross-town route, and its successful conversion made a case for buses on heavy surface routes. Far more buses than planned, though, were required to accomplish this changeover.

Trackless trolleys, with their access to a virtually unlimited power supply, high passenger carrying capacity, and rapid acceleration, were more promising than buses for phasing out streetcars on trunk routes.[a] The Elevated had converted the Harvard–Lechmere line in Cambridge and seven[2] Malden and Everett lines from streetcar to trackless trolley between 1936 and 1939. These conversions clearly demonstrated that trolley coaches could easily handle routes with heavy ridership, and led the company to plan an extensive and rapid expansion of its trackless trolley network.

At the end of the 1930s, the Boston Elevated Railway was still operating approximately 142 route miles[b] of surface streetcar track, despite earlier conversions of many of its lighter lines and a few high-ridership routes to bus or trackless trolley operation.[3] This was one-way street mileage. If the second track, sidings, carhouse, and yard trackage are taken into account, the total track mileage operated at this time[c] was approximately 318 miles.[4]

At its peak in 1918, the company was operating 492 miles of surface track overall.[5] So, by 1940, the Boston Elevated was still running a hefty 65 percent of the surface streetcar track miles that it did in 1918. This situation was due in part to the boost in track miles that came with the Boston Elevated Railway purchase in 1936 of the Eastern Massachusetts Street Railway Chelsea Division. The Chelsea Division was an important group of heavy surface lines serving Chelsea, East Boston, Everett, Malden, and Revere.

In 1940 the Boston Elevated carried 294 million passengers.[6] The company had lost 86 million annual riders between 1929 and 1933 to the Great Depression.[7] Since 1934 the El had gained back only 26 million, about one-third of the riders it had lost.[8] It was difficult in 1940 to justify the large physical plant that was still in place in light of this loss of ridership, but the picture would soon change.

World War II brought many new riders, their numbers increasing steadily throughout the conflict and into 1946. In fact, the company's peak ridership year was 1946, when the El carried 433 million revenue riders.[9] Strong ridership growth, coupled with government restrictions and shortages of tires and motor fuel, ensured that virtually no streetcar service would be eliminated before the end of the war.

---

[a] The terms, "trackless trolley," "trolley coach," and "trolley bus" are equivalent, and are interchangeable in this book.

[b] The total mileage owned or leased was actually 150.6 miles. This figure included 8.3 miles of usable but non-revenue trackage in various parts of the system. These segments are discussed later in the book. Leased trackage totaled 15.6 route miles and was located in West Roxbury and Stoneham and leased from the Eastern Massachusetts Street Railway; on Hyde Park Avenue and leased from the Hyde Park Transportation District of the City of Boston; and the High-Speed Trolley Line from Ashmont to Mattapan and leased from the Transit Department of the City of Boston. These leased lines are also included in the system mileage total.

[c] The total track mileage owned or leased, as with the one-way or route mileage, was also greater than the mileage operated. The Boston Elevated operated 317.9 miles but actually owned or leased 334.8 miles. The 16.9-mile difference, again, was non-revenue trackage.

However, beginning in 1947, ridership began to drop sharply when private automobiles and gasoline again became widely available. In 1950 the MTA annual report showed only 308 million revenue passengers, way down from the 1946 level, but still greater than the ridership level in 1940.[10]

The MTA was operating 103 route miles of streetcar track in 1950 versus the 142 of its predecessor in 1940, and a total of 227 track miles in 1950 including second track and non-revenue rail versus 335 in 1940.[11] Thirty-nine route miles of surface track had been abandoned since 1940. However, despite the steady reduction of track, 46 percent of the maximum surface track miles in 1918 was still in operation in 1950!

Abandoned Lines

In the 1940s, many track segments of car lines that had been previously converted to bus or trackless trolleys or abandoned completely were left in the street, sometimes with trolley wire still suspended over the rails.[12] Some of this track was still active, and had survived for streetcars carrying school students, work cars, and Night Cars,[d] and to maintain connections between sections of the trolley system.

Much of this former revenue trackage, together with the many remaining car lines still in service, created the look and feel of the far more extensive system of the past. Railfans of the day often scheduled fan trip cars on intact but seldom used segments of former car lines to explore and relive a bygone era.[13] Some of this track was eventually reclaimed for the replacement needs of the El or "mined" as scrap for the war effort. Much abandoned track, however, remained in the streets well after the war.

The tracks on Dover Street between Tremont and Washington Streets and on Washington Street between Dover and Northampton Streets were a good example of rail kept in place for operating convenience. The car line between Dudley Street Station and North Station had used this trackage, and the tracks were retained after regular service ended on March 5, 1938. Owl Car service and cars for school students, however, regularly used the tracks until December 25, 1948.

Tracks also continued on a short stretch of Dover Street from Washington Street east to Harrison Avenue. Here the Dover Street tracks connected to a single track on Harrison Avenue, another remnant of a former car line. In its last years, the track on Harrison Avenue ran only from Dover Street to the former Albany Street Shops.

The last segment of these shops, the brass foundry, was closed on January 5, 1940, but work cars still used the Harrison Avenue track to get to a material storage yard that had remained on the Albany Street site.[e] Extra cars for services at

Boston Elevated 4400, a former Eastern Massachusetts Street Railway car, pauses on Dover Street at the Main Line Elevated Dover Street Station on January 14, 1940, during a fan trip. This non-revenue trackage connected with the Harrison Avenue track and ultimately Albany Street Shops. *Charles A. Duncan*

This fan trip with center-entrance car 6202 used the tracks on Washington Street between Northampton and Dover Streets on July 13, 1941. The shot was taken right outside the Cathedral of the Holy Cross. *Charles A. Duncan*

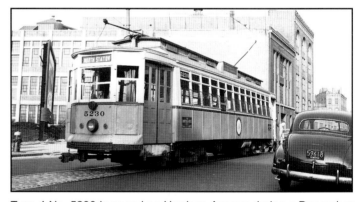

Type 4 No. 5230 is posed on Harrison Avenue during a December 5, 1948, Boston Chapter NRHS fan trip. *Stanley M. Hauck*

the Cathedral of the Holy Cross in the South End occasionally laid over on this trackage. This trackage was a railfan favorite, and photos show a Boston Chapter NRHS charter, car 4400 no less, rumbling along this iron on January 14, 1940.[14] Another trip here featured Type 4 No. 5230 on December 5, 1948, only weeks before the abandonment of this track on Christmas Day.

---

[d] The official use of the term *Owl Car* began about 1942, and gradually replaced *Night Car* as the decade ended.

[e] This was also the site of the former Central Power Station and a former trolley freight station. There was still trackage in the yard area. In 1940, 378

feet of this track was abandoned in the yard on land that the Elevated had leased from the United Shoe Machinery Company.

School cars and extras often used track that was no longer in use for regular revenue operation. At left, Type 5 school car 5605 turns from Tremont Street onto Dover Street. Another purpose of the tracks on Dover Street and Harrison Avenue was to allow work cars to get to and from Albany Street Yard and the rest of the system. At right, motor flat 2015, used to deliver supplies and parts between the El's many carhouse and shop facilities and equipped with a derrick for loading and unloading, turns into the yard from Harrison Avenue.

Both, Charles A. Duncan

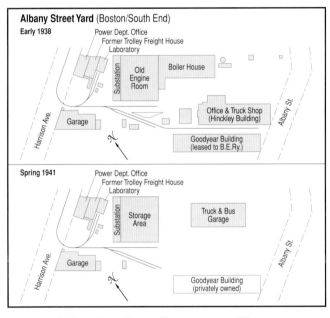

An assortment of interesting work equipment was stored at Albany Street Yard. In this January 14, 1940, view we see former open car 2858, which hauled trash around the yard, beside the former trolley freight station, and boxcar 231, a former 25-foot passenger car converted into a wire car in 1922. *Charles A. Duncan*

The Surface Streetcar Fleet

In 1940 the Boston Elevated streetcar fleet was largely obsolete. By 1950, however, most of the older conventional streetcars had been scrapped or sold, and many lines had been converted to trackless trolley, bus, or PCC car operation. The 1940 annual report of the Boston Elevated listed 1,033 streetcars, one of which was a PCC.[15] By 1949 the annual report of the successor Metropolitan Transit Authority showed 922 cars, 271 of which were PCC cars.[16] The descriptions of the types of rolling stock covered below include references to chapters where extensive photographs of each car type can be found.

PCC car 3001, built by the St. Louis Car Company and delivered in 1937, was the newest car on the roster. (See Chapter 4 for a photograph of this car.) It offered a smooth, quiet ride, and had comfortable leather-upholstered seats for 59 pas-sengers. As the only PCC car on the property in 1940, 3001, dubbed the "Queen Mary," was the best streetcar the Boston Elevated could offer the riding public.[17] Because it lacked Tomlinson couplers and a left-hand door, 3001 only ran in the subway on occasional fan trips. In regular revenue service, 3001 was used on surface lines with loops at either end, principally south of the city.[f] In later years it operated sporadically, but remained on the active roster for the entire decade.

The Elevated's newest pre-PCCs were the fifteen 4400 series cars numbered 4400–4414. These 4400s were built in 1927 for the Eastern Mass. Street Railway and were later purchased by the Boston Elevated in two groups, ten in 1936, and five more in 1937.[18] The initial batch of 4400s was acquired

---

[f] Known assignments are the Charles River line in West Roxbury from 1937-41 and the Dudley–Humboldt line from 1945-47. The car was out of service from mid-1941 to early 1945 to allow its trucks to be used as spares for PCCs 3002-3021.

to replace ten older 4200 series cars included in the Elevated's purchase of the Eastern Mass. Chelsea Division.

The 4400s were refurbished by the Boston Elevated and performed so well that the company bought the second batch the following year. The 4400s had a compelling amenity: comfortable leather-upholstered seating, virtually unheard of on pre-PCC Boston Elevated equipment. Seating capacity was 42. Most of these cars remained in service in the Chelsea Division throughout the 1940s.[g] Type 5 cars replaced the 4400s in late 1949 and early 1950.[19] Chapter 8 has good photographs of the 4400 series.

The next newest cars in the fleet were 471 Type 5 cars built between 1922 and 1928 by Brill, Laconia, Osgood Bradley, and Wason. These cars were numbered 5500–5970. While twenty years is "young" in the life of a streetcar, by 1940 the Type 5 cars were already obsolete by contemporary standards, especially in light of available PCC technology.[20] The Type 5s were noisy, rough riding, and relatively uncomfortable, notwithstanding the company's questionably proud references in earlier times to their "hickory seat cushions." Type 5 cars seated 48 passengers.

Despite their lack of creature comforts, however, Type 5 cars were very reliable and the mainstay of the surface streetcar system and pictures of them are throughout the book. Like PCC 3001, their lack of Tomlinson couplers confined them primarily to surface lines that did not enter the subway.[h] All 471 of these cars remained in service during the 1940s, steadily replacing older equipment as it was retired.

Next in age were the 405 center-entrance cars, built by Brill, Kuhlman and Laconia from 1917 to 1921. These cars were the "ugly ducklings" of the surface fleet, but what they lacked in beauty, they more than made up for in utility. The large center doors, spanning a distance of 6-feet 6-inches with a low step well, were the most noteworthy features of these cars. Their wide doors allowed center-entrance cars to handle large numbers of riders quickly,[i] and the cars were soon nicknamed "crowd swallowers." Center-entrance cars had seats for 56 passengers.[21]

The majority of the center-entrance fleet could run in multiple unit operation in trains of up to four cars.[j] When operated in revenue service, though, they virtually never ran with more than three cars. A conductor collected fares and issued transfers, allowing the motorman to focus on his primary duty of running the car. In trains, each car had a conductor, so a three-car train had a crew of four. This fleet was numbered 6000–6404.

The mainstay of the surface car fleet in the 1940s were the 471 Type 5 cars. Here, No. 5643 stops at Broadway and the Northern Artery in Somerville to let off a passenger in March 1946.

Charles A. Duncan

Rapid loading and unloading, the high passenger capacity per train achieved with multiple-unit capability, and the efficient use of a two-man crew made the center-entrance cars a natural choice for the heaviest lines of the company. Accordingly, they were extensively used on lines running into the present-day Green Line, or Tremont Street Subway.

During the Great Depression, ridership dropped and so did the need for these two-man cars. Starting in 1934, the Boston Elevated began converting some center-entrance cars to sand and salt service and in one case, a school instruction car.[k] Other center-entrance cars, mostly in the 6000-series, were put into dead storage. Many 6000s and 6300s were scrapped between 1936 and 1940, leaving only 231 center-entrance cars on the roster at the end of 1940.[22] Center-entrance car photos are well represented in Chapter 5.

World War II stopped the scrapping in a hurry. Suddenly passenger carrying capacity was critical. By the end of 1941, the Boston Elevated reported that it had 50 rapid transit cars and 73 surface cars under refurbishment.[23] Many of these surface cars were center-entrance cars, and all were in good condition and available for revenue service in 1942.[24] With the conversion of the school instruction car back to revenue service in 1942, the roster showed 232 center-entrance cars.

The arrival of large wartime orders of PCC cars from 1944 to 1946, totaling 225 units, made it possible for the Boston Elevated to retire most center-entrance cars. However, in 1947 the MTA extensively rehabilitated 30 center-entrance cars for subway service and for special events. Most of these refurbished cars remained in service until 1953.

Even older than most of the center-entrance cars were the 4300-series cars built by Laconia in 1917 and 1918 and acquired from the Eastern Mass. with the Chelsea Division. These 39 cars numbered 4305–4399 had 44 thatched cane-upholstered seats and were far more comfortable than the rock-hard

---

[g] Boston Elevated records show that four 4400s were assigned to Salem Street Carhouse from March 15, 1937, to April 1, 1940, and three thereafter until March 17, 1941.

[h] Night or Owl Car service in the subway was usually run with Type 5s.

[i] This low stepwell was really a low floor platform that speeded up loading and unloading. A similar concept is incorporated into the new Type 8 low floor cars for the Green Line.

[j] 6300–6404 were built for single-unit operation.

[k] School instruction cars were used to train future motormen. School student cars were assigned to certain lines for students, primarily at the junior high and high school levels.

The crowd-swallowing ability of the center-entrance cars can be seen in this view of a three-car train loading at Harvard and Commonwealth Avenues in 1945.

Charles A. Duncan

seats of the Boston Elevated's native fleet.[25] The 4300s soldiered on until 1944, when the Boston Elevated scrapped the first of them. The remaining cars were scrapped steadily through April 1947, bringing this small fleet to an end.[26] Chapter 8 features many photos of 4300s.

The oldest surface cars of all in passenger service were the Type 4 cars and their somewhat younger running mates, the center-entrance trailers. The earliest Type 4 cars dated from 1911, and by 1914, 275 numbered 5191–5465 had been placed in service. During 1915 to 1919, they were equipped with Tomlinson couplers and appropriate electrical connections to haul trailers. For many years thereafter, the Type 4 and trailer duo was a common sight on Boston streets. As of 1940, there were 265 Type 4 cars still in service. A school instruction car, 5295, was returned to revenue service at this time, raising the total to 266.[27]

During the war, the Type 4 cars required constant maintenance. Despite continuous attention, the fleet was worn out by the end of the conflict. The arrival of PCC cars in large numbers and the availability of Type 5 cars released from lines that had been converted to bus or trackless trolley operation allowed the Elevated to remove Type 4s from the active roster. Scrapping began in earnest in 1945, and by the end of 1949, only 84 remained.[28] Like the Type 5 and the center-entrance cars, the Type 4s were equipped with hard wooden seats which were fine for short trips and minimal maintenance, but rough on the riding public. Seating capacity of the Type 4s was 52.[29]

After the Egleston Station accident of April 12, 1948, the MTA reviewed its use of Type 4 cars. In September 1948, the Authority decided to replace most of the Type 4s at the Arborway, Eagle Street, and City Point Carhouses with Type

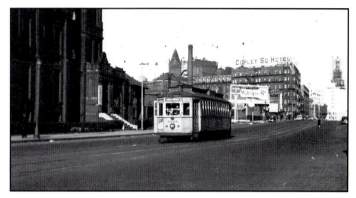

Type 4 No. 5239 passes the Mechanics Building outbound on Huntington Avenue on New Year's Day of 1941. Scenes such as this would be possible only for another six weeks, as beneath the road lies the new Huntington Avenue Subway, which would open on February 16, 1941. *Horton Banks, Stephen P. Carlson Collection*

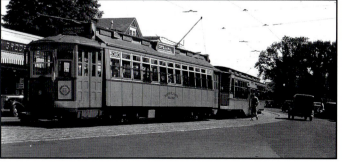

Railfan charters often used older equipment, either recreating scenes of the past or bringing it to locations where it did not run in revenue service. During a nine-hour trip on July 14, 1940, Type 4 No. 5380 and center-entrance trailer 7040 are seen at the upper loop of Sullivan Square Station (top) and on the way to the Charles River Loop (bottom). *Top, Horton Banks, Stephen P. Carlson Collection; bottom, Charles A. Brown*

– 5 –

5s. The Type 5s would soon become available after the conversion from streetcars to trackless trolleys of the lines based at Park Street Carhouse in Dorchester. The Authority also planned, however, to retain a limited number of Type 4 cars at Arborway, City Point, and Watertown for subway service.

What actually happened, however, was close to these plans, but slightly different. Shortly after the Egleston Square accident, Type 5s replaced Type 4s on the Mattapan–Egleston and Mattapan–Ashmont lines. During 1949, Type 4s were also withdrawn from East Boston routes and from City Point. After December 1949, the Type 4s were left on lines based at Watertown, Bennett Street, and Arborway stations. These lines were Watertown–Arlington Heights, Watertown–Central Square (Cambridge), Park Street Station–Braves Field Loop, Egleston Station–North Station, and Park Street Station–Heath Street.[30] The remaining Type 4s also served as spares. Good photos of these cars in operation are in Chapters 3, 4, 6, and 8.

A fleet of 225 center-entrance trailer cars built by Brill, Kuhlman, and Laconia were placed in service from 1915–1918 for use with Type 4s. The trailers bore more than a passing resemblance to their cousins, the center-entrance motor cars, and they shared the same great crowd eating capabilities. These cars seated 62 on the usual hard wooden seats favored by the Boston Elevated.[31] Most of them were still active in the early 1930s, but steady scrapping had left only 12 (7002, 7004, 7009, 7019, 7025, 7040, 7050, 7055, 7104, 7115, 7164, and 7174) by 1940. Type 4s with trailers were used in East Boston and Revere for service to the Suffolk Downs racetrack and to Revere Beach until 1944, when the trailers were finally scrapped.[32] Shots of Type 4 and trailer trains are found in Chapter 8.

The coming of the PCC by the hundreds would modernize and substantially change the entire equipment roster. In 1941 the Boston Elevated placed 20 new PCC cars in service on the Watertown–Park Street Station route. The Pullman-Standard Car Manufacturing Company of Worcester, Massachusetts, built these cars and all subsequent PCC orders for Boston. One hundred PCC cars equipped for multiple-unit operation were ordered in 1942 and 75 more in 1943. However, of the 175 cars on order in 1943, the War Production Board, responding to the recommendations of the Office of Defense Transportation as to where the most significant need for new transit vehicles existed, authorized the construction and delivery of only 150.[33]

No PCC cars were delivered in 1943, but 100 were received in 1944. However, ridership was so heavy that only 36 of the aging center-entrance and Type 4 cars could be retired that year. It was clear that the El needed more new equipment, and the company ordered 100 additional PCC cars in 1944.[34]

Another 112 PCC cars were delivered in 1945, and the balance of 38 arrived in 1946.[35] An active participant in on-going industry-wide PCC improvement efforts, the company allowed the last 25 cars to be constructed to the new postwar all-electric design, without multiple-unit capability. At this time the PCC fleet comprised 271 cars numbered 3001–3271. PCC cars are shown primarily in Chapter 5. There were a number of different types of PCC cars, and a quick review of the photographs in that chapter will show the basic types.

The October 1945 edition of *Co-operation* reported studies that had been conducted by the Boston El on ways to improve PCC car ventilation and riding quality.[36] The first ventilation studies had been conducted in June 1944 with the installation of interior fans on car 3017. This experiment led to ventilating fans on the 25 all-electrics and the retrofit of fans on 100 more cars, starting in 1947. To speed up subway operations, longitudinal seating replaced cross-seats on one side of the forward part of the cars. The Elevated also experimented with FM communication on PCC cars at this time, using the trolley wire to transmit the signal, and the rail for return.[37] This experiment was short-lived and was never widely applied.

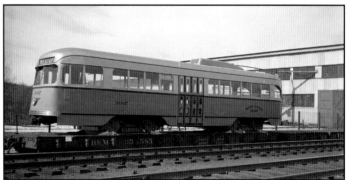

Modernization of the car fleet began in 1941 with the delivery of 20 PCC cars from Pullman-Standard in Worcester, Massachusetts. Here, PCC 3007 has been loaded on a flatcar for delivery to Boston. *Arthur Ellis*

Officials of the Boston Elevated Railway made an inaugural run through the subway on February 19, 1941, using PCC 3002. Standing in front of the car, from left to right, are Willis B. Downey, general counsel; Patrick J. Welsh, trustee; John H. Moran, vice-president and treasurer; Edward E. Whiting, chairman, Board of Public Trustees; and Henry J. Smith, secretary, Board of Public Trustees. In the doorway are Ernest A. Johnson, trustee (left); and Edward Dana, president and general manager. *BERy*

Members of the New England Transit Club on an outing visited Everett Shops on March 9, 1944, where they inspected and posed with the first of the new multiple-unit PCC cars.   *BERy, Daniel R. Cohen Collection*

The Boston Elevated and the MTA also maintained and operated a large roster of service cars that lasted throughout the 1940s. Many of these cars were home-built from former passenger streetcars. This equipment included Type 3 snowplows, Type 2 compressor cars, electrical test cars and rail grinders made from early closed electric cars, and school instruction cars.[38]

The most unusual cars in this maintenance fleet included a shifter car, No. 3123, at the South Boston tie treating plant and a trash car, No. 2858, used at Albany Street in 1940, then stored at Everett Shops. Both cars were made from former 12-bench open cars and were true relics of the distant past.[39]

The service fleet also had work cars that were manufactured by outside builders. This work equipment included sweepers, rail grinders, pavement plows, bottom and side dump cars, and a tank car originally built for trolley freight service.

Many service cars had been scrapped by the end of the 1940s.[l] A representative collection of these cars, however, ended up preserved at the Seashore Trolley Museum in Kennebunkport, Maine. Shots of work cars occur throughout the book, but no attempt has been made to present a compilation of them.

Finally, in addition to the Boston Elevated rolling stock discussed above, cars of the Eastern Massachusetts Street Railway also ran over Boston Elevated lines in two places:[m]

1.   **Sullivan Square Station, Charlestown–Sheepfold, Stoneham** (on the through line to Stoneham Center)

Despite the dislike of the "all-electric" concept by Superintendent of Rolling Stock & Shops Ralston B. Smythe, the El agreed that a 25-car group of PCCs it had ordered during World War II could be built to the postwar PCC specification to give Pullman-Standard the opportunity to gain experience with the new design. The first all-electric is seen here shortly after delivery in 1946.   *BERy*

2.   **Fields Corner Station–Neponset** (on the through line to Quincy)

The Quincy and Stoneham lines had heavy ridership, and they were important feeders to the Boston Elevated Fields Corner and Sullivan Square rapid transit stations, respectively. As Eastern Mass. bus lines, the Quincy and Stoneham lines continued long after the abandonment of streetcar service.

Twelve Eastern Mass. 4300-series cars ran on the Stoneham line. These cars were numbered 4381–4397 with a gap between 4391 and 4396 and were identical to the 39 cars of the same series acquired by the Boston Elevated with the former Eastern Mass. Chelsea Division. Chapter 7 has many photographs of this car type as operated by the Eastern Mass.

---

[l] The NRHS newsletter, *The Turnout*, noted in its September 1949 issue that the MTA was then scrapping its ex-Eastern Mass. snow fighting equipment and some of its own work cars. Also mentioned was an "endless parade of Type 4 cars to the bonfire." *The Turnout*, 8 (September 1949), 115.

[m] While Eastern Mass. cars were on Boston Elevated property, they were operated by Boston Elevated motormen.

Nineteen of the Eastern Mass. 7000-series cars, 7001–7048 with numbering gaps,[40] ran on the Quincy line, supplemented by six[41] Eastern Mass. 4200s used in service for high school students and during rush hours.[n] The 7000s were of the same type as those sold to the El in 1936-37 that the El renumbered in the 4400 series. The 4200s were a year older than the 4300s but otherwise were virtually the same, the only major difference being in the type of control system. The 4200s assigned to Quincy were numbered 4201, 4205, 4214, 4241, 4287, and 4289. Chapter 3 has a section devoted to the Quincy operations of the Eastern Mass.

Equipment Assignments

Each year in the 1940s the Boston Elevated and the MTA made four system-wide service adjustments, usually in March or April, June, September, and December, called *rating changes*. At the time the rating changes were made, the rush hour equipment requirements and operating personnel for each line were set to cover the planned service levels for the next three months. Supplemental rating changes were made when needed.

Using Boston Elevated and MTA rush hour car requirement listings by lines, which were prepared for each rating change, the streetcar types assigned to each line and their periods of use have been discussed in detail later.[o] This information has also been summarized in Appendices 2–8, which correspond to the respective chapters in this book.[p]

Rating changes also affected the personnel assigned to a given line. Rating changes were posted in the rating stations, usually in the operators' lobbies at the carhouses. The available work was based on the expected service requirements for the coming season. Operating employees picked their working hours based on their seniority, or *rating*, in strict succession of their employment date.[q] Thus the longest-term employees, who had the best ratings, could pick first and pick the best work.

Eastern Mass. 4241 and a 7000 series car are seen in Quincy Square on July 5, 1942. They will soon turn the corner from Hancock Street onto Temple Street for the completion of their trips to the Fore River Shipyard.   *Winthrop Greene, BSRA Collection*

Service Levels and Line Statistics

The level of service provided on Boston Elevated streetcar lines varied widely during the 1940s. Appendix 9 presents a snapshot of the levels of weekday service and line statistics on most Boston Elevated streetcar lines. Most of this information is for the Spring 1945 rating, a time of very high ridership. In a few cases, however, information has been included for lines that were not running at this time, so the rating dates are different and listed accordingly. Appendix 9A has similar information for the car lines of the Eastern Massachusetts Street Railway.

Appendices 9 and 9A list the routes by public map number; internal route number; route name, round-trip mileage; average round-trip running time in minutes; morning rush hour, midday base, afternoon rush hour, and evening headways, or service frequencies; number of daily trips; peak number of streetcars operated in the morning and evening rush hours; the rating date for which the information applies; and notes for selected entries.[r] Unless specifically defined otherwise, when line distances or mileage are refered to in this book, the round-trip distance is meant. Similarly, running times cited are always round-trip running times.

The line numbers and physical distances remained much the same throughout the 1940s, but the service level statistics including headways, numbers of trips, and peak vehicle levels varied widely. Appendix 9 primarily covers the Spring 1945 rating, and the reader can quickly grasp from this information the comparitive activity of the lines and judge their relative importance. For the few routes that are not covered in this rating, but for which the data are available for other years, the reader should take this distinction into account before making any comparisons.

---

[n] Frequently, 4200s used to make local trips for school students would run all the way to Fields Corner to maintain the schedule. This occurred often between 1941 and 1945.

[o] This information is intended to give the reader an idea of the types of equipment that were running at various times and where. It is not a comprehensive analysis. Newer equipment than that used during rush hours was often run in off-peak service. For example, PCC cars were not normally used on the Charles River and Watertown–Central lines at peak times, but they were often run middays, evenings, and on weekends and holidays. Where off-peak car use information is available, it has been included in this book.

[p] When a phrase such as "the March 6, 1940, rating" is used in the book with regard to rolling stock, it refers to the specific rush hour car requirements established at that time for the line being discussed.

[q] It had been long-standing practice to use black letters on white roll signs, also known as "paper signs," the reverse of the usual white letters on black, for temporary and experimental routes. In accordance with the union work agreements with the Elevated, such routes could only be run for seven days before the work had to be formally posted at the rating station for picking.

[r] The Boston Elevated and its successor, the MTA, used route numbers on maps and Night Service timetables, but, unlike many other transit properties, did not display these numbers on the vehicle destination signs. Internally, both the Elevated and the MTA used entirely different sets of route numbers to handle route variations. See Appendix 9 for the public route numbers and their four-digit internal equivalents.

A BRB&L Railroad train on the Winthrop Loop enters Playstead Station for the trip to the ferry to downtown Boston. It is November 13, 1939, and this scene would be repeated only for a few more months. *Seashore Trolley Museum Collection*

The Prewar Years, 1940-41

Boston, Revere Beach & Lynn Abandonment

The Boston, Revere Beach & Lynn Railroad,[s] known locally as the *Narrow Gauge*, abandoned its harbor ferry service between Boston and East Boston and its lines from East Boston to Lynn and Winthrop on January 27, 1940.[42] This loss of service became a major problem that would grow as World War II continued, ultimately setting the stage for the East Boston Tunnel extension to Revere.

The Massachusetts Legislature had authorized this extension as far as Day Square, East Boston, in 1945 and to Orient Heights in 1946.[43] In 1947 the Metropolitan Transit Authority drew up new plans for a further extension from Orient Heights to a future station near the Revere Beach Loop, now known as Wonderland Station. When it opened as far as Orient Heights in 1952, this extension would be concurrently accompanied by the complete abandonment of all streetcars in East Boston, Chelsea, and Revere.

The St. Valentine's Day Blizzard of 1940

Metropolitan Boston was struck by a major snowstorm on Wednesday, February 14, 1940. This snow was heavy, wet, and sticky, and was accompanied by northeast gales. The accumulation was not record shattering, but the composition of the snow made it unusually tough to plow and remove.[t]

There were widespread service interruptions from the storm, and the system did not return to normal operation until Thursday, February 22. In addition to impassable streets blocked by snow, abandoned vehicles left in the travel lanes also confronted the Boston Elevated. In the course of reopening its lines, the El's snow fighting force dug out more than 300 surface transit vehicles and 3,300 private cars and trucks.[44]

Anyone for a little snow? The storm on St. Valentine's Day, February 14, 1940, was one that Bostonians would not soon forget. The storm paralyzed streetcar traffic and scenes such as that recorded the next day of Type 5 No. 5928 near Fields Corner were common. It was quite some time before things returned to normal.

Pitt Holland

On the day after the storm Type 3 snow plow 5175 and snow sweeper 3263 lead a parade of Type 4 cars across the Charles River on the Watertown–Central Square, Cambridge, line.

Horton Banks, Stephen P. Carlson Collection

Record snowfalls would happen during the winters of 1944-45 and 1947-48. None of these storms, however, would match the system shutdown wrought by the 1940 St. Valentine's Day Blizzard.[u]

Opening of the Huntington Avenue Subway

The completion of the Huntington Avenue Subway was celebrated on February 16, 1941, at a well-attended public

---

[s] The abbreviation BRB&L Railroad will be used in this book interchangeably with Boston, Revere Beach & Lynn Railroad.

[t] At that time weather forecasters considered the density of snow from a normal snowfall to be 6 pounds per cubic foot. The snow density of this storm was 11 pounds per cubic foot, and 14 inches dropped on the Hub.

[u] The Boston Elevated Railway and the MTA regularly plowed all streets on which transit lines were located. This effort was a substantial burden to the company, which often did a superior job to that done by the cities and towns on neighboring streets to Boston Elevated routes. The October 1948 edition of *Co-operation* gave a rundown of these snow clearing efforts. The MTA Engineering and Maintenance department was responsible for plowing 23 miles of trackless trolley lines, 154 miles of bus lines, 25 miles of yards and terminals, 5 miles of car lines, and all caryards and terminals. In addition, the MTA Transportation Department plowed 21 miles of trackless trolley lines and 100 miles of car lines. "The MTA Battle with Snow and Ice Begins Each Year in the Spring," *Co-operation*, 27 (October 1948), 45-47.

Opening day for the Huntington Avenue Subway was February 16, 1941. The inaugural train of center-entrance cars with 6204 leading and followed by 6283 and 6291 is about to pick up the waiting crowd of dignitaries at Opera Place (Northeastern) and commence operation of the new facility.
Stanley M. Hauck

ceremony. Construction by the Boston Transit Department began on September 18, 1937, as a Works Progress Administration (WPA) project.[45] Originally, the subway was intended to end near the Mechanics Building at West Newton Street and Huntington Avenue. The project scope was changed by extending the subway to Opera Place and Huntington Avenue and by adding two stations, Mechanics and Symphony.

A related project, the Huntington Avenue vehicular underpass under Massachusetts Avenue, was opened on November 6, 1941. This roadway was engineered to fit between the twin tubes of the new subway.

The World War II Years, 1942-45

Wartime Ridership Growth

Wartime ridership expanded rapidly because of war industry commuting and reduced automobile travel caused by gasoline and tire rationing. Military personnel were very evident, traveling to the Boston Army Base and the adjoining Naval Dry Dock in South Boston, the Boston Navy Yard in Charlestown, shipyards in Quincy and Hingham, the Watertown Arsenal, and many smaller war production sites.

The El had noticed a ridership increase in April 1941, well before the declaration of war. In its 1941 annual report, the company acknowledged a 4.2 percent increase for 1941 over the previous year. The 1941 annual report added, however, that the system still had excess capacity. Significantly, years before in 1926, the railway had carried 371 million riders versus the 307 million that it carried in 1941, yet most of the infrastructure from the earlier time was still in use.[46]

There was another difference between the 1926 and 1941 ridership. In 1941, unlike 1926, there were sharp riding peaks in the morning and evening rush hours. To relieve this problem, the Elevated suggested that businesses adopt staggered

working hours.[47] State, city, insurance, and retail store workers first tested this measure on October 1, 1942.[48] In 1942 many private companies and schools also adopted staggered hours.

In 1943, the Boston El carried 418 million riders, 37 million more than the 381 million of 1917, the previous high.[49] The number of riders dropped slightly in 1944, to 417 million, but 1944 was still the second highest ridership year to date.[50]

During 1945 the Boston Elevated hauled 420 million riders, another new record. In its 1945 annual report, the Elevated said that it had carried a staggering 1.6 billion riders during the war, while operating 224 million miles of service. In a nod to its long-suffering patrons, the company said,

> The most important single factor that enabled the railway to meet the challenge of wartime transportation was the cooperation of the riders. We wish to state here that without the understanding of the riders of the problems that were facing the railway, and without their willingness to put up with an unusual degree of crowding and without co-operation of many of them who refrained from riding during the rush hours the job of maintaining efficient transportation under wartime conditions would have been much more difficult, if not impossible. In this connection we wish also to thank the employees of the railway for their fine spirit of cooperation in helping to keep the wheels rolling. A further important factor in the railway's ability to carry a greatly increased number of passengers arose from the fact that over the years the railway plant had been kept in good operating condition, and thus was able, without a substantial expansion of its facilities, to take care of the greatly increased number of riders.[51]

The end of gasoline rationing after the war led to heavy increases in motor vehicle traffic. Nevertheless, the Elevated's

Staggering work hours was a successful strategy during the war, often reinforced with newspaper ads such as this one produced in 1943.   *BERy*

when they came to a stop. Passengers were required to leave and to seek shelter. For rapid transit trains and streetcars in subways, passengers were required to leave the car or train after it had stopped but could remain on the station platform.[55]

A number of other steps related to blackouts were also taken. On August 10, 1942, Frank A. Goodwin, Massachusetts Registrar of Motor Vehicles, issued regulations designating many coastal communities as *Dimout Areas*. A number of inland communities near the coast were defined as *Low Beam Areas*.[56]

In Dimout Areas, from sunset to sunrise motor vehicles were restricted to 3 candlepower headlamps and a top speed of 15 miles per hour. These low power lights were difficult to spot at a great distance. Many other transit companies nationwide took similar steps in instances where their routes ran along the coastline and could be seen at sea. The only Boston Elevated line in a Dimout Area was the Broadway–Beachmont bus line loop on Winthrop Avenue, Crescent Beach, and Crescent Avenue, in the Beachmont section of Revere.[57]

In Low Beam Areas, motor vehicles were restricted to low headlamp beams and a top speed of thirty miles per hour. Other than the Beachmont line mentioned above, the entire Boston Elevated system was located in a Low Beam Area. As an added precaution to ensure the low light levels required in Low Beam Areas, the upper half of the headlights on buses and on many other motor vehicles of the Boston El were blacked out.

ridership remained high, establishing an all-time record in 1946 of 433 million passengers.[52]

Blackouts and Other Protective Measures

Blackouts were a wartime action taken to minimize damage from possible bombing raids by Axis warplanes. The Boston Elevated participated in the first practice blackout and air raid drill held in Boston on February 17, 1942, from 10 p.m. to 10:20 p.m. Test blackouts were carried out on a number of other dates at different evening hours and in the suburbs as well.[53]

Blackout rules for transit vehicles were simple. When a blackout began, surface transit vehicles stopped at the first level place. Trolley cars and rapid transit trains in subways were run to the next station, and passengers were allowed to remain inside.

Surface vehicles were darkened; rapid transit cars and trolleys in subways kept their lights on. Underground stations remained lit. Lights were extinguished at outside rapid transit stations and at surface vehicle stations, garages, carhouses, and on all other railway property. After the "all-clear" signal was given, service immediately resumed. Always revenue conscious, the El reported that its receipts were noticeably down on the days that the tests were conducted.[54]

Later the blackout rules were changed for surface vehicles

Conservation

The April 1943 issue of *Co-operation* discussed government restrictions placed on the El during World War II. Measures of the Federal Office of Defense Transportation (ODT) were highlighted.[58]

On March 25, 1942, Joseph B. Eastman, Director of the ODT, issued a nationwide order: "No carrier or railroad, in respect of the transportation of passengers, shall substitute a bus or buses for any vehicle or vehicles theretofore operated on rails, over any existing line or route of such carrier by railroad, unless it shall have been authorized to do so by this office."[59]

This order was effective April 1, 1942. It shelved plans by transit companies and railroads everywhere in the United States for bus substitutions for the duration of World War II. The order was revoked on August 31, 1945, after the war had ended.[60]

A memorandum from the ODT dated April 6, 1942, went a little further. The memo directed transit companies to notify the Special Projects Salvage Section Field Representatives if rail removal was imminent on any unused car line not already covered over. The memo added, "where the car lines are intact, (ODT) wishes to be advised so that they may determine whether national policy may better be served if the tracks remained for future use."[61]

The Clarendon Hill–Sullivan Square via Broadway and the Salem Street–Sullivan Square via Winter Hill lines were the only two Boston Elevated streetcar routes immediately and directly affected by this order, both lines lasting beyond the end of the war. The El had converted two routes between Clarendon Hill and Lechmere from streetcar to trackless trolley in November 1941, and the Broadway line was next. The Salem Street–Sullivan line had been run with buses in off-peak hours and had been steadily drifting toward full-time bus operation.

Where streetcars could easily replace buses, such as on streetcar lines that were run with buses during off-peak hours, car service was completely restored. The Salem Street–Sullivan line mentioned above and the Harvard–Massachusetts Station[v] line were examples, as well as six Owl Bus routes running where active car tracks were available.

To further conserve rubber and gasoline, the Elevated ended bus service on three lightly used routes that were near or paralleled car lines or other bus lines. These routes included the Dudley–Dover–Tremont, the Shawmut Avenue and Dover Street to Berkeley and Stuart Streets, and the Magoun Square–Sullivan Square Station bus lines. All three were discontinued because nearby streetcar service was available.

Some bus lines were shortened to serve only their heavily used sections. Examples included the Granite Bridge line, which was cut back to Gallivan Boulevard. The Cypress Street loop was eliminated on the Kenmore–Cypress line, and the section of the Massachusetts Station–Bowdoin line between Bowdoin Square and Charles Street was also cut. A number of other bus lines were switched to limited hours operation, including Arlington Center–Clarendon Hill, Copley Square–South Station via Stuart Street, and Kendall Square–Lafayette Square.[62]

The ODT had recommended that transit stops be spaced at least 500 feet apart and, optimally, 600 to 1200 feet apart. To comply with these guidelines, the Elevated eliminated 106 stops system-wide, dropping the average number of stops to 6.7 per mile.

Because of low gasoline supplies, on May 25, 1943, the ODT ordered a 20 percent reduction in Boston Elevated bus mileage. During this cutback, the heavily crowded surface streetcars shouldered even more of the burden. The cut ended on August 16, 1943, and while it was short-lived, it saved 540,000 bus-miles.[63]

If these measures were not enough, a widespread shortage of spare parts and stringent government measures to conserve rubber, gasoline, copper and scrap metal made the job of providing reliable public transportation even harder. In 1944, the railway's largest budget item, coal, was limited to a 25-day supply.[64] An acute shortage of heavy-duty tires for buses and

Newspaper delivery cars were another gasoline conservation measure. Here we see one of the Type 4s used in this service being loaded on Beverly Street near North Station in June 1943. *BERy*

trackless trolleys forced the Elevated to increase its use of synthetic rubber for tires and recaps. Synthetic rubber had not been perfected, and extra care was required to use it. For a time in 1944, the Elevated was concerned that it might have to curtail some bus and trackless trolley service due to the tire situation, but the company somehow managed to keep all its routes in operation.[65]

To maintain passenger carrying capacity, the El was forced to run many older buses beyond their normal service lives. No new buses were available and the El had to "make do" with the fleet on hand.

Other conservation measures included scrap drives. A showcase example was the well-publicized demolition of the Atlantic Avenue Elevated Line, which began on January 24, 1942, and was finished on June 10.[w] Scrap steel from the Atlantic Avenue Elevated went to the war effort along with abandoned streetcar rails from many other parts of Boston. Since all steel was scarce and in high demand, and fabricated steel for transit rails even more so, the Boston Elevated had many run-ins with the ODT over the company stock of rails for system maintenance. The ODT viewed the El stockpiles

[v] Massachusetts Station was the official name of this station, but it was locally known as "Mass. Station."

[w] A short stretch of the Atlantic Avenue Elevated from Keany Square (Tower C) to Bent 201 opposite North End Park on Commercial Street was left for car storage. By January 29, 1942, rails, feeders, and station equipment had been removed from the rest of the Atlantic Avenue Elevated for reuse.

as unnecessarily generous and felt that they could be better applied directly to the war effort.

Copper was also a critical material in short supply. The scarcity of copper led to the eventual system-wide elimination of pole-mounted trolley wheels for current collection and the adoption of trolley shoes with carbon inserts. In 1942 and 1943, the Boston Elevated replaced trolley wheels on 321 cars with carbon insert trolley shoes.[66] Wear on the bronze trolley wire, a copper alloy, was also greatly reduced by this substitution.[67] Later, all new PCC cars were delivered with trolley shoes, and trolley wheels soon became a thing of the past.

To save gasoline, in 1943 the *Boston Post* and the *Boston Globe* jointly chartered Type 4 cars to carry newspapers to parts of Boston and its inner suburbs. Leaving from a distribution point at Causeway and Beverly Streets, five Type 4s were used between 3 and 6 a.m. on weekdays delivering papers to West Roxbury; Mattapan and Dorchester; Brighton and Newton; Medford; and to Cambridge. This service was gradually introduced between May 29 and July 8, 1943,[68] and ended October 31, 1944.[69] The Boston El had run newspaper cars as early as 1905 and at other times thereafter, but the practice had ended well before this wartime measure.

In its 1945 annual report, the Boston El summarized the wartime conservation program. The company had taken many actions, some drastic, including using substitute materials, such as 2,135 synthetic tires for buses and trackless trolleys, and the use of strip-mined coal when better grades were unavailable. The Elevated had also converted oil-heating equipment back to coal operation where possible and had saved 725,900 gallons of heating fuel. The company had made 37,800 tons of scrap steel, iron and copper available for the war effort and had saved 1,310,647 gallons of gasoline and 21,353,874 bus tire miles by reducing bus mileage.[70] Chartered bus service was curtailed except for military trips and for trips directly connected with wartime needs.[x]

Wartime Employment

Many additional employees were needed to handle the extremely heavy wartime ridership. In direct conflict with this need was the need of the nation for men fit for military service. In 1943, 699 Boston Elevated men were serving in the armed forces.[71] In 1944 the number of El men in the armed forces had risen to 982.[72] By the end of the war, 1,052 Boston Elevated employees had served or were in active military service.[73] This loss of manpower was particularly felt in the ranks of "blue uniform" operating personnel.

As the war went on, the Elevated was forced to make rapid and dramatic changes, including hiring women for positions in the Operations Department. Women had worked for the

Rubber and gasoline were in short supply for domestic use during the war. One conservation measure was to replace Gray Line tour buses with horse-drawn excursion buses riding on hard tires such as this one photographed outside the Statler Hotel on November 7, 1942.
Clarke Collection

Boston El for many years, but mainly as office employees. A major exception to this practice was the employment of women only as fare collectors on the rapid transit lines until 1928. Some men had worked in this position after 1928, but the wartime manpower shortage compelled the company to begin staffing fare collector positions again exclusively with women. On January 12, 1943, the company reverted to hiring only women as collectors.[74]

The Boston Elevated Railway Operations Department, had always been a "man's world," and hiring female employees for work on transit vehicles was something that had never been done before in Boston. On July 6, 1943, women began replacing men as conductors on the Reservoir–Lechmere and Lake Street–Lechmere subway-surface lines.[75]

Local newspapers had reported earlier that the El was considering employing female conductors. In mentioning this interest of the press, the March 1943 issue of *Co-operation* said, "Not for a long time has news coming from the 'El' aroused so much public curiosity as the announcement that we are considering women as *conductorettes* (emphasis added) to replace men called into the armed forces."[76] The term *conductorettes* stuck and is still remembered by retired employees.

By the end of 1943, the railway had also hired women as rapid transit guards, as machinists' and electricians' helpers in the shops, and as storeroom clerks. In 1945, the company annual report said that the El had trained 2,270 new employees for its blue-uniformed force, including 114 women as conductors and rapid transit guards, and 86 women for shop work. At the end of the conflict, most of the El's female workers returned to their prewar lives having proven that they could effectively handle the heavy work traditionally given to men. The Boston Elevated expressed its appreciation to these women in its 1945 annual report for agreeing to do this work and for doing it very well.[77]

A long-standing employee benefit was changed during the war. Before April 1, 1944, employees were issued tickets for

---

[x] On August 21, 1942, the ODT banned the use of buses for sightseeing service. In Boston, horse-drawn vehicles between 50 and 75 years old were brought out of retirement to allow visitors to tour the city's historic places.

The Boston El augmented its wartime labor force with women working in a wide variety of positions. Above, the first women hired as conductors on some surface streetcar lines pose for an official photograph with President Dana. From left to right are Lillian Campbell, Josephine E. Burri, Flora M. McKenzie, Hannah J. Lynch, Doris R. Notrem, Mary S. Scribner, Harriet W. Critcher, Louise M. Henshaw, and Mary A. Roddy. At top right, a drill press operator at Everett Shops makes precision parts, while at lower right, women workers help in the war effort in the Shops' farebox repair area.   *All, BERy*

free transportation. After this date, employee passes were issued instead of tickets. When this benefit was first given to the workforce, there was a 30-day waiting period for new hires to get their passes.

Safety and *Co-operation*

Despite great increases in wartime traffic, the Boston Elevated said in its 1945 annual report that it had "maintained

BOSTON ELEVATED RAILWAY

Co-operation

Volume 21   NOVEMBER, 1942   Number 4

FACSIMILE OF AMERICAN TRANSIT ASSOCIATION SAFETY PLACQUE AWARDED
TO THE "EL" FOR SAFE OPERATION IN 1941

collision accidents on a mileage basis at about the same low rate that on six (prior) occasions had won the railway national recognition for safety."[78] In 1941 the Boston El had managed to win the American Transit Association (ATA) safety award for the sixth time. After this success, the ATA had barred the El from further competition in an effort to encourage other transit companies to continue to compete for the award.

Co-operation, the employee magazine of the Boston Elevated and later the MTA, was a champion of corporate safety. The publication celebrated its silver anniversary with the January 1947 issue, having started the same month in 1922 as a personal project of General Manager Edward Dana. Throughout the years, the magazine promoted safe operating practices and safety in general. *Co-operation* also provided a superb record of the company's operations and activities, including many interesting photographs.

During the war, *Co-operation* ran many photos of the Elevated's men and women at the front, greatly boosting employee morale. Publication of *Co-operation* ended in 1953 as a cost-cutting measure and was a serious loss for effective communications between MTA employees and management.

Two-Way Radio

A little-known milestone occurred on March 26, 1943,with the introduction of the first two-way radio-equipped inspectors' car. Before this almost all internal communication took place over a private company network of street and subway telephones. The Elevated's use of radio expanded rapidly, and the August 1946 edition of *Co-operation* ran a feature article on radio operation.[79] At that time, eight inspectors' cars, two wreckers, one wire truck, and several supervisory automobiles from the Maintenance and Power Departments were radio-equipped.

On December 2, 1949, the MTA began broadcasting from its own radio station, KCA 573, using an antenna located at the Albany Street Yard. The MTA was then using 19 radio-equipped vehicles, including eight Transportation Department supervisors' cars, four Rolling Stock & Shops emergency trucks, four Engineering & Maintenance supervisors' cars, and an emergency truck and two supervisors' cars from the Power Department.[80]

The Postwar Years, 1946-50

Plans for the Postwar Period

In its 1944 annual report, the Boston Elevated called for the completion of pre-war plans to convert car lines in Somerville, Medford, Dorchester, and Roxbury to trackless trolley operation using 128 new trackless trolleys. The company also said that it planned to increase its use of PCC cars, primarily in subway operations.[81]

The Elevated also planned to acquire part of the right-of-way of the former BRB&L Railroad and to use it for high-speed streetcar service from Bennington Street, East Boston, east of Ashley Avenue, to Revere Beach Loop. The Elevated had already purchased land in East Boston bounded by Washburn Avenue,[82] Belle Island Inlet, Bennington Street, and the Gladstone Loop for a carhouse site.[83]

The 1945 annual report of the Boston Elevated mentioned the legislative authorization to extend the East Boston Tunnel

Despite the deprivations of war, Americans managed to retain their healthy sense of humor. The famous wartime phrase, "Kilroy was here," prompted the Boston Elevated, the American Transit Association, and the Yankee Mutual Network to present car 4362 in time for Christmas to Francis Kilroy of Halifax, Massachusetts. Kilroy had won the car in a contest to establish authorship of the phrase. In this scene, the car is loaded at Everett Shops on December 24, 1946, for shipment to Kilroy's house to provide an extension for living quarters for six of his nine children. *BERy*

line from Maverick Square to Day Square, East Boston. To support the new extension, the El planned to reroute several car lines and substitute trackless trolleys for streetcars on other routes.

Streetcar service would continue between Gerrish Avenue and Maverick Station via Meridian Street. Buses or streetcars would serve Jeffries Point, Lexington Street, and the inner section of Bennington Street. Revere Beach streetcars would be retained on Ocean Avenue, but would originate from the new Day Square Station and run via Bennington Street.[84]

Two trackless trolley lines would run from Day Square to Revere Beach Loop via Eastern Avenue and Broadway. At Beach Street and Broadway, one line would follow Beach Street to Revere Beach Loop. The second line would continue on Broadway to Revere Street and then follow Revere Street to Revere Beach Loop. Another trackless route would run from Revere Carhouse to Day Square via Broadway and Central Avenue.[85]

The plan to run high-speed streetcar service over the former BRB&L right-of-way was still very much alive as well. The Boston Elevated Trustees had authorized the acquisition of the right-of-way from the Revere–East Boston boundary line to a point near Revere Beach Loop. This land would give the railway complete ownership of the former BRB&L between Ashley Avenue, East Boston and Revere Street, Revere. Streetcars would use this right-of-way rather than follow Washburn and Ocean Avenues.[86] The high-speed streetcar proposal was quietly dropped when plans changed later for the East Boston Tunnel line extension to continue from Day Square to Revere.

Looking at the downtown area, the 1945 annual report pointed out the need for a second tunnel to eliminate the single tunnel bottleneck between Scollay Square and Park Street Stations, and for platform enlargement at both stations. Both of these projects, the report predicted, would markedly improve subway service.[87]

The Coolidge Commission

Bolder plans than those in the 1944 and 1945 Boston Elevated Annual Reports were in the works, however, and forces outside the Boston Elevated were making them. On June 11, 1943, the Massachusetts Legislature established a special commission consisting of one member of the Senate, three members of the House of Representatives, and the commissioners of the Department of Public Utilities. Arthur W. Coolidge of Reading was appointed chairman. Under the leadership of Coolidge, first as the Senate representative and later as lieutenant governor of Massachusetts, two remarkable reports were produced. The recommendations in these reports still impact Boston area transportation planning.

The first document, *Report of the Legislative Commission on Rapid Transit – 1945*, was published on April 2, 1945. The commission proposed the creation of a Metropolitan Transit Authority (MTA) in response to shifting population patterns in the Metropolitan Boston area. The report said that this agency, "should be empowered to secure the provision of an adequate, integrated and efficient system of rapid transit, and the improvement thereof, within the area and to manage the same."[88]

The Commission recommended that the Commonwealth of Massachusetts purchase the Boston Elevated Railway and related agencies. The Boston Elevated Railway itself would constitute the core infrastructure of the MTA. The Boston Metropolitan District would raise the money for the acquisitions through the sale of bonds.[89]

The creation of the MTA would also respond to a festering political problem. The Public Control Act of 1918 had left the Boston Elevated Railway under public control but private ownership. The Commonwealth of Massachusetts extended the Act in 1931 under new terms that included reducing the dividend rate on the stock held by the private owners of the Boston Elevated and providing for the eventual acquisition of the company.

The original Public Control Act required municipalities served by the Boston Elevated to make payments proportionate to the service provided to cover the annual operating deficit of the El. Operating deficit payments were funded by local property tax assessments. Most taxpayers knew that part of the operating deficit payment would be used to pay dividends to Boston Elevated shareholders. Given the fact that the Elevated was in essence a monopoly providing an essential public service, popular sentiment against the deficit payments grew over time. Especially grating to many riders was that they paid twice: once as part of their property taxes, and once again in the farebox.

Under the MTA, the annual dividend payments to private shareholders would be eliminated. Many transit riders, however, would still pay for service twice through property taxes and fares, but now to a publicly owned and operated entity. This concept was more palatable to the public.

The Boston Elevated had steadily lost money during the 1930s and through 1941, but wartime conditions had raised revenue significantly. The company enjoyed surpluses from 1942 to 1945. In 1946, however, despite the highest ridership year in its history, the El again incurred a deficit.

Ominously, the 1946 Boston Elevated Annual report identified a "Serious Financial Problem Facing the 'El.'" Despite the collection of deficit assessments for 1941 amounting to $3.7 million, the Commonwealth of Massachusetts had not passed this money on to the El, and the 1946 deficit was almost $788,000. This left the company reserve fund almost completely dry, and the cash position of the company needed a boost to allow the company to pay its debts.

Furthermore, in 1947 the company faced $8 million in bond interest to cover subway rentals, property and motor vehicle taxes, and real estate taxes. The Federal Internal Revenue Service had already executed liens against the company, which was still a private corporation, for non-payment of federal taxes.

The company was unable to borrow money to pay these obligations and petitioned the Legislature to allow the Boston Metropolitan District to loan funds to the railway up to the amount of the unpaid deficits. This became moot when on February 27, 1947, the Legislature passed Chapter 92 of the Acts of 1947 enabling the Boston Elevated to borrow $3 million. The company exercised this opportunity the following day. The loan was a temporary fix, and the larger financial concerns of the company were still very much alive. This situation set the stage for the creation of the Metropolitan Transit Authority in 1947, an event that is described later in this chapter.

The Commission also proposed five extensions, largely over railroad rights-of-way, to the existing rapid transit lines of the Boston Elevated. These routes were intended to provide balanced service from all parts of Metropolitan Boston into the city. Dramatic color plates of proposed high and low platform articulated PCC cars for these routes were included in the 1945 report. Some of these vehicles suggested in appearance the then new "Electroliners" of the Chicago, North Shore & Milwaukee Railroad, or today's articulated light rail cars in the Tremont Street Subway.

The proposed extensions were:

1. **Braintree to Arlington Heights** *via the Cambridge Subway and East Watertown*[90]
2. **Dedham to Reading** *via the Washington Street Tunnel*
3. **Needham and Riverside to Park Street Station** *via the Boston & Albany Railroad (B&A Railroad) Highland Branch and the Boylston and Tremont Street Subways*
4. **Riverside to Woburn** *via the B&A Railroad Main Line, the Boylston and Tremont Street Subways, and the Boston & Maine Railroad (B&M Railroad) New Hampshire Division*
5. **Bowdoin Square Station to Lynn** *via the East Boston Tunnel, Airport and Revere Beach*

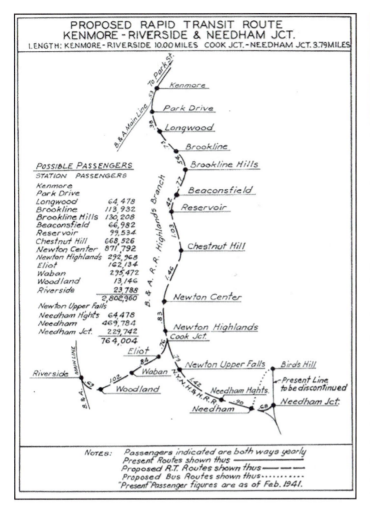

PROPOSED RAPID TRANSIT ROUTE
KENMORE - RIVERSIDE & NEEDHAM JCT.
LENGTH: KENMORE - RIVERSIDE 10.00 MILES COOK JCT.- NEEDHAM JCT. 3.79 MILES

POSSIBLE PASSENGERS

STATION	PASSENGERS
Kenmore	
Park Drive	
Longwood	64,478
Brookline	113,932
Brookline Hills	130,208
Beaconsfield	66,982
Reservoir	99,534
Chestnut Hill	668,526
Newton Center	871,792
Newton Highlands	292,968
Eliot	162,134
Waban	295,472
Woodland	13,146
Riverside	23,788
	2,802,960
Newton Upper Falls	
Needham Hghts	64,478
Needham	469,784
Needham Jct.	229,742
	764,004

NOTES: Passengers indicated are both ways yearly
Present Routes shown thus ——————
Proposed R.T. Routes shown thus — — —
Proposed Bus Routes shown thus ·········
*Present Passenger figures are as of Feb. 1941.

PLATE NO. III

TYPE OF CAR PROPOSED FOR
RIVERSIDE-NEEDHAM-WOBURN AND ARLINGTON HEIGHTS ROUTE

The end of the war brought calls for change in mass transit in the Boston area and nationwide. The Coolidge Commission reports of 1945 and 1947 profoundly changed the way Boston commuters got to work, and many new proposals were made in these documents. One of the more interesting ideas was the creation of new rapid transit lines and the extension of existing ones over railroad rights-of-war. At left is a proposed extension from the Kenmore subway station to Riverside and to Needham Junction over the Highland Branch of the Boston & Albany Railroad. The portion of this route to Riverside would be accomplished in 1959. To operate this service, the Coolidge Commission called for the purchase of 35 articulated cars for the Riverside route and 18 for the Needham Junction line. Although described as "a postwar adaptation of what is today the newest equipment known as the P.C.C. car," the illustration in the report (Plate III, above) in fact showed an articulated car based on the Brilliner, ACF-Brill's unsuccessful competitive design.   *Both, 1945 Coolidge Commission Report*

As a matter of historical record, parts of proposed extensions 1, 2, 3, and 5 were eventually built and run today. Parts of 4 and 5 are still under consideration. The Coolidge Commission Report was pace setting in its freshness of thought. It shook the deeply rooted and inbred thinking of the transit establishment at a time when there was a good opportunity for change.

The Coolidge Commission heightened public interest in mass transit, and on July 25, 1945, the legislature revived the Commission and increased its membership by one member of the Senate and four members of the House of Representatives. On April 1, 1947, the Commission issued a second document, *Report of the Legislative Commission on Rapid Transit–1947*,[91] again under the direction of Coolidge, who by now was lieutenant governor of Massachusetts.

The 1947 report proposed changes and additions to the rapid transit extension plans presented in the 1945 report. The later report also considered a number of other topics, including the decline of commuter rail service, additional rapid transit extensions, and the gradual curtailment of surface streetcar operations wherever possible.

Most importantly, the report proposed legislation for the acquisition of the Boston Elevated Railway by the Commonwealth of Massachusetts and the creation of the Metropolitan Transit Authority. With the constraints of war behind them,

but the previously described financial difficulties of the Boston Elevated still confronting them, Massachusetts Legislators were very receptive to the concept of the MTA, and passed Chapter 544 of the Acts of 1947, which enabled the MTA to come into being. Governor Robert F. Bradford approved this legislation on June 19, 1947, and the agency soon became a reality.[92]

From Boston Elevated to MTA

The Boston Elevated Railway had been under public control since July 1, 1918. At this time, five trustees, Louis A. Frothingham (Chairman), William M. Butler, Stanley R. Miller, John F. Stevens, and Galen L. Stone, were appointed to run the company by Governor Samuel W. McCall. However, ownership of the company remained in the hands of its shareholders.

At noon on August 29, 1947, the publicly owned Metropolitan Transit Authority acquired the assets of the privately owned Boston Elevated Railway Company. In a well-attended ceremony in the directors' room of Eastern Gas & Fuel Associates at 250 Stuart Street in downtown Boston, Carroll L. Meins, Chairman of the MTA, handed a check for $20.3 million to Patrick A. O'Connell, Chairman of the Boston Elevated.[y] Meins had purchased for the Commonwealth of Massachusetts the outstanding stock of the Boston Elevated Railway Company.

Interestingly the Boston Elevated was only under the control of the trustees originally defined by the 1918 legislation

---

[y] The Eastern Gas & Fuel Associates directors' room had been loaned for the occasion.

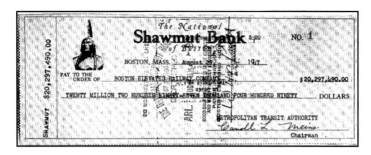

At noon on August 29, 1947, Caroll L. Meins, Chairman of the Board of Trustees of the Metropolitan Transit Authority, handed Metropolitan Transit Authority check No. 1 (above) to Patrick A. O'Connell, Chairman of the Boston Elevated Railway Company. For this payment of $20,297,490, the Commonwealth of Massachusetts now owned Boston's transportation system.   *Both, BERy*

until July 2, 1947. At that time, the new trustees of the Metropolitan Transit Authority assumed control of the railway property, and ran it as the Board of Trustees of the Boston Elevated Railway for an interim period of almost two months under the terms of the 1918 Public Control Act.

This situation occurred because the enabling legislation creating the MTA provided that the public trustees of the new MTA, on their qualification date, would succeed to the offices of the public trustees of the Boston Elevated. The qualification date was July 2, 1947, and at this time, Governor Bradford swore in the new six-man board: Carroll L. Meins (Chairman), Joseph Gannon, John F. Hurley, Henry Parkman, Harold D. Ulrich, and Edward E. Whiting.

Whiting, former Chairman of the Board of the Boston Elevated, accepted a transitional position as one of the new MTA public trustees until September 1947. Henry Parkman, who was returning from a government assignment in post-war Europe, replaced Whiting.

At this time, Patrick A. O'Connell became the new Chairman of the Board of the Boston Elevated Railway. O'Connell would handle the outstanding business concerns of the Boston Elevated and would disburse the funds from the sale of the company to its shareholders.

As previously mentioned, legislation passed in 1931 had extended the lease of 1918 and had provided for the takeover of the Boston Elevated Railway by the Commonwealth of Massachusetts. Chapter 544 of the Acts of 1947 required the MTA trustees to exercise this provision by August 30, 1947. On July 8, 1947, the MTA trustees notified Boston Elevated Chairman O'Connell of their intention to purchase the assets of the company. Finally, on August 29, the MTA Public Trustees, while operating the Boston Elevated Railway, invoked the provision by purchasing the Elevated and assumed control of their new entity, the Metropolitan Transit Authority.

In their first Annual Report, the trustees of the MTA cited several high-priority projects that they intended to promptly pursue. The first of these was the construction of a second subway tube between Scollay Square and Park Street Stations. The Boston Elevated had proposed this idea in its postwar plans mentioned earlier. This has always been an enormous bottleneck and remains so today, the project never having been started.[93] A second plan was to join Boylston and Park Street Stations with continuous platforms.[94] This, too, never happened.

Other projects included construction of a branch of the Cambridge–Dorchester subway over the New Haven Railroad Old Colony right-of-way to Quincy and Braintree, completed in 1980; the extension of the East Boston Tunnel Rapid Transit Line to Revere, started in May 1947 and completed in 1954; removal of the remaining Main Line elevated structure, a long process that began in the 1975 and was completed in 1992; and the substitution of trackless trolleys for streetcars on most lines in Roxbury and Dorchester.[95] The last project was completed in 1949 and is discussed below and more extensively in Chapter 3.

The MTA issued new badges to its employees starting on February 19, 1948. The old Boston Elevated badges, which were similar in appearance, were retired and exchanged for the new ones. Apart from changes in uniforms and a new logo, to the riding public, the property looked much the same as it had under the Boston Elevated. It took several more years for new equipment and other physical changes to create a fresh image.

On August 3, 1949, the MTA acquired the remaining transit facilities in the MTA district not owned by the Authority.[z] At this time the functions, powers, and personnel of the Boston

---

[z] The enabling legislation were Acts of 1949, Chapter 572, and Acts of 1947, Chapter 544, Section 8A.

Transit Department (formerly the Boston Transit Commission), and title to the subways and other transit properties owned by the City of Boston, were purchased by the MTA for $40.2 million.[96] This acquisition freed the MTA from making annual lease payments to the city for these facilities.

Abandonment of Dorchester/Roxbury Streetcar Lines

Starting on Christmas Day 1948, the MTA began replacing streetcars with trackless trolleys on the major lines in the Dorchester and Roxbury Districts of Boston. Along with the Huntington Avenue Subway, this was the second of the two most significant physical changes to the system of the decade. Eight lines, including one previously converted from streetcar to bus, were changed to trackless trolley operation.

The experience of former Boston Elevated personnel, now working for the MTA, with trackless trolley conversions before and after the war made these changeovers virtually problem-free. The trackless trolley system would continue to expand well into the 1950s.

Night and Owl Service

The Boston Elevated Railway operated an extensive network of Night Cars and buses for many years. Run during the wee hours of the morning, this service continued long after the Boston El was acquired by the MTA. In January 1940, the Boston Elevated was running 29 Night Service lines, 13 with streetcars and the remainder with the modes indicated in parentheses:[97]

The conversion of the first of the car lines in Dorchester and Roxbury is about to take place. The East Loop at Dudley Street Station has been rebuilt for trackless trolleys, the overhead wire has been strung, and operators are being broken in. The date is December 20, 1948, and the fresh snow on the roof of Pullman-Standard coach 8407 confirms the season. On December 25, an improbable conversion date, the first trackless trolleys will enter revenue service. Note the reinforced concrete safety posts, later nicknamed "headstones" by the operators because of the number of collisions that occurred between the posts and the trolley buses. *MTA, Al Silloway Collection*

Route No.	Description
1	**City Point–Scollay Square Station**
2	**Fields Corner–Scollay Square Station**
3	**Neponset–Scollay Square Station**
4	**Milton (River and Standard Streets)– Dudley Station** (Bus)
5	**Ashmont Station–Dudley Station** (Bus)
6	**Gallivan Boulevard & Washington Street–Dorchester Avenue & Summer Street** (Bus)
7	**Mattapan Station–Scollay Square Station**
8	**Hyde Park (Cleary Square)–Scollay Square Station**
9	**Dedham Line–Scollay Square Station**
10	**Charles River Loop–Arborway Station**
11	**Boylston and Cypress Streets (Brookline)–Massachusetts Station** (Bus)
12	**Brighton and Commonwealth Avenues– Kenmore Station** *via Lake Street*
13	**Watertown Station–Lechmere Station** *via Brighton*
14	**Chestnut Hill and Commonwealth Avenues–Lechmere Station** *via Central Square* (Bus)
15	**Watertown Station–Harvard Square** (Bus)
16	**Harvard Square–Dudley Station** (Bus)
17	**Waverley–Harvard Square** (Bus)
18	**Arlington Heights and Harvard Square– Scollay Square Station (Surface)** (Bus)
19	**Arlington Center–Sullivan Square Station** (Bus)
20	**Clarendon Hill–Lechmere Station** *via Highland Avenue* (Bus)
21	**Sullivan Square Station–Scollay Square Station** *via Main Street or Bunker Hill Street*
22	**Clarendon Hill–Sullivan Square Station** *via Somerville Avenue* (Bus)
23	**Salem Street Carhouse–Sullivan Square Station** *via Winter Hill* (Bus)
24	**Salem Street Carhouse–Everett Elevated Station** *via Fellsway*
25	**Lebanon Street–Everett Elevated Station** (Trolley Bus)
26	**Linden–Everett Elevated Station** (Trolley Bus)
27	**Revere Beach Loop–Maverick Station** *via Chelsea*
28	**Beachmont and Orient Heights–Maverick Station**
29	**Maverick Station–Scollay Square Station (Under)** (Rapid Transit)

A January 1940 Night Service map is shown below.

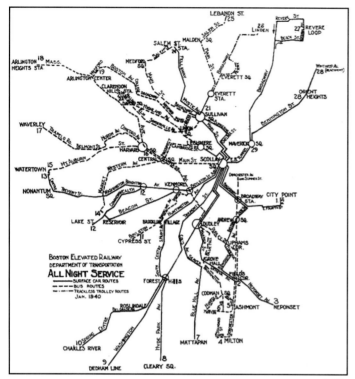

BERy

The Arborway was a terminal for night cars, and Type 5 No. 5732 shown here was likely a car from Charles River Loop. No other action is apparent in this magical view taken in the wee hours of the morning.
BERy

With the exception of the East Boston Tunnel line between Maverick and Scollay, the Boston Elevated did not run Night Service on the rapid transit lines. East Boston Tunnel Night Service trains, terminating at Scollay Under, looped at Bowdoin and returned to Scollay for the trip back to Maverick. In lieu of looping at Bowdoin, the trains on occasion used the crossover located before the southbound end of Scollay Under.

A number of Night Service car lines used the Tremont Street Subway and are shown in the table above as ending at Scollay Square Station. Once passengers on these Night Cars got off at Scollay, the cars continued empty to Canal Street Loop at North Station and returned to Scollay to begin their outbound trips.

Night Cars often ran over tracks that had been specially retained for Night Service but were no longer regularly used by daytime routes. Most Night Car service was run with Type 5 cars both on the surface and in the subway. Subway operation with Type 5s was a sharp departure from operating practices during normal hours.[98] The term "Owl" began to be used about 1942, and gradually replaced "Night" toward the end of the decade.

On September 12, 1942, the East Boston Owl Car, operating alternately every 30 minutes from Winthrop Avenue (Beachmont) or Orient Heights to Maverick was extended to Revere Beach Loop. This new Owl Service to Maverick connected with the East Boston Tunnel Owl Train service to downtown Boston.[99]

Also on September 12, 1942, the Owl Car from Watertown to Lechmere was cut back to North Station (Canal Street) run-

ning on a 30-minute headway. At the same time, the round-about Owl route from Commonwealth and Brighton Avenues to Kenmore via Lake Street, Reservoir, and Beacon Street was replaced by two routes operated alternately and hourly: Lake Street to Lechmere via Commonwealth Avenue and Reservoir to Lechmere via Beacon Street. Both lines were coordinated with the 30-minute Watertown–North Station service and this resulted in a 30-minute headway through the Subway.[100]

In 1945, five Owl Car lines, which had replaced Owl Bus routes early in the war, were converted back to bus:[101]

1. **Ashmont–Dudley Street Station** *via Washington Street*
2. **Arlington Heights–Scollay Square** *via Harvard Square*[aa]
3. **Waverley–Harvard Square** *via Huron Avenue*[bb]
4. **Watertown–Harvard Square** *via Mt. Auburn Street*
5. **Harvard Square–Dudley Street Station** *via Massachusetts Station*

On April 19, 1947, Owl Cars between Sullivan Square and Everett were abandoned. The Fellsway Owl Cars that had run through the lower level of Sullivan Station to Everett had provided this service. In their place, the Linden and Lebanon Street Owl Trackless Trolley lines were through-routed to Sullivan Square. Also at this time, the Fellsway Owl Cars were extended to Elm Street, having formerly run only from Salem Street.[102]

[aa] Before the war, this line used buses between Scollay Square and Harvard Square and either a streetcar or a bus from Harvard Square to Arlington Heights, depending on the specific trip. During the war, bus service between Harvard and Scollay was dropped, and streetcars only were used between Arlington Heights and Harvard. After the war, the line was run as it had been before the war.

[bb] Before the war, this line used buses when running via Huron Avenue, but made some trips using streetcars running via Mt. Auburn Street. During the war, the line was operated with streetcars only between Harvard Square and Waverley; no buses made the run via Huron Avenue. After the war, the service resumed its pre-war operating arrangement, but with fewer trips.

Starter Edward E. Wood poses in front of PCC 3041 in night duty on the Charles River line about 1946. Operator McCarthy is at the controls.
James E. Smith

Another change occurred on April 17, 1948, when the Owl Bus between Harvard and Dudley was routed via Massachusetts Avenue rather than over Northampton Street. This routing was also instituted for the regular midday and evening buses operated on the Dudley–Massachusetts Station line.[103]

Major Owl Service changes were made on December 25, 1948, at the time of the conversion of the first Dorchester and Roxbury area car lines to trackless trolleys.[104] The Neponset–North Station Owl Service had been run with buses from Neponset to Fields Corner. Riders transferred at Fields Corner to a streetcar to North Station (Canal Street Loop) via Meeting House Hill, Andrew Square, Dorchester Street, Broadway Station, and the Tremont Street Subway. This route was changed to run as a bus line from Neponset to Andrew Station (surface level). Passengers transferred at Andrew to an Owl Car, which ran to North Station on the same route from here as it did before.[cc]

The Fields Corner–Scollay Square Owl Car via Geneva Avenue, Grove Hall, Warren, Dudley, Washington, and Dover Streets was discontinued. A bus from Fields Corner to Broadway and Tremont Street replaced this car. The new bus line followed the same route as the streetcars except that inbound buses ran from Washington Street to the subway entrance via Broadway. Outbound buses returned to Washington Street via Tremont and Dover Streets. Outbound subway riders using the new Owl Bus line took the Andrew Station or Dedham Line Owl Car to the Broadway and Tremont Street subway portal to make the bus connection.

The Mattapan Owl Car to Egleston, Dudley, and North Station via Washington and Dover Streets was changed at Egleston to run via Columbus Avenue and Tremont Street to North Station. However, it was important to maintain Owl Service between Egleston and the subway via Dudley, and a new Owl Bus from Egleston to the Broadway and Tremont Street Portal was started via Washington Street. The bus line ran inbound via Washington Street and Broadway to the subway entrance. Outbound the buses ran via Tremont, Dover,

and Washington Streets. Outbound bus riders now took the City Point or Mattapan Owl Car to the Broadway and Tremont Street Portal for the bus connection.

With these changes, the track on Washington Street between Northampton and Dover Streets, and on Dover Street from Washington Street to Tremont Street, was finally abandoned. The branch on Dover Street to Harrison Avenue and on Harrison Avenue to the material yard at the former Albany Street Shops was also dropped at this time.

On September 13, 1949, because of the resurfacing of the Harvard Bridge, the through Harvard Square–Dudley Street Station Owl Bus service was temporarily discontinued. An Owl Bus detour between Harvard and Scollay Squares via Massachusetts Avenue, Vassar, and Main Streets replaced this service during reconstruction of the Harvard Bridge.[105]

In December 1949, the MTA was still very much in the Owl Service business and was running the following 33 car and bus lines:[106]

Route No.	Description
1	**City Point–Scollay Square Station**
2	**Fields Corner–Broadway and Tremont Streets** (Bus)
3	**Neponset–Andrew Station** (Bus)
4	**Andrew Station–Scollay Square Station**
5	**River and Standard Streets–Dudley Street Station** (Bus)
6	**Ashmont Station–Dudley Street Station** (Bus)
7	**Morton and Norfolk Streets–South Station** (Bus)
8	**Egleston Square–Broadway and Tremont Street** (Bus)
9	**Mattapan Station–Scollay Square Station**
10	**Hyde Park–Scollay Square Station**
11	**Dedham Line–Scollay Square Station**
12	**Charles River Loop–Arborway Station**
13	**Cleveland Circle–Lechmere Station** *via Subway*
14	**Boston College–Lechmere Station** *via Subway*
15	**Boylston and Cypress Streets–Massachusetts Station** (Bus)
16	**Cleveland Circle–Lechmere** *via Central Square* (Bus)
17	**Watertown Station–Scollay Square Station**
18	**Watertown Station–Harvard Square** (Bus)
19	**Waverley Square–Harvard Square** *via Aberdeen Avenue* (Bus)

cc The surface station at Andrew was kept open all night, and the stairways and escalators to the Cambridge–Dorchester Subway were all blocked off for night operation on the upper level of the station.

20   **Harvard Square–Dudley Street Station**
      (Bus)

21   **Arlington Heights and Harvard Square–
      Scollay Square Station (Surface)** (Bus)

22   **Clarendon Hill–Lechmere Station** *via
      Highland Avenue* (Trolley Bus)

23   **Clarendon Hill–Sullivan Square Station**
      via Somerville Avenue (Bus)

24   **Sullivan Square Station–Haymarket
      Square** *via Main Street or Bunker Hill
      Street* (Bus)

25   **Arlington Center–Sullivan Square Sta-
      tion** (Bus)

26   **Salem Street Carhouse–Sullivan Square
      Station** *via Winter Hill* (Trolley Bus)

27   **Elm Street and Fellsway–Sullivan Square
      Station** *via Fellsway*

28   **Lebanon Street–Sullivan Square Station**
      (Trolley Bus)

29   **Linden– Sullivan Square Station** (Trolley
      Bus)

30   **Woodlawn–City Square** (Bus)

31   **Maverick Station–Scollay Square Station**
      (Rapid Transit)

32   **Revere Beach Loop–Maverick Station** *via
      Chelsea*

33   **Revere Beach Loop–Maverick Station** *via
      Orient Heights*

While the number of Owl streetcar operations had dropped since 1940 to twelve, the track miles they commanded were substantial. A December 1949 map of these late decade Owl Service lines is shown below.

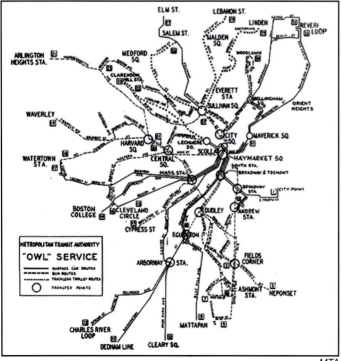

MTA

Owl operations would continue for many more years, ending as bus-only lines in 1960.

Fares

In 1940 the universal fare on the Boston Elevated was 10 cents with a free transfer, a system that had been in effect since 1919. There also was a local 5-cent fare for short rides on surface lines with no transfer, but often involving warrant forms.[dd] The Boston Elevated shortened the 5-cent local ride zones on December 19, 1939, and all local fares were discontinued on December 14, 1946, leading to a sharp drop in local ridership and a net loss of revenue system-wide.

The MTA increased fares with a new system introduced on August 6, 1949, using 5, 10, 15, and 20-cent fares with no transfers. Surface line fares were 5-cents and fares on rapid transit lines were 10-cents.[ee] A combination surface and rapid transit ride cost 15-cents, and a surface, rapid transit, and second surface ride was 20-cents.[ff]

This fare increase became a campaign issue for Boston mayoral candidate Walter A. O'Brien and inspired the song about Charlie on the MTA. The new system proved confusing and unwieldy, and the MTA replaced it on January 28, 1950, with a 15-cent system fare and the reinstatement of transfers. Local fares were also reestablished at 10-cents.

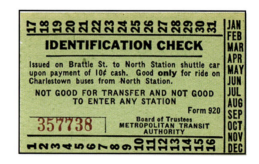

[dd] On pay-enter lines, if passengers boarding a surface vehicle bound for a rapid transit station or subway line wanted a local ride, they dropped five cents in the fare box and handed the operator another nickel. The operator gave the passenger a warrant form as a receipt, and if the rider left the car within the local fare limit, the warrant was returned to the operator for the second nickel. On lines where the fare was paid on leaving the vehicle, the rider dropped only 5 cents in the farebox if he got off before the station.

[ee] The 5-cent fare applied to 126 of 129 surface lines. The fare for pupils was also 5-cents and was unchanged.

[ff] Night car riders also paid a 15-cent fare.

He's The Man Who Never Returned…
The True Story of Charlie on the MTA

When the trustees of the Metropolitan Transit Authority decided to raise fares effective August 6, 1949, they never imagined that Bostonians would be singing about that fare increase nearly half a century later. But in their action to eliminate the system-wide free transfer—which had been a feature of Boston's transit system since 1887—the MTA trustees unwittingly created a folk hero who would "ride forever 'neath the streets of Boston."

To Walter A. O'Brien, Jr., a candidate for mayor of Boston in the 1949 fall election, the MTA fare increase was merely another effort to make working-class Bostonians shoulder the burden of post-war inflation. O'Brien, described in newspapers of the day as the "left-wing director of the Progressive Party," made the transit fare hike a central issue in his campaign.

In O'Brien's view, the creation of the MTA had been a bailout for the wealthy stockholders of the privately owned Boston Elevated Railway. The greatest single contributing factor to the deficit, O'Brien charged, was interest on bonds issued to buy the stock of the old Boston Elevated Railway at an inflated price. He favored an income tax on large downtown businesses to pay off those bonds.

But Walter O'Brien was a fringe candidate, running a campaign on a shoestring. He relied extensively on a rented sound truck, which was driven through the city's neighborhoods. Some of his young volunteers were musicians; so, to liven things up a bit, O'Brien asked them to write a few campaign songs. Jackie Steiner and Bess Hawes decided to tackle the transit fare issue.

Bess Hawes had been a member of the Almanac Singers, a pioneering political folk music group in the early Forties whose other members included Pete Seeger and Woody Guthrie. Bess' father, John Lomax, and her brother, Alan Lomax, were both noted folklorists who were largely responsible for the American folk revival in the Thirties and Forties. Jackie Steiner was a graduate student at Radcliffe College. Trained in classical music, she became interested in folk songs after her arrival in Cambridge.

The fare increase was the first since the MTA takeover of the transit system, and the trustees chose to make a dramatic change. Where riders had previously paid a dime for a ride anywhere on the system, the MTA adopted the so-called "5-10-15-20" cent fare structure: 5¢ for a surface ride on a streetcar, bus, or trackless trolley; 10¢ for a rapid transit ride; 15¢ for a combination surface and rapid transit ride; and 20¢ for a surface–rapid transit–surface ride.

Under the new system, many transit riders had to pay a nickel here, a dime there, and two or three times during a long trip, instead of paying just one fare. A few commuters paid less than before, some paid the same, but most people paid more. And on many of the busiest lines—including the car lines from the Central Subway—riders had to pay that extra nickel to get off a streetcar heading away from town.

The day after the fare increase, the Boston Herald told the tale of one woman who refused to pay the extra nickel. "That's all right with me," the motorman told her. "You'll stay on this car until you do." He closed the door and the trolley started up, with her still aboard.

The exit fare was a sore point with transit riders, so Jackie Steiner and Bess Hawes armed their song's protagonist with just "ten cents in his pocket." Lacking the extra nickel, Charlie couldn't get off that train.

For the tune, the two musicians turned to the hillbilly music hit, "The Wreck of the Old 97." It was a popular record, based on an even older song called "The Ship that Never Return'd," written by Henry Clay Work around the time of the Civil War. Steiner and Hawes adapted the chorus of Work's "Ship" song with the train imagery of the "Old 97," and the rest is legend. A half-dozen musicians went to a recording studio and came back with two 78-rpm records of the song, plus recordings of songs about other, now-forgotten campaign issues.

With the Almanac Singers, Bess Hawes had also played at a Transport Workers' Union rally in New York's Madison Square Garden in May 1941. There the Almanacs had performed another parody—unfortunately now apparently lost to posterity—of "The Wreck of the Old 97," about what would happen to that city's subway system if the bosses had their way.

On Election Day, Walter O'Brien placed last with just 3,653 votes, barely one percent of the total ballots cast. In the city's hottest municipal contest in years, City Clerk John B. Hynes tallied 138,790 votes to defeat Mayor James Michael Curley, who was seeking a fifth term.

The young progressives who had worked on O'Brien's campaign eventually moved on and scattered across the country. One of them pursued a musical career in San Francisco, where he sang the "MTA" song in clubs. There it caught the ear of Will Holt, who recorded it as a single for Coral Records in 1957.

Unknowingly, Holt's original recording included Walter O'Brien's real first name (although Holt, for reasons unknown, changed the middle initial to "J."). The Red Scare of the Fifties was still in full swing; when it was learned that Walter O'Brien was a "leftist" politician, Will Holt's record was promptly banned in Boston and elsewhere.

Another San Francisco folk group, the Kingston Trio, picked up the song, changing the lyrics to a fictitious "George" O'Brien. Released in June of 1959, the Trio's version of "MTA" spent 11 weeks on Billboard *magazine's "Hot 100" chart, peaking at number 15.* Life *magazine did a feature on the song, and the* Boston Globe *ran a cartoon showing PCC car 3001—ironically, the only PCC in Boston that never regularly ran in the subway—racing through Scollay Square station while Charlie's wife handed him a sandwich.*

Since then the MTA song has been a part of Boston's folklore, itself parodied in new political campaigns, usually involving transit issues. The lyrics have also been adapted for other cities and transportation modes, including trucks, the London Underground, Soviet spacecraft, and UFOs.

Walter A. O'Brien, Jr., the candidate who started it all, moved to Maine in the early 1960s. He ran a used bookstore there for many years, and passed away in July 1998 at the age of 83. Jacqueline Steiner lives in Connecticut, where she remains active musically; Elizabeth (Bess) Hawes is now retired after serving as head of the Folk Art Department at the National Endowment for the Arts in Washington, D.C.

And the fare increase? Just six weeks after Walter O'Brien lost the mayoral election, newspapers reported that the MTA would request a second fare hike. It seems that the politically appointed trustees had tried to "sugar coat" their first fare increase by lowering the price of local streetcar and bus rides to a nickel, against the advice of seasoned transit managers. It had been this low surface fare that required elimination of the system-wide transfer. But the fare hike did not bring in enough money, so a second increase was needed. On January 28, 1950—five months and 22 days after the first fare increase—surface fares were raised back to a dime, and rapid transit fares went to fifteen cents. The system-wide transfer was restored at fifteen cents, and Charlie's infamous exit fare was abolished.

The exit fare returned in 1961, when the transfer was eliminated for good—just two years after the Kingston Trio's record hit the charts.

—Charles Bahne

Power Stations

The MTA and Boston Edison began interchanging electric power on December 28, 1948. Both systems were entirely separate before this date. This move provided a needed backup for both systems during emergency conditions and allowed peak load sharing during periods of high power demand.

In October 1949, the Lincoln Power Station on Boston's waterfront was converted from coal to oil. This change allowed the MTA to use a cleaner, more easily handled fuel and

This mid-1940s shot of Edward Dana, then President and General Manager of the Boston Elevated Railway, was taken at his office in the Park Square Building in the Back Bay section of Boston. Mr. Dana was affectionately known as "Mr. Transit," with nationwide recognition in the transit industry. Much of the core system that Bostonians enjoy today was created during the 1907-1959 period that was Dana's era.   *BERy*

to eliminate an inefficient and costly coal storage and handling facility adjacent to the station.

The Employees

The managers and employees of the Boston Elevated Railway Company and the MTA in the 1940s and later can be described in one word: professional. Throughout the 1940s, including the early years of the MTA, politics took a back seat to sound policies and prudent decision-making.

However, the company also "had a heart." The sons and daughters of employees injured or killed in job-related accidents or wartime were often offered employment. The Boston Elevated and its successor were always family-oriented.

Notwithstanding the human side of their organizations, the Boston El and the MTA were public entities. Operating budgets were always tight, largely because of the high profile service assessments on cities and towns within the district that these agencies served.

Edward Dana, President and General Manager of the company, was its star employee. A graduate of Harvard College, he started working for the Boston El in 1907 as a conductor. After this basic training, he quickly moved into management. Dana had risen to Superintendent of Transportation by 1918 and was picked by the Public Trustees in 1919 to be General Manager. He held this position until 1932, when he was appointed Executive Vice President and General Manager. Dana became President and General Manger in 1936.

When the MTA was created, the new Public Trustees reappointed Edward Dana as General Manager, a position he held until his retirement in 1959. Selecting Dana for this position, despite the change in corporate identity, was easy: he

Edward Dana and his management team posed for an official photograph shortly after the establishment of the Metropolitan Transit Authority. In the front row (left to right) are Willis B. Downey, General Counsel; John H. Moran, Treasurer; Edward Dana, General Manager; Thomas A. Dunbar, Comptroller; and Charles A. McCarron, General Claims Attorney. In the back row (left to right) are E.B. Myott, Superintendent of Maintenance; Myron F. Freeman, Superintendent of Power; Ralston B. Smythe, Superintendent of Rolling Stock & Shops; Forrest W. Carroll, Purchasing Agent; John J. Sullivan, Superintendent, Rapid Transit Lines Transportation; and John P. Banks, Superintendent, Surface Lines Transportation. *BERy*

was clearly the best candidate for the job. His many years of experience had resulted in an unparalleled safety record in the industry, and his broad education made him receptive to change. He had an unusual ability (for a Boston Brahmin) to identify with other people, to solve their problems, to comfort them. Dana really felt and meant what he said, and his employees knew and appreciated these qualities.

Dana knew the players in the Massachusetts Legislature on Beacon Hill as well, and, after years of negotiations, was the "best of the best" for the high visibility job that he held. More than anyone else, though, Edward Dana was "Mr. Transit." He knew his transit system, his employees, and the industry. The legacy of Edward Dana would be a very difficult act to follow.

The level of professionalism exhibited by Dana was mirrored by the other corporate officers and by a phalanx of capable and loyal subordinates. Most of these people rose through the ranks and were transit-oriented to the core. The Board of Trustees itself was always selected with great care. Its members were often forced to make hard financial choices, particularly in the first years of the MTA, but the trustees generally gave Dana their full support.

The passing of the Boston Elevated Railway Company, the replacement of the rolling stock acquired before, during and just after World War I, and the beginning of large-scale surface track abandonments ended a significant period of transit development in Boston. In its place would come a new transportation authority, new PCC cars, buses, and trackless trolleys, new rapid transit extensions to Revere and to Riverside, and, most significantly, a new realization of the need for a coordinated regional approach to mass transit in Metropolitan Boston.

This major change in the collective mindset of the movers and shakers of public transportation in Massachusetts resulted in the creation of the Metropolitan Transit Authority in 1947, the Massachusetts Bay Transportation Authority in 1964, and the eventual completion of most of the goals of the Coolidge Commission.

The company and its employees were very civic-minded and often supported community-based charitable activities. A group of Operators and other "blue uniform" personnel gather at the Jackson Memorial Building of the Boston Floating Hospital as part of the "Come and See Tours" held here and at Children's Hospital in 1941. *BERy*

The surface level of Broadway Station was a gateway to South Boston residents and to many other Bostonians as well. Streetcars running between North Station and City Point, such as Type 4 No. 5397, passed through this station constantly, with some cars short turning here. During the summers in fact, streetcars shuttled all day and into the evening between this station and the alternate loop on Farragut Road at Marine Park. Broadway station was unusual, for it existed in three levels! The first was the surface transfer station on Broadway that we see here. A middle level consisted of a short streetcar subway tunnel and station immediately below the surface station but running crosswise under Dorchester Avenue. The lowest level was yet another tunnel and station used to the present day by the Red Line, then known as the Cambridge–Dorchester Subway. In 1919 after only two years' use by streetcars, the middle level was taken out of regular service, but saw annual use on St. Patrick's Day for many years as a pedestrian conduit for transferring the crowds going to and from the Red Line and Southie's famous parade.

Donald E. Shaw

– 26 –

Chapter 2
The South Boston Lines

South Boston in the 1940s was heavily residential with an extensive mix of commercial and industrial businesses. It remains this way today. The main streets were and still are Broadway, Dorchester Avenue, Dorchester Street, and Summer Street. Trolley lines ran along all of these streets and ridership was heavy.

Most of the housing was multi-family. An aquarium at Marine Park near City Point and area beaches, including L Street and Carson Beach, were popular with South Boston residents but drew people from other sections of Boston as well. South Boston was a streetcar suburb, but one within the city.

Service Overview

In 1940 four streetcar lines served South Boston, and all were based at City Point Carhouse.[a] These lines are listed below and are shown on Map 1.

Route No.[b]	Route Description
7	**City Point–South Station (Dewey Square)** *via P, East 4th, L, and Summer Streets*
8	**City Point–South Station (Dewey Square)** *via P, East 4th, and L Streets, Broadway, Dorchester Avenue and Summer Street*
9	**City Point–North Station** *via P, East 4th, and L Streets, Broadway, and Subway*
	Farragut Road–North Station (summer months)
10	**City Point–Dudley Street Station** *via P, East 4th, and L Streets, Broadway, Dorchester Street, Andrew Station, Southampton, Northampton, Washington, and Warren Streets*
	Farragut Road–Dudley Street Station (summer months)

Route 7 and its cutback at the Army Base, Route 9 with its direct connection to the subway, and Route 10 with an important destination—Dudley Street Station—offered comparable and frequent service all day. On Route 8, however, which nearly ended up as a rush-hour only line at the start of the decade, service was light compared to the other South Boston lines. See Appendix 9 for detailed information on service frequencies for all these routes.

Two other lines based at City Point Carhouse and are discussed in Chapter 3, which covers Dorchester and Roxbury.

16	**Franklin Park–Andrew Station** *via Columbia Road, Boston Street, and Dorchester Avenue*
47	**Dudley Street Station–Massachusetts Station** *via Warren Street, Washington Street (Roxbury, South End), Northampton Street, Columbus Avenue, and Massachusetts Avenue*

City Point Carhouse

South Boston car lines normally started at City Point Carhouse. This facility had two carbarn buildings at one time and a substantial amount of yard trackage. Much of the yard trackage was on the site of the former South Carhouse building. P Street, East First Street, Farragut Road, and East Second Street bounded the City Point complex. Double track was located on all of these streets, with leads from the buildings and yard emerging onto P Street, Farragut Road, and East Second Street.[c] Cars arriving at and leaving City Point ran on

---

[a] The Elevated also called this carhouse "North Point." This is the older name, and "City Point" will be the term used in this book.

[b] The route numbers shown here are from the Boston Elevated Railway System Route Map No. 5, which represents the system as it was in early December 1941. Cutbacks, not assigned their own route numbers, are indicated by "cb" in brackets before the description. Between 1940 and 1941, the route numbers used in the maps handed out to the public underwent the last of a series of changes. The route numbers in the 1941 map were used in subsequent maps for many more years and are the numbers that many readers will remember. The streetcar line listings, however, are the same as they were in 1940. All subsequent chapters will use streetcar line listings as of 1940 and route numbers from the 1941 map. Route numbers were generally assigned in an ascending pattern. Starting in South Boston, and moving clockwise around the Boston hub, the route numbers steadily increased, with the highest numbers generally ending up in Revere. Also, as mentioned in an earlier footnote, the route numbers shown on the public maps had four-digit equivalents used by the company internally. See Appendix 9 for a listing of the public map numbers and their internal counterparts.

[c] The eastbound track on East First Street was connected to the southbound P Street track but did not cross the intersection. The eastbound track resumed on the east side of P Street and connected with the trackage on Farragut Road.

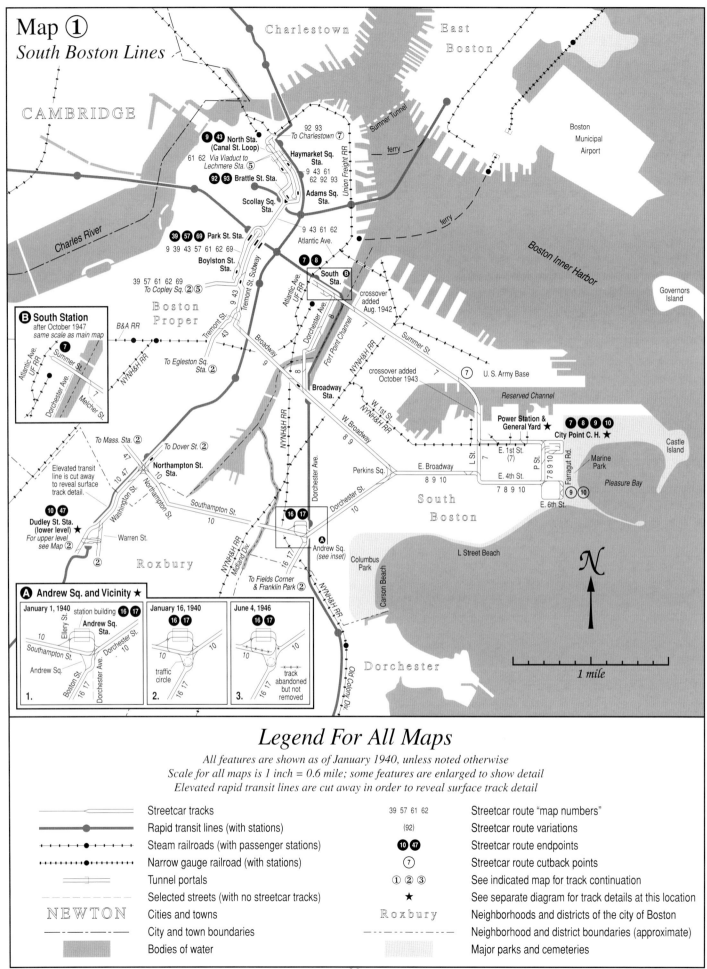

Map ①
South Boston Lines

CAMBRIDGE

Charlestown   East Boston

9 43 North Sta.
(Canal St. Loop)
61 62 Via Viaduct to Lechmere Sta. ⑤

92 93 Brattle St. Sta.

Scollay Sq. Sta.

Haymarket Sq. Sta.
92 93
To Charlestown ⑦

Adams Sq. Sta.
9 43 61 62 92 93

Sumner Tunnel

ferry

Boston Municipal Airport

39 57 69 Park St. Sta.
9 39 43 57 61 62 69

Boylston St. Sta.

39 57 61 62 69
To Copley Sq. ②⑤

Boston Proper

Tremont St. Subway

Charles River

9 43 61 62
Atlantic Ave.

⑦ ⑧ South Sta. **B**

crossover added Aug. 1942

ferry

Boston Inner Harbor

Governors Island

B South Station
after October 1947 same scale as main map

⑦

Atlantic Ave.
UF RR

Summer St.

B&A RR

Dorchester Ave.

Melcher St.

NYNH&H RR

⑦

Atlantic Ave. UF RR

To Egleston Sq. Sta. ②

Broadway

Tremont St.

43

9

8

Dorchester Ave.

Fort Point Channel

NYNH&H RR

crossover added October 1943

Summer St.

⑦

⑦ U. S. Army Base

Reserved Channel

Power Station & General Yard ★

⑦ ⑧ ⑨ ⑩
City Point C. H. ★

Castle Island

Marine Park

Pleasure Bay

Broadway Sta.

W. 1st St.

NYNH&H RR

E. 1st St.
(⑦)

E. 4th St.

7 8 9 10

L St.

P St.

Farragut Rd.

7 8 9 10

⑨ ⑩

E. 6th St.

South Boston

L Street Beach

To Mass. Sta. ②

To Dover St. ②

47

Elevated transit line is cut away to reveal surface track detail.

Northampton St. Sta.

10

10 47 Dudley St. Sta. (lower level) ★
For upper level see Map ②

Washington St.

Warren St.

Northampton St.

Southampton St.

W. Broadway
8 9

E. Broadway
8 9 10

Perkins Sq.

Dorchester Ave.

Dorchester St.

10

16 17

Andrew Sq. (see inset)

Columbus Park

Carson Beach

Roxbury

②

NYNH&H RR
Midland Div.

To Fields Corner & Franklin Park ②

Old Colony Div.

Dorchester

A Andrew Sq. and Vicinity ★

1. January 1, 1940   station building **16 17**
Ellery St.
Andrew Sq. Sta.
Southampton St.
Andrew Sq.
Boston St.
Dorchester Ave.
Dorchester St.
10   16 17

2. January 16, 1940
16 17
10
traffic circle
16 17

3. June 4, 1946
16 17
10
10
16 17
track abandoned but not removed

N
1 mile

Legend For All Maps
All features are shown as of January 1940, unless noted otherwise
Scale for all maps is 1 inch = 0.6 mile; some features are enlarged to show detail
Elevated rapid transit lines are cut away in order to reveal surface track detail

Streetcar tracks	39 57 61 62 — Streetcar route "map numbers"
Rapid transit lines (with stations)	(92) — Streetcar route variations
Steam railroads (with passenger stations)	**10 47** — Streetcar route endpoints
Narrow gauge railroad (with stations)	⑦ — Streetcar route cutback points
Tunnel portals	①②③ — See indicated map for track continuation
Selected streets (with no streetcar tracks)	★ — See separate diagram for track details at this location
NEWTON — Cities and towns	Roxbury — Neighborhoods and districts of the city of Boston
City and town boundaries	Neighborhood and district boundaries (approximate)
Bodies of water	Major parks and cemeteries

P Street between the carhouse and East Fourth Street.

As mentioned above City Point was also the rating station for two routes primarily outside South Boston: Franklin Park–Andrew Station and Dudley Street Station–Massachusetts Station. These lines will be discussed in Chapter 3. City Point provided the operators and Type 5 cars that were assigned to these routes in the 1940s.

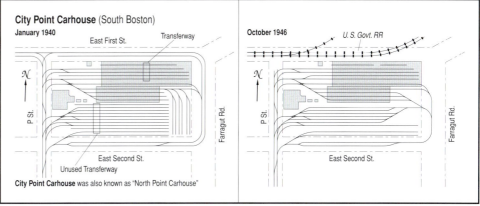

City Point Carhouse (South Boston)
January 1940
East First St.
Transferway
N
P St.
Farragut Rd.
East Second St.
Unused Transferway
City Point Carhouse was also known as "North Point Carhouse"

October 1946
U. S. Govt. RR
N
P St.
Farragut Rd.
East Second St.

In 1942 two tracks and an unused transferway were removed from the yard on the former site of the South Carhouse, and 104 feet of another yard track were written off.[107] In 1944 six yard storage tracks were removed, and a curve track was installed between Farragut Road and the South Carhouse yard adjoining East Second Street. The new curve completed a loop from P Street through the yard and was installed with PCC operation in mind. Also at this time a second transferway was removed from the North Carhouse, and a former stub-end track was connected to an adjacent track.[108] A second yard track was joined to the yard lead onto Farragut Road in May 1945, providing storage for cars that used the loop.[109] Later in 1945, all but three of the remaining South Carhouse yard storage tracks were joined to the Farragut Road yard lead.[110] Early in 1946, 192 feet of additional storage track was added to the three remaining stub-end yard tracks.[111]

In October 1946, as part of roadway resurfacing by the City of Boston, 721 feet of track was removed from Farragut Road, and 203 feet was covered over on East Second Street.[112] The track affected was the outer one nearest Pleasure Bay and ran on Farragut Road between East First Street and East Second Street, then around the corner on East Second Street to the crossover.

A view of the caryard and buildings on the south side of City Point Carhouse. Type 4 and 5 cars abound in this scene taken from P Street on January 1, 1941.
Stanley M. Houck

Center-entrance sand car 6317 and Type 4 No. 5405 bask in the late afternoon sun in front of the northerly carhouse building at City Point. One of several tanks in a tank farm near the carhouse looms in the background in this view taken in April 1942.
Charles A. Duncan

Major repairs were made to the trackwork on P Street beside the carhouse and elsewhere on P Street between East First Street and East Fourth Street in the late summer and early fall of 1947.[113] Between East Second and East Fourth Streets, the track was completely rebuilt. Between the carhouse special work and East Second Street, the tracks were resurfaced, and the remaining abandoned rails on P Street from East First Street to the special work at City Point Carhouse were removed. Finally, special work at East Second Street and the carhouse was renewed. This work was also done as part of a City of Boston roadway-resurfacing project.

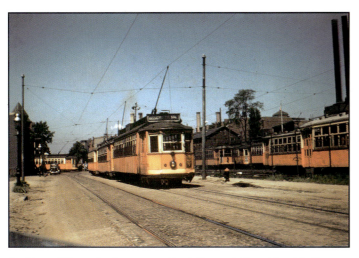

A string of Type 4s line up on East Second Street beside the car yard at City Point in 1941. East Second Street, while a public way, was used by the Boston Elevated to store cars that were soon to go into service.
Charles A. Duncan

Marine Park, a popular South Boston destination, was located on the shore of Pleasure Bay and featured an aquarium. Streetcars from Dudley Street Station and North Station directly served the park, ending their runs at these parallel layover tracks on Farragut Road. This terminal point was used during the summer and on fair weather days in the spring and fall as an alternative destination to City Point Carhouse, located a few blocks away along Farragut Road. The all-electric PCC and the two Type 4 cars are facing inbound in this scene, taken in 1946.   *Charles A. Duncan*

Farragut Road Loop (Marine Park)

Cars on Routes 9 and 10 were often routed to a special loop with a layover point on Farragut Road rather than to City Point Carhouse during milder weather in the summer ratings. The layover was a few blocks south of the carhouse and directly served the local beaches and Marine Park, the site of a City of Boston Aquarium. The loop location is shown on Map 1. When this loop was in operation, service generally ran from 10 a.m. to 11 p.m. seven days a week during all but the early morning and late evening hours.

Outbound cars were routed over the loop from East Fourth Street, then south onto P Street, in the opposite direction from the carhouse. From P Street, the track turned east onto East Sixth Street, and then north onto Farragut Road adjacent to Marine Park. Here two layover tracks and three crossovers provided ample storage and switching capability. Cars returned inbound via East Fourth Street directly to North Station or to Dudley Street Station. The loop was single track on P Street, East Sixth Street, and East Fourth Street.

Bill Grimes remembers…

A seven-year-old, tired after a day of splashing in the waves at City Point, maybe a little sunburned, you finish the last fried clams in the white cardboard box from Kelly's Landing and head for the streetcar for home. With a final glance at the plump copper fish impaled on the weather vane above the Aquarium, you climb the steps into the first car in line—most likely a Type 4 signed "North Station via Subway," laying over on one of the two parallel tracks on Farragut Road, usually the one closest to the sidewalk and the ocean.

Scampering to a vacant window seat, you slide across the sun-warmed red seat slats to peer through the black metal grating at the Type 4s lined up on the other track and bound for a mysterious, yet undiscovered destination called "Dudley." First one car's compressor cuts in and then another, each chugging at its own pitch, like a group of elderly South Boston ladies gossiping on a bench by the shore. Finally the operator climbs aboard, cranks the accumulated coins through the farebox, and releases the brakes in a burst of escaping air. The Type 4 groans into motion; we clatter over the switches and head up East Fourth Street, homeward bound.

William J. Grimes, BSRA Publications Director, grew up in South Boston.

Farragut Road had only two Type 4 cars in attendance on this sunny summer day, July 10, 1945. The Type 4 nearest us will soon depart for Dudley Street, while the second will likely head for North Station. *Charles A. Duncan*

Equipment Assignments

The Type 5 was the predominant car type based at City Point. In the April 1, 1940, rating there were 90 cars, including spares. The roster consisted of 53 Type 5s and 37 Type 4 cars.

The December 12, 1949, rating showed 20 PCC cars and 96 Type 5s, totaling 116 cars including spares. As of this rating, Salem Street Carhouse in Medford became a substation of City Point. The 18 Type 5s required for the Fellsway line and the single Type 5 for the North Station–Brattle Street Station shuttle car and their spares are included in the 116-car total. Physically, however, cars for the subway shuttle and the Fellsway remained at Salem Street Carhouse.

Car assignments by type of car and by line during the 1940s are presented in detail in Appendix 2. Type 5 cars were used almost exclusively during the 1940s on the City Point–South Station via Dorchester Avenue and the City Point–South Station via Summer Street lines, including the Army Base service.

City Point–North Station was assigned Type 4s until September 1946. Two PCCs were assigned to this line in the October 22, 1945, rating, following the installation mentioned above of a turning loop at City Point in 1944. All-electric PCC cars entered service here on July 8, 1946. In the September 3, 1946, rating, the line was completely converted to PCC operation, but Type 4s continued to fill in as spares. Type 5s were used on the cutback, City Point–Broadway Station.

Type 4 cars were operated on the City Point–Dudley line almost exclusively until the June 20, 1949, rating. Peak service at this time was entirely converted to Type 5s. After the Egleston Station accident in April 1948, the MTA made every effort to remove Type 4 cars from service. The move to Type 5s reflected this intention and the fact that the Type 5s were newer and in better condition. PCC cars were introduced on City Point–Dudley in November 1946 but were generally operated only in weekday off-peak hours and all day on Sundays.

East Sixth Street was part of the Farragut Road summertime loop. Here we see a Type 4 on East Sixth Street single track about to take the switch onto one of the two storage tracks around the corner on Farragut Road on July 10, 1945. *Charles A. Duncan*

East First Street

Double tracks on East First Street ran about four-tenths of a mile between Summer Street and P Street and saw limited use. The East First Street tracks paralleled those on nearby East Fourth Street, a few blocks to the south. As late as February 1942, the El was running ten outbound morning trips and seven inbound evening trips for the Summer Street line over East First Street.

In response to a request from the United States War Department, the Elevated stopped using East First Street on March 5, 1942. The War Department had its own freight railroad tracks on East First Street, and traffic over the freight line had increased tremendously during the war. Most of the cargo consisted of live ammunition and petroleum products. The Elevated, under contract from the War Department, removed most of the streetcar track from East First Street by the end of the year. This track included the leads into the yard of the South Boston Power Station.

Type 5 No. 5566 turns from East First Street onto Summer Street on May 17, 1940. The roll sign reads ARMY BASE, so the car may run between that destination and South Station. Note the railroad track to the right of the trolley tracks. *Charles A. Duncan*

The South Boston Power Station (1), with its outdoor coal storage facility, is seen in the center of this aerial photograph looking north taken by an aircraft from Naval Air Station Squantum on October 8, 1941. To the left is the Boston Edison power plant, while the City Point Carhouse (2) is two blocks east of the Power Station.

U.S. Navy, Boston National Historical Park Collection

The track arrangement on East First Street was quite unusual. Prior to the removal of the streetcar track, a single railroad track was located on the south side of the street. One railroad rail was to the south of the eastbound streetcar track and the second railroad rail was located between the two rails of the same streetcar track. This construction obviously prevented the simultaneous operation of railroad equipment and eastbound streetcars.

This overlapping rail arrangement continued as far as the South Boston Power Station, at which point, the railroad track turned north onto O Street, crossing both streetcar tracks to serve the power station and a tank farm on the east side of O Street. There were also two freight sidings between Summer Street and the Elevated's power station that crossed the streetcar tracks into the Boston Edison power plant property. After the streetcar tracks were removed, double railroad tracks were installed and extended along East First Street almost as far as Farragut Road. Here the railroad tracks turned north onto private land.

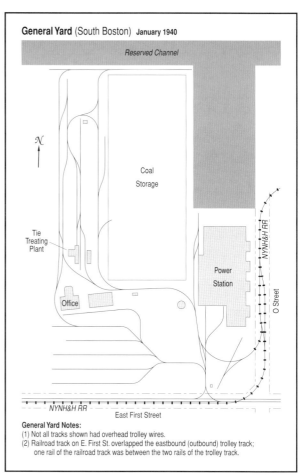

General Yard Notes:
(1) Not all tracks shown had overhead trolley wires.
(2) Railroad track on E. First St. overlapped the eastbound (outbound) trolley track; one rail of the railroad track was between the two rails of the trolley track.

South Boston Power Station and the General Yard

South Boston Power Station was the main electricity generating facility of the Boston Elevated Railway Company. It opened in 1911 and was in use until 1981. At the time the station closed, it was the last power generating facility still run in the United States by a transit entity.

The General Yard of the company was also part of the South Boston Power Station complex. The yard tracks connected to East First Street and to an adjoining tie-treating plant. The General Yard was used chiefly for work cars and material

The entrance to the South Boston Power Station from East First Street brackets the last Type 5 built, 5970, as it wends its way toward the complex's storage yard. The station buildings and coal handling towers seen over the top of the car set the theme of this scene rather well. *Charles A. Duncan*

This view of the tie treating plant at the General Yard in South Boston shows work car 3123, a former 12-bench open passenger car, beside bundles of ties on flat cars about to enter the processing shed. This shot was taken in April 1922; the yard would see many more years of service before closing in 1948. *BERy*

Cars using the middle level at Broadway Station entered and left through this incline near West Fourth Street and Broadway. In this November 27, 1941, scene, it had been 22 years since cars last used it. The City of Boston began filling in the incline in December 1941 as a WPA project. The northerly entrance to the middle level subway remains to this day yet was never used for through service. *BERy*

storage, but there are good photos of Type 5 cars in temporary storage here as well.[d] In 1944 the Elevated removed 385 feet of track that ran to the site of a coal trestle, which had been demolished in 1937.[114]

As previously mentioned, the yard was isolated from the rest of the system in 1942 with the removal of the streetcar track on East First Street at the behest of the War Department. However, the yard still retained its connection to the freight railroad track.

The Boston Elevated had operated a creosote tie-treating plant at the General Yard since 1916. While this treatment facility was very cost effective, retaining it in the late 1940s in the light of the system-wide decline of streetcar lines could not be financially justified. The plant was sold to the Mari-Trop Trading Company, a division of the United Fruit Company, on November 10, 1948.

Two interesting work cars were used at the tie-treating plant. Former 12-bench open car 3123 and car 3604 were used as shifters; 3123 served as an office as well. They were sold for scrap on November 15, 1948. In May 1949, the MTA Maintenance Department removed much of the track and special work that had been abandoned with the closing of the tie-treating plant.[115]

Broadway Trolley Station Incline

In December 1941, the City of Boston began filling in the unused Dorchester Avenue surface car incline near West Fourth Street[116] and Broadway as a WPA project.[117] This south ramp to the former underground Broadway trolley station had been unused since October 14, 1919. The trolley station was in active use less than two years, having opened on December

15, 1917 with the rest of the Broadway Station complex.[e] The north portal of the Broadway trolley station tunnel, fronting on Foundry Street, was never removed and remains to this day secured by massive gates.

7 City Point–South Station (Dewey Square) *via Summer Street*

This line left City Point Carhouse and turned south onto P Street, west onto East Fourth Street, then north onto L Street, which ran into Summer Street at East Second Street. The line followed Summer Street all the way to South Station. On the way it crossed a drawbridge over the Reserved Channel; a bridge near B Street, which ran over the New York, New Haven & Hartford Railroad (New Haven Railroad) line to the docks, Naval Dry Docks, and Army Base; and a drawbridge across the Fort Point Channel. The tracks entered Boston Proper over the middle of the Channel.

At Dorchester Avenue, just beyond the Fort Point Channel, the cars joined a double-track connection with the second City Point–South Station line, Route 8, described later. Just beyond this intersection, off the outbound rail on Summer Street, there was a passing siding with a short storage spur at its downtown end.

---

[d] One such example was in 1938, after the famous Hurricane had affected part of City Point Carhouse.

[e] The Broadway Station complex included a subway station at the lowest level for the Cambridge–Dorchester subway line, today's Red Line. The underground trolley station was located on the middle level. A surface transfer station was built at the street level on Broadway, and it remained in use for streetcars until 1953. It was also used for buses over the years, and a new but unused surface station occupies the same site today.

Type 5 No. 5566 running inbound on Summer Street passes the Boston Army Base on April 18, 1948. The Wharf Shed at left became the Black Falcon Cruise Terminal in 1985. *Foster M. Palmer*

Car 5568 outbound on Summer Street near Melcher Street on its way to City Point passes the Colonial Wool Company in this scene on July 5, 1941. *Stanley M. Hauck*

The Summer Street line continued to South Station to a *trailing point* crossover located just before Atlantic Avenue.[f] Here cars lay over after changing ends for the return trip to City Point. Route 7 was 5.006 miles round-trip and the average round-trip running time was 28 minutes.

On March 12, 1946, the drawbridge on Summer Street over the Fort Point Channel was closed for repairs, and the car line temporarily ended at a crossover at Melcher Street on the South Boston side of the bridge.[118] During the repairs, which were completed July 19, 1946, passengers were required to walk across the bridge to South Station.

The MTA completely rebuilt the end of the line from Dorchester Avenue to Atlantic Avenue in the early fall of 1947.[119] This new construction produced a *Y* track configuration, centered in the street by using a diamond switch.[g] The City of Boston had wanted the line to end centered in a new traffic island with protection for pedestrians on both sides; the reconstruction provided this improvement. Also during this work, the track connections at Dorchester Avenue for the City Point–South Station via Dorchester Avenue line were removed along with the passing siding on Summer Street and its storage spur. Map 1, Inset B shows these track changes.

Route 7 ended at South Station in the middle of Summer Street at Dewey Square. This shot of 5969 was taken June 14, 1949, after the MTA rebuilt the double track stub-end configuration to a Y configuration with pedestrian safety islands. *Leon Onofri*

A cutback started in 1943 ran between South Station and the Boston Army Base. A trailing point crossover was located north of the Reserved Channel next to the Army base. A new *facing point*[h] crossover was installed south of the Reserved Channel on Summer Street in 1943.[120] Either crossover was available for the Army Base cutback. This extremely short 2.227-mile round-trip route was operated in rush hours and evenings from May 1943 through December 1949. The average round-trip running time was 10 minutes.

Between the May 17 and the September 3, 1943, ratings, Route 7 service was only operated between the Reserved Channel and South Station, evidently while bridge repairs were taking place.

---

[f] A *trailing point* switch was installed with the movable part of the switch facing away from the direction of travel of the oncoming streetcar. Once the car had passed over the switch, the trailing point design required the operator of the car to reverse the direction of the car to take the switch. The operator usually threw the switch manually with a *switch stick*, also called a *switch iron*. Cars with primary operating controls at one end, such as PCCs, required *facing point* switches in normal operation. Boston PCCs did have a backup controller, however, so it was possible for them to use a *trailing point* switch if necessary.

A *trailing point crossover* required cars to change operating ends and reverse direction before taking the crossover, making *trailing point* crossovers far safer to use than *facing point* crossovers.

[g] The term *Y* should not be confused with the railroad term, "wye." A *Y* termination point on a Boston car line was quite literally shaped like the letter "Y." Two tracks converged through a switch, into one stub-end, where double-ended streetcars could change ends for the return trip. Sometimes the single leg of the *Y* was centered using a diamond, or *Y*, switch; at other times it ended up on the left or right-hand side of the road using a *facing point or a trailing point switch*.

---

[h] A *facing point* switch was installed with the movable part of the switch facing the direction of travel of the oncoming streetcar. This design allowed the operator of the car to select the direction permitted by the switch, right or left, and continue on through the switch. The operator manually threw most switches with a *switch stick*, but switches at busy locations were often electrically thrown from the car to save time. Cars normally operated with controls at one end, such as PCCs, required *facing point* switches in normal operation.

A *facing point crossover* allowed cars to move directly onto the rail running in the opposite direction. Since this type of move invited a collision between cars traveling in the opposite direction, *facing point* crossover moves have always been made with extreme caution.

On April 18, 1947, lumbering Type 4 No. 5434 crosses the Reserved Channel drawbridge having completed a trip to the Boston Army Base. A crossover on this side of the bridge added in 1943 will be the turnback point for the return trip of 5434 to South Station. *Stanley M. Hauck*

8 City Point–South Station (Dewey Square)
via Broadway and Dorchester Avenue

This line left City Point the same way as the Summer Street line. One block after turning onto L Street, however, the line turned west onto East Broadway and followed it to Perkins Square, which is the junction of East Broadway, West Broadway, and Dorchester Street. Tracks on the latter two streets formed a *Y* configuration with the East Broadway track. A double-track curve connection at Perkins Square between Dorchester Street and West Broadway was used for the Owl Cars traveling between Andrew Station and the Tremont Street Subway.

Cars for South Station bore right onto West Broadway and followed it to Dorchester Avenue, crossing a bridge near B Street over the New Haven Railroad line to the docks. Just before the Broadway Station subway-surface transfer facility, the line turned north onto Dorchester Avenue, crossed the Fort Point Channel drawbridge into Boston Proper, and ran to Summer Street. The line turned northwest onto Summer Street, joining the City Point–South Station via Summer Street line for the few remaining blocks to South Station, and changing ends there for the return trip. This line was 5.844 miles long, round-trip, and the average running time was 37 minutes.

North of the Fort Point Channel on Dorchester Avenue there was a short passing siding off the northbound rail beside the channel. This was the "snow dump track," and it started about 1000 feet south of Summer Street, running 700 feet toward the Dorchester Avenue drawbridge. About 500 feet of this track was on the sidewalk directly adjacent to the channel. The City of Boston began road and sidewalk repairs in this area in the fall of 1940. As part of the work, on October 3, the Elevated tore the track up from the sidewalk but left the connections with the main line intact.

This line had low ridership and on June 5, 1940, it became a rush hours-only route. The line had originally been slated for afternoon rush hour service only, but the El decided at the

Most of Route 8, City Point–South Station via Dorchester Avenue, was shared trackage with Routes 7 and 9. Its only unique trackage was on Dorchester Avenue between Broadway and Summer Street. At top, car 5606 travels inbound to South Station having just crossed the Dorchester Avenue drawbridge over the Fort Point Channel. The snow dump track that ran alongside the channel is in the foreground. Above, Type 5 No. 5965 has just passed the South Postal Annex and is about to turn from Dorchester Avenue onto Summer Street. *Both, Charles A. Duncan*

last moment to include morning rush hour trips as well. Restricted operation continued throughout the war, but service requirements grew steadily. By 1946 the line was running all day from about 6 a.m. to 6 p.m.

In anticipation of the reconstruction of the Dorchester Avenue drawbridge over the Fort Point Channel, streetcar service across the bridge was discontinued December 2, 1946.[i] The line was broken into two parts: Dorchester Avenue Bridge–South Station, .890 miles round-trip with a running time of 5 minutes, and the much longer City Point–Dorchester Avenue Bridge via Broadway, 4.746 miles round-trip and a running time of 28 minutes. One Type 5 was assigned to Dorchester Avenue Bridge–South Station, and three Type 4s to City Point–Dorchester Avenue Bridge. Both segments were abandoned on April 4, 1947.

The seven-tenths of a mile of rail on Dorchester Avenue was the only track not shared with other routes and unique to this line. Removal of track on the north side of the drawbridge began on August 30, 1948. Track removal was about half done when the work was suspended on September 7. The project resumed on April 14, 1949, and it was completed April 18. The track connections to Summer Street had been removed in 1947 as previously mentioned.

---

[i] Actual reconstruction of the bridge did not begin until February 15, 1947.

Route 9, City Point–North Station, was the most important South Boston line. PCCs entered service on this route in July 1946, and on September 3, took over most service with Type 4s running only as spares. This shot was taken on September 3, 1946, and veteran Type 4 No. 5433 waits at P and East Second Street to begin its run in town, one of the last it would make in regular revenue service. *Stanley M. Hauck*

9 City Point–North Station *via Subway*

This line was the most important of the South Boston lines, providing direct service to downtown Boston via the Tremont Street Subway. Leaving City Point Carhouse, Route 9 followed the same route as the City Point–South Station via Dorchester Avenue line as far as Dorchester Avenue. Here, instead of turning north, the line crossed Dorchester Avenue and entered Broadway Station, where riders could transfer to the Cambridge–Dorchester Subway.[j]

Cars then ran across the Broadway Bridge over the New Haven Railroad yards and the Fort Point Channel into Boston Proper, and then crossed another bridge over the New Haven Railroad and B&A Railroad main lines. At Tremont Street, cars entered the subway through a now-abandoned portal. Once underground the cars ran through a flying junction with the Egleston line and continued on to Canal Street Loop at North Station, turning around there for the return trip.[121] A Route 9 round-trip between City Point and North Station was 8.157 miles, making this the longest of the South Boston lines. The round-trip running time averaged 54 minutes.

As previously mentioned, during fair weather in the summer, service was operated from the layover track on Farragut Road rather than the carhouse during most hours of the day. This alternate route was 8.141 miles round trip to North Station and took 55 minutes.

Repairs on the Broadway Bridge interrupted service on this line between May 17 and September 3, 1943. During this period, the Elevated operated a temporary cutback using Type 4 cars as far as the Broadway Bridge crossover. Owl Cars that usually crossed the bridge ended at the Broadway Bridge crossover, and a second Owl Car shuttle ran from North Station to a crossover on Broadway near the Broadway and Tremont Street subway portal essentially to make up for the lost subway service.

On March 17, 1947, the Elevated instituted a regular cutback of Route 9 that ran from City Point to Broadway Station. This line, 4.377 miles round-trip with a running time of 27 minutes and a duplication of the temporary cutback in 1943, would replace the City Point–Dorchester Avenue Bridge service on Route 8 previously mentioned and would continue through the end of the decade and beyond.

Type 4 No. 5442 heads toward downtown Boston having just turned from L Street onto East Broadway. *Charles A. Duncan*

Type 4 No. 5435 heads down West Broadway toward City Point. By the time this shot was taken in September 1945, PCC cars were slated to replace these Type 4s on the line to North Station.

Charles A. Duncan

All-electric PCC 3209 has just crossed the Broadway Bridge over the Fort Point Channel and is making its way to the Broadway and Tremont Street subway portal and downtown Boston.

Paul M. Paulsen

---

[j] Because this surface station had an island platform situated between the inbound and outbound tracks, buses that also used this station were specially equipped with a left-hand door for loading and unloading. The streetcars, of course, already had left-hand doors.

Two Type 4 cars head outbound for South Boston on Broadway near Shawmut Avenue in this 1941 scene.   *Charles A. Duncan*

10 City Point–Dudley Street

The City Point–Dudley line shared track with Routes 8 and 9 as far as Perkins Square. Here, City Point–Dudley bore left onto Dorchester Street, and ran directly into Andrew Square.[k] At Andrew Square, the track ran straight through to Southampton Street in both directions.[l] However, the City Point–Dudley cars turned north at Andrew Square onto Dorchester Avenue and then immediately west into the northerly prepayment station platform at Andrew surface station. Here a transfer could be made to the Cambridge–Dorchester Subway, the car lines to Franklin Park and Fields Corner, or to the Savin Hill Station bus line. Leaving Andrew Station, the Dudley-bound cars turned south onto Ellery Street, then west onto Southampton Street.[m]

---

[k] Andrew Square is the intersection of Boston Street, Dorchester Avenue, Dorchester Street, and Southampton Street. Map 1, Inset A, Panel 1 shows the tracks in and around Andrew Square as of January 1, 1940.

[l] Between January 2 and January 16, 1940, in conjunction with the construction of a traffic circle in Andrew Square, a new loop track was built around the traffic circle to the south. The new loop connected the southbound Boston Street track with the northbound Dorchester Avenue track, and allowed cars going directly from Southampton Street to South Boston to conform to the traffic circle flow.

To make way for the traffic circle and the new track curve, connecting trackage from Dorchester Street to Boston Street was removed. This trackage ran between a switch off the westbound track on Dorchester Street to the southbound track on Boston Street, via the southbound Dorchester Avenue track. This change now required cars going from South Boston to Boston Street to loop through Andrew Station first. Map 1, Inset A, Panel 2 shows these changes.

On June 4, 1946, the Boston Elevated abandoned the westbound track on Dorchester Street and Southampton Street, from the northbound switch on Dorchester Street that connected to Dorchester Avenue, to Ellery Street. A short stretch of the eastbound track was also abandoned, from the northbound switch on Southampton Street that connected to Dorchester Avenue, to the switch on Dorchester Street from Dorchester Avenue. The special work from the eastbound and westbound Southampton Street tracks that crossed the Dorchester Avenue track was removed at this time. This change forced all cars from South Boston to Southampton Street to go through Andrew Station first. Details of these changes in 1946 are shown in Map 1, Inset A, Panel 3.

[m] The car lines to Franklin Park and Fields Corner from Andrew followed the same street routing into Andrew Station as the Dudley Street cars. However, the Franklin Park and Fields Corner cars used the southerly platform track and they turned east onto Southampton Street from Ellery Street and then south onto Boston Street.

City Point housed the Type 5s used on the Franklin Park–Andrew and Dudley–Massachusetts Station lines. Here, No. 5829, dead-heading to Andrew Square, pauses on Broadway at Perkins Square before taking the switch onto Dorchester Street.   *Charles A. Duncan*

Eastern Massachusetts Street Railway car 7010 provides a rare daytime photo opportunity on the special loop used by Owl Cars from Dorchester Street to West Broadway. The date is May 2, 1948, and the car is on the way to Everett Shops to be scrapped following the abandonment of the Eastern Mass. Quincy lines.

Foster M. Palmer

Andrew Square saw many track changes in the 1940s as evidenced by this 1950 scene. Here we are looking directly into Andrew Square from Dorchester Street. The cross street is Dorchester Avenue. Type 5 No. 5558 has rounded the traffic circle to the left of the square and will soon enter Dorchester Street and return to City Point. Tracks going north to the right run to Andrew Station and tracks on the other side of the square veering off from the right are coming from Andrew Station and Southampton Street.   *MTA*

All-electric PCC 3209 is turning from Ellery Street onto Southampton Street following its departure from Andrew Square Station in the background.
Clarke Collection

All-electric PCC 3206 sporting the new MTA map decal practically has the street to itself as it heads for Andrew Square in this scene taken June 16, 1948, at Dorchester and East Ninth Streets.
Charles A. Duncan

Cars going from Dudley Street to City Point on Southampton Street also turned north onto Dorchester Avenue at Andrew Square and then entered the station on the same track and in the same direction as the cars from City Point. Leaving Andrew Station, outbound City Point cars turned south onto Ellery Street, east onto Southampton Street, southeasterly toward Boston Street, and rounded the Andrew Square traffic circle before entering Dorchester Street. Outbound City Point cars, then, made a complete circle through Andrew Station before continuing to South Boston.

Westbound City Point–Dudley cars now continued on Southampton Street, crossing a bridge over the New Haven Railroad Old Colony line, and then entering Roxbury and running under the New Haven Railroad Midland Division Bridge. The line then crossed Albany Street. At this point Southampton Street became Northampton Street. The line continued on Northampton Street, entering the South End section of Boston Proper near Harrison Avenue and shortly thereafter turning south onto Washington Street.[n] The line continued on Washington Street, soon crossing back into Roxbury.

Dudley-bound cars followed Washington Street to Warren Street, meeting a double-track connection on Warren Street, and bearing left onto Warren Street to Dudley Street Station. Here the cars turned west into the North Yard of the lower station level to drop off and take on riders. Cars leaving Dudley Street Station for South Boston turned north onto Washington Street for their return trip.[122]

Starting from City Point Carhouse, this line was 7.88 miles round-trip, which made it the second-longest South Boston line. It had an average running time of 49 minutes. As with Route 9, summer service was usually operated from the lay-

The Main Line Elevated is behind 5858 as it rumbles down Northampton Street toward Andrew Square.
Paul M. Paulsen

A Type 5 runs under the Main Line Elevated on Washington Street on its way to Andrew Station from Dudley around 1943.
BERy

---

[n] The Northampton Street tracks continued across Washington Street and were used from this point by the Dudley–Massachusetts Station cars.

A Type 4 heads for City Point at Washington and Warren Streets, passing a Type 5 from Massachusetts Station going to Dudley Street. The building at right that housed Ferdinands Furniture is still there. *BERy*

The lead into the South Yard at Dudley Street is where the Type 5 on Washington Street will end up in a moment or two. The date is June 4, 1946. *BERy*

The North Yard at the lower lever of Dudley Street Station was the arrival and departure point for cars to City Point. Here PCC 3203 enters the station from Warren Street. The operator has already changed the roll sign from DUDLEY to CITY POINT in preparation for a quick return. *MTA*

over on Farragut Road. The round trip distance from here to Dudley Street was 7.864 miles and also took 49 minutes to complete.

The balance of the decade in South Boston would be uneventful. Major changes loomed on the horizon, however, and these would be played out in the early 1950s with the replacement of all South Boston streetcar service by buses.

Type 5 No. 5742 from Jamaica Plain Loop bound for Dudley Street Station passes a Mack bus headed for Allston on Roxbury Street in historic John Eliot Square. This scene was taken about 1948, and ten years earlier, the Allston line would have been running with Type 5 cars as well. The Eliot Congregational Church in the background could be in any New England country town, but this building is just two miles or so from downtown Boston.

Robert A. Kennerly

Chapter 3

The Dorchester, Roxbury, & Quincy Lines

Dorchester and Roxbury, both former colonial towns, are adjoining districts of Boston. Dorchester was annexed to Boston in 1870 and Roxbury in 1868. By the 1940s these districts had well-developed commercial, industrial, and residential sections, and the local car lines were in heavy use.

Both districts also had good rapid transit service. The Cambridge–Dorchester rapid transit line stopped at Columbia, Savin Hill, Fields Corner, Shawmut, and Ashmont Stations in Dorchester. The New Haven Railroad Midland Division also served Dorchester, stopping at a number of stations, depending on the year, between 1940 and 1947. The Main Line Elevated served Roxbury with stations at Dudley Street and Egleston Square.

Many streetcar lines originated at rapid transit stations, some lines running between stations and enjoying heavy ridership in both directions. The Franklin Park Zoo was a major recreational traffic generator, and was directly served by streetcar lines on Blue Hill Avenue, Seaver Street, Humboldt Avenue, and Columbia Road.

The City of Quincy, located southeast of Dorchester across the Neponset River, is known as the birthplace of Presidents of the United States John Adams and John Quincy Adams. The city is also the site of the Granite Railway, the first railroad in America. Its principal industry was the Fore River Shipyard, probably the most important reason for the retention of streetcars here until 1948. Quincy also had significant commercial and light industrial activity and was quite residential as well. In addition to the Quincy Shipyard and Houghs Neck streetcars of the Eastern Massachusetts Street Railway, the New Haven Railroad provided service in Quincy on its Granite Branch and Old Colony Division.

More changes took place in Dorchester and Roxbury in the 1940s than in any other section of the transit system. The Metropolitan Transit Authority converted most of the streetcar lines in this area to trackless trolleys in 1948 and 1949. The Authority also transferred two more car lines in 1948 from Park Street Carhouse in Dorchester to its nearby neighbor, the Arborway. For clarity, some lines are discussed both in this chapter and Chapter 4.

Quincy, too, saw the end of its last streetcar lines in 1946 and 1948. Buses replaced the streetcars on these two routes, however.

Service Overview

In 1940, fourteen streetcar lines served Roxbury and Dorchester. Nine lines were assigned to Park Street Carhouse in Dorchester. Two more lines ran out of City Point Carhouse in South Boston, and another three lines were based at Arborway Carhouse in Jamaica Plain.

The nine Park Street Carhouse lines are listed below and are shown on Map 2.

Route No.	Route Description
15	**Uphams Corner–Dudley Street Station** *via Columbia Road and Dudley Street*
17	**Fields Corner Station–Andrew Station** *via Geneva Avenue, Bowdoin Street, Meeting House Hill, Hancock Street, Columbia Road, Boston Street, and Dorchester Avenue*
19	**Fields Corner Station–Dudley Street Station** *via Geneva Avenue and Warren Street*
20	**Fields Corner Station–Neponset Loop** *via Geneva Avenue, Park Street, Dorchester Avenue, Gibson Street, Adams Street, and Neponset Avenue*
22	**Ashmont Station–Dudley Street Station** *via Dorchester Avenue, Talbot Avenue, Codman Square, Talbot Avenue, Blue Hill Avenue, Grove Hall, and Warren Street*
23	**Ashmont Station–Dudley Street Station** *via Dorchester Avenue, Talbot Avenue, Codman Square, Washington Street (Dorchester), Grove Hall, and Warren Street*
28	**Mattapan Station–Ashmont Station** *via High-Speed Trolley Line*
29	**Mattapan Station–Egleston Station** *via Blue Hill Avenue, Seaver Street, and Columbus Avenue*
[cb]	**Morton Street Crossover–Egleston**[a]
45	**Grove Hall–Dudley Street Station** *via Blue Hill Avenue and Dudley Street*

[a] Cutbacks, not assigned their own route numbers, are indicated by "cb" in brackets before the description. Some readers may recall that MTA operators in the 1950s referred to this cutback as "Johnston Road," and some car roll signs at that time read BLUE HILL AVENUE TO JOHNSTON ROAD. However, the cutback in the 1940s was located just north of Morton Street.

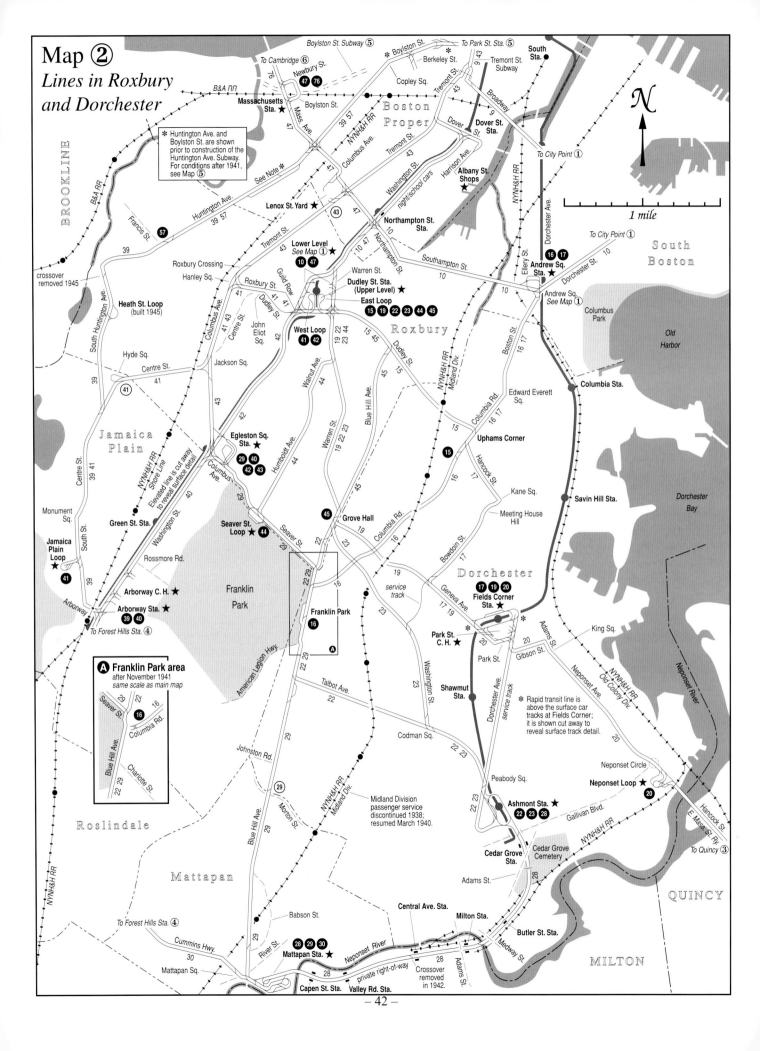

Map ②
Lines in Roxbury
and Dorchester

* Huntington Ave. and
Boylston St. are shown
prior to construction of the
Huntington Ave. Subway.
For conditions after 1941,
see Map ⑤

Boylston St. Subway ⑤
To Cambridge ⑥
* Boylston St.   To Park St. Sta. ⑤
Newbury St.   * Berkeley St.
47 76   Copley Sq.
Tremont St. Subway
South Sta.

B&A RR
Massachusetts Sta. ★
Boylston St.
Boston Proper
Dover St.
Dover St. Sta.

BROOKLINE

Huntington Ave.   39 57
Francis St.
57
crossover removed 1945

Heath St. Loop (built 1945)

Lenox St. Yard ★
43
Lower Level See Map ① ★
10 47
Roxbury Crossing
Hanley Sq.
Roxbury St.
Dudley St. Sta. (Upper Level) ★
East Loop
15 19 22 23 44 45

Albany St. Shops ★
night/school cars
Northampton St. Sta.
Southampton St.
To City Point ①
To City Point ①
16 17
Andrew Sq. Sta. ★
Andrew Sq. See Map ①

South Boston

Columbus Park
Old Harbor

Hyde Sq.
Centre St.
41
Jamaica Plain
Monument Sq.
Green St. Sta. ★
Jamaica Plain Loop ★
41

Centre St.
John Eliot Sq.
West Loop
41 42

Egleston Sq. Sta. ★
29 40
42 43

Seaver St. Loop ★ 44
45
Grove Hall

Columbia Sta.
Edward Everett Sq.
Uphams Corner
15
Kane Sq.
Meeting House Hill
Savin Hill Sta. ★
Dorchester Bay

Franklin Park
Franklin Park
16
Ⓐ

service track
Dorchester
17 19 20
Fields Corner Sta. ★
Park St. C. H. ★
Park St.
Shawmut Sta. ★

Ⓐ Franklin Park area
after November 1941
same scale as main map
29 22
16
16
Columbia Rd.
22 29

American Legion Hwy.
Talbot Ave.
22
Codman Sq.
22 23

Johnston Rd.
29
29
NYNH&H RR Midland Div.
Midland Division passenger service discontinued 1938; resumed March 1940.

King Sq.
Neponset Ave.
Neponset Circle
Neponset Loop ★
20

Roslindale
Mattapan
Blue Hill Ave.
Morton St.
29

Peabody Sq.
22 23
Ashmont Sta. ★
22 23 26
Cedar Grove Sta. ★
Cedar Grove Cemetery
Adams St.
To Quincy ③

To Forest Hills Sta. ④
Cummins Hwy.
River St.
30
28 29 30
Mattapan Sta. ★
Mattapan Sq.
Babson St.
Neponset River
Central Ave. Sta.
Milton Sta. ★
Capen St. Sta. ★   Valley Rd. Sta.
Crossover removed in 1942.
Butler St. Sta. ★
MILTON
QUINCY

* Rapid transit line is above the surface car tracks at Fields Corner; it is shown cut away to reveal surface track detail.

N

1 mile

Most of these lines were very busy, characterized by high service frequencies and large numbers of trips each weekday. The 392 daily trips offered on Route 29 combined with its cutback were the most by far. Next in number of trips was Route 20, followed by Routes 28, 23, 15, 45, 17, and 22, in that order. Fields Corner–Dudley via Geneva Avenue, Route 19, had the fewest daily trips, 41, and ran during rush hours only. See Appendix 9 for service frequencies and related information.

The heaviest service on the entire system was operated in two places: Warren Street in Roxbury between Walnut Avenue and Dudley Street, and on Massachusetts Avenue north of Harvard Square as far as North Cambridge Yard. Appendix 9 shows this information for Cambridge, but because the Warren Street routes operated from two different rating stations and Appendix 9 information is structured by rating station, the Warren Street information will only be mentioned here.

Warren Street saw 605 trips per day, which resulted from the combined service offered by Routes 19, 22, and 23, all Park Street lines and by Route 44, an Arborway line. The morning rush hour headway on Warren Street was 0.9 minute, and the evening headway was 1.0 minute, very high service frequencies! In the Cambridge location, the combined service also totaled 605 trips per day with the same headways, but reversed between morning and evening rush hours from those in Roxbury.

The Quincy lines of the Eastern Massachusetts Street Railway are covered later in this chapter and are shown on Map 3. The main line into Quincy connected with Boston Elevated Route 20 at Neponset, providing through service between Quincy and Boston. Service on this route was exceptionally heavy, and service frequencies are presented in Appendix 9A.

The two City Point car lines were:

16   **Franklin Park–Andrew Station** *via Columbia Road, Boston Street, and Dorchester Avenue*

47   **Dudley Street Station–Massachusetts Station** *via Warren Street, Washington Street (Roxbury, South End), Northampton Street, Columbus Avenue, and Massachusetts Avenue*

Both of these routes were busy, but Dudley–Massachusetts Station was especially so in the morning rush hour, with a 2.6-minute headway. Appendix 9 details this information.

The three lines based at Arborway were:

41   **Jamaica Plain Loop–Dudley Street Station** *via South Street, Centre Street, Jackson Square, Columbus Avenue, Roxbury Street, and Dudley Street (Guild Row westbound)*

42   **Egleston Station–Dudley Street Station** *via Washington Street*

44   **Seaver Street Loop–Dudley Street Station** *via Humboldt Avenue, Walnut Avenue, and Warren Street*

All three routes were heavily patronized lines. Seaver–Dudley led with 185 daily trips, followed by Egleston–Dudley via Washington Street, then Jamaica Plain–Dudley in that order. See Appendix 9 for more detailed information.

Park Street Carhouse

Park Street Carhouse and its surrounding yard were situated on a trapezoid-shaped plot of land, adjacent to Fields Corner Station. Faulkner Street, Freeman Street, and the rapid transit station bounded the carhouse site on the north. Geneva Avenue bounded the parcel on the west, Park Street on the south, and Dorchester Avenue on the east.

The complex consisted of a large carhouse building located roughly in the southerly section of the site. Storage trackage was located in two yards, one on either side of the carhouse. The carhouse lobby was situated between the north yard tracks and Faulkner Street.[123] Most of the storage tracks were parallel passing sidings. There was a loop on the north side of the carhouse yard beside Geneva Avenue and three stub-end spur tracks were located within the loop.

Cars could exit the yard north or south on Dorchester Avenue, leave north on Geneva Avenue towards Fields Corner Station, or directly access the Park Street reservation on the south. There was also a direct track connection to Fields Corner Station itself. During the 1940s, there were large numbers

Type 4 No. 5231 runs on Dorchester Avenue at Center Avenue on the service track between Ashmont and Park Street Carhouse on February 10, 1948, just two days before the end of streetcar service in this area.   *Foster M. Palmer*

of Type 5 cars at this station and a smaller number of Type 4s. Many work cars were stored here as well.

The El maintained a double-track service line on Dorchester Avenue between Fields Corner and Peabody Square, connecting to Ashmont Station. This line was primarily used for pull-in, pull-out equipment moves and trips for school students.

Equipment Assignments

Appendix 3 shows equipment assignments by line, carhouse, and date. In the April 1, 1940 rating, 153 cars were assigned to Park Street Carhouse. The roster consisted of 60 Type 4s, 89 Type 5s, and 4 Eastern Mass. cars. The Elevated also stored 50 Type 4 cars at Mattapan Yard, a substation of Park Street Carhouse.

The Eastern Mass. cars at Park Street were used in the jointly operated service between Fields Corner and Neponset. These cars continued from Neponset to Quincy where additional Eastern Mass. cars were based. All total, the Eastern Mass. used nineteen[124] of the 7000-series cars on the Quincy lines and the line to Fields Corner, supplemented by six Eastern Mass. 4200s for high school students and rush hour service.[b] This equipment was discussed in Chapter 1.

By the end of the 1940s, no streetcars remained at Park Street Carhouse. The last rating to show streetcars for all the lines running in 1940 was dated January 5, 1948 and listed 159 cars, consisting of 58 Type 4s, 97 Type 5s, and four cars from the Eastern Mass. The December 27, 1948 rating was the last rating to show any streetcars at all at Park Street Carhouse. By this time, the first conversions to trackless trolley operation had occurred and only 90 Type 5 cars remained.

The Type 5 was the predominant streetcar on the Dorchester and Roxbury Lines. During the 1940s, these cars were exclusively assigned to Fields Corner–Neponset, Fields Corner–Andrew, Uphams Corner–Dudley, Fields Corner–Dudley, Grove Hall–Dudley, and both Ashmont–Dudley lines, all based at Park Street Carhouse.

Type 4 cars also ran in this area, but to a lesser extent than the Type 5s. Type 4s saw service on two lines in particular: Mattapan–Ashmont and Mattapan–Egleston. Both routes were based at Park Street Carhouse, and the use of Type 4s on these lines will be discussed later in this chapter. Most Type 4s were stored at Mattapan, a substation at that time of Park Street. Type 4s were also used as spares and were observed occasionally on many of the lines based at Park Street.

Type 5s, based at City Point Carhouse, were exclusively assigned to the Dudley–Massachusetts Station and the Franklin

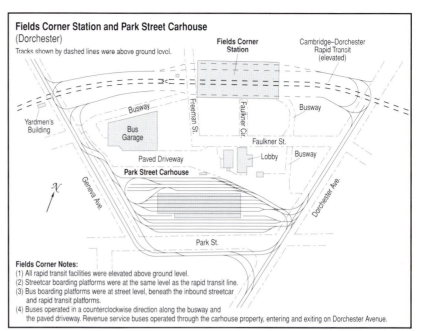

Fields Corner Station and Park Street Carhouse (Dorchester)
Tracks shown by dashed lines were above ground level.

Fields Corner Notes:
(1) All rapid transit facilities were elevated above ground level.
(2) Streetcar boarding platforms were at the same level as the rapid transit line.
(3) Bus boarding platforms were at street level, beneath the inbound streetcar and rapid transit platforms.
(4) Buses operated in a counterclockwise direction along the busway and the paved driveway. Revenue service buses operated through the carhouse property, entering and exiting on Dorchester Avenue.

This January 23, 1947, view of the yard at Park Street Carhouse adjacent to the corner of Park Street and Geneva Avenue was probably taken from the bus garage. A little more than a year later, the streetcars would be gone and replaced by trackless trolleys. *MTA*

Type 4 cars were often assigned as spares to routes normally run with other cars. In this January 1944 scene, No. 5196 running on Geneva Avenue has just left Fields Corner Station, the overpass of the Cambridge–Dorchester rapid transit line crossing the street in the background. Park Street Carhouse is behind the fence on the right. *Charles A. Duncan*

[b] Frequently, as mentioned earlier, 4200s used to make local trips for school students would run all the way to Fields Corner to maintain the schedule. These trips occurred often between 1941 and 1945.

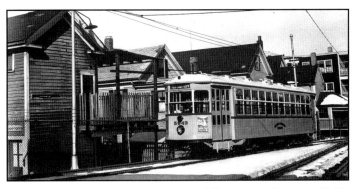

Cars from Andrew, Dudley Street, and Neponset all ran to Fields Corner. Type 5 No. 5943 has dropped off its inbound riders on the south side of the station and is now entering the north side for a trip to Dudley Street or Andrew Station. The date is March 14, 1941.

Stanley M. Hauck

Park–Andrew Station lines. Finally, Type 5s from the Arborway were assigned throughout the 1940s to the Jamaica–Dudley Street Station, Seaver Street–Dudley via Humboldt Avenue (with the exception of one PCC, usually 3001), and the Egleston Station–Dudley line.

Streetcar assignment information for City Point Carhouse has been presented in Chapter 2, and similar information for Arborway will be given in Chapter 4.

Eddie Collins remembers…

In the spring of 1942, I was planning to begin working for the Boston El. I also knew from a member of my local draft board that I would soon be called for military service. I was fortunate, and began working for the Elevated as a streetcar conductor on June 2 from the Reservoir Carhouse. I had established myself as an employee!

Just nineteen days later, on June 21, I was called for military duty. I spent the next four years in the service and was discharged in March 1946. My short stint with the Elevated qualified me to return to my job, and I went back to the El in April.

The transit rider of today would have a hard time imagining the amount of work involved in running a streetcar in the 1940s, especially an older car like a Type 5. Just running the car took some doing: sweeping the heavy controller handle to speed up, and pulling it back to prepare to stop. Operating the brake handle was an art. It took a deft touch and quite some time to learn to do properly. The sander handle for slippery conditions, the two door handles for the four doors, the hand-operated windshield wiper, the foot gong, and the wobbly motorman's seat stool were also part of this package which was primitive by contemporary standards.

Add that the motorman made change with a Johnson or McGill change maker, handed out transfers, changed the direction of the seats on stub-

end lines, and changed the trolley poles as well, and you had a busy employee! The motorman also had to be well-coordinated, for operating the car often occurred while making change, handing out transfers, cranking the farebox, and preparing for the next stop—all at once. These were the working conditions I returned to and readily accepted at the time, but hard to imagine today by operators working in air-conditioned comfort on the modern streetcars of the Green Line.

I was assigned to the Park Street, Dorchester rating station near Fields Corner and was given three day's instruction on operating a streetcar. Normally, a new hire would have been given eight weeks of "break-in" time, but 1946 was the busiest year ever for the El. It simply was not possible to provide the usual training period.

With this hasty and inadequate introduction, I was immediately put into service, running on lines with which I was totally unfamiliar. In the first few weeks I got into many accidents which resulted from my lack of experience and training. A coal truck and several automobiles were one day's toll!

Fortunately, none of these events resulted in an injury, but I was afraid that someone would get hurt. I begged my stationmaster for more instruction time, but he was unable to provide it. I quit!

The stationmaster asked me to reconsider, and sent me to see John Banks, the Superintendent of Transportation. Banks told me to see the personnel director, and the personnel director told me to see a doctor. The doctor saw me and thought that my desire to quit was quite normal; he told me to go back to Banks.

I did so, and Banks said that I should take an unpaid leave of absence, get my feet on the ground (after four years in the military), and return to work when I felt up to it. A while later, I was back on the job.

This time, however, my stationmaster had spent some time reviewing my record. I spent two weeks with an instructor and two more weeks with various streetcar operators who analyzed my performance. In this time, I learned the routes and the nuances of daily streetcar operation, and when I was back on my own, I never had another problem.

The Boston El truly cared for its employees and did its best to help them through tough times. The patience shown toward an inexperienced kid in those early days started me on a long and successful career, and I will never forget it.

Edward P. Collins retired from the MBTA in 1980, having served as Superintendent of Surface Transportation and in many other positions with the MBTA, the MTA, and the Boston Elevated Railway in a 38-year career.

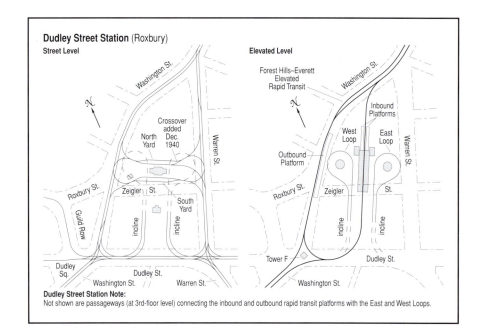

Dudley Street Station (Roxbury)

Street Level

Elevated Level

Forest Hills–Everett Elevated Rapid Transit

Washington St.

Crossover added Dec. 1940

North Yard

Warren St.

Roxbury St.

Zeigler St.

South Yard

Guild Row

incline

incline

Dudley Sq.

Dudley St.

Washington St.

Warren St.

Inbound Platforms

West Loop

East Loop

Outbound Platform

Zeigler St.

incline

incline

Tower F

Dudley St.

Washington St.

Dudley Street Station Note:
Not shown are passageways (at 3rd-floor level) connecting the inbound and outbound rapid transit platforms with the East and West Loops.

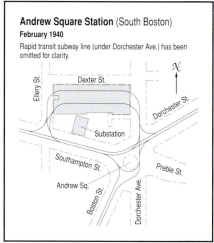

Andrew Square Station (South Boston)

February 1940

Rapid transit subway line (under Dorchester Ave.) has been omitted for clarity.

Ellery St.

Dexter St.

Dorchester St.

Substation

Southampton St.

Andrew Sq.

Boston St.

Preble St.

Dorchester Ave.

Routes Based at Park Street Carhouse

15 Uphams Corner[c]–Dudley

This route started in Dorchester at a set of crossovers on the Columbia Road reservation. The crossovers were located on the south side of the Hancock Street intersection two blocks south of Uphams Corner. Cars changed ends here and ran northeast on Columbia Road over the double-track connection with Hancock Street.

The cars turned northwest at Uphams Corner onto Dudley Street, and continued to Dudley Street Station, crossing under the Midland Division Bridge of the New Haven Railroad. The car line then crossed the Dorchester–Roxbury boundary just before a double-track intersection at Blue Hill Avenue and Dudley Street. After crossing Warren Street, the line turned north into the East Loop of Dudley Street Station. A round-trip run on this very short line was 3.2 miles and averaged 19 minutes.

17 Fields Corner Station–Andrew Station *via Meeting House Hill*

This line entered and left Fields Corner Station on two ramps that led from Geneva Avenue to the rapid transit platform level. The ramps were connected in both directions to Geneva Avenue on the west side of the station. On the east side of the station, the southerly ramp was connected in both directions to Dorchester Avenue, while the northerly ramp was connected to Dorchester Avenue from the south only. The ramps were also connected to each other by loop trackage at each

The end of trolley service was near for Route 15 in this view taken at Dudley and Clifton Streets in Roxbuty on December 22, 1948. Three days later, on Christmas Day, trackless trolleys like 8409 shown here in test service would replace the streetcars between Dudley Street Station and Uphams Corner. *Charles A. Duncan*

Signed UPHAMS, Type 5 No. 5620 runs outbound on Dudley Street just past the intersection of Blue Hill Avenue in this circa 1947 scene. *Charles A. Duncan*

---

[c] Uphams Corner is the intersection of Columbia Road, Dudley Street, and Stoughton Street. At one time it was also known as "Columbia Square."

end. These loops utilized part of the outer rail on Geneva Avenue and Dorchester Avenue, respectively.[125] There was also an additional loop at the Dorchester Avenue end of the station, within the station property. Just before entering the station, the northerly ramp track fanned out with a second track, a passing siding, into the platform area. Cars entering the station could use either platform track, and upon leaving the station, they returned to the main ramp track.

Cars arriving at Fields Corner from Andrew entered the station by ascending a ramp on the inbound rapid transit side of the station and stopped on the paid fare section of the platform nearest Geneva Avenue. Andrew cars then descended the ramp toward Dorchester Avenue. Here they could take either of the two loop tracks to reverse direction and climbed the ramp from Dorchester Avenue to the outbound rapid transit side of the station to board their passengers. Cars boarded on the northerly rail furthest from the rapid transit tracks.

Leaving Fields Corner Station, cars on this line turned northwest onto Geneva Avenue and ran to Bowdoin Street.[d] Here the line turned northeast and followed Bowdoin Street to Hancock Street, then turned northwest onto Hancock Street. Along the way, the line ran over historic Meeting House Hill.

The line continued on Hancock Street and turned northeast onto Columbia Road. Here it joined the Franklin Park–Andrew line, and crossed the double-track connection onto Dudley Street used by the Uphams Corner–Dudley Line. The tracks then continued on Columbia Road through Edward Everett Square and onto Boston Street.[e] The tracks on Columbia Road ran in a reservation, but when they entered Edward Everett Square, they ran in pavement both in the square and on Boston Street.

The line then ran on Boston Street past the Dorchester-South Boston boundary, crossed a bridge over the New Haven Railroad, and finally turned north onto Dorchester Avenue at Andrew Square. Here the trolleys crossed Dorchester Street, and turned west into the southerly platform track in Andrew

Cars on Route 17, Fields Corner–Andrew, ran along Bowdoin Street as depicted here by car 5886 on April 24, 1948, at the intersection of Bowdoin Street and Geneva Avenue. Trackless trolley overhead wire is already up for the conversion later that year.

Foster M. Palmer

No. 5560 picks up passengers on Columbia Road near Uphams Corner, Dorchester, on its way to Andrew Station in this scene taken in the late 1940s. The doublewide overhead bracket arms were a distinctive feature on Columbia Road. *MTA*

Station. A round-trip on this line was 5.981 miles and the average running time was 36 minutes.

Cars returning to Fields Corner exited the station south on Ellery Street, turned east onto Southampton Street, and southeast back onto Boston Street. There was a loop track at this point that ran around a traffic circle in Andrew Square. This track connected the southbound track on Boston Street with the northbound track on Dorchester Avenue.[f]

---

[d] At Geneva Avenue and Bowdoin Street, a single-track connection to Washington Street (Dorchester) ran over Bowdoin Street. It connected the outbound track on Bowdoin Street to Fields Corner with the outbound track on Washington Street to Codman Square and Ashmont. This track was disconnected at the Geneva Avenue end in 1940 and abandoned. The parallel track on Bowdoin Street between Geneva Avenue and Washington Street in the opposite direction had been abandoned in 1935. The special work from both tracks at Geneva Avenue was removed between March 25 and April 18, 1941.

[e] Edward Everett Square is the intersection of Boston Street, Columbia Road, and Massachusetts Avenue.

[f] As noted in Chapter 2, the loop was installed between January 2, 1940 and January 16 in connection with the construction of a new traffic circle in Andrew Square. As part of this work, the southbound track from Dorchester Street to Boston Street was removed. This required cars going to Boston Street from South Boston to loop through Andrew Station.

Boston Street was the last leg of the run from Fields Corner to Andrew Station as well as for the Franklin Park–Andrew cars. Here we see 5811 at Boston and Rawson Streets near the South Boston–Dorchester boundary line heading outbound from Andrew Square on March 25, 1948. *Foster M. Palmer*

19 Fields Corner–Dudley *via Geneva Avenue*

This line ran rush–hours only. The routing through Fields Corner Station was the same as for the Fields Corner–Andrew line discussed above. Leaving Fields Corner Station, the cars turned northwest onto Geneva Avenue, ran past Bowdoin Street and under the New Haven Railroad Midland Division Bridge, and then crossed Columbia Road. The cars continued to Blue Hill Avenue, crossing from Dorchester into Roxbury. At Blue Hill Avenue, the cars turned north, and passed through Grove Hall.[g]

Almost immediately, the cars turned northwest onto Warren Street and continued all the way to Dudley Street. At Dudley Street, the line turned west then continued to the East Loop ramp at Dudley Street Station. The round-trip distance of this line was 5.892 miles and the running time was 35 minutes.

20 Fields Corner–Neponset

Cars arriving at Fields Corner from Neponset and Quincy were routed through the station the same way as the cars from Andrew Station and Dudley Street Station. There were two differences, however, one on each side of the station. Inbound, the Neponset and Quincy cars stopped in the unpaid section of the platform nearest Dorchester Avenue. Outbound, these cars boarded on the southerly rail, nearest the rapid transit tracks.

Neponset and Quincy-bound cars then followed Geneva Avenue southeast a short distance past the Park Street Carhouse. Here, the tracks turned east onto Park Street. The track on Park Street ran only one block in a private reservation that remains to this day for the use of MBTA buses.

From Park Street, the cars turned south onto Dorchester Avenue, then east almost immediately onto Gibson Street.[126] The line then ran to Adams Street, turned southeast onto Adams Street, and then bore left after one block onto Neponset Avenue. The cars then ran all the way in a southeasterly direction to Neponset Loop, located on Neponset Avenue south of

Route 19 running from Fields Corner to Dudley Street via Geneva Avenue was a rush-hour route only. Normally, Type 5 cars plied this route, but not here on December 5, 1948, when the Boston Chapter NRHS ran a system-wide fan trip with Type 4 No. 5230 shown in a scene taken from the New Haven Railroad bridge over Geneva Avenue. *Stanley M. Hauck*

Gallivan Boulevard. From here, Eastern Massachusetts Street Railway Company cars continued on to Quincy Square and the Quincy Shipyard. A round-trip between Fields Corner and Neponset Loop was 4.024 miles and took 21 minutes.

A 7000-series lightweight car nears the end of its run from Quincy at Fields Corner Station on a hot summer day. Boston Elevated and MTA motormen were responsible for revenue operation of Eastern Mass. cars over the tracks from Neponset to Fields Corner, while Eastern Mass. operators ran between Neponset and Quincy. *Charles A. Duncan*

Brrr! The kids on the corner of Park Street and Dorchester Avenue don't mind the cold, but the lady across the street who has to wade through major snow piles sure does. It is February 1945 and Type 5 No. 5929 is making its way off the private reservation onto Dorchester Avenue for a trip to Neponset. *Charles A. Duncan*

---

[g] Grove Hall is the intersection of Blue Hill Avenue, Warren Street, Washington Street, Geneva Avenue, and Georgia Street.

Type 5 No. 5564 makes an inbound trip on Neponset Avenue amid the remnants of a heavy snowfall in this February 10, 1948, scene. *Foster M. Palmer*

Traffic circles were usually a timesaver for Boston streetcars, which often ran straight through them. On May 17, 1947, 7039 made the Boston El trackage at Neponset Circle look like an Eastern Mass. line. *Robert A. Kennerly*

Neponset Loop (Dorchester)

Gallivan Blvd.
Neponset Circle
Neponset Ave.
Shelter
NYNH&H RR
Track south of this line owned & operated by Eastern Mass. St. Ry.
Neponset River
Neponset Bridge

22 Ashmont–Dudley *via Talbot Avenue*

Starting at Ashmont Station, this line turned more than 180 degrees from the southeasterly loading track on the outbound station platform northbound onto Dorchester Avenue. Following Dorchester Avenue about 600 feet, the tracks turned northwest onto Talbot Avenue at Peabody Square. The route continued along Talbot Avenue, passing through Codman Square[h] and under the Midland Division Bridge of the New Haven Railroad to Blue Hill Avenue.

Here the line turned north onto Blue Hill Avenue, joining the Mattapan–Egleston line. The track on Blue Hill Avenue ran in a reservation from Babson Street near Mattapan Square all the way to Washington Street at Grove Hall.[i] At Columbia Road, the Franklin Park–Andrew line diverged to the right, and at Seaver Street, the Mattapan–Egleston line diverged to the left. Both the Egleston and Talbot Avenue streetcar lines crossed the boundary here from Dorchester to Roxbury.

The Ashmont–Dudley via Talbot Avenue line continued to follow Blue Hill Avenue to Grove Hall, crossing the tracks entering from Washington Street and Geneva Avenue.[127] The line then veered left onto Warren Street and joined the Ashmont–

Dudley via Washington Street and the Fields Corner–Dudley lines for the final leg along Warren Street to the East Loop of Dudley Street Station. This line was the longest Park Street Carhouse route, with a round-trip distance of 8.552 miles and an average round-trip running time of 47 minutes.

23 Ashmont–Dudley *via Washington Street*

Ashmont–Dudley via Washington Street cars loaded on the center outbound track at Ashmont Station. This line followed the same route as the Ashmont–Dudley via Talbot Avenue line between Ashmont Station and Codman Square. At Codman Square, however, the line diverged to the north onto Washington Street, crossing the service track on Bowdoin Street mentioned earlier, and continuing on Washington Street all the way to Blue Hill Avenue. Here the line crossed into Roxbury from Dorchester. Just before intersecting Columbia Road, the Washington Street trolleys crossed a bridge over the New Haven Railroad Midland Division.

---

[h] Codman Square is the intersection of Talbot Avenue, Washington Street, and Norfolk Street.

[i] A distinction should be made between Washington Street, Dorchester, and Washington Street, Roxbury. The two streets survive from the formerly separate towns of Dorchester and Roxbury, and their names were not changed when these towns were annexed to Boston. Washington Street, Dorchester, extends in a southeasterly direction from Grove Hall (Blue Hill Avenue) to Dorchester Lower Mills (River Street). By 1940 only the section from Grove Hall to Codman Square (Talbot Avenue) still had streetcar tracks. Washington Street, Roxbury, was an extension of Washington Street in downtown Boston, which continued in a southwesterly direction all the way to the Dedham–Boston boundary in the West Roxbury District (and ultimately to the Rhode Island state line in South Attleboro). En route it passed through the South End, Roxbury, Jamaica Plain, Roslindale, and West Roxbury Districts of Boston. Streetcar tracks were still in place in the 1940s the entire length of this street from the South End to West Roxbury, and the Main Line Elevated ran above the street from the South End to Forest Hills.

Looking into Ashmont from Dorchester Avenue, we see a Type 4 entering the station. To the right is the busway. The shot was taken in 1946, and it was not long after that the surface track shown entering the station and the cars that used it would be gone, replaced by trackless trolleys. *Charles A. Duncan*

At Grove Hall, the Washington Street cars turned right onto Blue Hill Avenue, and crossed the tracks coming in from Geneva Avenue. The line then bore left onto Warren Street, joining the Ashmont–Dudley via Talbot Avenue and Fields Corner–Dudley lines for the last part of the run to the Dudley Station East Loop. Ashmont-Dudley via Washington Street was shorter than the Talbot Avenue route, a round-trip comprising 7.545 miles and taking less time, 43 minutes.

Type 3 snowplow 5100 clears the way along Talbot Avenue on February 16, 1940, trailed by a motorist who knows an opportunity when he sees one. *Charles A. Duncan*

No. 5622 turns from Talbot onto Blue Hill Avenue in May 1948. *Charles A. Duncan*

Talbot Avenue car 5626 bound for Ashmont runs over the Blue Hill Avenue reservation at Wayne Street near Grove Hall on October 22, 1948. *Foster M. Palmer*

Type 5 No. 5879 has just boarded passengers for Ashmont and is turning from the East Loop at Dudley Street Station onto Dudley Street itself on May 29, 1948. *Foster M. Palmer*

Car 5928 approaches Blue Hill Avenue on Warren Street at Brunswick Street on its way to Ashmont on December 7, 1948. This car will soon complete its run via Washington Street, the companion route to the Talbot Avenue line. *Foster M. Palmer*

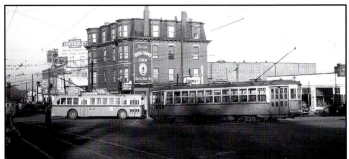

Grove Hall presents a stark contrast of new and old on Christmas Eve 1948. A trackless trolley on a test run enters Geneva Avenue while Type 5 No. 5558 enters Grove Hall from Washington Street. By January 8, 1949, the car line would be converted to trolley coach operation. *Foster M. Palmer*

The roll sign of car 5910 in this 1946 scene says ASHMONT WASH ST, but Talbot Avenue and Fields Corner cars also used this track at Warren Street and Walnut Avenue. *Charles A. Duncan*

28 Mattapan–Ashmont *High-Speed* Trolley Line

The newest streetcar line in the Metropolitan Boston area served Dorchester and the northern edge of the town of Milton. In 1940 the Mattapan–Ashmont High-Speed Trolley Line was only eleven years old. Its moniker came from the fact that it operated entirely over private right-of-way, completely separated from local streets except for two grade crossings. The intermediate stations were the same as those of today: Cedar Grove, Butler Street, Milton, Central Avenue, Valley Road, and Capen Street. This line was quite popular and very busy.

Well before the High-Speed Trolley Line had been opened in 1929, the Transit Department of the City of Boston had leased the future route to the Boston Elevated. The High-Speed Line would be part of the Dorchester Rapid Transit Extension, and the lease document was signed October 17, 1924.[j] This lease ended August 3, 1949, when the MTA acquired the property of the Boston Transit Department.

Cars for Mattapan started at Ashmont Station on the northeasterly loading track on the outbound platform nearest the Cambridge–Dorchester rapid transit tracks. Mattapan-bound cars crossed over the rapid transit line on a short concrete trestle, enroute to the first stop at Cedar Grove. For about a fifth of a mile after leaving Ashmont, the streetcar line was paralleled by rapid transit tracks that ran to Codman Yard, south of Gallivan Boulevard. Both sets of tracks crossed bridges over Van Winkle Street and Gallivan Boulevard.

Just after Cedar Grove Station, the high-speed line ran under Adams Street and entered the Cedar Grove Cemetery. The tracks continued under a cemetery road, rounded a sharp bend, and climbed an overpass that crossed the Neponset Branch of the New Haven Railroad at the southeasterly edge of the cemetery. The line then descended to Butler Street, where an overhead pedestrian bridge provided access to the center island station platform. Freight tracks of the New Haven Railroad paralleled the trolley line on both sides at Butler Street.

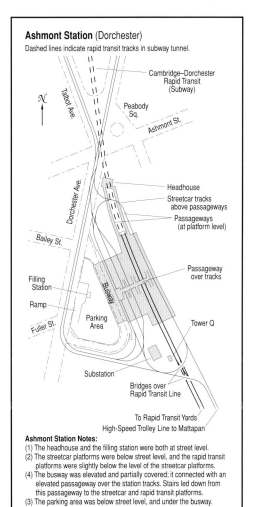

Ashmont Station (Dorchester)
Dashed lines indicate rapid transit tracks in subway tunnel.

Cambridge–Dorchester Rapid Transit (Subway)
Talbot Ave.
Peabody Sq.
Ashmont St.
Dorchester Ave.
Headhouse
Streetcar tracks above passageways
Passageways (at platform level)
Bailey St.
Passageway over tracks
Filling Station
Busway
Ramp
Fuller St.
Parking Area
Tower Q
Substation
Bridges over Rapid Transit Line
To Rapid Transit Yards
High-Speed Trolley Line to Mattapan

Ashmont Station Notes:
(1) The headhouse and the filling station were both at street level.
(2) The streetcar platforms were below street level, and the rapid transit platforms were slightly below the level of the streetcar platforms.
(4) The busway was elevated and partially covered; it connected with an elevated passageway over the station tracks. Stairs led down from this passageway to the streetcar and rapid transit platforms.
(3) The parking area was below street level, and under the busway.

From here the cars ran under Medway Street and crossed the Neponset River on a short bridge into the Town of Milton, stopping at Milton Station. The line ran under Adams Street again, crossed Central Avenue at grade, and entered Central Avenue Station. Two more stops were located at Valley Road and Capen Street. The line then crossed Capen Street at grade and the Neponset River a second time, reentering Dorchester and arriving at Mattapan Station. A round-trip on this line totaled 5.393 miles and took a fast 19 minutes to complete.

This early example of the "light rail" concept remains today. It is the last vestige of streetcar operation in Boston other than the Green Line and its branches. Appropriately, the last PCC cars in revenue service on the MBTA run here. The MBTA, in concurrence with its predecessors, views the Mattapan–Ashmont service as a continuation of the Red Line, although Mattapan–Ashmont is operated and supervised by Green Line personnel.

Mattapan Station

Mattapan Station consisted of an operators' lobby, a combination sand house and shifters' lobby, passenger loading platforms, a busway, and loops at each end of the station for turning cars from the High-Speed, Blue Hill Avenue, and Cummins Highway lines. There was also an adjoining yard with a number of passing sidings used for storage and one long stub-end spur. Much of this infrastructure remains intact today. Between August 10 and 21, 1942, the El removed a crossover at Central Avenue Station and relocated it to Mattapan Station yard.

29 Mattapan–Egleston *via Blue Hill Avenue*

Egleston-bound cars left Mattapan Station and turned north onto Blue Hill Avenue at Mattapan Square. The line soon entered a private streetcar reservation at Babson Street. Egleston-bound cars followed Blue Hill Avenue as far as Seaver Street. Shortly after leaving Mattapan Square, near Woodhaven Avenue, the line crossed a bridge over the Midland Division of the New Haven Railroad.

There was a crossover north of Morton Street for cutbacks from Egleston Station. Just south of Talbot Avenue,

---

[j] This line was the first example in the Boston area of the purchase and conversion of a railroad right-of-way for light rail use, in this case the Shawmut Branch of the New York, New Haven & Hartford Railroad. The inner segment of this railroad branch, from Dorchester Avenue to Ashmont, was converted to third-rail rapid transit operation, and the outer segment, from Ashmont to Mattapan, became the High-Speed Trolley Line.

One of two lines that regularly saw Type 4s in Roxbury and Dorchester was the High-Speed Trolley Line between Ashmont and Mattapan. With Ashmont Station behind it, 5283 has just crossed the Dorchester rapid transit line en route to Mattapan.

Charles A. Brown

The railroad crossing signs at the Capen Street crossing in Milton betray the railroad origins of the High-Speed Trolley Line. Type 4 No. 5204 heads inbound to Ashmont in this scene taken August 27, 1948.

Robert A. Kennerly

Roaring across the Neponset River, No. 5282 heads for Mattapan on a cold January day in 1947.   *Foster M. Palmer*

Car 5202 will soon be on its way to Egleston Station via Blue Hill Avenue. In this 1943 view, it is standing right beside the starter's shack before moving up the platform to board for departure. *BERy*

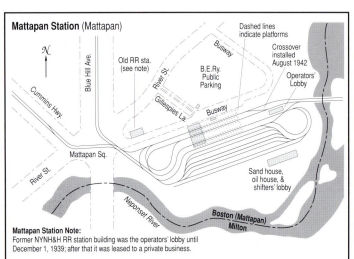

Mattapan Station (Mattapan)

N

Blue Hill Ave.

Cummins Hwy.

River St.

Old RR sta. (see note)

River St.

Gillesplies La.

Busway

B.E.Ry. Public Parking

Busway

Dashed lines indicate platforms

Crossover installed August 1942

Operators' Lobby

Sand house, oil house, & shifters' lobby

Mattapan Sq.

River St.

Neponset River

Boston (Mattapan) Milton

Mattapan Station Note:
Former NYNH&H RR station building was the operators' lobby until December 1, 1939; after that it was leased to a private business.

there was another crossover and a passing siding on the east side of Blue Hill Avenue. At Talbot Avenue, tracks of the Ashmont–Dudley via Talbot line joined the Blue Hill Avenue tracks. The Franklin Park–Andrew line diverged from the Blue Hill Avenue line at Columbia Road. On Blue Hill Avenue south of Columbia Road, there was a third track for the Andrew Station cars to change ends, which will be described later.

At Seaver Street and Blue Hill Avenue, Egleston cars turned from Dorchester to Roxbury northwest onto Seaver Street and entered another reservation. Cars on the Talbot Avenue line continued north on Blue Hill Avenue towards Grove Hall and Dudley Street Station.

Continuing on Seaver Street, Egleston-bound cars crossed the leads to the loop at Humboldt Avenue, which was used by the Dudley–Humboldt line. Seaver Street became Columbus Avenue at Walnut Avenue, the western boundary of Franklin Park. At Walnut Avenue, the cars left the Seaver Street reservation for street-paved tracks on Columbus Avenue and ran down a moderate grade to Egleston Station.

Route 29 as a Park Street Carhouse line was second only to the Ashmont–Dudley via Talbot Avenue route in length, a round-trip on Route 29 comprising 7.752 miles and an average running time of 40 minutes. The cutback service between Egleston and Morton Street was much shorter, with a round-trip distance of 4.987 miles and a running time of 25 minutes.

Egleston Station, once the site of a carhouse, was laid out with two concentric track loops running in opposite directions. The inner loop was single track, ran clockwise entirely within the station, and was used by the cars from Mattapan. The outer loop ran counterclockwise, on the street and in the station, and handled the lines from Arborway, Dudley Street Station, and North Station. The outer loop from Columbus Avenue through the station had a passing siding for layovers along much of its length.

The crossover in the background for the cutback near the intersection of Blue Hill Avenue and Morton Street shown here provides a good backdrop for Type 4 No. 5199 on its way to Mattapan in the mid-1940s.   *BERy*

Cars from Mattapan entered Egleston at the south side of the station on the inner loop. Mattapan-bound cars exited the station through the same side that they entered, crossing as they departed over the inbound track lead to the inner loop and the outer loop trackage.

Blue Hill Avenue Reservation Changes

The reservations on Blue Hill Avenue and Seaver Street adjoining Franklin Park were located on the side of the road from American Legion Highway and Blue Hill Avenue to Walnut Avenue and Seaver Street. From Mattapan to American Legion Highway, the reservation was in the center of the roadway.

To speed up traffic flow along busy Blue Hill Avenue, the City of Boston began an aggressive program in 1940 to widen the street. This work entailed relocating the streetcar tracks

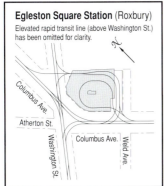

Two Type 4s have arrived in Mattapan Square from Egleston Station on a tranquil day in September 1945. Soon they will turn right into Mattapan Station and loop for a return trip. The tracks running across the lower part of the photo from left to right were used by Cummins Highway cars.   *Charles A. Duncan*

where they ran in the reservation on the side of Blue Hill Avenue to the center of the road. The tracks were then set in pavement and separated with a concrete island. The Boston Elevated Maintenance Department starting relocating the line from American Legion Highway to a point north of Charlotte Street on October 5, 1940. This work was completed on November 12, at which time the City of Boston began removing the reservation.

The program continued in 1941, when the Elevated centrally relocated the rail from north of Charlotte Street to a point just north of Columbia Road.[128] Center islands replaced the reservation as before. Again, in 1950, the reservation was removed from Columbia Road to Seaver Street, and the track was relocated with center islands.[129]

The remaining reservation was changed in the section between Babson Street and the New Haven Railroad Midland Division Bridge near Woodhaven Street in 1950. The City of Boston installed granite curbing on both sides of the reservation, and the MTA realigned the tracks and a crossover near Babson Street and set them in paving. New signs reading, "Reservation – Danger" were installed at each end of this section.[130] This work was part of a traffic safety improvement program.

The Egleston Station Tragedy

On April 12, 1948, elderly Type 4 car 5246, making a trip on the Mattapan–Egleston line, went out of control and ran wild down Seaver Street and Columbus Avenue into Egleston Station. The 36-year-old car derailed as it entered the inner loop at Egleston, and crashed into the station wall alongside Columbus Avenue. The car brought down two vertical steel support beams and demolished a newsstand before finally smashing into the starter's booth. The car was destroyed down to the top of the seats, and it was subsequently scrapped. All eight passengers aboard the car had significant injuries.

Motorman Alphonse MacDonald suffered the loss of both his legs in attempting to stop the runaway. On April 13, 1948, MacDonald was awarded $5,000 and the MTA Medal of Honor for his bravery.

Seven days after the accident, on April 19, 1948, the Mattapan–Egleston and Mattapan–Ashmont lines were transferred to the Arborway rating station. Both lines were still fully operated with Type 4 cars. When it later became clear that a faulty air valve—a problem that had also been associated with an earlier serious accident involving a Type 4, had caused the accident—the MTA ended the use of these cars on both lines.[k]

---

[k] Type 4 car 5193 bound from Egleston to Mattapan on February 28, 1939, ran away on Seaver Street, derailing at Seaver Street and Blue Hill Avenue, and overturning on the sidewalk. Six persons were killed and there were many injuries. The car was scrapped. The 1948 incident was not the end of woes with Type 4 cars. There was yet another mishap on the Heath Street–Park Street Station subway line on July 31, 1949, as described in Chapter 5.

Blue Hill Avenue Reservation Changes

Until 1940/41, the reservation alongside Franklin Park and Blue Hill Avenue was on the side of the roadway adjacent to Franklin Park. Near the park entrance, a third center track was used by cars from Andrew Square to change ends as we see here. To the left of the Andrew car, a Dudley via Talbot Avenue car passed on its way to Dudley Street Station.   *BERy*

Changes are afoot in this view of the move of the tracks from the reservation alongside Franklin Park to the middle of Blue Hill Avenue taken on October 22, 1941. One of the Elevated's Type 2 compressor car, 5060, was supplying air for tie tamping. The Type 5 is likely an Ashmont-bound car from Dudley Street Station.   *Charles A. Duncan*

The "improvement" to Blue Hill Avenue saw the removal of the reservation at the edge of Franklin Park, seen at left, and the installation of a concrete center island between the traffic lanes. Done to increase the capacity of the street for automobiles, it greatly slowed down streetcars such as this Type 4 southbound to Mattapan by forcing them to mix with other traffic.   *MTA*

This was not due to brake failure, but rather was believed to be from the deliberate action of a boy releasing the brakes.

A tragic scene greeted onlookers on April 12, 1948, after Type 4 No. 5246 ran away on Columbus Avenue, entered Egleston Square Station, and practically tore the place down. Motorman Alphonse MacDonald, who lost both legs trying frantically to halt the onrushing car, received the MTA Medal of Honor (above) for his "outstanding act of public service."

The April 5, 1949, rating eliminated Type 4 cars on the Mattapan–Ashmont line and replaced them with Type 5s. Some Type 4s were still assigned to the Mattapan–Egleston line, but 11 Type 5s were now in use as well. By the June 20, 1949, rating, Mattapan–Egleston was also completely operated with Type 5s.

45 Grove Hall–Dudley

Grove Hall–Dudley started from a crossover on Blue Hill Avenue between Geneva Avenue and Warren Street. The line followed Blue Hill Avenue north to Dudley Street, turning northwest and following Dudley Street to the East Loop of Dudley Street Station.

Grove Hall–Dudley was another very short route. It was only 3.987 miles in length round-trip with an average running time of 22 minutes.

The Egleston Station tragedy hastened the final withdrawal of Type 4 cars throughout the system. In 1949 Type 5s replaced Type 4s on the Mattapan–Egleston line. Here we see 5666 leaving Egleston Station for Mattapan.   *Raymond E. McMurdo*

Type 5 No. 5626 rounds the corner on Blue Hill Avenue at Dudley Street on its way to Grove Hall on the last day of operation of this line, December 24, 1948.   *Foster M. Palmer*

A lone Type 5 has changed ends at Grove Hall for the return trip to Dudley Street Station. This shot looking north on Blue Hill Avenue toward Dudley Street was taken about 1945.   *BERy*

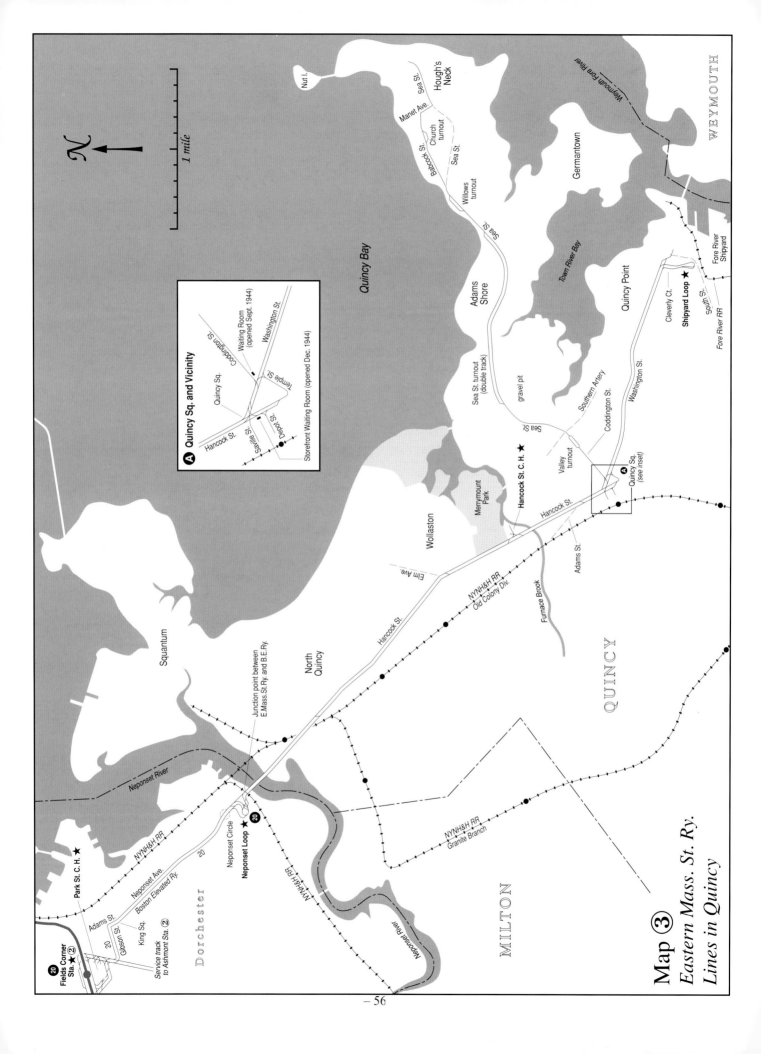

Quincy Bay

Nut I.

Hough's Neck

Sea St.

Manet Ave.

Church turnout

Sea St.

Babcock St.

Willows turnout

Sea St.

Adams Shore

Sea St. turnout (double track)

gravel pit

Germantown

Town River Bay

Quincy Point

Fore River Shipyard

Cleverly Ct.

Shipyard Loop ★

South St.

Fore River RR

Sea St.

Valley turnout

Southern Artery

Coddington St.

Washington St.

A **Quincy Sq. and Vicinity**

Coddington St.

Waiting Room (opened Sept. 1944)

Washington St.

Quincy Sq.

Temple St.

Hancock St.

Saville St.

Depot St.

Storefront Waiting Room (opened Dec. 1944)

Hancock St. C. H. ★

Merrymount Park

Wollaston

Hancock St.

Quincy Sq. (see inset)

Adams St.

Elm Ave.

Furnace Brook

NYNH&H RR Old Colony Div.

QUINCY

Squantum

North Quincy

Junction point between E.Mass.St.Ry. and B.E.Ry.

Neponset River

Neponset Circle

20

Neponset Loop ★ **20**

NYNH&H RR

Granite Branch

MILTON

Neponset River

NYNH&H RR

Neponset Ave.

Boston Elevated Ry.

20

Park St. C. H. ★

Dorchester

Adams St.

20

Gibson St.

King Sq.

Service track to Ashmont Sta. ②

20 **Fields Corner Sta.** ★ ②

WEYMOUTH

Weymouth Fore River

𝒩

1 mile

Map ③
Eastern Mass. St. Ry. Lines in Quincy

Eastern Massachusetts Street Railway

Quincy Shipyard and Houghs Neck Lines

While not shown on the system route maps of the Boston Elevated Railway, tracks owned by the Eastern Massachusetts Street Railway Company continued to Quincy from the Neponset Loop terminal of the Boston Elevated. The Quincy line crossed over the Neponset River and ran along Hancock Street to Quincy Square.[1] Cars crossed the Boston-Quincy boundary at the center of the Neponset River Bridge. Eastern Mass. 7000s and 4200s served this line, providing local service over the Boston Elevated tracks from Fields Corner to Neponset as well in addition to the Type 5s of the El.

Quincy Carhouse

On Hancock Street near Carruth Street, the Eastern Mass. maintained a carbarn and storage yard. There was a single carhouse building here, which had been divided into three sections, one for the streetcars and the other two segments for bus storage and maintenance. The west side of the building used for streetcars had five stub-end spurs inside. There was also a track lead that fanned into six stub-end storage spurs in a storage yard on the east and north sides of the building.

Cars from Neponset accessing the carhouse property could use either of two crossovers on Hancock Street located on either side of the carhouse lead tracks to get to the inbound rail and enter the yard. Cars from Quincy Square entered the yard directly from the outbound rail.

Quincy Square

At Quincy Square, there was a full loop on Hancock, Temple, and Washington Streets around the Church of the Presidents. There was also a stub-end spur on Saville Street and another on Depot Street.[131] Houghs Neck cars used the Saville Street spur as a turnback before World War II. The Depot Street track was used to store snow-fighting equipment before storms. Track details in and around Quincy Square are shown on Map 3, Inset A.

Most cars did not end their trips at Quincy Square, but some did on a run-as-directed basis to fill service gaps. Cars ending at Quincy Square used the loop to return to Fields Corner or the carhouse. Between Fields Corner and Quincy Square, the round-trip distance was 10.461 miles and required a running time of 54 minutes.[m]

Lightweight cars 7027 and 7033 are lined up outside the Eastern Massachusetts Street Railway's Quincy Carhouse on Hancock Street in this 1948 view. A bus garage adjoined the carhouse as evidenced by the bus to the right of car 7033.
Robert A. Kennerly

A modern waiting room in Quincy Square (below) served riders on the Houghs Neck line.
Clarke Collection

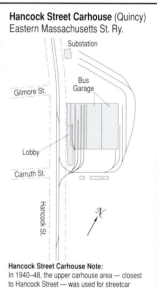

Hancock Street Carhouse (Quincy)
Eastern Massachusetts St. Ry.

Substation

Gilmore St.

Bus Garage

Lobby

Carruth St.

Hancock St.

N

Hancock Street Carhouse Note:
In 1940–48, the upper carhouse area — closest to Hancock Street — was used for streetcar storage and maintenance. The middle carhouse was used for bus storage, and the lower carhouse was used for bus maintenance.

Through cars to the Quincy Shipyard followed Hancock, Temple, and Washington Streets, turning east toward the shipyard from Temple Street. Cars returning from the Shipyard continued west on Washington Street to Quincy Square, then turned north onto Hancock Street. Cars could turn directly from Hancock Street southbound onto Washington Street eastbound to go to the shipyard, but only did so if they were disabled or diverted for special events such as a parade.

In October 1943 the Eastern Mass. trustees voted to build two waiting rooms in Quincy Square, the first on the west side of Hancock Street between Depot and Seville Streets for eastbound Quincy Shipyard riders. This waiting room was opened in an existing storefront in December 1944.[132]

The second waiting room was located on a traffic island at Coddington and Washington Streets for passengers bound for Houghs Neck. It opened in September 1944.[133] This facility was a new building and was built with financial assistance from the City of Quincy.[134]

---

[1] The Boston El track on Neponset Avenue ended 20 feet south of the New Haven Railroad Mattapan Branch grade crossing. The Eastern Mass. owned all the track on the Neponset Bridge and 169 feet of track on the Boston mainland.

[m] The round-trip distance between Neponset and Quincy Square was 6.438 miles.

Quincy Shipyard Service

From Quincy Square, the track followed Washington Street to the Fore River Shipyard, turning south into a loop with a passing siding at Cleverly Court. The tracks also continued a short distance past Cleverly Court to Washington and South Streets, where they merged into a single track on the side of the road. The single track continued under live wire another 300 feet and was used to store and turn snow fighting equipment and disabled cars. The round-trip distance between Fields Corner and Quincy Shipyard was 13.752 miles and took 78 minutes to complete.[n]

Until the end of Quincy streetcar service in 1948, the Eastern Mass. and the Boston Elevated pooled equipment between Fields Corner and Neponset. Through cars for Quincy provided about half the service on the Boston Elevated's part of the line. Eastern Mass. and Boston Elevated streetcar operators and their respective fare boxes changed at Neponset. Generally, a Boston El car preceded an Eastern Mass. car inbound or outbound during the rush hours to Fields Corner, since the Eastern Mass. cars were usually full. Interestingly, on the Stoneham line north of Boston, another joint operation, operators took fare box readings for their respective companies rather than physically changing the boxes.

At Fields Corner, Boston Elevated motormen usually signed the Quincy cars "Quincy Square."[135] At Neponset, if a car was going to the Quincy Shipyard, Eastern Mass. motormen would change the sign to read "Shipyard."

There was no direct outbound track connection on Neponset Avenue outside the loop. Quincy-bound cars had to use the loop trackage as part of the route. There was, however, an inbound track connection for cars from Quincy to bypass the loop and proceed directly to Fields Corner. This track was used for non-revenue or special moves that did not need to use the loop, or for the temporary storage of work or revenue equipment. The outer and inner loop trackage was used interchangeably for regular movements or for car storage, depending on service requirements and the whim of the motormen.

During World War II, Boston Elevated Type 5 cars were operated through to Quincy, with Eastern Mass. motormen taking over at Neponset.[o] The April 1943 issue of *Co-operation* discussed this operation.[136] The El had arranged to lend the Eastern Mass. twelve cars for through operation to Quincy, although at that time the article in *Co-operation* said, the Eastern Mass. had only exercised the option for four.[p] Peak riding

[n] Between Neponset and the Quincy Shipyard, the round trip distance was 9.729 miles.

[o] A local observer has reported that the Eastern Mass. motormen disliked the Type 5s because of their wooden motorman's seat, the two-piece front window and the long reach for the door handle.

[p] A Quincy resident has reported that he saw Type 5 cars 5875, 5876, 5877 and 5889 in this service with "Quincy Square" and "Shipyard" added to their roll signs. He also recalls as many as six Type 5s in operation at one time on Washington Street.

Eastern Mass. cars provided local service between Neponset and Fields Corner. At top, lightweight 7048 rumbles along Geneva Avenue toward Fields Corner on the night of April 29, 1948, two days before the end of Eastern Mass. streetcar service. Above, some eleven weeks earlier, on February 10, 1948, 7004 climbs the northerly ramp to Fields Corner Station. *Both, Foster M. Palmer*

On the last day of operation of the Quincy Division, May 1, 1948, Eastern Mass. car 7010 lays over at Neponset Station.

Robert A. Kennerly

Eastern Mass. 7013 has just left Neponset Loop and is crossing the Neponset River drawbridge on its way to Quincy Square on October 4, 1947. *Lawson K. Hill, Stephen P. Carlson Collection*

A rider alights on Hancock Street from Shipyard-bound lightweight car 7033 on the sunny spring morning of May 17, 1947.

Robert A. Kennerly

Car 7001 rounds the bend from Hancock to Temple Street in Quincy Square early in 1947. The Church of the Presidents is in the background.

Robert A. Kennerly

Eastern Mass. car 7012 pulls onto Washington Street from Temple Street in Quincy Square on May 1, 1948. The trolley station is in the background, but a Mack bus waits beside it on Coddington Street.

Robert A. Kennerly

The winter of 1947 is nearing the end in this scene at Washington and Elm Streets as car 7048 heads for the Quincy Shipyard.

Robert A. Kennerly

hours to the Fore River Shipyard in Quincy came earlier in the morning than the Boston Elevated peak hour, and the Eastern Mass. returned the cars each day in time for the Boston Elevated rush hour service.

The Eastern Mass. discontinued streetcars between Quincy Square and Quincy Shipyard on April 4, 1948, replacing them with buses. The last car, 7003, left Quincy Square at 12:25 a.m. and was operated by Motorman Raymond Thomas. Streetcars remained in operation on the section of the line between Neponset and Quincy Square. To compensate for the reduction in Eastern Mass. streetcar service, the MTA immediately increased the number of its own cars between Fields Corner and Neponset Loop.

During World War I, the United States Navy had paid the cost of changing the line on Washington Street and Cleverly Court from single to double-track. The predecessor of the Eastern Mass., the Bay State Street Railway, had agreed at this time not to abandon this streetcar trackage without the permission of the Navy, and the agreement still bound the Eastern Mass. In 1946 the company applied for permission to abandon this line, but the Navy did not see fit to grant the request until March 1948.[137]

On May 1, 1948, the Quincy Square–Fields Corner streetcar service came to an end. Car 7012 had the honor of making the final run about 10 p.m. MTA Starter Frederick W. Battle blew the departure whistle, and MTA operator Thomas Buchan began the final run from Fields Corner to Neponset. Eastern Mass. operator Robert J. Egan, a 47-year streetcar veteran, ran the car jammed with railfans and regular riders from Neponset to Quincy Square. The starter and both operators were Quincy residents.

Bus operation began at once for the last runs of the day, but only between Quincy Square and Neponset. Full through bus operation from Quincy to Fields Corner began the following day, May 2, the buses running non-stop between Neponset and Fields Corner. The Quincy line was the last remaining rail operation of the sprawling 1000-mile track system of the Bay State Street Railway.[q] The Bay State had become the Eastern Massachusetts Street Railway twenty–nine years earlier, just a month to the day, on June 1, 1919.

A month and a half later, on June 19, 1948, the MTA replaced its own streetcars on the Fields Corner–Neponset line with buses, which ran from the lower busway of Fields Corner to the street outside the Neponset Loop.[r] The buses would later be replaced by trackless trolleys.

[q] Eastern Mass. trackage actually remained in operation after this date, but it was operated by the MTA under lease from the Eastern Mass. These tracks comprised a group of leased lines in the West Roxbury District of Boston, which the MTA purchased from the Eastern Mass. in 1951 and 1952. This transaction is discussed in Chapter 4.

[r] By December 1948, after renovations at Fields Corner for trackless trolleys had been completed, the Neponset buses began using the upper level at Fields Corner Station. When the line changed from bus to trackless trolley operation on December 10, 1949, the trolley coaches used the upper level as well.

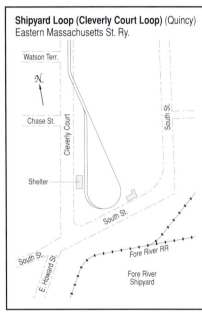

Shipyard Loop (Cleverly Court Loop) (Quincy)
Eastern Massachusetts St. Ry.

A simple wooden waiting station accommodated thousands of workers at the Quincy Shipyard over the years, particularly during World War II. On May 17, 1947, cars 7031 and 7043 had a brief respite before returning to Fields Corner Station. *Robert A. Kennerly*

The last leg of the Shipyard line featured double-track, side-of-road running on Cleverly Court between Washington Street and Shipyard Loop. Car 7041 has just passed another 7000-series car in this short segment on a sunny May 17, 1947. *Robert A. Kennerly*

Shipyard Loop saw considerable traffic during World War II as the Eastern Mass. transported the thousands of workers who constructed warships for the United States Navy at Bethlehem Steel's Fore River Shipyard. One of the best known "Quincy-built" ships was the aircraft carrier USS *Wasp* (CV-18), seen here ready for launching on August 17, 1943. *Naval Historical Center*

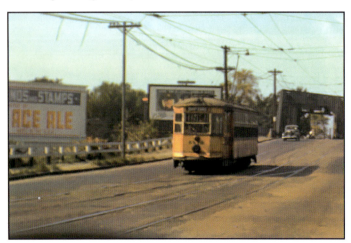

The heavy ridership generated by the Shipyard led to the Eastern Mass. borrowing Boston Elevated cars to supplement its own fleet. This June 1943 view shows an El Type 5 bound for the Shipyard on Hancock Street, Quincy, having just passed over the New Haven Railroad near Atlantic Station. *Charles A. Duncan*

Houghs Neck Line

Physically connected to the line between Fields Corner and the Quincy Shipyard was a throwback to an earlier time: a single-track line with turnouts running from Quincy Square to Houghs Neck. This route was operated as a shuttle, never running through to Fields Corner. On June 30, 1946, Houghs Neck was converted to buses. The Eastern Mass. reported that the Houghs Neck line, "had always been a bad accident hazard," which was not surprising considering the amount of single track running in both directions on this line.[138] The last Houghs Neck car was 7012, which later made the last run from Quincy Square to Fields Corner. The operator of the last Houghs Neck car was Motorman William McNeil.

After the start of World War II, the Houghs Neck line left Quincy Square from the site of the previously mentioned waiting room on Coddington Street, and after September 1944, from the waiting room itself. Before World War II, the Houghs Neck line had crossed Washington and Hancock Streets and had ended on the Saville Street spur.[s]

During the war the line ended at Coddington and Washington Streets in deference to the heavy motor vehicle and streetcar traffic in Quincy Square. Cars from Houghs Neck usually changed ends for the return trip at the waiting room, but they also could turn right onto Washington Street toward Quincy Square and reverse direction at a nearby crossover located just before the intersection of Washington and Hancock Streets. The latter scenario often occurred when a school extra on Houghs Neck was directed by an official to become a Shipyard extra on the main line.

From Quincy Square, the line followed Coddington Street, Sea Street, Babcock Street, and Manet Avenue, before returning to Sea Street. The rails stub-ended at Sea and Bayview Avenue. Most of the track on this line ran on the side of the road, with the exception of the Coddington Street track nearest Quincy Square. In this instance, the track was in the center of the roadway. The round-trip distance from the Coddington Street waiting room to the end of the line at Sea and Macy Streets was 6.868 miles. The round-trip running time was 36 minutes.

There were four turnouts on this line. The first was Valley Turnout on Coddington Street. Two more turnouts were located on Sea Street, the very long Sea Street Turnout (essentially a long stretch of double track) that ran from Merrymount to Adams Shore, and the short Willows Turnout. Last was the Church Turnout on Babcock Street between Oswego and Winthrop Streets.

The Boston Chapter NRHS newsletter, *The Turnout,* mentioned in its May 1948 issue that the cars sometimes did not run all the way to the end of the line if the tide was high, a curious and quaint nod to Mother Nature.[139] During rough

---

[s] The round-trip distance from the end of track on Saville Street to the end of the Houghs Neck line was 7.098 miles.

A 7000 waits on Coddington Street outside the trolley shelter. Soon the car will be making the run to Houghs Neck. *Lawson K. Hill*

A pair of 4200s including 4241 approach the Southern Artery on the way from Quincy Center to Houghs Neck. Note the street railway signal on the line pole, an important safety feature on a single-track line like this one. *Charles A. Duncan*

Cars 4287, 4289, and 7041 converge at the Church Turnout on Babcock Street toward the end of the Houghs Neck line. This was the shortest of the four turnouts on the line. *Charles A. Duncan*

The Houghs Neck line harkened to a slower, more relaxed time, and the lad in the sailor cap gazing out the rear of car 7011 as it ambles along certainly sets the mood in this 1944 scene.

Leon Onofri

Portions of the Houghs Neck line skirted the sea, and were often subject to flooding when high tides and storm runoff combined, as evidenced by the view at right of a 7000 splashing through the water near the end of the line. Sometimes the water depth was great enough to prevent the cars from running all the way to the end of the line. This was not a problem on a bright, sunny June 3, 1946, above. Service on the line would continue only until the last day of the month. *Above, Lawson K. Hill, Stephen P. Carlson Collection; right, Charles A. Duncan*

weather, the tide occasionally covered the rails in the lower places along the roadway on Sea Street at Manet Avenue. During the preparation of this book, a Quincy resident mentioned that the Eastern Mass. often used 4200s on this line because they rode higher than the 7000s and could handle minor flooding.

Al Jenness remembers…
The Missing Trolley Car

This little story occurred on a beautiful spring day in 1944. An operator on the spare board was assigned a run on the Houghs Neck line, replacing a man who had called in sick. At that time, the line had three cars in base service on a 15-minute headway. Running time was about eighteen minutes with allowed time of twenty minutes outbound and twenty-five minutes inbound.

It was early afternoon when another operator on the line called the foreman and said that his leader was missing and that only two cars were on the line. An inspector confirmed the situation and notified the Starter in Quincy Square. Neither official could explain the matter. Meanwhile, a car was diverted from the Quincy to Fields Corner main line to fill the gap on Houghs Neck.

The obvious and next step was to check cars on the main line between Quincy and Fields Corner.

Service seemed unusually good here, and the matter soon became clear with the arrival of the operator and his car at Quincy Square. When the passengers got off, the Inspector and Starter asked the operator the reason for his leaving the Houghs Neck line. The operator said that he was tired of running on the Houghs Neck line and thought he might "enjoy" a change by making a trip to Neponset.

In the transit business, "enjoyment" is not an employee benefit, and the operator was suspended for a few days. Normal discipline for such a severe infraction would have been much worse, but this operator was lucky because he was badly needed because of the wartime labor shortage. I am sure that this case merited a stronger response, but many other things were also overlooked at that time.

Albert S. Jenness of Quincy, a well-known trolley fan now deceased, ran streetcars for the Eastern Massachusetts Street Railway Company for a number of years.

Routes Based at City Point Carhouse

16 Franklin Park–Andrew Station

Route 16 was based at City Point Carhouse, which was described in Chapter 2. At the beginning of the 1940s, Andrew Station cars laid over in the side-of-the-road reservation on Blue Hill Avenue, next to Franklin Park. Outbound cars on Columbia Road crossed the traffic lanes of Blue Hill Avenue before turning left into the reservation and ran 500 feet south, entering a stub-end center track located near Glen Lane. The southbound main line jogged around the center track and allowed regular Blue Hill Avenue cars to bypass the Columbia Road cars as they lay over.

This stub-end center track was nearly 600 feet long, providing storage space for extra cars. It brought passengers from Andrew Station practically to the main entrance of Franklin Park. After reversing direction at the south end of the center track, Columbia Road cars immediately took a crossover onto the northbound track and turned right onto Columbia Road.

In 1941, with the removal of the Blue Hill Avenue streetcar reservation, the physical connection was cut between the Columbia Road and Blue Hill Avenue tracks. The special center cutback track on Blue Hill Avenue and southbound main line bypass were removed at the same time. A double crossover for the Columbia Road cars to turn back was installed on Columbia Road between Old Road and Blue Hill Avenue.[140] This change is shown in Map 2, Inset A.

The Columbia Road track ran in a reservation in the center of the road. Leaving Blue Hill Avenue, cars followed Columbia Road northeast, crossing tracks on Washington Street and Geneva Avenue, and running under a wide railroad bridge of the New Haven Railroad Midland Division. At the Hancock Street junction, just before Uphams Corner, the Fields Corner–Andrew line came in from the southeast. The two lines then shared the track into Andrew Station on Columbia Road, Boston Street, and Dorchester Avenue as previously described. Post-1941, Franklin Park–Andrew was 4.995 miles long, round-trip, with a running time of 27 minutes.

No. 5565 emerges into Ellery Street from Andrew Station as it starts a trip on Route 16 to Franklin Park on April 27, 1948.

Foster M. Palmer

The New Haven Railroad bridge across Columbia Road was an important landmark on the Franklin Park–Andrew line. Here we see 5566 on its way to Franklin Park on October 11, 1947.

Foster M. Palmer

Columbia Road car 5546 pauses at Washington Street on November 14, 1947, as 5558 headed on Washington Street for Ashmont rips across the intersection. Columbia Road was one of the few places on the system where double bracket arms supported the trolley wire..

Robert A. Kennerly

Until 1941, the Franklin Park–Andrew line crossed Blue Hill Avenue and changed ends on a special layover track between the running rails. Relocation of the Blue Hill Avenue tracks to the center of the roadway forced the cutback of this line to a scissors crossover on Columbia Road shown here in this April 1945 scene. The Type 5 cars will return to Andrew, while the Type 4 behind them are holding down Egleston or Ashmont–Dudley via Talbot Avenue service.

Charles A. Duncan

47 Dudley–Massachusetts Station

Dudley–Massachusetts Station was also based at City Point.[t] This line started at the lower level of Dudley Street Station. Cars from Massachusetts Station entered the South Yard from Washington Street and let their passengers off in the paid area of the platform near Washington Street. The cars then looped over Warren Street and reentered the station in the North Yard prepayment platform to pick up passengers for the trip back to Massachusetts Station.

Leaving Dudley Street Station, the cars turned north onto Washington Street and continued northeast on Washington Street crossing from Roxbury to Boston Proper before arriving at Northampton Street. The cars turned left onto Northampton Street, and ran northwest to Columbus Avenue, crossing the Egleston–North Station line at Tremont Street.[u] The line then turned northeast and ran one block on Columbus Avenue.

The tracks on Northampton Street bypassed parallel Chester Square, a jewel of Victorian design, which was located in the block of Massachusetts Avenue between Shawmut Avenue and Tremont Street. The lanes of the roadway were diverted around the sides of the park to maintain a solid open space, and streetcars never operated on this section of Massachusetts Avenue.

From Columbus Avenue, the line turned northwest onto Massachusetts Avenue, and crossed a bridge over the New Haven Railroad main line. The tracks continued across the Huntington Avenue car line, passing Symphony Hall and crossing a bridge over the Boston & Albany Railroad main line before reaching Newbury Street.

The cars turned east onto Newbury Street, then almost immediately south into the westerly loop track at Massachusetts Station. As previously mentioned, this line was extremely busy, but it was also extremely short, having a round-trip length of only 3.393 miles. The round-trip running averaged 28 minutes, however, which reflected heavy city traffic and heavy ridership.

Returning cars turned west from the station onto Boylston Street, then south onto Massachusetts Avenue for the return trip to Dudley Street Station. Cars used this routing at Massachusetts Station through the end of 1946, but by February 1947, they were entering Massachusetts Station from the Boylston Street end, using the easterly loop track, and exiting onto Newbury Street before returning to Massachusetts Avenue.

---

[t] This line was once part of a longer line from Harvard Square to Dudley Street which was split into two segments on July 27, 1930: Harvard–Massachusetts Station, and Massachusetts Station–Dudley. Night car service continued to operate directly between Harvard and Dudley, however.

[u] Cars coming from Massachusetts Station could reach Lenox Street Yard by using non-revenue tracks on Columbus Avenue beyond Northampton Street that ran directly to the yard. Between July 9 and 12, 1946, the Boston Elevated removed this track connection.

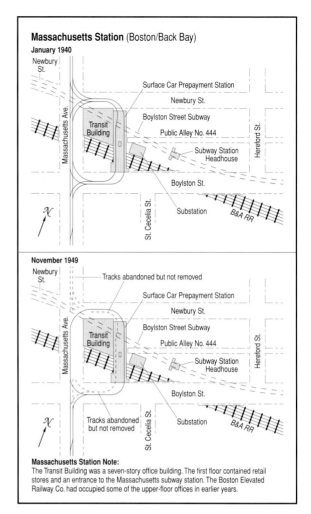

Massachusetts Station (Boston/Back Bay)

January 1940

Newbury St. — Surface Car Prepayment Station — Newbury St. — Boylston Street Subway — Public Alley No. 444 — Subway Station Headhouse — Boylston St. — Substation — B&A RR — Massachusetts Ave. — Transit Building — St. Cecilia St. — Hereford St.

N

November 1949

Newbury St. — Tracks abandoned but not removed — Surface Car Prepayment Station — Newbury St. — Boylston Street Subway — Public Alley No. 444 — Subway Station Headhouse — Boylston St. — Tracks abandoned but not removed — Substation — B&A RR — Massachusetts Ave. — Transit Building — St. Cecilia St. — Hereford St.

N

Massachusetts Station Note:
The Transit Building was a seven-story office building. The first floor contained retail stores and an entrance to the Massachusetts subway station. The Boston Elevated Railway Co. had occupied some of the upper-floor offices in earlier years.

From Dudley Street Station to Northampton Street, this line shared tracks with the City Point–Dudley route. At Northampton Street, cars for City Point turned southeast onto Northampton Street.

On April 17, 1948, buses replaced streetcars on Dudley–Massachusetts Station weekdays from 9:40 a.m. to 3:06 p.m. and after 7 p.m. The buses operated on Massachusetts Avenue, between Columbus Avenue and Washington Street, in-

The twin portals of the Boylston Street end of Massachusetts Station clearly show behind car 5531 as it starts its trip to Dudley Street Station. *Charles A. Duncan, Seashore Trolley Museum Collection*

Type 4 No. 5381 and a Type 5 proceed along Massachusetts Avenue in the Back Bay beside Symphony Hall. This is the Schoolboy Parade day in June 1942, and the Type 4 was rerouted to Massachusetts Station from the Tremont Street line, while the Type 5 is handling the regular service over this track between Massachusetts Station and Dudley Street Station.

Charles A. Duncan

Cars on Route 47 used narrow Northampton Street to get from Columbus Avenue to Washington Street, avoiding Chester Park which occupied the center of Massachusetts Avenue between Shawmut Avenue and Tremont Street. At right, a Dudley-bound Type 5 is about to turn into Northampton Street after having traversed the one block from Massachusetts Avenue. Tracks in the foreground lead to the Columbus Avenue end of Lenox Street Yard. Below right, a Type 5 on the Dudley–Massachusetts line passes Type 4 No. 5377 on Northampton at Tremont Street.

Right, BERy; below right, Charles A. Duncan

stead of the streetcar routing via Columbus Avenue and Northampton Street. Buses also began all day operation on Sundays and holidays. On Saturdays, cars were still operated from the early morning hours until 9:40 a.m. This service mix lasted for quite some time, and streetcars would continue on this route during hours of heavy riding until 1953.

At Dudley Street Station, cars from Massachusetts Station unloaded in the South Yard of the lower level (left), then looped onto Warren Street and into the North Yard prepayment platform (above) to take on riders for the return trip.   *Left, BERy; above, Charles A. Duncan*

Routes Based at Arborway

41 Jamaica–Dudley

This route originated at the Jamaica Plain Loop off South Street, Jamaica Plain. The loop once adjoined the site of a carhouse, but through most of the 1940s it consisted of a loop track with one passing siding used for storage, a stub-end spur, and a waiting shelter. A second stub-end spur ran off the first, parallel to the storage track, but this stub was removed in late August 1940 in conjunction with track renewal work elsewhere on the loop.

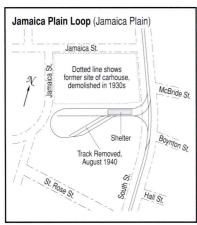

Jamaica Plain Loop (Jamaica Plain)

Jamaica St.

Jamaica St.

Dotted line shows
former site of carhouse,
demolished in 1930s

McBride St.

N

Boynton St.

Shelter

Track Removed,
August 1940

St. Rose St.

South St.

Hall St.

Cars leaving Jamaica Plain for Dudley turned north onto South Street and shared the tracks with the Arborway–Huntington line as far as Centre Street and South Huntington Avenue. Here Jamaica–Dudley cars diverged right and followed Centre Street to Jackson Square at Columbus Avenue, passing under the main line of the New Haven Railroad just before arriving at Jackson Square. A loop for short-turning cars from Dudley Street was located at Hyde Square, the junction of Centre and Perkins Streets and the boundary between the Jamaica Plain section of West Roxbury and Roxbury.

Cars turned north onto Columbus Avenue, sharing tracks with the Egleston–North Station line, and then turned east onto

Jamaica Plain Loop, the terminal of the Dudley–Jamaica line, was just up South Street from the Arborway. Here in 1947, two Type 5 cars pause between trips, although the one at the terminal will leave shortly. Jamaica Loop was the site of a large carhouse in earlier years. *Robert A. Kennerly*

Type 5s Nos. 5752 and 5721 pass under the New Haven Railroad bridge across Centre Street in Roxbury in 1947. The Jamaica Plain Loop–Dudley line was always busy and one of the more interesting Dudley car lines. In the distance, Fort Hill with its distinctive water tower looms up. Check out the fancy New Haven semaphore signals. *Robert A. Kennerly*

Type 5 No. 5720 roars through Cornelius T. Maloney Square (Hyde Square) on Centre Street on the way to Jamaica Plain Loop in June 1949. *Stanley M. Hauck*

Roxbury Street at Hanley Square, one block before the intersection known as Roxbury Crossing. Following Roxbury Street, the line passed through historic John Eliot Square before running onto Dudley Street over single track. Eastbound cars followed Dudley Street across Washington Street and turned into the West Loop of Dudley Street Station, dropping off their riders at the rapid transit platform level. This line was moderately long, a round-trip consuming 6.134 miles and requiring a running time of 36 minutes.

Cars leaving the West Loop turned west onto Dudley Street. At Washington Street, they bore northwest on single track onto Guild Row, and then ran back onto Roxbury Street, which was also single track at this point. Cars continued back to John Eliot Square for their return trip to Jamaica Plain. At John Eliot Square, the single track on Roxbury Street reentered double-track territory.

The MTA created a cutback between Hyde Square and Dudley Street Station in the April 12, 1948, rating using the loop at Hyde Square to turn cars. The round-trip distance was 3.588 miles with a running time of 22 minutes. The cutback was dropped in the June 1948 rating but was reinstated in September and lasted until the end of service on the through route from Jamaica Plain Loop to Dudley Street Station on June 8, 1949.

Jamaica cars approached Dudley Street Station on Dudley Street itself, on single track from John Eliot Square on Fort Hill. They left Dudley via Guild Row, shown here, turned onto Roxbury Street, and returned to John Eliot Square, where they rejoined the inbound track on Roxbury Street.   *BERy*

42 Egleston–Dudley *via Washington Street*

This line turned northeast onto Washington Street from the outer loop of Egleston Station. The cars followed Washington Street to Dudley Street, where they turned east, then entered the West Loop.

The return trip required a turn from the West Loop west onto Dudley Street, southwest onto Washington Street, and southeast onto Columbus Avenue. The cars then entered Egleston Station. A round-trip on this line was only 2.613 miles with a running time of 16 minutes.

Starting its run from Dudley Street Station to Egleston Station, Type 5 No. 5662 turns from Dudley onto Washington Street under the elevated about 1948. Note the single track in the foreground. This was actually on Dudley Street and used by Jamaica Plain Loop cars to get from John Eliot Square to the station.   *Clarke Collection*

The run from Dudley to Egleston was almost entirely under the Main Line Elevated. No. 5691 is just north of Townsend Street on March 25, 1948.   *Foster M. Palmer*

Already signed for its return trip to Egleston, 5723 ascends the West Loop at Dudley Street Station on June 10, 1949.
William V. Kenney, Anthony F. Tieuli Collection

44 Seaver–Dudley

This line connected Seaver Street Loop on the northeast side of Franklin Park with Dudley Street Station.[v] Leaving the loop, inbound cars turned northwest onto the Seaver Street tracks, which also carried the Mattapan–Egleston cars, and then immediately turned northeast onto Humboldt Avenue.[w]

Cars bound for Dudley ran northeast down Humboldt Avenue, turned right onto Walnut Avenue, and then north onto Warren Street. From here the line proceeded to the Dudley East Loop, sharing the route with Fields Corner–Dudley and the two Ashmont–Dudley lines. This was a short but busy line, with a round-trip distance of 3.245 miles and a 20-minute running time.

---

[v] Cars assigned to this line pulled out from the Arborway, followed Washington Street to Columbus Avenue, then Columbus Avenue and Seaver Street to the Seaver Street Loop. Pull-backs to the carhouse followed the reverse route.

[w] Outbound cars arriving at Seaver Street turned right from Humboldt Avenue onto Seaver Street, and then left into the loop. There were also connections allowing outbound cars on Humboldt Avenue to turn left directly onto Seaver Street and head towards Mattapan, and for cars from Egleston to enter the loop.

Seaver Street Loop (Roxbury)

Humboldt Ave.

Seaver St.

park entrance road

Seaver Street Loop Note:
The reservation along Seaver St. was part of the public way, owned by the Boston Public Works Department. The loop itself was owned by the Boston Elevated Railway. The other land south and west of Seaver St. was part of Franklin Park.

The only line in Roxbury that regularly saw a PCC car was Route 44, Seaver–Dudley. Generally, the only PCC used on this line was No. 3001, based at the Arborway. In this February 1945 scene, 3001 has emerged from Humboldt Avenue onto Seaver Street and is about to enter the Mattapan–Egleston streetcar reservation to access Seaver Street Loop. *Charles A. Duncan*

This line was regularly operated with Type 5 cars. However, Seaver Humboldt was off the beaten path geographically and was the Arborway's "odd" line. It was fitting that the line would be assigned the Arborway's "odd" car as the only example of PCC operation in this area. PCC service began on March 31, 1945. This assignment was officially made in the April 2, 1945, rating, which showed a single PCC car on the route. This assignment continued until the September 15, 1947, rating, and photographs and official records show that this car was usually 3001—the "Queen Mary."

On January 25, 1943, Route 44 was extended from Seaver Street Loop to Egleston Station as an experiment to stimulate outbound riding. This effort appears to have failed, and the line resumed its normal termination point at Seaver Street Loop at the start of the spring rating. The round-trip running time

Type 5 No. 5781 is at Walnut Street going onto Humboldt Avenue on September 15, 1948, on its way from Dudley Street to Seaver Street Loop. *Charles A. Duncan*

on the extended route was 27 minutes, an increase of 7 minutes over the regular run to Seaver Street Loop.

Trackless Trolley and Bus Conversions

Preparations

Change was in the offing in 1948 for most of the streetcar lines in Roxbury and Dorchester. A general conversion of these lines to trackless trolleys would soon begin. Early in 1948, the MTA began dual overhead wire construction. The first test run of a trackless trolley took place on June 16, 1948, between Fields Corner Station and Andrew Station via Meeting House Hill using coach 8333 on loan from Salem Street Carhouse in Medford. To ensure that the trip would be trouble-free, a line truck preceded the trolley bus the entire way.

Many changes were made at Andrew, Ashmont, Dudley Street, and Fields Corner Stations to accommodate trackless trolleys. The August 1948 issue of *Co-operation* discussed this work in detail.[141] The changes varied in complexity, but the work at Dudley Street Station surpassed by far the work done at the other three stations.

Car 5784 pulls into Seaver Street Loop deadheaded from the Arborway on March 25, 1948. It will enter revenue service shortly with an inbound trip to Dudley Street Station via Humboldt Avenue. *Foster M. Palmer*

Dudley Street was one of the earliest rapid transit stations in Boston. It was a busy terminal, opening for the interchange of rapid transit and surface streetcar riders in 1901. In 1948 the station was a veritable antique, and modifying it for trackless trolleys was difficult. On the other hand, Andrew Station, which had opened in 1918, Fields Corner in 1927, and Ashmont in 1928, all in the age of the automobile, were much more easily changed.

Most of the work at Dudley Street centered on rebuilding the East Loop. This loop and the matching West Loop had handled streetcars since the station opening. Cars turned into both loops from Dudley Street and climbed a short, steep ramp over ballasted trackwork to the rapid transit level of the station. Here riders made a convenient, across-the-platform transfer between streetcars and rapid transit trains. As part of this project, for the first time ever, cars from the East Loop were diverted to the West Loop. This was a major and expensive change, coming as it did at the eleventh hour of streetcar operation for the lines using the East Loop.

Starting on May 19, 1948, the MTA built double track curves and switches east from Dudley Street into the West Loop, making a half-grand union with the existing curves and switches at the bottom of the incline. This work was completed on July 16, 1948, and the two Ashmont–Dudley lines, and the Uphams Corner, Fields Corner, Grove Hall, and Humboldt Avenue lines were diverted to the West Loop until their conversion to trackless trolley operation.

Beginning on August 16, 1948, the rail on the East Loop and the ramp special work at Dudley Street were removed. The tracks on Dudley Street were repaved, and on September 30 the trackwork was finally completed.

Meanwhile the steel superstructure of the East Loop and much of the support steel were removed, and new columns were installed. A new asphalt-topped reinforced concrete roadway replaced the car tracks. A new superstructure with skylights and windows and a new stairway and lobby were built. Reinforced concrete safety posts[x] seven feet apart were installed between the passenger walkway and the trackless trolley roadway, and a concrete retaining wall was built on the inner side of the roadway.

Work at Andrew, Ashmont, and Fields Corner was much less extensive. The tracks were regraded and paved with macadam around the rails. After the cars had been abandoned, the macadam was replaced with a permanent asphalt surface. To handle the wider turning radius required by trackless trolleys, roadway-opening enlargements were made at both ends of the Andrew and Fields Corner platforms, and at both ends of the outbound platform at Ashmont.

At both Andrew and Fields Corner, the track grading and paving was done on one track at a time. During the off-peak periods, streetcars loaded and unloaded on the track not under construction. Special fare collection facilities were used in these instances.

Additional work took place at Fields Corner. Reinforced concrete walls were installed on the inclines and through the station on both sides. The underpass at the Dorchester Avenue end of the station was widened, and a bridge over Freeman Street was strengthened. Upon completion of the inclines and station lanes, buses were diverted from the street level busway to the upper level of the station to allow the busway floor to be reinforced.

At Ashmont Station, reinforced concrete walls were built on the north and south loops, and the south viaduct and north bridge were both widened. These changes required the relocation of the rapid transit trainmen's lobby at the north end of station.

New shop equipment was installed at Park Street Carhouse. Between May 3 and August 13, 1948, selected rails in the carhouse and yard were removed. The carhouse yard was regraded and temporarily paved with macadam for use while the cars were still running. When trackless trolleys replaced the streetcars, the yard area was permanently paved.

On the Park Street reservation, tracks were regraded and the reservation was paved. A crossover and a switch to a lead track beside the caryard on the Geneva Avenue side of the Park Street Carhouse were removed.[142]

While all these modifications were under way, overhead line construction was also in progress, continuing into the late fall. By mid-December, the stage was set.

Streetcar to Trackless Conversions

On Christmas Day, December 25, 1948, in an unprecedented but planned move, the first trackless trolleys operated from Park Street Carhouse. These coaches replaced streetcars on the Uphams Corner–Dudley Street Station (later extended to Kane Square), and Grove Hall–Dudley Street lines.[y]

On December 30, 1948, the seventieth trackless trolley of a 128-coach order was delivered from Pullman–Standard in Worcester, Massachusetts.[143] Seventy coaches were the minimum number that the MTA needed to begin the Dorchester and Roxbury conversions. Their delivery on time beat a promised delivery date of the end of the year by a day.

Conversions continued rapidly. Three more lines were changed to trackless trolleys on January 8, 1949:

19	**Fields Corner Station–Dudley Street Station** *via Geneva Avenue*
22	**Ashmont Station–Dudley Street Station** *via Talbot Avenue*
23	**Ashmont Station–Dudley Street Station** *via Washington Street*

---

[x] These posts were hit frequently but accidentally by the trackless trolleys during their first few months of service, incidents that were widely reported in the local press. MTA operators quickly nicknamed the posts "headstones."

[y] Kane Square is the junction of Hancock and Bowdoin Streets.

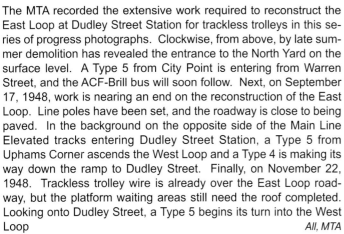

The MTA recorded the extensive work required to reconstruct the East Loop at Dudley Street Station for trackless trolleys in this series of progress photographs. Clockwise, from above, by late summer demolition has revealed the entrance to the North Yard on the surface level. A Type 5 from City Point is entering from Warren Street, and the ACF-Brill bus will soon follow. Next, on September 17, 1948, work is nearing an end on the reconstruction of the East Loop. Line poles have been set, and the roadway is close to being paved. In the background on the opposite side of the Main Line Elevated tracks entering Dudley Street Station, a Type 5 from Uphams Corner ascends the West Loop and a Type 4 is making its way down the ramp to Dudley Street. Finally, on November 22, 1948. Trackless trolley wire is already over the East Loop roadway, but the platform waiting areas still need the roof completed. Looking onto Dudley Street, a Type 5 begins its turn into the West Loop

All, MTA

In addition to these lines, the service line from Fields Corner to Ashmont via Dorchester Avenue was also converted to trackless trolleys at this time.

The next line to change from streetcar to trackless was Dudley–Seaver Street via Humboldt Avenue, on January 29, 1949. This route was reassigned from the Arborway to the Fields Corner rating station, since no trackless trolleys were then based at the Arborway.

The last conversion in this round of changes from streetcars to trackless trolleys came on February 12, 1949, on the Fields Corner–Andrew line. Eight Type 5 cars remained at Park Street Carhouse to cover the service the last night. These cars were sent the next day to Everett Shops for disposition.

Streetcar to Bus Conversions

As previously discussed, on June 19, 1948, the MTA changed the Fields Corner–Neponset line from streetcars to buses. This line would later be converted to trackless trolleys.

The 1945 Boston Elevated annual report mentioned that the busy Jamaica–Dudley line was under consideration for conversion from streetcar to trackless trolley. The Jamaica–Dudley line was eventually converted, but not until June 8, 1949, and to buses, not to trackless trolleys. The use of trolley buses would have required additional renovations at Dudley Street, and this expense was avoided by the simple expedient of running buses to the lower level of the station.

The new bus line was routed between Jackson Square and John Eliot Square via Centre Street rather than on Columbus Avenue and Roxbury Street. In doing so, the buses followed a former car line that had once used tracks on Centre Street.

On September 17, 1949, Dudley–Egleston was also converted to buses. This line was the last one to use the West Loop at Dudley Street Station. The real purpose of this route was as a connecting track to the Arborway, and the end of the streetcars on the Jamaica–Dudley and Seaver–Humboldt lines had made the Dudley–Egleston trackage unnecessary.

The Dudley West Loop was abandoned and was never

While the greatest changes for the conversion to trackless trolleys were made at Dudley Street Station, the work done at Fields Corner, shown here on August 20, 1948, was significant. Here we see a trolley crane car in action on the ramp from the south side of the station to Dorchester Avenue. The trackless trolley wire is already up, and the remaining work will focus on roadway construction. *MTA*

paved for bus or trackless trolley operation. The loop with its unused trolley tracks remained in plain view for many years, a reminder of an earlier time.

The Final Steps

The final trackless trolley conversions in Dorchester and Roxbury took place on December 10, 1949. The Franklin Park–Andrew line was converted from streetcar to trackless trolley, and at this time it was also transferred from City Point to the Park Street rating station. On the same day, Neponset–Fields Corner was changed from bus to trackless trolley, having gone from streetcar to bus a year and a half earlier, on June 19, 1948.

And that was it. At the beginning of 1950, only three streetcar lines were still running through Dorchester and Roxbury: the Mattapan–Ashmont High-Speed Trolley Line, which survives to the present day; Dudley–Massachusetts Station, which ran until 1953; and Mattapan–Egleston, which survived until 1955. This last route might have lasted even longer had not the City of Boston been so eager to appropriate parts of its reservation for motor vehicle use.

Adjacent car lines still running were Mattapan–Arborway via Cummins Highway (at the southwestern corner of Dorchester), and the lines from Egleston Station (on the southwestern border of Roxbury) to Arborway and to North Station.

Work car 924, a former Boston Elevated Railway parlor car, now works for the Metropolitan Transit Authority as a day laborer at Ashmont Station in July 1948. Soon the work 924 is doing will bring trackless trolleys and the end of her kind.

Stanley M. Hauck

Belgrade Avenue, West Roxbury, is seen in 1940. This Type 5 has stopped over the loop switch to Corinth Street near Roslindale Square to board passengers headed in the direction of Charles River.

BERy

Chapter 4

The Arborway Lines

Arborway Station was located in Jamaica Plain.[144] It served the largely residential Hyde Park, West Roxbury, and Roslindale areas of Boston and parts of the inner city, including Dorchester, Roxbury, the South End, Jamaica Plain, and the Back Bay. Arborway cars also ran into the Central Subway.

The Arborway lines were known for heavy ridership, heavy service levels, and heavy vehicle requirements. Today, the car lines that operated from Arborway are almost completely gone. The line on Huntington Avenue to Heath Street still runs, but it is based at Reservoir. This remaining vestige is no accident, for the Arborway–Huntington line, of which the Heath Street service was a part, was one of the busiest lines on the system.

The New Haven Railroad also served Roslindale and West Roxbury at stations on the Needham Branch and the Main Line. The Main Line Elevated, replaced by today's Southwest Corridor Orange Line, stopped at Egleston and Green Street Stations and ended at Forest Hills, the principal transfer point for surface cars.

Important destinations along routes based at Arborway Station included the Arnold Arboretum, the Museum of Fine Arts, the Isabella Stewart Gardner Museum, Boston Latin School, Symphony Hall, the Boston Opera House, the Mechanics Building, Harvard Medical School, Horticultural Hall, Northeastern University, the Calvary and Mt. Hope cemeteries, and several hospitals.

The main changes here in the 1940s were service revisions and the exchange of lines between the Arborway and its neighboring rating station, Park Street, Dorchester. For clarity some lines are discussed in this chapter, while others are covered in Chapter 3 on Dorchester and Roxbury and Chapter 5, which covers the Central Subway.

Service Overview

In 1940 nine streetcar lines were based at Arborway Station, located at Washington Street and the Arborway in Jamaica Plain.[a] These lines are listed below and are shown on Map 4.

Route No.	Route Description
30	**Mattapan Station–Arborway Station** *via Cummins Highway and Hyde Park Avenue*
32	**Cleary Square–Arborway Station** *via Hyde Park Avenue*
33	**Cummins Highway and Washington Street (Roslindale Square)–Arborway Station** *via Cummins Highway and Hyde Park Avenue*
34	**Dedham Line–Arborway Station** *via Washington Street*
	[cb] **Washington and LaGrange Street Crossover–Arborway** *via Washington Street*
36	**Charles River Loop–Arborway Station** *via Spring Street, Centre Street, Belgrade Avenue, Corinth Street, and Washington Street*
	[cb] **Centre and LaGrange Street Crossover–Arborway** *via Centre Street*
39	**Arborway Station–Park Street Station** *via Arborway, South Street, Centre Street, South Huntington Avenue, Huntington Avenue, Boylston Street, and Subway*
40	**Arborway Station–Egleston Station** *via Washington Street*
43	**Egleston Station–North Station** *via Columbus Avenue, Tremont Street, and Subway*
57	**Francis Street and Huntington Avenue[b]–Park Street Station** *via Huntington Avenue and Subway*

This chapter covers all of these lines except Arborway–Park Street and Francis Street–Park Street. Francis Street–Park Street and its successor, Heath Street–Park Street, were essentially cutbacks of Arborway–Park Street yet treated as separate routes. All three routes are more appropriately discussed in the context of the Central Subway, covered in Chapter 5.

---

[a] The Arborway is a highway and is part of Boston's Metropolitan Parkway System.

[b] The intersection of Francis Street and Huntington Avenue is known today as Brigham Circle.

Map ④
The Arborway Lines

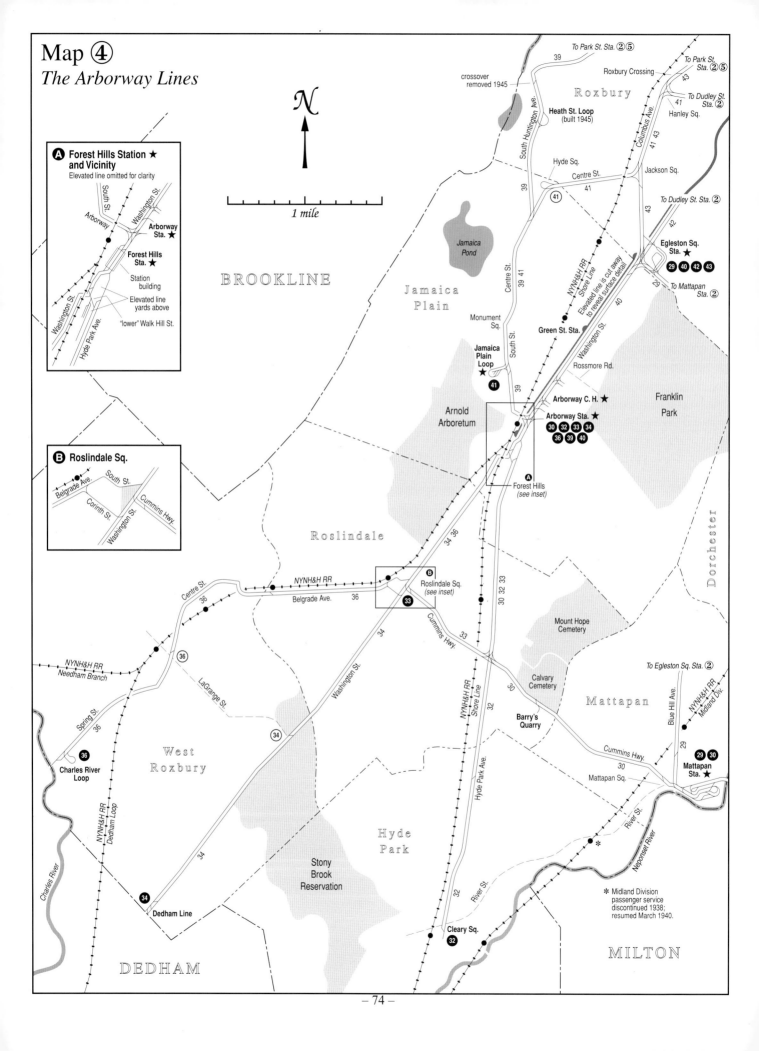

N

1 mile

Ⓐ Forest Hills Station ★ and Vicinity
Elevated line omitted for clarity

South St.
Washington St.
Arborway
Arborway Sta. ★
Forest Hills Sta. ★
Washington St.
Station building
Elevated line yards above
Hyde Park Ave.
"lower" Walk Hill St.

Ⓑ Roslindale Sq.

Belgrade Ave.
South St.
Corinth St.
Cummins Hwy.
Washington St.

To Park St. Sta. ②⑤
39
Roxbury Crossing
To Park St. Sta. ②⑤
43
To Dudley St. Sta. ②
41
Roxbury
crossover removed 1945
South Huntington Ave.
Heath St. Loop (built 1945)
Hanley Sq.
Columbus Ave.
41 43
Hyde Sq.
Jackson Sq.
Centre St.
41
㊶
43
To Dudley St. Sta. ②
42
Egleston Sq. Sta. ★
㉙ ㊵ ㊷ ㊸
㉙
To Mattapan Sta. ②

BROOKLINE

Jamaica Pond

Centre St. 39 41

Jamaica Plain

NYNH&H RR Shore Line
Elevated line is cut away to reveal surface detail
40

Monument Sq.
South St.
Green St. Sta.
Washington St.

Jamaica Plain Loop ★
㊶
39
Rossmore Rd.

Franklin Park

Arnold Arboretum

Arborway C. H. ★
Arborway Sta. ★
㉚ ㉜ ㉝ ㉞
㊱ ㊴ ㊵

Ⓐ **Forest Hills** (see inset)

Dorchester

Roslindale

34 36

Centre St. 36

NYNH&H RR
Belgrade Ave. 36

Ⓑ **Roslindale Sq.** (see inset)
㉝

30 32 33

Mount Hope Cemetery

NYNH&H RR Needham Branch
㊱
LaGrange St.
㉞

34

Washington St.

Cummins Hwy.
33

Calvary Cemetery

33
30
Barry's Quarry
32

To Egleston Sq. Sta. ②

Spring St. 36
West Roxbury

Mattapan

Blue Hill Ave.
NYNH&H RR Midland Div.
㉙
Cummins Hwy.
30
㉙ ㉚
Mattapan Sta. ★

Charles River
㊱
Charles River Loop

NYNH&H RR Dedham Loop
34

Mattapan Sq.

Hyde Park Ave.
32
River St.

Neponset River

Hyde Park

Stony Brook Reservation

River St.
✳

㉞
Dedham Line

32

✳ Midland Division passenger service discontinued 1938; resumed March 1940.

Cleary Sq.
㉜

DEDHAM

MILTON

– 74 –

This splendid view of the Arborway shows the waiting shelter with the lobby building behind. To the left center we see a center-entrance car on one of the tracks leading from the carhouse yard. In the foreground, a center-entrance car signed SUBWAY prepares to leave for a trip along the Arborway line and into the sybway at Arlington and Boylston Streets in the Back Bay. The Type 5 car will soon head into Forest Hills Station bound for Mattapan, Cleary Square, or Roslindale Square via Cummins Highway, and the ACF bus waits on the busway.   *BERy*

The busiest Arborway routes, including cutbacks for those that had them, were Routes 39, 36, 43, 34, and 32, in that order. A second tier of lines, Routes 57, 30 and 40, and 33, offered significantly fewer trips also in order. See Appendix 9 for detailed operating information.

The trackage of five lines, Mattapan–Arborway, Roslindale Square–Arborway via Cummins Highway, Dedham Line–Arborway, Charles River–Arborway, and the segment of Cleary Square–Arborway from Forest Hills to the Hyde Park–Boston boundary was leased by the Boston Elevated from the Eastern Massachusetts Street Railway under an agreement signed June 9, 1920.[145] This lease was effective throughout the 1940s, only ending in the early 1950s when the MTA terminated the lease by purchasing the lines outright from the Eastern Mass.[146]

The Boston El leased the section of the Cleary Square line from the Hyde Park–Boston boundary to Cleary Square from the Transit Department of the City of Boston on August 23, 1923.[147] This trackage was transferred to the MTA on August 3, 1949, when the Authority took possession of the property of the Boston Transit Department, which has been previously discussed.

Three other lines were based at Arborway, but were operated from Dudley Street Station. These routes were discussed in Chapter 3 but are listed here for reference since they are mentioned in this chapter. These routes were:

41   **Jamaica Plain Loop–Dudley Street Station** *via South Street, Centre Street, Jackson Square, Columbus Avenue, Roxbury Street, and Dudley Street (Guild Row westbound)*

42   **Egleston Station–Dudley Street Station** *via Washington Street*

44   **Seaver Street Loop–Dudley Street Station** *via Humboldt Avenue, Walnut Avenue, and Warren Street*

Route 44 was transferred to Park Street Carhouse in Dorchester on January 29, 1949, with the conversion of the line to trackless trolley operation.

In a special rating change made almost immediately after the Egleston Station accident of April 12, 1948, both the Mattapan–Ashmont and Mattapan–Egleston lines were transferred on April 19, 1948, from Park Street, Dorchester, to the Arborway. This drastic move was previously discussed in Chapter 3.

These later route transfers and the conversion of Routes 41 and 42 changed the number of car lines based at the Arborway from twelve to eleven. Thus, in 1950, this rating station was running only one less car line than it did in 1940!

Arborway Station

Arborway was a sprawling complex, consisting of two side-by-side carhouse buildings and adjacent caryards, a large operator and administrative lobby, a bus garage, and a heating plant. The carhouses had six track bays. A shifting loop ran partly on Washington Street and the yard track parallel to Brookley Road before running through the carhouses and back onto Washington Street. The loop track also connected the repair and storage tracks inside the buildings to the caryards.

A small yard located between the northwest side of the carhouses and Washington Street had three parallel tracks.[148] A much larger yard on the southern side of the property had two parallel loops for cars that had come from Forest Hills and were turning around for their next outbound trips and a parallel bus loop as well.

These loops were located between the public waiting shelter and Washington Street. Riders for Mattapan, Cleary Square, and Roslindale Square via Cummins Highway boarded on the loop nearest the waiting shelter. Patrons for Dedham Line and Charles River loaded on the loop track nearest Wash-

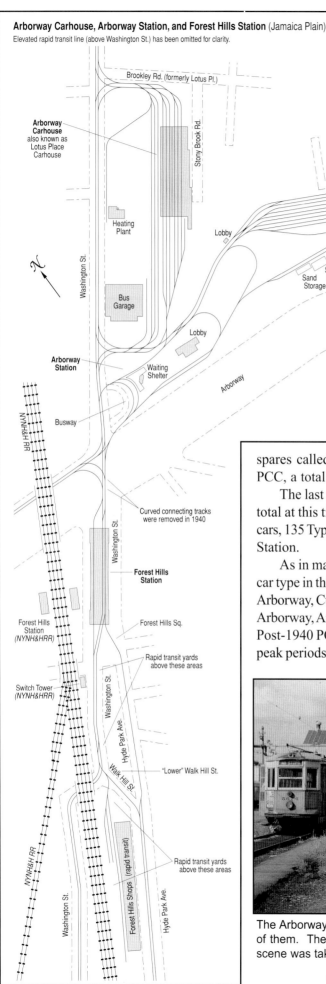

Arborway Carhouse, Arborway Station, and Forest Hills Station (Jamaica Plain)
Elevated rapid transit line (above Washington St.) has been omitted for clarity.

Approximate Scale
for all carhouse and station diagrams

500 feet
1 inch represents approximately 360 feet

Brookley Rd. (formerly Lotus Pl.)

Stony Brook Rd.

Arborway Carhouse
also known as Lotus Place Carhouse

Lotus St.

Forest Hills St.

Heating Plant

Lobby

Washington St.

Bus Garage

Lobby

Sand Storage

Salt Platform

Arborway Station

Waiting Shelter

Arborway

Busway

NYNH&H RR

Curved connecting tracks were removed in 1940

Washington St.

Forest Hills Station

Forest Hills Station *(NYNH&HRR)*

Forest Hills Sq.

Rapid transit yards above these areas

Switch Tower *(NYNH&HRR)*

Washington St.

Hyde Park Ave.

"Lower" Walk Hill St.

Walk Hill St.

Washington St.

Forest Hills Shops *(rapid transit)*

Hyde Park Ave.

Rapid transit yards above these areas

NYNH&H RR

Washington St.

ington Street. Once cars had left the loop, a second boarding would take place shortly thereafter at Forest Hills Station. Cars bound for Boston on the Arborway line boarded adjacent to the waiting station, but on the track coming from the loop around the lobby.

Further back was the main storage yard with two loops near the front and a third loop at the back of the yard. Connected to the rear yard loop were four parallel passing sidings for storage, and six more stub-end storage tracks.[149]

Equipment Assignments

Arborway equipment assignments are shown in detail for each line in Appendix 4. The April 1, 1940, car requirements including spares called for 104 Type 5s, 51 Type 4s, 46 center-entrance cars and one PCC, a total of 202 cars.

The last rating of the decade was December 5, 1949. The station streetcar total at this time was 265 cars, including spares. The roster showed 34 Type 4 cars, 135 Type 5s, 26 center-entrance cars, and 70 PCCs assigned to the Arborway Station.

As in many other parts of the system at the time, in 1940, the predominant car type in this district was the Type 5. Type 5s were assigned to Cleary Square–Arborway, Cummins Highway and Washington Street–Arborway, Dedham Line–Arborway, Arborway–Egleston, and Mattapan–Arborway, throughout the 1940s. Post-1940 PCC cars were also assigned to the Mattapan–Arborway line in off-peak periods.

The Arborway Carhouse buildings form a backdrop to the small storage yard in front of them. There were also storage yards parallel to the building and behind it. This scene was taken around 1947.

Clarke Collection

A trolley pole ahead of 5752 reveals that it is in a queue on the departure track for the Arborway–Egleston line on July 14, 1940. Ahead of both cars is the Main Line Elevated running over Washington Street. *Charles A. Duncan*

The car storage yard beside the Arborway Carhouse complex was used for active equipment. This scene on July 13, 1941, shows an impressive lineup of center-entrance cars and a Type 4 peeking out at left. *Charles A. Duncan*

Charles River–Arborway used a mix of Type 4s and Type 5s. Type 5 cars ran in varying numbers through September 1947. Starting in December 1948, Type 5s alone continued through the end of the 1940s. In the December 1942 rating, half of the Type 5 cars were replaced by Type 4s. This assignment lasted until the June 1943 rating, when the line went entirely to Type 5 operation. Type 4s returned in small numbers during the evening rush hours in September 1943 and continued until the June 1947 rating. From this time to the September 1947 rating, Type 5 cars alone were used on the line. The pendulum swung back in September 1947, when Charles River changed completely to Type 4 cars, continuing with them exclusively until the December 1948 rating. From this time on, Type 5 cars again handled all of the service.

The sole PCC car on the property in 1940, 3001, was assigned to Arborway. It usually saw service on the Charles River line, since loops were available at both terminals for this single-end car. With the March 1942 rating, 3001 was shown as a spare with no line assignment. This car spent most of the war on a temporary platform made of wooden barrels; its trucks were used as spares for the new fleet of Pullman PCCs that had arrived in 1941. Moreover, 3001 was plagued with electrical problems as it aged. This car would remain on the sidelines until 1945, when it was reassigned to the Seaver–Humboldt line, remaining there until September 1947.[c] After this time, the official car assignment sheets showed it as a spare through the September 12, 1949, rating.

In May 1946, post-1940 PCC cars began running on the Charles River line weekday and Saturday evenings after the rush hours and on Sundays. Operators of the speedy cars were instructed not to exceed 15 mph on Belgrade Avenue between Corinth and Iona Streets in either direction. A starter at Forest Hills was stationed beside the left-hand door to issue transfers for passengers who had to change to other lines to complete their trips.

As mentioned before, a week after the Egleston Station accident of April 12, 1948, 56 Type 4 cars were transferred in a special rating change from Park Street, Dorchester to the Arborway. Also transferred were the Mattapan–Ashmont and Mattapan–Egleston lines. Type 4s continued in use on both lines until the April 5, 1949, rating, when the Mattapan–Ashmont line was completely converted to Type 5 operation. Also, at this time, 11 Type 5 cars supplanted an equal number of Type 4s on the Mattapan–Egleston line. With the June 20, 1949, rating, Type 5s replaced Type 4 cars on Mattapan–Egleston completely. The retention of Type 4 cars at the Arborway was largely due to this transfer.

Type 4s ran on the Egleston–North Station line almost exclusively through December 1944. Between September 1940 and March 1941, a few center-entrance cars operated here as well. In the December 11, 1944, rating, the twenty-car PCC fleet originally assigned to Watertown–Park Street Station in 1941 was transferred to the Arborway for service on this line. These PCCs replaced most of the Type 4s.[d] Type 4s, however, would remain here until the end of the decade and beyond, running sporadically in regular assignments and as spares. This small group of PCCs was destined to operate on Egleston–North Station for many more years. Because the line ran over Tremont Street in Lower Roxbury and the South End, and through the Tremont Street Subway as well, the cars were nicknamed *Tremonts*.

The short-lived Lenox Street Yard–North Station cutback was assigned five Type 4s in the April 1948 rating. By September 1948, this service had ended.

Car assignments for Arborway–Park Street Station, Northeastern University–Park Street, and for Francis Street–Park Street and Heath Street–Park Street are discussed in Chapter 5, which covers the Central Subway.

---

[c] The May 1947 Boston Chapter NRHS newsletter, *The Turnout*, mentioned that PCC 3001 was back in service after a long absence with new paint and upholstery. The car's mechanical and electrical weaknesses were mentioned as well. *The Turnout*, 6 (May 1947), 3.

[d] At this time, the ROSSMORE ROAD destination appeared on PCC car roll signs. This was the last surface stop on Washington Street before the Arborway Yards. Cars completing their runs from North Station entered Egleston Station and were signed up ROSSMORE ROAD. These cars then carried revenue passengers as far as the Rossmore Road stop and continued on empty to the caryard entrance at Brookley Road.

30 Mattapan–Arborway

Route 30 cars left Mattapan Station and crossed Blue Hill Avenue onto Cummins Highway. Arborway–bound cars followed Cummins Highway northwest to Hyde Park Avenue, crossing a bridge over the New Haven Railroad Midland Division near Mattapan Square. The line crossed into West Roxbury from Dorchester at the Calvary Cemetery. At Hyde Park Avenue, the cars turned north and shared the track to the Arborway on Hyde Park Avenue and Washington Street with the Cleary Square and Roslindale Square cars.

At lower Walk Hill Street, the outbound and inbound tracks separated, the inbound track continuing on Hyde Park Avenue to Washington Street before entering Forest Hills Station.[e] The cars then continued to the Arborway along Washington Street. The round-trip distance on this line was 6.911 miles; the running time was 34 minutes.

Outbound cars for Mattapan, Cleary Square, and Roslindale Square left on the center track at Forest Hills, ran onto Washington Street, and switched to the single track on lower Walk Hill Street to get to Hyde Park Avenue. A facing point switch ran from the lower Walk Hill Street track under the elevated structure at Forest Hills. This switch branched into three stub-end spurs that were used for work equipment storage and disabled cars.

There was a siding off the Cummins Highway eastbound rail three-eighths of a mile before Hyde Park Avenue. The spur ran into Barry's Quarry, a source of ballast for the Boston Elevated. This siding was just across the street from the Calvary and Mount Hope Cemeteries. On Memorial Day, extra cars to the cemeteries were stored on the quarry siding. A crossover west of the siding allowed cemetery extras to return to the Arborway.

During the late summer and fall of 1948, the line operated on single track across the New Haven Railroad Midland Division Bridge on Cummins Highway as the bridge was rebuilt.[150] Streetcar and motor vehicle traffic alternated on either side of the bridge during the project.

32 Cleary Square–Arborway

This line started at a stub-end track on Hyde Park Avenue just south of Cleary Square. Inbound cars immediately entered double track and followed Hyde Park Avenue north to Forest Hills Station. The cars crossed the tracks on Cummins Highway with its inbound connections to Hyde Park Avenue.

---

[e] Walk Hill Street existed in two segments, which were separated by a short stretch of Hyde Park Avenue. The segment between Washington Street and Hyde Park Avenue has been designated in this book as "Lower Walk Hill Street" to clarify to the reader the section of Walk Hill Street that is being discussed. The term "Lower Walk Hill Street" was also used by Boston Elevated employees for the same reason, but it was not the official name of the street.

Type 4 cars were often transferred via the Cummins Highway line between Mattapan, where they ran regularly, and Arborway, where they were serviced. Here, in June 1945, 5316 has only to cross the New Haven Railroad Midland Division and then nearby Blue Hill Avenue to enter Mattapan yard. Sometimes passengers were carried during these transfer moves.   *Charles A. Duncan*

Cummins Highway was wide and streetcar friendly. Here we see all-electric PCC 3218 at Cummins Highway and Seminole Street on the way to Mattapan on October 31, 1948.   *Foster M. Palmer*

Hyde Park Avenue was the other half of the Mattapan–Arborway line. Here car 5637 turns north onto Hyde Park Avenue for the completion of its trip to Forest Hills Station and Arborway.

Foster M. Palmer

Barry's Quarry, located opposite Calvary Cemetary off Cummins Highway, was the principal source of gravel for the Boston Elevated for many years, but the public best remembers Barry's Quarry as the place that cars turned around when taking them to the Calvary and Mount Hope Cemetaries on Memorial Day. At left, 5804 has already changed ends and awaits the starter's signal to return to Forest Hills. At a completely different time of year, on October 22, 1948, dump car 3271 is seen at right ready to leave the Quarry with a fresh load of gravel. Later that same day, below, the work car was captured approaching the loop at Seaver Street and Humboldt Avenue.

Left, Charles A. Duncan; right and below, Foster M. Palmer

After leaving Arborway, outbound cars for West Roxbury, Hyde Park, and Mattapan ran below the ornamental elevated structure to Forest Hills Station to pick up waiting riders. Type 4 No. 5240 trundles south on Washington Street to the station behind a Type 5 already well on its way.

Charles A. Duncan

PCC 3220 leaves Forest Hills for Charles River or Mattapan in this shot taken on July 16, 1948. Of the five lines south of Forest Hills, these were the only two that had loops at both ends, a necessity for operation of the single-end PCCs.

Charles A. Duncan

Hyde Park, Mattapan, and Roslindale cars all used Hyde Park Avenue between Forest Hills and Cummins Highway. This procession consisting of a Type 5 with two Type 4s close behind passes Mt. Hope Street on May 30, 1945.

Charles A. Duncan

Type 5 No. 5666 changes ends on Hyde Park Avenue at Cleary Square in February 1944. This was literally the end of the line, although in earlier years the tracks continued further south to the Readville Trotting Park and were operated by the Eastern Mass. Street Railway.   *Charles A. Duncan*

From Cummins Highway to Forest Hills, the Cleary Square cars shared the track with the Roslindale Square–Arborway and Mattapan–Arborway lines. Outbound cars used the center track at Forest Hills Station for loading. This line was 6.654 miles long, round-trip, with a running time of 32 minutes.

33 Cummins Highway and Washington Street (Roslindale Square)–Arborway

Route 33 began at a trailing point crossover on Cummins Highway near Washington Street in Roslindale Square. Cars ran southeast down Cummins Highway, turned north onto Hyde Park Avenue, and shared the remainder of the route to Forest Hills and the Arborway with the Cleary Square and Mattapan lines. Just before entering Hyde Park Avenue, the line crossed a bridge over the New Haven Railroad main line. A round-trip on this route was 4.598 miles and took 23 minutes to complete.

At Roslindale Square, the track on Cummins Highway continued from the crossover onto Washington Street, making an inbound double-track connection. This connection was not used for revenue cars. Outbound passengers at Forest Hills Station boarded cars for this line on the center track. Map 4, Inset B shows the track arrangement at Roslindale Square.

34 Dedham Line–Arborway

Dedham Line–Arborway began at the Dedham–Boston boundary line on Washington Street. Here there were three crossovers for cars to change ends.[f] The line followed Wash-

At the intersection of Hyde Park Avenue and Cummins Highway, cars bound for Roslindale Square turned onto Cummins Highway in the opposite direction from that taken by Mattapan cars. This shot of outbound car 5668 was taken at Cummins Highway and Sherwood Street on September 6, 1947.   *Foster M. Palmer*

Type 5 No. 5752 changes ends at Cummins Highway and Washington Street at Roslindale Square. The double-track connection with the tracks on Washington Street provided flexibility to add cars as needed or to send surplus ones back to the Arborway.
Charles A. Duncan

---

[f] Until June 12, 1932, Eastern Mass. cars used the third crossover, the one closest to the Dedham line, to change ends before returning to Dedham, Westwood, Norwood, and Walpole. When the track south of the Dedham–Boston boundary line on Washington Street was removed, the third crossover ended up so close to the boundary line that no car had enough room to clear the switch point and change ends for the return trip on the inbound rail. The third crossover was essentially useless, and the Elevated removed it between December 16 and 31, 1943, making this scarce special work available for use elsewhere on the system.

Dedham Line, Route 34, literally ended at the Dedham–Boston boundary line. This view of 5735 shows both poles up, a sure sign of changing ends in this view taken in 1942. *BERy*

Route 34, Dedham Line, had a cutback near Washington and LaGrange Streets. Here in June 1945, two Type 5s from Boston await a third which is taking the crossover and providing added seating capacity on the inner section of the run. *Charles A. Duncan*

ington Street northeast to Roslindale Square. The Charles River line joined the Washington Street tracks at Corinth Street. From here the Dedham Line and Charles River routes shared the tracks on Washington Street to the Arborway. Shortly after Corinth Street, the Washington Street tracks crossed the connection to Cummins Highway.

Before entering Forest Hills Station, the line passed under the main line embankment of the New Haven Railroad Shore Line and crossed the single-track outbound rail onto lower Walk Hill Street. After passing through Forest Hills, the line ended at the Arborway. The round-trip distance of Dedham Line–Arborway was 8.221 miles and a complete trip took 36 minutes.

Outbound riders boarded cars on the right-hand track at Forest Hills, nearest the railroad embankment but through the left-hand doors of the cars, since the clearance on the wall side of the track was very tight.

A Type 4 from Charles River turns onto Corinth Street from Belgrade Avenue in September 1942. This location is just to the west of Roslindale Square. *Charles A. Duncan*

At LaGrange and Washington Streets, there was a trailing point crossover for a cutback to the Arborway. A round-trip between LaGrange Street and the Arborway was 5.470 miles and took 25 minutes. Between LaGrange Street and the Dedham–Boston boundary, the line was located in a private reservation in the center of the roadway.

36 Charles River–Arborway

This busy line started at the Charles River Loop located off Spring Street in West Roxbury. Charles River Loop had no sidings. The Spring Street track continued a short distance beyond the loop, ending as a single track *Y* at the Dedham–Boston boundary in the middle of the bridge over the Charles River. This track was a remnant of an earlier line through Dedham to Needham, and it was used by the Boston Elevated before the construction of the loop for reversing cars.

Leaving Charles River Loop, the line turned northeast onto Spring Street, crossed under the New Haven Railroad Dedham Loop, and turned north onto Centre Street. At LaGrange and Centre Streets there was a trailing point crossover for a cutback to the Arborway, and a round-trip between here and the Arborway comprised 6.595 miles and required 32 minutes to complete.

The line continued on Centre Street, crossing a bridge over the New Haven Railroad Needham Branch, and running to Belgrade Avenue. Here the cars turned right and crossed a bridge over the Needham Branch a second time.

Approaching Roslindale Square, inbound cars turned southeast onto Corinth Street on single track, and ran to Washington Street. From here Charles River cars turned northeast onto Washington Street and shared the track with the Dedham Line cars straight into Forest Hills Station. Route 36 was

Charles River Loop was located at the end of Route 36, off Spring Street very close to the Charles River, the boundary line at this point between Boston and Dedham. The track going past the loop continued to the middle of the bridge over the river and was used to store disabled cars and work equipment such as snowplows. One Type 4 has arrived from Forest Hills while the second is ready to leave in this early morning February 1946 scene. *Charles A. Duncan*

A Type 4 parades along Centre Street, West Roxbury, in October 1945. *Charles A. Duncan*

Cars 3029 and 5299 pass on March 25, 1948, at Centre and LaGrange Streets in West Roxbury. The PCC is on its way to Charles River Loop, but the Type 4 has just cut back at the crossover in the foreground. *Foster M. Palmer*

The Queen Mary, PCC 3001, making an inbound trip on Washington Street between Roslindale Square and Forest Hills in 1942 was a splendid sight. The contrast with the ancient Type 4 which had just passed it is dramatic. *Charles A. Duncan*

very long. The round-trip distance was 8.878 miles, and the running time averaged 40 minutes.

At Roslindale Square, outbound cars turned west off Washington Street onto South Street, which was single track, before running onto Belgrade Avenue. A curved track connection from Belgrade Avenue to Corinth Street, allowed outbound cars to loop around Roslindale Square and return to Forest Hills. The last scheduled use of this loop was by the special wartime newspaper cars during 1943 and 1944, which were mentioned in Chapter 1. Track details at Roslindale Square are shown on Map 4, Inset B.

Boarding passengers at Forest Hills Station got on cars on the right-hand track nearest the railroad embankment. Passengers normally boarded through the left-hand doors of the cars, including the single left-hand door of the PCC cars later assigned to the line. PCC 3001 was a special case because it had no left-hand door. When this car entered the station, it used the center track that was normally reserved for Hyde Park Avenue, Mattapan, and Roslindale Square cars. A former operator on this line notes that when this happened, the rush of passengers and the ensuing confusion was memorable. For this reason, management tried to avoid using the Queen Mary during rush hours.

40 Arborway–Egleston

The Arborway–Egleston line turned northeast onto Washington Street from the Arborway. Cars ran directly to Egleston Station, turning right onto Columbus Avenue and into Roxbury, then left into the station. Returning cars turned left directly out of the station onto Washington Street and followed it back to the Arborway. Cars changed ends for the return trip on the trackage near the entrance to the yard near the bus garage.

This line was one of the shortest trolley routes on the system, 2.506 miles round-trip, and operators nicknamed it the "Back and Forth." The round-trip running time was also short, averaging 14 minutes.

Tony Tieuli remembers…
The "Back and Forth" Line

Streetcar operators always knew the Arborway–Egleston surface line underneath the elevated structure on Washington Street as the "Back and Forth" or "B&F". One type 5 car ran during the day on a 20-minute headway. It was supplemented in the morning and evening rush hours by another car. This extra car reduced waits to 10 minutes. Some operators loved the line and had as many as 11 round-trips a day on this one service. As a very young boy, it was MY personal territory. I would leave the Mary E. Curley Junior High School promptly and take the Arborway car to the end of the line. Once there, I would run over to the "B&F" car stop near the bus garage. Soon my motorman friend Bill Rusk would rumble in on a car from Egleston Square. Bill was a big man with red hair and a happy disposition. He lived on my street.

The rest of the afternoon into the evening rush hour was spent riding the car between Egleston Square and the Arborway. I had my duties too! I squeezed myself between the hand brake wheel and a stanchion near the right front window. There I could move the door handle to open and close the front or rear door. That was the most important job and I had to be a good lookout.

At the Arborway the car switched into a single track. Then the trolley poles and seats had to be reversed. That was my job. It took much strength to pull the pole off the wire and then swing it down to the left and under the hook! The pole seemed to weigh more than me.

Bill took the brake, reverser, and door handles from one end of the car to the other. He would not let me take the heavy farebox, but he did let me carry the yellow "car card." This card matched the numbers shown on the fare box. The numbers told how many fares were collected on the route. It was a very important document and was always placed in a box near the destination sign handle. *Another card in the box had a printed list of items that could be checked off if the car developed any faults in service. This information was essential for the carhouse repairers. I'll never forget the farebox though—Bill would move a lever and all the coins would drop from view through a trap door. Then he would manually turn a crank on the side several times until all the coins dropped through a chute into a tray.*

Unlike today, operators collected all of the money and put it into cloth sacks. Each motorman had a "bank" of money to work with, including numbered paper transfers, and a "coin changer" mounted on his belt. This chrome affair held tokens, quarters, dimes, and nickels in separate coin barrels. With a couple of clicks, the motorman made the correct change when a passenger presented a bill or coin that exceeded the fare. At the end of the day's run, all of the money collected had to agree with the yellow car card figures. The total was turned in to the carhouse "treasurer." If the card and money turned in did not agree, the operator had to make up the difference from his own pocket!

Occasionally, we had an adventure! Sometimes we would come back from Egleston Square and a Starter would frantically wave his hands to Bill. Bill would run over to see him while I changed the seats and poles. On his return, Bill would say, "We are going in town. There is a holdup somewhere and all of the cars have left the station. No cars are coming back." At the car stop in front of the bus garage was a track switch controlled by a lever in a big green painted box mounted on a pole. Bill ran up to the pole and moved the lever. Whump! The track switch changed to the left and to the direction of Forest Hills and the Huntington Avenue line. Off we went humming along at full speed to fill the gap in PCC car service. I was always late for supper when that happened!

Anthony F. Tieuli has had a life-long interest in Boston streetcars, writing about and modeling them extensively.

Type 5 No. 5741 has just arrived at Egleston from the Arborway on the "Back and Forth" line and is waiting in line for its return trip in this 1945 scene. *BERy*

Washington Street near Egleston Station was a picture of total congestion on the day after the Valentine's Day Blizzard of 1940. Two stalled Type 5s lead this streetcar lineup, with Type 3 snowplow 5184 in exactly the wrong position—bringing up the rear!

Charles A. Duncan

43 Egleston–North Station

This heavy subway–surface line left Egleston Station from the outer loop, running directly out the west exit and across Washington Street onto Columbus Avenue. Cars returning to Egleston continued across Washington Street on Columbus Avenue and entered the station at the south entrance.

Going inbound the line followed Columbus Avenue north to Jackson Square, at Centre Street. From this point, the Egleston–North Station and Jamaica–Dudley lines shared track as far as Hanley Square, at Roxbury Street, paralleling the viaduct carrying the New Haven Railroad main line. North Station-bound cars continued on Columbus Avenue through Hanley Square to Roxbury Crossing, where Columbus Avenue intersects Tremont Street.

Egleston–North Station cars then followed Tremont Street generally northeast all the way to the subway portal at Broad-

Route 43 was a heavy subway-surface route between North Station and Egleston Station. It lasted as a completely intact streetcar line until 1956, when it was cut back to Lenox Street. This scene is at Egleston Station with its combinations of dank shadow and exuberant light and shows center-entrance car 6369 laying over before a trip to North Station. Behind it is Type 5 5389 destined for Arborway or Dudley Street Station.

BERy

way and Tremont Street. From here the cars continued through the Tremont Street Subway to the Canal Street Loop at North Station. A round-trip on this line was 8.934 miles and the running time was 55 minutes.

While on Tremont Street, North Station-bound cars entered the South End section of Boston Proper near the Lenox Street Yard, crossed the Dudley–Massachusetts Station line at Northampton Street, and intersected the tracks on Dover Street, which still were used by streetcars in Owl, school student, and work service. Finally, the North Station cars crossed a bridge over the main lines of the B&A and the New Haven Railroads.

Type 4 No. 5353 has the road all to itself in this wartime shot taken on Columbus Avenue looking inbound from Egleston Square in June 1944.

Charles A. Duncan

"Tremont" PCC No. 3021 races through Jackson Square at Tremont and Centre Streets in September 1945. This car was the last of the group acquired in 1941 for the Watertown–Park Street Station line and later assigned to Route 43.

Clarke Collection

This scene from 1945 shows "Tremont" PCC 3004 enroute to North Station midway on Tremont Street approaching the South End.

Charles A. Duncan

Car 6237 leads a two-car center-entrance train in school service headed for the subway on Tremont Street in the South End in 1949.
Paul M. Paulsen

All-electric PCC 3218 heads outbound on Tremont Street at Worcester Street followed closely by PCC 3013 in this May 4, 1948, view.
Foster M. Palmer

In 1947 the Columbus Avenue tracks from Washington Street to Centre Street were rebuilt with a series of concrete islands between them. This construction was similar to the earlier median work on Blue Hill Avenue, but in this case was an upgrade since it did not replace a private reservation. This project was prompted by the City of Boston, which resurfaced the roadway at that time and built the concrete islands.[151]

As on Route 39, a sister Arborway route, the Elevated and MTA operated school service along Route 43 throughout the 1940s. The Route 43 school trips were primarily for students at Boston English High School. This service was extensive before and during World War II, but it steadily decreased toward the end of the 1940s. Most of these trips were run with center-entrance and Type 4 cars, the latter type disappearing rapidly as the 1940s came to an end. Interestingly, two-car trains of center-entrance cars were used in this service until February 17, 1941, and from December 11, 1944, until the end of the decade. This was the only known multiple-unit operation on this line in the 1940s.

A new line, Lenox Street Yard–North Station, was created in the April 1948 rating. This route was a cutback of the Egleston–North Station main line and lasted only until the September rating.[g] The line was 5.127 miles long, round-trip, and had a running time of 35 minutes.

---

[g] This line should not be confused with the later route, Lenox Street Loop–North Station, that ran between 1956 and 1961.

Looking up Tremont Street from Massachusetts Avenue toward Lenox Street in June 1942, Type 4 No. 5282 is seen at the end of a string of cars lined up to handle the crowds for the annual Boston Schoolboy Parade. To the right, high school and junior high school cadets in military attire will soon muster in the Back Bay for their march.
Charles A. Duncan

Lenox Street Yard

Work cars primarily used the Lenox Street Yard. Over the years, however, service extras and disabled cars were temporarily put up here as well. The site of the former Lenox Street Carhouse adjoined the yard, and the carhouse site was the location many years later of the well-known Lenox Street Loop, installed for the cutback of Route 43 in 1956.

A distinctive feature of this yard was a large circular sand house made from a former gasometer building. Cars used a single entryway to enter and exit the building, running into the building and over a trestle about ten feet above the floor around the entire interior perimeter. Dump cars discharged their loads onto the floor, and a traveling bucket elevator located in the center of the building loaded sand cars and dump trucks. Exiting cars crossed over the entry track and ran back onto the yard lead track.

Lenox Street Yard
(Boston/South End)

Columbus Ave.

Snow HQ Erected Dec. 1940

Garage

Salt Platform

Sand House

Camden St.

Westfield St.

Tremont St.

Lenox St.

Dotted line shows former site of Lenox Street Carhouse

Lenox Street Yard Note:
The tracks on Columbus Ave. were removed in July 1946.

Lenox Street yard adjoined the former Lenox Street Carhouse site. In this view we see the cab of a trolley crane on the rail opposite Type 4 No. 5358, which is about to make a run to North Station on the short-lived cutback that ran between April and September in 1948.
Charles A. Duncan

One of the two most important changes to surface transportation in Boston in the 1940s was the end of scenes such as this one, when the Boston Elevated Railway opened the Huntington Avenue Subway. This major improvement eliminated street running of surface streetcars from Northeastern University to the subway portal near Boylston and Arlington Streets opposite the Public Garden, including this trackage in Copley Square. Traffic density in this area was usually very high and the streetcars ran on one of the heaviest lines in the city, a combination that was difficult at best and simply chaotic during the rush hour. Pictured here on Huntington Avenue in Copley Square is Type 4 No. 5354 bound for the Arborway on February 16, 1941, the last day of service for this surface track. This section of the roadway is now part of the large public park across Dartmouth Street from the Boston Public Library and in front of Trinity Church.

Stanley M. Hauck

Chapter 5

The Central Subway and Its Branches

Today, the MBTA Green Line includes most of the surviving trackage of the Boston Elevated Railway. This system of subway and surface lines consists of the Tremont Street, Boylston Street, and Huntington Avenue Subways, the Lechmere Viaduct, and surface branches to Boston College, Cleveland Circle, and Heath Street.[152] A branch to Riverside that opened in 1959 was not part of the Boston Elevated system.

The Central Subway and its branches have long been the busiest part of Boston's transit network. In its 1946 annual report, the Elevated said that the capacity of the Boylston and Huntington Avenue Subways had been reached.[153] Schedules for the winter of 1946-47 called for 97 trains comprising 204 cars between 8 a.m. and 9 a.m. between Copley and Boylston Stations. This schedule represented one train every 37 seconds. Three-car trains of PCC cars, introduced on September 16, 1946, offered the possibility of increasing subway capacity even more.

September 1, 1947, was the golden anniversary of the opening of the Tremont Street Subway, the first subway in America and the fourth subway in the world.[a] This event was marked by a flurry of articles in the local press and in *Cooperation*. The Boston Chapter NRHS made its September 1947 issue of *The Turnout* a commemorative edition to mark the subway's fiftieth year.[154]

In 1940 nine streetcar lines ran through the subway, but by 1950, three of these routes had been converted to bus. Car lines entered the subway in 1940 at portals north of Haymarket Station, at Tremont Street and Broadway, on Boylston Street beside the Public Garden, on Commonwealth Avenue at Blandford Street, and on Beacon Street at St. Mary's Street. When the Huntington Avenue Subway and the portal at Northeastern University were opened in 1941, the Boylston Street portal was closed.

The two center tracks of the subway between Brattle Street Station and Canal Street Loop were still in use in 1940. The northbound segment of the subway under Cornhill Street was in use at that time as well, running to Washington Street and through Adams Square Station before rejoining the southbound tube south of Haymarket Station.[b]

The area covered by this chapter includes parts of the Brighton and Jamaica Plain sections of Boston, downtown Boston, and sections of the Town of Brookline, the City of Newton, and the Town of Watertown. Brighton and Jamaica Plain were primarily commercial and multi-family residential and remain so today. The downtown section of Boston, capital of Massachusetts, has long been known for its educational institutions and as a major manufacturing, commercial, and financial center. Despite the business and governmental orientations in downtown Boston, there was and is a surprising amount of residential housing in the heart of this major city, particularly in the adjacent neighborhoods of the Back Bay, Beacon Hill, the North and West Ends, Bay Village, and the South End.

Newton, skirted by the Watertown–Park Street Station line cutting through its northeast corner, and Brookline, served by the Beacon Street line, were both primarily residential. Watertown had considerable manufacturing activity but much residential property as well. The surface lines of the Boston Elevated were the primary source of public transportation in these municipalities, with few other services.

Newton, Watertown, and Brookline all were served by buses of the Middlesex & Boston Street Railway Company (M&B), which connected at several points with the Boston Elevated and provided service primarily to points west of these areas. The B&A Railroad main line operated through Brighton and Newton, making several stops, and the Highland Branch of the B&A also offered frequent commuter service to stations in Brookline and Newton.

Service Overview

The nine streetcar lines in the Central Subway of 1940 are illustrated in Map 5 and are listed below.

---

[a] The Metropolitan Railway subway in London was the very first, opening on January 10, 1863. This was a conventional railroad, however, and is generally regarded as an underground railway tunnel rather than a *mass transit subway* as the term *subway* is generally understood today. The world's first electrically powered subway, the City & South London Railway, opened on December 18, 1890. Next was the Budapest Földalatti, which opened May 2, 1896. Glasgow, Scotland, was third, opening the cable-powered District Subway on December 14, 1896.

[b] A new tunnel replaced this section of the subway in October 1963 to make way for construction of the new Boston City Hall.

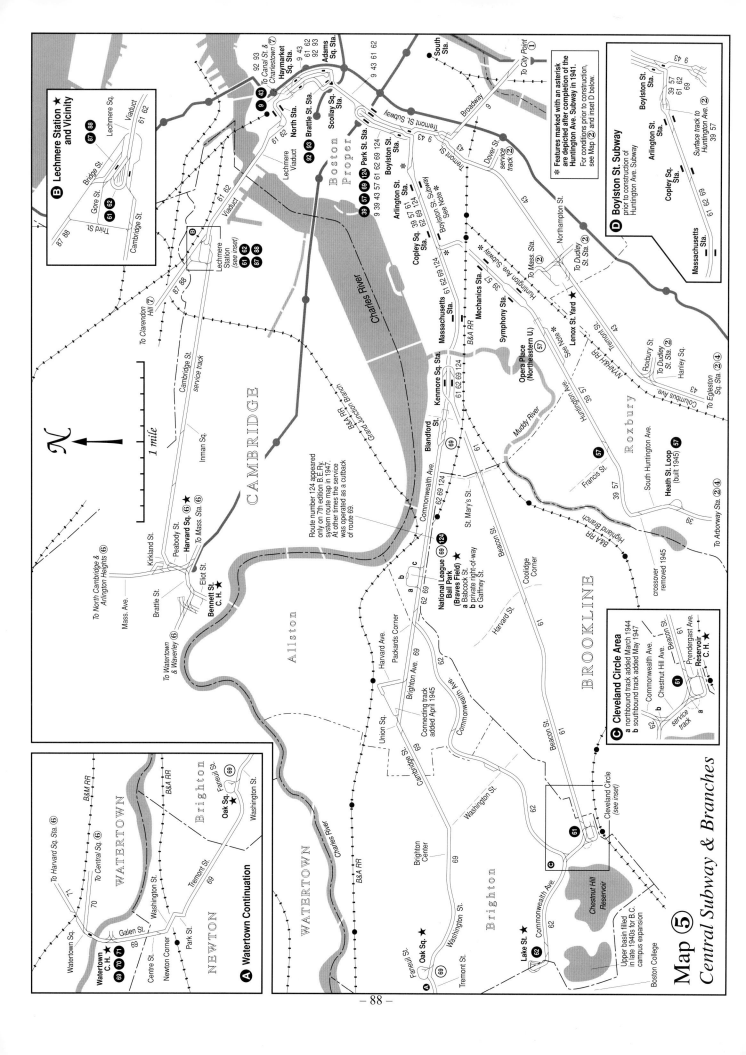

Map ⑤
Central Subway & Branches

Route No.	Route Description
9	**City Point–North Station** *via P, East 4th, and L Streets, Broadway, and Subway*
	Farragut Road–North Station (summer months)
39	**Arborway Station–Park Street Station** *via Arborway, South Street, Centre Street, South Huntington Avenue, Huntington Avenue, Boylston Street, and Subway*
43	**Egleston Station–North Station** *via Columbus Avenue, Tremont Street, and Subway*
57	**Francis Street and Huntington Avenue–Park Street Station** *via Huntington Avenue, Boylston Street, and Subway*
61	**Reservoir–Lechmere** *via Beacon Street and Subway*
62	**Lake Street–Lechmere** *via Commonwealth Avenue and Subway*
	[cb] **Blandford Street–Park Street Station**
69	**Watertown Carhouse–Park Street Station** *via Galen Street, Centre Street, Washington Street, Park Street, Tremont Street, Washington Street, Cambridge Street, Brighton Avenue, Commonwealth Avenue, and Subway*
	[cb] **Oak Square–Park Street Station**
92	**Sullivan Square Station–Brattle Street Station (Scollay Square)** *via Main Street, Causeway Street, and Subway*
93	**Sullivan Square Station–Brattle Street Station (Scollay Square)** *via Main Street, Bunker Hill Street, Chelsea Street, Main Street, Causeway Street, and Subway*
	[cb] **Elm and Bunker Hill Streets–Brattle Street Station**

The number of daily trips for all these routes are tabulated in Appendix 9. Route 61 had the highest service frequency, with a whopping 423 daily trips, followed by Routes 62, 39, 69, 43, 93, 57, 9, and 92 in that order. Appendix 9 details this information.

Charlestown, South Boston, and Arborway Routes

92 Sullivan Square Station–Brattle Street Station *via Main Street*
93 Sullivan Square Station–Brattle Street Station *via Bunker Hill Street*

Two lines ran from Sullivan Square Station through Charlestown and the Tremont Street Subway to Brattle Street Station: Route 92, Sullivan Square Station–Brattle Street Sta-

The Starter at Sullivan Square Station points to the BRATTLE–BUNKER HILL sign on Type 5 No. 5502 on New Year's Eve 1948.
Raymond E. McMurdo

tion via Main Street and Subway; and Route 93, Sullivan Square Station–Brattle Street Station via Bunker Hill Street and Subway. By far, the heavier of the two lines was Bunker Hill Street. The Main Street line was converted to buses on April 3, 1948, and the Bunker Hill Street route followed on July 2, 1949. These two lines were based at Salem Street Carhouse in Medford. The surface sections of these routes are covered in Chapter 7.

Both lines entered the subway system from Causeway Street at the Canal Street Loop and ran directly into the subway through the Haymarket Portal. Type 5 cars were assigned to both routes throughout the 1940s.[c] At that time Type 5s did not have Tomlinson couplers, and they were kept separate from the rest of the equipment operated in the subway, except for the cars with which they shared the Canal Street Loop tracks. Between the Haymarket Portal and Brattle Street Station, the Charlestown cars used the two center subway tracks exclusively all the way to Brattle. A round-trip on Route 92 was 4.360 miles with an average running time of 29 minutes; on Route 93 a round-trip was 5.173 miles and the running time was 35 minutes. The cutback between Elm and Bunker Hill Streets and Brattle Street was 3.164 miles round-trip and had a running time of 26 minutes.

Brattle Street Station consisted of a platform located adjacent to the platform of Scollay Square Station but separated from Scollay by heavy fencing. Scollay was a prepayment area with system-wide subway connections and Brattle was not.

The Charlestown cars stopped at Haymarket Station on their way to and from Brattle Street Station. Fencing separated the platform between the inner and outer tracks here as well, again because the inner tracks at Haymarket were for

---

[c] Equipment assignments are discussed in Chapter 7 and summarized in Appendices 5 and 7.

Charlestown local fare riders only, while the outer tracks accommodated all other system passengers. Both Charlestown lines were local fare routes, and passengers had to pay an additional fare for access to the rapid transit system. Charlestown riders accessing the rapid transit system usually did so at Haymarket with a paper transfer.

Passengers boarding or leaving at Canal Street did so at stops on Causeway Street, just outside the loop area. Cars to and from Charlestown passed directly through the Canal Street loop area itself without stopping, again preserving the separation between the local and the system-wide services.

To replace the subway service after the Charlestown car lines were abandoned, and to provide a connection to buses from Charlestown, the MTA began operating a single-car shuttle between North Station and Brattle Street Station on October 15, 1949. The route was only 1.160 miles round-trip, with a running time of six minutes. Cars loaded on the unused track on the Haverhill Street side of the North Station Loop.[d]

The North Station–Brattle Street Station shuttle was operated with cars from Salem Street. To reach the subway, the shuttle cars used the surface tracks of the former Charlestown Main Street line, which had been kept in place between Sullivan Square and Canal Street. The track also provided a connection between the Central Subway and the MTA facilities at the Charlestown yard complex and beyond to the Everett Shops. At least for the evening return trip which was made about 6:55 p.m., riders could board at Brattle or Haymarket and ride all the way back to Salem Street carhouse, using the formally abandoned Main Street tracks. There were a few regular commuters that took advantage of this service, and a long-time observer has noted that once north of Canal Street, the motorman would dutifully ask each "through" passenger to put another nickel in the farebox.

Beginning on December 1, 1951, the shuttle service was significantly reduced. It was discontinued completely in September 1952.

9 City Point–North Station

From the south, Route 9, the City Point–North Station line from South Boston via Broadway, entered the portal at Tremont Street and Broadway. It ran to Canal Street Loop at North Station and was based at City Point Carhouse. A round-trip, as previously mentioned, was 8.157 miles with a running time of 54 minutes. Summer service was usually operated from the layover track at Farragut Road near Marine Park. The round trip from this alternative starting point was 8.141

All-electric PCC 3209 emerges from the Tremont Street Subway portal at Broadway and Tremont Street bound for City Point in South Boston. The Metropolitan Theater in the background is now the Wang Center for the Performing Arts.   *Paul M. Paulsen*

miles and the running time was 55 minutes. This line used a special "flying junction" inside the portal at Tremont Street and Broadway to join the Route 43 car line from Egleston Square.

Type 4 cars primarily provided service on this line until the September 3, 1946, rating, when the route was completely converted to PCC car operation. PCCs had been introduced in 1945 in the off-peak hours.[e] The surface operation of the City Point–North Station line was covered in Chapter 2.

43 Egleston–North Station

Egleston–North Station, Route 43, also entered the subway at Broadway and Tremont Street, using the "flying junction" to join Route 9 from City Point and continuing on to Canal Street Loop at North Station. Route 43 was based at the Arborway, and the surface section was covered in Chapter 4. The round-trip distance was 8.934 miles, as previously discussed, and the running time was 55 minutes.

Type 4 cars mainly ran on this line until the December 11, 1944, rating. At this time 20 PCC cars, the original PCC fleet assigned to Watertown–Park Street Station, replaced most of

---

[d] This track continued out of the loop reservation area onto Haverhill Street, then turned right onto Causeway Street. It had been used by Eastern Mass. cars until June 9, 1936, for the Mystic Wharf–Brattle shuttle. In 1940, the track on Haverhill Street itself was abandoned, but the connecting trackage on the property at Canal Street Loop was retained as a stub-end for car storage.

[e] Equipment assignments are discussed in Chapter 2 and are summarized in Appendices 2 and 5.

This unusual view at left of PCC 3007 about to swing across Broadway and enter Tremont Street from the Broadway and Tremont subway portal was taken from the roof of the Brandeis Vocational High School. The lower tracks lead to South Boston via Broadway. In the more conventional view of the portal above, Type 4 No. 5236 heads for Egleston on a school trip.

Both, Paul M. Paulsen

the older cars. This assignment left Egleston–North Station with one Type 4 in regular service. Type 4s would continue to run on this line in varying numbers, however, though the end of the decade and beyond.

Two center-entrance cars were used on this line from September 1940 to March 1941. Center-entrance cars continued to appear here from time to time during the war, including 6309, which one observer clearly recalls having ridden down Tremont Street in 1943.[f]

From April 12 through September 13, 1948, a short-lived cutback of the Egleston–North Station line ran between Lenox Street Yard and North Station. As previously mentioned, the round-trip distance was 5.127 miles with an average running time of 35 minutes. Type 4 cars were used for this service.

The Canal Street surface loop at North Station was the northern terminal point of lines entering the subway through the Broadway and Tremont Street portal. Type 4 No. 5341, operating on Route 43, Egleston–North Station, waits at Berth 1 on March 29, 1940, as departing riders make their way toward Causeway Street and North Station, which looms in the background.

BERy

Al Silloway remembers…

On April 12, 1948, I was sent to the Opera House with an extra car for the theater crowd. I pulled out a Type 4 and on the way discovered that the brakes were slack. When I arrived at the Opera House, the inspector unexpectedly sent all of the extra cars, including mine, deadhead to North Station.[g]

At North Station, I was sent back deadhead to Park Street. There, a starter boarded my car and told me to sign up Egleston. The reason for this special trip was that there had been a serious collision at Egleston Station.[h] Extra cars were needed on the

Egleston–North Station line. We pulled down to the stop to load; the car was soon jammed with people. With slack brakes on a car carrying an unusually heavy load, I was reluctant to run the car, and I said so to the starter.

The starter took the controls and ran to Boylston Station. Here, we took on a few more riders. At this point the starter and I were pressed against the windshield. After leaving Boylston Station, the starter lost control of the car because of the slack brakes. The Type 4 was going very fast down the hill and leaned badly on the curve at the bottom of the grade. It seemed to me that the roof of the car brushed the subway walls at one point! Fortunately we cleared the switch (at the flying junction) without derailing and arrived at Tremont and Broadway intact.

[f] Equipment assignments are discussed in Chapter 4 and are summarized in Appendices 4 and 5.

[g] The term "deadhead" refers to the practice of sending cars to a destination with no passengers, usually for a special assignment.

[h] This was the runaway accident discussed in Chapter 3.

The starter opened the front door and quickly left the car. The last I saw of him, he was hurrying along Tremont Street back downtown. For the rest of the trip, needless to say, I ran the car very slowly. At Jackson Square, because of the emergency activity at Egleston, I was diverted onto Centre Street and sent back to the Arborway. I was glad to return in one piece!

Al Silloway worked for 36 years for the MBTA, MTA, and Boston Elevated Railway. He is the former Arborway District Supervisor.

39 Arborway–Park Street Station *via Huntington Avenue*

From the Southwest, Route 39, Arborway–Park Street Station, entered the subway at the portal on Boylston Street. The present day Heath Street service is a cutback of the Arborway line.

The Arborway line started in Jamaica Plain at Arborway Station, which was described in Chapter 4. Passengers boarded on the track coming from the loop around the lobby at a point adjacent to the waiting station.

Following essentially the same route that they did until service ended in December 1985, inbound cars pulled out southwest onto Washington Street, and continued a short distance to a stretch of private right-of-way, which was actually located on part of the Arborway itself.[i] Cars turned west onto this reservation and passed through an impressive arch, part of a stone viaduct carrying the main line of the New Haven Railroad. The cars soon left the reservation and turned north onto South Street.

The line continued on South Street past Jamaica Plain Loop, the end of the Jamaica–Dudley line. At the Civil War Monument, cars bore northeast onto Centre Street and ran through the Jamaica Plain business district. At Centre Street and South Huntington Avenue, Arborway cars followed South Huntington Avenue to the left and north, and Dudley cars followed Centre Street northeast to the right. The line crossed the boundary between the Jamaica Plain section of West Roxbury and Roxbury just north of Perkins Street. Late in 1945, the Boston Elevated opened a turn back loop at Heath Street and South Huntington Avenue, which will be described later.

At South Huntington and Huntington Avenues, the line turned east onto Huntington Avenue and ran to Brigham Circle. Here the tracks entered a private reservation in the center of the road. Two crossovers were located here for the Francis Street–Park Street Station service.

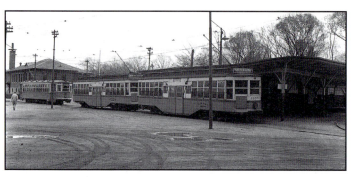

Route 39 was one of the principal lines in the system. Multiple-unit trains of center-entrance and PCC cars operating from Arborway to Park Street, Type 4s on the Francis Street and Heath Street curbacks, and a few Type 5 school cars were the usual mix on this line throughout the 1940s. Here, on April 28, 1946, 6250 leads 6276 in a train preparing for departure to Park Street Station. A Type 5 waits behind.
Stanley M. Hauck

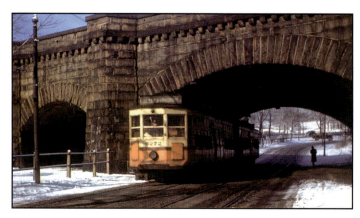

A center-entrance train has just passed under the stone bridge carrying the main line of the New Haven Railroad. This scene taken in March 1946 shows the unique paved private right-of-way for the streetcars.
Charles A. Duncan

PCC 3023 charges up South Huntington Avenue in an early view of a two-car PCC train taken in November 1946. *Charles A. Duncan*

The line continued down Huntington Avenue in a generally northeasterly direction past the Museum of Fine Arts, crossing the boundary between Roxbury and Boston Proper at Ruggles Street. Starting near the Museum, a 1,881-foot passing siding ran around the inbound rail almost all the way to Gainsborough Street.[j] The passing siding left the reservation

---

[i] Until 1940 track connections between the Arborway reservation tracks and those on Washington Street south of Arborway allowed cars coming from South Street to run into Forest Hills Station directly.

[j] After the opening of the Huntington Avenue Subway, this passing siding was shortened to 1,400 feet, running only as far as the southerly end of the Opera Place (Northeastern University) Station platform.

A two-car train of center-entrance cars on the street was a formidable sight to motorists, who kept their distance. Here 6045 is the trailing car in an inbound train making its way past Heath Street on South Huntington Avenue in May 1942. *Charles A. Duncan*

Center-entrance car 6309 built for non-train operation heads outbound on Huntington Avenue near the Museum of Fine Arts. In the foreground is the long inbound passing siding that ran almost to Gainsborough Street before the opening of the Huntington Avenue Subway. This shot was taken in May 1943, and by then, the siding had been cut back and rejoined the main line just before the platform at Opera Place (Northeastern University). *Charles A. Duncan*

The reservation on Huntington Avenue was fine for streetcars, but what was a poor boarding passenger to do? There are major differences in safety standards between now and this scene from February 1943. *BERy*

In order to maintain operation during the construction of the Huntington Avenue Subway, a wooden trestle was constructed over the incline and subway portal at Northeastern University. Inbound Type 4 No. 5304 follows a center-entrance car over this structure in January 1941. *Seashore Trolley Museum Collection*

and swung into the street, merging with the paving for its entire length. This siding allowed inbound streetcars to bypass cars stored on the inbound main line rail near the Opera House. Inbound cars using the passing siding had to merge with automobile traffic, always a hazardous move.

A trailing point crossover near the Opera House connected the section of inbound main line rail bypassed by the passing siding to the outbound rail. The crossover allowed extra cars to wait on the inbound main line for the Opera House curtain call, the end of performances at nearby Symphony Hall, and to provide heavy daily service to the Northeastern University community. Cars signed "Back Bay Schools" also used this cutback. These trips for school students originated at the Arborway and served many institutions along the way. The round-trip distance via the Huntington Avenue Subway was 11.383 miles between Arborway and Park Street Station, and the running time was 57 minutes.

Before the opening of the Huntington Avenue Subway, the Arborway line continued on Huntington Avenue past North-

eastern University. At Symphony Hall, Arborway cars crossed the Massachusetts Avenue tracks of the Dudley–Massachusetts Station car line, where there was an impressive three-quarter grand union. Arborway cars continued past the Mechanics Building and through Copley Square to Boylston Street.[k] Map 2 shows this trackage in detail. The cars continued on Boylston Street directly into a subway incline in the center of Boylston Street between Arlington Street and Charles Street beside the Public Garden. This incline is shown on Map 2 and on Map 5, Inset D.

Because the Huntington Avenue Subway ran under Exeter Street before joining the Boylston Street Subway, the round-trip distance between Arborway and Park Street actually increased by 0.175 miles after the subway opened. Thus the round-trip distance of the Arborway–Park Street Line before the opening of the subway was only 11.208 miles, but the run-

---

[k] Prior to 1969, Huntington Avenue continued straight across Copley Square through what is now a park and ended at the junction of Boylston and Clarendon Streets.

Route 39 only operated on Huntington Avenue to Copley Square and then to the subway portal at Arlington and Boylston Streets until February 1941. Above, outbound center-entrance car 6228 has turned from Boylston onto Huntington Avenue at Copley Square around 1938. Henry Hobson Richardson's masterpiece Trinity Church is at the right. Above right, in this 1940 scene, a two-car center-entrance train follows a procession of cars on Boylston Street toward Berkeley Street, illustrating well the traffic congestion the Huntington Avenue Subway would eliminate.

Above, Horton Banks, Stephen P. Carlson Collection; above right, BERy

Surface running on Boylston Street ended with a direct entrance to the Tremont Street Subway slightly beyond Arlington Street beside the Public Garden. This platform on private right-of-way just outside the incline kept streetcars and riders alike separate from the hustle and bustle of automobile traffic. The street trackage on both sides of the incline had been abandoned by this time and connected with unused tracks on Charles Street straight ahead. *BERy*

ning time was 68 minutes, 11 minutes greater than the subway route.

At Boylston and Berkeley Streets, there was a double-track spur about 400 feet long with switches to Berkeley Street in both directions from Boylston Street. This trackage was used as an emergency turnback for diverting equipment to avoid subway blockages, to handle disabled cars, and to store equipment for special events. A crossover in the middle of the spur connected both tracks. In earlier years, this track had continued south to Tremont and Dover Streets. The Berkeley Street tracks are shown on Map 2.

Arborway–Park Street Equipment Assignments

Center-entrance cars and a much smaller number of Type 4s were used in 1940 on the Arborway–Park Street Station line. Then, from June 1941 to the spring rating in March 1942, Type 4s were used almost exclusively. After that the center-entrance cars predominated through the end of the war. Type 4s continued on this line in small numbers throughout the decade, however, usually during the fall, winter, and spring ratings.

The April 1943 issue of *Co-operation* discussed the heavy use of two-car trains of center-entrance cars on the Arborway line.[155] These cars could be run in trains, which increased the capacity of the subway because the signals interpreted each two-car train as an individual car.

Starting on December 17, 1945, PCC cars completely replaced the center-entrance cars in regular service. The first two-car trains of PCCs followed on January 25, 1946.

A small number of center-entrance cars continued in use as extras and spares and for special events through the early 1950s. These cars were kept for their fast loading and multiple-unit capabilities, features that made them useful in the subway.

The Schoolboy Parade

The annual Schoolboy Parade, usually held in early June, was a high-traffic event for the Boston El. This parade was an old tradition in the Boston Public Schools. Schoolboys from the public junior high and high schools all over the city participated, practicing throughout the school year for this event. Dressed in military cadet uniforms, they marched on a number of different routes until the early 1960s.

Special streetcars and buses carried students from schools to the downtown muster areas. The El fielded an army of extra inspectors, switchmen, and other officials to ensure smooth operation and to minimize service disruptions. The company insisted that operators of buses and streetcars stay

Prior to the opening of the Huntington Avenue Subway, it was common practice during the Schoolboy Parade to store cars and buses on one or both rails of Route 39 between Copley Square and Massachusetts Avenue. This practice was a magnet to railfans, and on June 6, 1939, Charles A. Duncan found Type 5s near the Mechanics Building (above left), between there and Exeter Street (above), and in front of the Boston Public Library in Copley Square itself (left), their line being broken only by the need to keep cross streets open.
All, Charles A. Duncan

While the tracks on Huntington Avenue were tied up for car storage during the Schoolboy Parade, regular service was diverted to Massachusetts Station in the Back Bay. At left, 6287 and 6283 turn from Massachusetts Avenue onto Huntington. The three-quarter grand union at this location came in handy after the parade, as cars could be dispatched in many directions. At right, Type 5 No. 5592 carries a full load as it turns onto Massachusetts Avenue in the direction of Dudley Street Station. *Both, Charles A. Duncan*

with their vehicles at all times, no doubt because of the rambunctious nature of the clientele.

Until 1940, starting as early as 8 a.m., cars on the Arborway–Huntington line were rerouted from Huntington Avenue onto Massachusetts Avenue and run to Massachusetts Station in the Back Bay. This diversion was necessary because part of the main line inbound and outbound to Copley Square was usually reserved to store streetcars during the parade. Starting in 1941, the subway replaced the surface tracks on that section of Huntington Avenue, and the Elevated ended most of the special steps it took on the Arborway line for the parade. In later years, however, parade day service on the Arborway line was increased in the afternoon hours.

The Schoolboy Parade also affected route 43, Egleston–North Station. As on the Arborway Line, the tracks on the inner section of Tremont Street between Massachusetts Av-

Type 5s seldom entered the subway during daytime hours. A rare exception was on the day of the annual Schoolboy Parade, as we see on this fine day, June 7, 1938. *Charles A. Duncan*

enue and Dover Street and sometimes further south were often used to store streetcars for the end of the parade. When this happened, cars from this line were diverted to Massachusetts Station as well.

The Huntington Avenue Subway

The Transit Department of the City of Boston, under the auspices of the WPA, started building the Huntington Avenue Subway on September 18, 1937. This subway was badly needed to speed up the traffic-choked segment of the Arborway line in Boston's Back Bay.

As originally conceived, the subway came to the surface near West Newton Street and Huntington Avenue near the Mechanics Building. During construction in 1938, however, the Boston Transit Department modified the project and decided to extend the subway to the Opera House, build Mechanics[l] and Symphony Stations, and construct the Massachusetts Avenue automobile underpass.

As finally built, the incline tracks of this subway were supported on raised side beams over an open excavation, in a way similar to the Commonwealth Avenue incline, opened in 1932. This construction was made to expedite a possible future extension of the subway on Huntington Avenue. In fact, the subway shell extended full-depth as far as Opera Place, and was located under and near the southerly end of the present-day Northeastern University Station platform.[m]

After nearly five years in the making, the twin-tunnel, 4,398-foot Huntington Avenue Subway opened on February 16, 1941. In a ceremony at 2:30 p.m. that day, Boston Mayor Maurice J. Tobin drove a golden spike on the subway ramp near the Opera House. Following the ceremony, the mayor, officials of the Boston Transit Department and the Boston Elevated Railway, and local civic representatives rode a special 3-car train of center-entrance cars through the subway. Regular service began when the first outbound revenue car left Park Street Station at 3:30 p.m. The first inbound revenue car left Northeastern University at 3:35 p.m.

All Huntington Avenue cars were immediately rerouted into the new subway, and travel time reductions resulted right away. According to the April 1941 edition of *Co-operation*, the company saw a noticeable increase in riders with the opening of the subway. On February 10, before the subway opened, a count at Gainsborough Street had shown 22,413 riders. On March 3, a few weeks after the subway opened, a count at nearby Opera Place showed 28,239, an increase of 5,826 riders–almost 26 percent![156]

The surface tracks between Northeastern University and the subway incline on Boylston Street were abandoned, and the Boston El wasted no time in uprooting the rails. A day after their abandonment, February 17, 1941, the company began tearing up the tracks on the Boylston Street Incline and from there on Boylston Street to Arlington Street. This work

[l] The name of a cross street of Huntington Avenue, Garrison, was originally selected for the station which was later named Mechanics and ultimately, Prudential.

[m] As part of Green Line reconstruction in the 1980s, the MBTA filled in the hollow section of the Northeastern incline and the extension to Opera Place.

Temporary wooden-planked roadways were used to allow traffic to pass along Huntington Avenue while subway construction proceeded below. Above, this view taken at Garrison Street near the Mechanics Building on March 29, 1939, shows the rails in place, but much decking remains to be done. A year later, below, center-entrance car 6283 heads inbound at the same location over a more finished temporary structure. *Both, BERy*

Construction of the Huntington Avenue Subway was nearly complete when this shot was taken of a work car near the crossover near Mechanics Station on September 12, 1940. *BERy*

To provide passengers access to Copley Station, the new subway diverted from Huntington Avenue onto Exeter Street and then to a junction with the Boylston Street Subway. This view from about 1940 shows construction at the intersection of Huntington and Exeter. *BERy*

It's officially open! The first train enters the Huntington Avenue Subway on February 16, 1941, with a large crowd of onlookers on both sides of the incline at Northeastern. *Stanley M. Hauck*

Once the Huntington Avenue Subway opened, the City of Boston and the Boston Elevated Railway lost no time in removing the surface tracks and repaving Huntington Avenue and Boylston Street. Like the subway itself, the work, seen here in the late spring of 1941 at Copley Square, was undertaken by the WPA. *BERy*

was completed on February 20. That same day the Elevated set to work on the remaining surface tracks, beginning with the section on Huntington Avenue between Gainsborough and Exeter Streets. The removal of these tracks was completed on May 10.

Also at this time the special work at Massachusetts and Huntington Avenues was removed as part of the roadway rebuilding that was required for the Huntington Avenue automobile underpass. This track project took from March 3 to August 9, 1941, to complete.

The City of Boston was eager to rebuild Huntington Avenue from Exeter to Boylston Street, and Boylston Street from Huntington Avenue to Arlington Street. Before the roadways could be rebuilt, however, the track on these streets had to be removed. There was also abandoned surface track on Boylston Street from Arlington Street to Charles Street on both sides of the abandoned subway incline. Additional special work was located at Charles and Boylston Streets and was connected to unused surface track on Charles Street. Finally the emergency spur tracks on Berkeley Street remained. The Elevated started removal of all these surface tracks, except those on Charles Street, on April 12, completing the work on November 8, 1941.

Subway tie-in tracks were taken up at the foot of the Boylston Street Incline. Active tracks in this area were rebuilt and included the installation of a 303-foot crossover under Charles Street. This work took place between June 15 and August 31, 1941.

57 Francis Street/Heath Street–Park Street Station *via Huntington*

Route 57, Francis Street–Park Street Station, was a cutback of the Arborway line. At first it ran to Park Street Station from a set of crossovers at Francis Street and Huntington Avenue. The round-trip distance was 5.657 miles with a running time of 25 minutes. After December 15, 1945, Route 57 was operated from the newly-opened Heath Street Loop, and the round-trip distance increased to 7.884 miles with a running time of 36 minutes.

This line was primarily run with Type 4 cars until Heath Street opened. A few center-entrance cars were used here as well in the spring of 1943 and in the spring and fall of 1944.

In anticipation of PCC operation and the need to shortturn these single-end cars, the Elevated purchased land for a loop at South Huntington Avenue and Heath Street. This parcel had been occupied by an automobile service station. The Elevated began construction on September 14, 1945, and on December 15, 1945, Heath Street Loop was officially opened and placed in service. From November 20-30, 1945, the Elevated removed a nearby trailing point crossover on South Huntington Avenue between the new loop and Huntington Avenue.

Before Heath Street Loop opened in 1945, Francis Street and Huntington Avenue, also known as Brigham Circle, was the site of a cutback. Cars between here and Park Street Station operated as Route 57. In this March 21, 1940, view, riders board a Type 4 for the run downtown. The process of changing ends is incomplete, as both trolley poles are up. *BERy*

PCC cars entered Heath Street service on January 3, 1946. The March 1946 rating showed four PCCs and four Type 4s assigned to this run. Combinations of PCCs and Type 4s ranging from zero to several of each continued on this line through 1950.

An odd accident started at Heath Street on July 31, 1949. Type 4 car 5228, which had been laying over at Heath Street Loop, rolled away down Heath Street onto South Huntington Avenue to the corner of Huntington Avenue, where it derailed. The car came to rest outside 891 Huntington Avenue, where a utility pole that crashed through the window of her apartment injured a resident of the building. It is believed that a boy released the brakes of the car and jumped out as it began rolling.[157]

Northeastern University (Opera Place)[n]– Park Street Station

In June 1947, the Boston El began running a shuttle between Park Street Station and Opera Place Station. Type 4 cars were used exclusively. The run was discontinued in June 1949, but reappeared again a few years later. This route was 4.027 miles round-trip with a running time of 20 minutes.

---

[n] On May 21, 1947, the Boston Elevated trustees voted to change the name of the station at Opera Place to Northeastern University.

Heath Street Loop, opened in December 1945, was intended to replace Francis Street as a cutback point, yet cars continued to turn back at Francis Street off and on for many more years. The Boston Elevated envisioned using PCC cars on Route 57, which was now extended to Heath Street, but Type 4s such as 5292 entering the loop on March 21, 1947, continued on this route mixing with PCCs through the end of the 1940s. *Stanley M. Hauck*

Opera Place Station (Northeastern University) was a busy stop on the Arborway line. Here, on March 26, 1950, we see two Type 4 cars awaiting work, and an outbound PCC at the platform. Underneath the platform from the subway incline about as far as Opera Place, the side street to the viewer's left, was the tunnel shell of a future extension of the Huntington Avenue Subway. Note the inbound Boston & Worcester ACF-Brill bus on the right. *Foster M. Palmer*

The third track at Northeastern University ran off the reservation in the street and freed up a lot of space for car storage on the inbound reservation running rail, scarcely used on this occasion by the center-entrance train on an almost vacant track. Two Type 4 cars move right by in June 1942. *Charles A. Duncan*

The Reservoir Lines

Two of the present-day Green Line branches entered the subway from the west: Route 61, Reservoir Carhouse–Lechmere via Beacon Street; and Route 62, Lake Street–Lechmere via Commonwealth Avenue.[o] Both lines were based at Reservoir Carhouse.

The Lake Street line shared track on Commonwealth Avenue with the line from Watertown between Brighton Avenue (Packard's Corner) and Blandford Street. Two cutback routes originated in this section during the 1940s: Blandford Street and Braves Field to either Park Street Station or North Station.[p] These cutbacks were usually based at Watertown or occasionally at Reservoir.

Reservoir Carhouse

This large carhouse and yard complex dates from the start of the Beacon Street line in 1889. It is primarily located in Brookline along the Brookline–Brighton boundary line. In 1940 it consisted of a large car repair building with a yard loop and storage tracks. Reservoir Carhouse has undergone many changes over the years and still exists, but as an entirely new carhouse building and yard opened in 1983.[q]

There were two exits from the property, a double-track line onto Chestnut Hill Avenue, and a single-track line along Prendergast Avenue onto Beacon Street. The single track on Prendergast Avenue connected with the outbound and inbound Beacon Street tracks in their respective directions. There was also an unusual connection with the inbound track in the outbound direction from Prendergast Avenue.

On May 4, 1940, the Elevated completed a new carhouse addition at Reservoir. This project entailed expansion of the carhouse and various track modifications to permit the transfer of the Lake Street line from Bennett Street Carhouse in Cambridge to Reservoir. Before this date, the Lake Street service required pull-ins and pull-outs from Bennett Street.

The March 1944 issue of *Co-operation* mentioned track work modifications for PCC operation at Reservoir that had recently been completed, including adding a new lead to the loop in the rear of the yard. Eight stub-ended storage tracks were also connected to another new lead from the front caryard, effectively forming a second loop for the single-end PCC cars

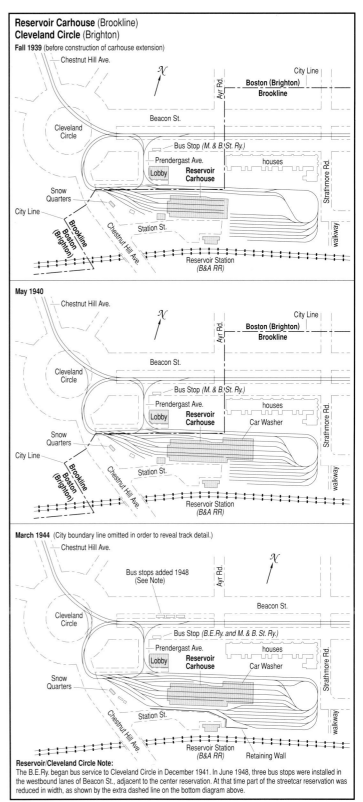

Reservoir Carhouse (Brookline)
Cleveland Circle (Brighton)
Fall 1939 (before construction of carhouse extension)

May 1940

March 1944 (City boundary line omitted in order to reveal track detail.)

Reservoir/Cleveland Circle Note:
The B.E.Ry. began bus service to Cleveland Circle in December 1941. In June 1948, three bus stops were installed in the westbound lanes of Beacon St., adjacent to the center reservation. At that time part of the streetcar reservation was reduced in width, as shown by the extra dashed line on the bottom diagram above.

---

[o] The "Reservoir" destination at the end of the Beacon Street line of the 1940s is now known as "Cleveland Circle." As a result of an expansion of the Boston College campus from Newton into Brighton the Boston Elevated trustees voted to change the "Lake Street" designation to "Boston College" on May 21, 1947. The MBTA still uses the term "Lake Street" to refer to the light rail storage and maintenance facility at this location. The in-town terminal points of the Cleveland Circle and Boston College lines have also changed at various times over the years.

[p] The Braves Field–Park Street Station line was given its own route number, 124, in the Boston El seventh edition system route map in 1947. This number did not appear in earlier or later editions of the map.

[q] The MBTA began demolishing the old carhouse buildings in 1982.

to change direction.[158] To get the space for these changes, the Elevated purchased part of Station Street, a private way, from the B&A Railroad.[r] Part of the embankment supporting the street was removed to make way for the new track, and a 332-foot long, 23-foot high retaining wall was constructed against the embankment to support the remainder of Station Street.

---

[r] This name should not be confused with Station Street in Brookline Village, also adjacent to the B&A Railroad.

Reservoir Carhouse dated to the start of the Beacon Street line in 1889. We are looking into the yard in front of the building from Chestnut Hill Avenue on October 9, 1941, and see an assortment of Type 4 and center-entrance cars. *Charles A. Duncan*

Reservoir–Lechmere, Lake Street–Lechmere Equipment Assignments

In the May 6, 1940, rating, 179 cars including spares were based at Reservoir Carhouse to handle the Blandford Street, Beacon Street, and Lake Street lines. Of this total, 149 were center-entrance cars and 30 were Type 4s. These cars were stored at Lechmere Station and Lake Street Yard as well as at Reservoir. The Type 4s were normally used on the Blandford Street cutback and after 7 p.m. and on Sundays on all lines. Forty-eight center-entrance cars were assigned to the Beacon Street line, and 54 to Lake Street.

The use of center-entrance cars increased during the war, peaking in December 1943. The arrival of the PCC cars in large numbers in 1944 and 1945, however, soon resulted in a sharp reduction in center-entrance cars. The last exclusive assignment of center-entrance cars on the Beacon Street line was 57 units in the December 11, 1944, rating. On the Lake Street line, center-entrance cars were last used exclusively in the April 16, 1945, rating.

The March 1944 issue of *Co-operation* said that the Elevated had received 30 out of 150 PCC cars authorized by the War Production Board.[159] During operator training, these cars would be assigned to Reservoir-Lechmere, and later to other lines as well. Delivery of 35 more PCC cars was expected by the end of March, another 35 during the summer, and the final 50 during the fall of 1944 or early 1945.

PCC cars appeared as spares on the Beacon and Lake Street lines in the May 1944 rating.[160] In July 1944, 8 PCCs were shown at Lake Street with 31 more at Reservoir. These cars were used in the evenings, as Owl Cars, and in Sunday service.

In 1945 PCC cars entered regular service on the Beacon Street and Lake Street lines. On April 14, 1945, the first two-car multiple unit PCC trains entered regular service on the Beacon Street line. Two days later, in the April 16, 1945, rating, PCCs completely replaced the Beacon street center-entrance cars except as spares.

In June 1945, 42 PCCs were assigned to Lake Street. Fourteen center-entrance cars remained but regularly assigned PCCs replaced them in the December 10, 1945, rating. Center-entrance cars remained as spares, however, until the November 29, 1947, rating.

Center-entrance cars continued as spares for Beacon Street through 1950 and beyond. On September 16, 1946, 11 center-entrance cars reappeared on the Beacon Street line as a regular assignment, along with 55 PCCs. The number of center-entrance cars on Beacon Street increased to 24 in November 1947, and the number of PCCs dropped to 42. For a while thereafter, these numbers varied with ratings. In the February 14, 1949, rating, however, the number of center-entrance cars used on Beacon Street rose to 30 and remained there through 1950. In this later period, the PCC level remained at 42.

All PCC cars on order had been received by May 1946. On July 13, 1946, a three-car PCC train was first used in revenue service on Beacon Street, running as a baseball extra. On September 16, 1946, the first regularly scheduled three-car PCC trains began running on Beacon St.

There still were not enough PCCs to handle all the rush hour subway traffic, and this was the reason for holding onto the remaining center-entrance cars. The war had extracted a severe toll from these survivors, and heavy maintenance would be needed if these cars were to remain in service.

The MTA began a program to rehabilitate thirty center-entrance cars, and on February 10, 1948, the first three-car train entered service. These cars featured new longitudinal subway seating and green interiors. This new paint scheme was in sharp contrast to the traditional red interiors and cross seating previously used. A rider remembers them as "sharp-looking and cavernous." These cars were used to beef up subway service and handle sporting and special events at Braves Field, Fenway Park, and Boston Garden.

In the September 12, 1949, rating, 176 cars were based at Reservoir Carhouse. Of these cars, 13 PCCs were stored overnight at Lechmere, 44 PCCs were stored at Lake Street, and 46 center-entrance cars and 70 PCCs were stored at Reservoir. Three PCCs ran in Owl Service.

PCC cars entered service on the Beacon Street line as spares in 1944. This shot of 3029 at Cleveland Circle was taken that spring. Note the tan roof as opposed to the silver used later. This was said to be a wartime measure to make the cars less visible from the air.

Charles A. Duncan

61 Reservoir–Lechmere

The line on Beacon Street was part of the original electric line of the West End Street Railway. This line opened in 1889 and still runs today, well over a century later. Beacon Street is a heavily developed residential area, in no small part due to the car line in the middle of the roadway.

This line was simplicity in itself. The cars started on Prendergast Avenue in Brighton, a narrow alley beside the lobby at Reservoir Carhouse. Streetcars turned right onto Beacon Street and then almost immediately entered Brookline, running completely in a private reservation to the subway portal at St. Mary's Street, which was also the boundary line between Brookline and Boston Proper.[161] Cars then continued through the subway to Lechmere, crossing from Boston Proper into Cambridge on the East Cambridge Viaduct over the Charles River.[s] The round-trip distance was 13.600 miles with a running time of 63 minutes.

The Chestnut Hill Avenue Service Tracks

At Cleveland Circle, the Beacon Street line ended, and the track split in two directions along Chestnut Hill Avenue. Turning southeast, the main line track continued on Chestnut Hill Avenue into the Reservoir Carhouse. Turning northwest, a service track ran in the street two blocks along Chestnut Hill Avenue to Commonwealth Avenue where it connected inbound and outbound. The Chestnut Hill Avenue service track was used for pull-in and pull-out moves, and equipment transfers between Reservoir and Lake Street. Tracks at Cleveland Circle and the surrounding area are shown on Map 5, Inset C and with the Reservoir Carhouse diagrams.

---

[s] In 1959 the present-day Riverside line began using the subway, entering at a new portal from the west near the roadway overpass at Park Drive and running into the Beacon Street tunnel between St. Mary's Street and Kenmore Station.

A center-entrance train with 6106 bringing up the rear enters Coolidge Corner, Brookline, the intersection of Harvard and Beacon Streets, in March 1946. *Charles A. Duncan*

The signature equipment consist on the Beacon and Commonwealth Avenue lines was the three-car train of center-entrance cars. Here 6185 takes up the rear of an outbound train on Beacon Street on April 18, 1947. *Stanley M. Hauck*

Type 4 No. 5464 picks up inbound riders at the St. Mary's Street stop in January 1941. Note the illuminated sign above the boarding passengers showing the running time to Park Street Station, a feature at both the St. Mary's Street and Blandford Street portals.

Clarke Collection

In 1944, as part of the PCC track work at Reservoir, the Elevated completed the connection of the two double-track segments on Chestnut Hill Avenue. A connecting track from the southbound rail between Commonwealth Avenue and Cleveland Circle to the southbound rail of the segment from Beacon Street to the carhouse had been installed in 1939. Beginning on February 23, 1944, and ending on March 15, the northbound rail on Chestnut Hill Avenue between the carhouse and Beacon Street was joined to the northbound rail from Beacon Street to Commonwealth Avenue. This change allowed carhouse pull-outs onto Chestnut Hill Avenue to proceed directly to Commonwealth Avenue.

A connecting track from Commonwealth Avenue westbound to Chestnut Hill Avenue southbound was added between April 28 and May 31, 1947. This allowed outbound cars on Commonwealth Avenue to run directly to Cleveland Circle.

A PCC train led by car 3033 is headed down the Chestnut Hill Avenue service trackage to the Reservoir in July 1944. This is one of the earliest photographs of a three-car PCC train on the Boston Elevated Railway system.
Charles A. Duncan

Lake Street Yard

Lake Street Yard was and is a satellite of Reservoir Carhouse. The Lake Street facility straddles the Boston–Newton city boundary near the Boston College campus. Lake Street Yard had two concentric loops with inner passing sidings used for storage. The yard capacity was limited and was insufficient for all the cars the line required.[162] For this reason, cars for the Lake Street line were also housed at Reservoir and in the small yard at Lechmere.

Until 1940 additional Lake Street cars were also stored at Bennett Street Carhouse in Cambridge. These cars routinely accessed the Central Subway at Lechmere, deadheading in trains through Harvard Square in Cambridge and running more than two miles along Cambridge Street before they entered the subway system.[†] This deadhead mileage was a costly operating nuisance. To eliminate it, an addition mentioned earlier was completed at Reservoir Carhouse in May 1940, which provided more car storage for the Lake Street line much closer to the actual point of use.

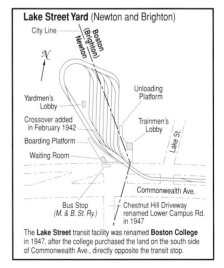

Lake Street Yard in Brighton was one of three storage points for Route 62, Lake Street–Lechmere Station. In February 1944, a center-entrance train with No. 6167 on the end has just arrived from downtown Boston.

Charles A. Duncan

Lake Street Yard (Newton and Brighton)
City Line
Boston (Brighton)
Newton
N
Yardmen's Lobby
Crossover added in February 1942
Boarding Platform
Waiting Room
Unloading Platform
Trainmen's Lobby
Lake St.
Commonwealth Ave.
Bus Stop (M. & B. St. Ry.)
Chestnut Hill Driveway renamed Lower Campus Rd. in 1947
The **Lake Street** transit facility was renamed **Boston College** in 1947, after the college purchased the land on the south side of Commonwealth Ave., directly opposite the transit stop.

62 Lake Street (Boston College)–Commonwealth Avenue–Lechmere

The Lake Street line followed the same route it does today completely situated in a private reservation. The Lake Street line followed Commonwealth Avenue from Lake Street Yard to Chestnut Hill Avenue, where a track connection to Reservoir Carhouse previously described was located.[163] The Lake Street line then continued along Commonwealth Avenue to Washington Street where there was a passing siding located off the westbound rail. A crossover between the main line rails was located west of the Washington Street end of this siding for cutbacks.

[†] The Harvard–Lechmere streetcar line had been converted to trackless trolleys in April 1936. Because of the storage arrangement at Bennett Street for the Lake Street line, streetcars continued to ply busy Cambridge Street for four more years. The 2.27 miles of track on Cambridge Street were formally abandoned in 1940.

The Commonwealth Avenue line was known for heavy service over hill and dale running. This August 1941 photo portrays the scenario well, a two-car train making a typical roller coaster run near Washington Street. *Charles A. Duncan*

A passing siding on the Commonwealth Avenue reservation located at Washington Street allowed cars to lay over before cutting back at a crossover just beyond this point. A September 1947 fan trip using two Type 5 cars was getting out of the way of regular service here.
Charles A. Duncan

Outbound business is brisk near the Boston University Bridge during the evening rush hour on November 20, 1941. Newfangled PCC car 3002 has been in service on the Watertown line since the spring, and the Type 4 and center-entrance train ahead of it, a whole lot longer here and elsewhere. *Charles A. Duncan*

A three-car train approaches Commonwealth and Harvard Avenues in this colorful scene taken in May 1942. *Charles A. Duncan*

A two-car train of center-entrance cars headed by car 6148 rolls outbound to Lake Street near Boston University in 1940. *BERy*

The line continued along Commonwealth Avenue to Brighton Avenue and joined the line from Watertown.[u] Both routes continued inbound on Commonwealth Avenue, passing Braves Field Loop and crossing a bridge over the main line of the B&A Railroad near the end of the Boston University Bridge. From here the line continued to Blandford Street, a cutback point where there was a center track with crossovers. Here the cars entered the subway, joining the Beacon Street line at Kenmore and running to Lechmere. Route 62 covered a distance of 16.101 miles round-trip and took 74 minutes to complete.

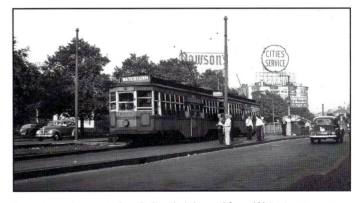

A center-entrance train, obviously inbound from Watertown, pauses at the Blandford Street incline entrance to the Boylston Street Subway in 1946. Note the Cities Service sign, the forerunner of the current landmark Citgo sign in Kenmore Square. *Richard L. Wonson*

[u] The section of Commonwealth Avenue between Chestnut Hill Avenue and Brighton Avenue consisted then and now of four divided roadways—two in each direction—separated by three median strips. Between Chestnut Hill Avenue and Warren Street, the car line tracks occupied the center median strip. Between Warren Street and Brighton Avenue, however, the car line was located in the northern median strip, between the westbound traffic lane and the westbound service road.

– 103 –

A center-entrance train from Boston makes its way along the final stretch of the viaduct into Lechmere Station in this scene taken in 1941. The Type 5 is looping from Cambridge Street onto Bridge Street, traveling from the inbound side of the station, where it has just dropped off passengers, to the outbound side, where it will pick up new riders for Clarendon Hill, Somerville. *Charles A. Duncan*

The yard at Lechmere Station is filled with PCC cars for the afternoon rush hour in this shot taken around 1948. PCC 3224 is boarding for downtown and Boston College and will soon be underway. *MTA*

The Boston Elevated Railway was a pioneer in the concept of "Park n' Ride." Here, on December 9, 1941, we see a near-full parking lot at Lechmere with a two-car center-entrance train in the background climbing the viaduct and headed in town. *BERy*

Lechmere Station

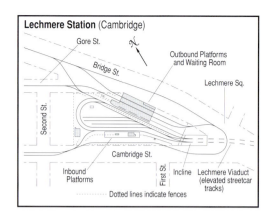

In 1940 Lechmere Station was the northern terminal of the Central Subway system. There were two loops and three storage tracks at Lechmere. There was also a transfer station for connections to surface trackless trolleys for Harvard Square, for streetcars to Clarendon Hill via Somerville Avenue and via Highland Avenue, and for buses to Arlington Center.

The service track to Harvard Square via Cambridge Street was still connected to the station trackage to allow Lake Street pull-outs from Bennett Street Carhouse to enter service. The station trackage also connected to the surface tracks on Bridge Street. These connections to the surface system were severed in 1940 and 1941. The service track to Harvard Square was abandoned in 1940, and the streetcar lines to Clarendon Hill were both converted to trackless trolleys in 1941.

As they are today, cars were stored at Lechmere throughout the 1940s. At first, a single Type 4 for the Blandford Street service was stored here, but with the September 1942 rating, the Type 4 was joined by 12 center-entrance cars. Thirteen center-entrance cars were stored at Lechmere in the May 1944 rating, but a single PCC displaced one of them in April 1945. Finally, 13 PCC cars were stored here in June 1945, an assignment that continued into 1950.

The Lechmere Viaduct was built as an ornamental structure in the long stretch from Leverett Circle to the Prison Point Bridge. Here we see a three-car train approaching the drawbridge over the Charles River locks in October 1940. *Charles A. Duncan*

69 Watertown–Park Street Station

Route 69, Watertown–Park Street Station, entered the subway portal near Blandford Street and Commonwealth Avenue until 1969. The Brighton–Newton–Watertown line, as it was also known, had cutbacks at Oak Square, Braves Field, and Blandford Street. With its cutbacks and special baseball storage track bypass loop on Cambridge Street and Harvard Avenue, the line was a system unto itself.

Route 69 was based at Watertown Carhouse, a large carhouse and yard storage facility located on Galen Street, Watertown, just across the Charles River from Watertown Square.[v] Leaving Watertown Carhouse, the line turned south onto Galen Street, climbed the hill to the Newton-Watertown boundary, and entered Newton Corner. At the city line, Galen Street became Centre Street. At Newton Corner, the line turned southeast onto Washington Street, crossed a bridge over the main line of the B&A Railroad, and then turned south onto Park Street.[w]

The cars followed Park Street for two blocks, then turned southeast onto Tremont Street, and followed Tremont Street to the Boston city line, which was located about halfway to Oak Square. At the city boundary, the tracks entered the Brighton District of Boston and continued on Tremont Street to Washington Street at Oak Square. A turn-back loop was located here, partly on the site of the former Oak Square Carhouse.

From Oak Square the line continued east on Washington Street, passing through Brighton Center and veering northeast onto Cambridge Street. At Union Square in the Allston section of Brighton, the main line bore to the right and ran down Brighton Avenue in a private reservation. At Packard's Corner, the line joined the Commonwealth Avenue tracks and ran directly into the subway just beyond Blandford Street. A round-trip run to Park Street Station and back was 14.859 miles and required 66 minutes to complete.

Jim Gately Remembers…

I grew up on Tremont Street in Brighton along the Watertown car line. I was born in 1941, and my earliest memories are of this line. As a little kid, I lay awake listening to the Owl Cars passing by my house.

Tremont Street in Newton and Brighton had a long, straight stretch of level track. I lived at the first curve, at a stop called "clubhouse" (named for a long burned clubhouse belonging to the local Catholic Church). The cars would build up a lot of speed, and because of the curve, they would have to noisily apply their brakes.

Work car 2001 appears to be engaged at the starting platform for the Park Street Station cars at Watertown Carhouse. It is June 1942, and the beautiful weather might lull the viewer into the belief that this is a casual affair. It is not. This is wartime on a busy line, and the work car must complete its tasks quickly and get out of the way of revenue service. *Charles A. Duncan*

Newly-arrived PCC car 3002 gobbles up inbound riders in this 1941 view at Newton Corner, an important transfer point between Boston Elevated streetcars and buses of the Middlesex & Boston Street Railway Company. *Charles A. Duncan*

A local judge would not allow my father to be drafted because he had a child to support, namely me. My dad was required, however, to act as the local air raid warden and black-out light enforcer. His post was at the corner of Waverley Avenue and Tremont Street, just over the Newton city line from our house. He had many stories about his duties, but the ones I remember most concerned the streetcars. When an alert was in effect, my father stopped all streetcars, ordered the riders off, and made the motorman extinguish all the lights. I always admired my dad for this awesome responsibility.

My father must have been a trolley fan but he would never admit to it. On a free Sunday, he would take me on a trolley trip that we came to call "going around the belt." For a single fare, we would ride the car to Watertown, change to the Harvard or Central car, and then get on an Ashmont train. At Ashmont, we rode the "High Speed Line," a real thrill to me, to Mattapan.

There we had another choice. We could take the Arborway car over Cummins Highway, or my favorite, the Blue Hill Avenue car to Egleston, with that great

---

[v] Watertown Carhouse is described in Chapter 6.

[w] Newton Corner, the intersection of Centre and Washington Streets, was also known as Nonantum Square.

piece of private right-of-way alongside Franklin Park. There was even an interesting little loop along the way, where you might catch a glimpse of a Humboldt Avenue car.

If we went to the Arborway, we took the Jamaica car to the subway. If we arrived at Egleston, however, we could take the North Station car through Roxbury and the South End, a more interesting ride. Once in the subway we boarded the Watertown car for home. This was one great outing for a single fare. If my father saw his way clear, a hot chocolate or an ice cream cone really topped off the day!

I must have witnessed the early PCC operation on Tremont Street, but my first recollection of them happened one wintry day. We used to sled down a very steep street called Cufflin Street, which was the last side street before crossing the city line into Newton. I can remember being at the top of the hill and seeing two PCCs go by, very close together. What was this? Upon further inspection, I realized that the two cars were coupled together and operating as a two-car train. This advance in streetcar technology stunned me.

Another function the trolley filled was taking people to the cemeteries on Memorial Day. Every year we journeyed from Brighton to the cemeteries in West Roxbury to decorate the graves of my ancestors. I loved these jaunts, not only because of the great number of extra cars that ran on the Charles River line, but also the very old extra buses that ran to the cemeteries.

Another branch of my family was buried in the cemeteries along Cummins Highway in Roslindale. There was a spur track into a Boston El-owned quarry where the El secured its ballast. On Memorial Day weekend, however, it stored extra cars for the crowds. My family would go to the graves, but I remained at the quarry to watch the great passing scene of Type 5s.

I also remember my first trolley photograph of a Type 5 with my friends. I was in full cowboy regalia posed in front so no one would think that I was really taking a picture of the streetcar!

James Gately served for many years as Treasurer of the Boston Street Railway Association and is now BSRA Librarian.

Watertown–Park Street Station Equipment Assignments

In the April 1, 1940, rating, 35 Type 4s and one spare based at Watertown Carhouse were used on the Watertown–Park Street Station line. The November 28, 1949, rating showed a dramatic change with 40 PCCs and 11 spares now assigned to this line.

Type 4 cars were exclusively used on the Watertown line until March 3, 1941. At that time 20 new single-unit PCC cars, 3002-3021, were assigned along with 8 Type 4s. This equipment was the first true fleet of PCCs on the system; there would be no more new PCC cars on the property until 1944. During 1944, deliveries of multiple-unit PCC cars steadily increased, and some of them were assigned to the Watertown line. By the end of the year, the original fleet of single-unit PCC cars has been reassigned from the Watertown line to the Egleston–North Station line, having been supplanted completely by the new multiple-unit cars.

As the war continued, the number of Type 4s rose steadily, reaching 18 in the December 20, 1943, rating. Thereafter, the number of Type 4s on the Watertown line dropped significantly. In September 1944, 33 PCC cars alone handled service. The PCCs increased to 43 by December 1946. A Type 4 was occasionally used during the late war years, but the route was purely PCC after 1946. Operating personnel and other observers of this period have mentioned that the Type 4s on this line were "very tired" toward the middle and end of the war.

Outbound Type 4 No. 5362 drops two ladies off at Washington and Lake Streets in Brighton in August 1941. *Charles A. Duncan*

Park and Tremont Streets, Newton, was the site of this derailment on February 25, 1942. PCC 3009 was apparently operating too fast and derailed at the corner, landing on the sidewalk and front yard of the Channing Unitarian Church. *BERy*

A number of reliable observers have also reported the use of 6000-class center-entrance cars on the Watertown line during World War II.

On February 25, 1942, PCC 3009, apparently running too fast outbound on Tremont Street, Newton, derailed at the corner of Park Street, injuring several passengers. The car ended up on the lawn and sidewalk of the Channing Unitarian Church overturned on its side

Oak Square Loop

Oak Square Loop, at Tremont, Washington, and Faneuil Streets in Brighton, was a holdover from the days when a carhouse occupied much of the site. The loop ran on part of the roadway in Oak Square and on part of the former carhouse property, which was still owned by the Boston Elevated. An adjacent substation, the company's first such automatic electric power facility, was also located here.

In 1946, the Boston Elevated Maintenance Department relocated the loop through track and reconnected an existing dead end track to the new through track to provide additional storage space.[164] The new second storage track rejoined the through track just before it exited the loop property onto the Washington Street inbound track.

Oak Square was a cutback of the Watertown Line. Cars generally looped here as required during the 1940s to maintain service headways. From April to November 1945, cars were regularly operated from Oak Square to Park Street Station weekdays and Saturdays from about 7 a.m. to 5 p.m. After November 1945, the service was cut back to 3 p.m. Beginning in December 1946, a few rush-hour trips were run with two-car trains of PCC cars. Service was suspended from Oak Square from June through September in 1947 and 1949, but cars were run in the summer of 1948.

The Oak Square–Park Street Station route was 11.688 miles round-trip and required 52 minutes to complete.

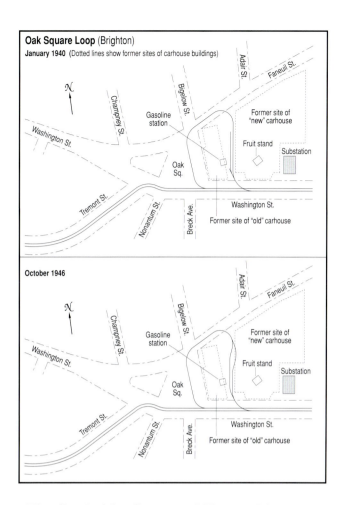

The Cambridge Street and Harvard Avenue Ball Game Bypass Loop

There was an inbound track switch to Cambridge Street at Union Square. Cars taking this connection ran straight ahead on single track to a point on Cambridge Street near Harvard Avenue. Here a switch led into double track, the outbound and the inbound rails of the former Allston–Dudley line. From the switch on Cambridge Street to Brighton Avenue, the outbound rail lay dormant; it was disconnected at Brighton Avenue. Cars followed the inbound rail from the switch to Harvard Street, turned right onto Harvard Street, and turned left onto Brighton Avenue to rejoin the main line inbound.

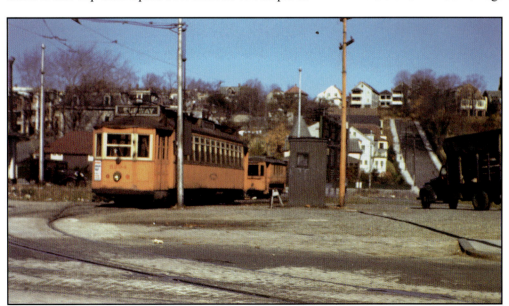

Type 4 No. 5294 and ancient work car No. 724, a rail grinder, form an odd duo at Oak Square Loop in October 1942. They represent two distinct generations of streetcars: old and very old. They both are fully functional, though, and will soldier on for many more years.

Charles A. Duncan

On ball game days, the El stored extra cars on the main line inbound rail on Brighton Avenue. Regular inbound cars were diverted onto the loop trackage down Cambridge Street.[x]

In 1945, a curved track connection between the outbound main line and the inbound Cambridge Street track was installed at Union Square.[165] This connection allowed outbound cars to be diverted via Cambridge Street and Harvard Avenue back to the subway. In 1946, the Boston Elevated began removing the unused outbound rail on Harvard Avenue between Brighton Avenue and Cambridge Street. The active inbound rail was resurfaced and regraded.[166]

Braves Field

Braves Field, located one-half block north of Commonwealth Avenue, was the home of the National League baseball team, the Boston Braves. A one-way single-track loop that left the reservation on Commonwealth Avenue and ran north onto Babcock Street served the baseball field. Here the cars turned east into a double-track boarding area beside Braves Field, and then emerged south onto Gaffney Street for their return to Commonwealth Avenue.

Braves Field was an important transit destination.[y] On May 11, 1946, the first night game at Braves Field was played. On August 16, 1947, the Braves Field Loop boarding area was made a prepayment station to speed up loading.

Originally, Braves Field–Park Street Station or North Station service was operated on ball game days. It also ran periodically in regular and rush hour service. Before November 1945, service was run during rush hours only. After this date, regular service ran all day, including weekdays and Saturdays, operating from approximately 6 a.m. to 8 p.m. The cars for Braves Field Loop service were initially based at Watertown. A round trip between Braves Field and Park Street Station was 6.849 miles and required 33 minutes to complete. The run between Braves Field and North Station was 8.466 miles round-trip with a running time of 43 minutes.

In September 1946, some cars began running to North Station as late as 10 p.m., and in December 1946 to 11 p.m. This evening service was cut back during the summer ratings to 7 p.m., but usually resumed in the fall and continued through the winter and spring.

Starting with the November 19, 1945, rating, PCC cars and Type 4s were assigned in varying numbers to the Braves Field service. After September 1946, Type 4s were the only

Using the connecting track onto Cambridge Street from Brighton Avenue installed in 1945, Type 4 No. 5309 short turns for a trip back to the subway on April 23, 1947. *Foster M. Palmer*

The bypass loop allowed inbound cars to Park Street to run around cars stored on the inbound rail for the crowds at the end of ball games at nearby Braves Field and Fenway Park. Here we are looking east and see a lineup of center-entrance cars at Union Square, Allston, on Brighton Avenue during World Series Game 2 on October 7, 1948. *Foster M. Palmer*

cars assigned from Watertown and were used through the end of the decade and beyond.

Braves Field service was increased in February 1949, using two-car center-entrance trains based at the Reservoir. The service was run to North Station weekdays-only from 8 a.m.

A two-car center-entrance train on a fan trip enters Commonwealth Avenue trackage from Gaffney Street, the outbound track from Braves Field, and heads toward downtown Boston. *Clarke Collection*

---

[x] Streetcars waiting for baseball fans were parked on Brighton Avenue presumably because they would not interfere with automobile traffic while they were in the center reservation.

[y] On April 4, 1945, the name "National League Park" was changed to "Braves Field." For five seasons between 1936 and 1940, however, the baseball team was renamed the "Boston Bees," and the ball park was popularly known as the "Bee Hive." It always retained the official name of "National League Park," however. The former team and park names were restored for the 1941 season.

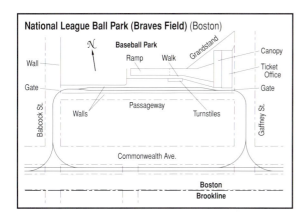

National League Ball Park (Braves Field) (Boston)

National League Park, popularly known as Braves Field, had its own streetcar loop to handle the crowds riding to and from the stadium. For this heavy traffic, center-entrance cars, renowned for their "crowd swallowing" wide center doors and low platform, were the trolley of choice. Here we see the end of car 6216 poking out from the end of the entrance to the ballpark. *Charles A. Brown*

to 4 p.m. using eight center-entrance cars. Ten center-entrance cars were assigned in the June 1949 rating, but this number was reduced back to eight in September, a level that continued into 1950.

Fenway Park extras were also short turned at Braves Field Loop. These cars handled heavy traffic from the Boston Red Sox, Boston's American League baseball team.

The Braves won the National League pennant in 1948, and three games of the World Series were played at Braves Field that year. In the October 5, 1948, edition of the *Boston Globe*, the MTA's plans for handling service for the World Series were published.[167] Cars would leave Park Street Station for Braves Field Loop every 45 seconds. From North Station to Braves Field the frequency was every minute.

Eighty extra cars would be used to achieve this level of service, and thirty MTA inspectors would be stationed on Commonwealth Avenue between Blandford Street and Packard's Corner to ensure swift service. A wire crew would be based at Kenmore Station, and repairmen would be stationed at various points in the subway to handle any breakdowns. Anticipating huge crowds, the MTA was taking no chances.

Looking into the two-track platform area at Braves Field, we see two two-car trains of center-entrance cars waiting for departing crowds. This platform was so busy that it later was equipped as a prepayment station with restricted access through turnstiles and past a collector's booth. *Charles A. Brown*

The Braves Field Loop featured this small, two-track yard beside the field on private land owned by the Braves. Each track could hold several cars, as this center-entrance train headed by No. 6250 illustrates in 1948. The gaping maw that comprised the open doorway on each car awaits the crowds to come. *Clarke Collection*

A three-car center-entrance train leaves Braves Field on Gaffney Street on May 2, 1948, but this time signed FENWAY PARK. Why? Because the loop at Braves Field was also used to turn cars for the Red Sox field at Fenway Park near Kenmore.   *Foster M. Palmer*

Blandford Street

At Blandford Street near the subway portal on Commonwealth Avenue, a third track was located between the inbound and outbound tracks of the main line. A series of switches connected the center rail to the main line tracks.

The Blandford Street track was used for cutbacks from the Central Subway. It was also a convenient point for storing Red Sox ball game extras for nearby Fenway Park.

The Blandford Street cutback was used intermittently. In April 1940, service between Blandford Street and Park Street Station was based at Reservoir Carhouse. It was then a cutback of the Lake Street line, Route 62. The round-trip distance was 4.619 miles with an average running time of 22 minutes. Type 4s were assigned, and they were used until September 1943. At that time this service was transferred to Watertown, continuing to operate with Type 4s.

The April 1945 rating showed regular service from about 8 a.m. to 9 p.m on weekdays and Saturdays from Blandford Street to Park Street Station. Some evening trips also ran from Blandford Street to North Station, a round-trip distance of 6.236 miles with a running time of 32 minutes. In the November 19, 1945, rating, the Braves Field cutback replaced regular service from Blandford Street.

On November 1, 1948, the Blandford Street service reappeared, but this time it was reassigned to Reservoir Carhouse and ran to North Station using eight center-entrance cars in two-car trains. Cars ran to North Station weekdays from approximately 8 a.m. to 4 p.m., with extra rush hour service. This route lasted until the June 1949 rating, when the rush hour service was curtailed. Rush hour trips returned with the September 1949 rating and continued into 1950.

The Brighton Avenue Reservation

On July 1, 1949, the MTA and the City of Boston began removing the reservation on Brighton Avenue between Commonwealth Avenue and Union Square. This work entailed track reconstruction and the placement of center islands between the rails. This project was completed on October 5, 1949.

Blandford Street was the cross street on Commonwealth Avenue near Kenmore Square where a third center track was located for cutbacks and baseball game storage. Here we see an outbound PCC approaching center-entrance car 6246 in May 1947.

Foster M. Palmer

Brighton Avenue had its own streetcar reservation until July 1949. Above, we see PCC 3134 running inbound on the reservation. Below, crane car 3605 rips up the track on July 28, 1949. It won't be long before the exclusive trolley right-of-way is appropriated for the use of private automobiles.   *Above, Norton D. Clark; below, MTA*

This project was quite similar to the earlier reservation replacements on Blue Hill Avenue along Franklin Park and on Columbus Avenue between Jackson Square and Washington Street. The change was intended to improve automobile traffic flow. By forcing the streetcars to mix with other traffic, however, the project became a contributing factor to the untimely demise of the car line.

In 1996 the car tracks were removed long after regular service had ended. Today a landscaped traffic median, the purpose of which is to "calm" traffic, has replaced the tracks–and the streetcar reservation that was removed 47 years earlier. In a sharp reversal of intent, current city policy is to enhance the quality of life by slowing traffic down rather than by speeding it up! It is fair to say that the streetcars did a much better job of this!

Subway Changes

A new loudspeaker system was placed in service above the southbound platform of Park Street Station on March 14, 1940. This system was used extensively during the war for emergency and service announcements.

Also in 1940, the maintenance pit track on the southbound side of Park Street Station was removed; the northbound pit remained. Abandoned track running southbound from beneath Hanover and Washington Streets to Adams Square Station and the track on the unused turn back loop at Adams Square was also removed in 1940.

The Kenmore busway was opened on November 4, 1943. It featured a direct stairway to the Boylston Street Subway and provided a covered waiting area for transferring riders. The busway also isolated buses from Kenmore Square traffic.

New illuminated signs that read "DRAW OPENING" were placed in service on March 17, 1944, on both sides of the Lechmere Viaduct drawbridge. The signs were lit when the bridge tender prepared to open the draw and were a major safety improvement.

The famous Park Street Information Booth was modernized in 1947, with stainless steel sheathing, modern glass, and fluorescent lighting. It replaced an earlier structure that had opened in 1923.

On September 16, 1948, the MTA reactivated the Lowell Street Siding, located between the inbound and outbound rails on the steel elevated structure leading to the Lechmere Viaduct. This track could hold six cars and was intended for use by the refurbished center-entrance cars that had entered subway service earlier in the year. Extras for Boston Garden sports events were frequently stored in the siding in the years that followed.

As built in 1912, the siding was awkward to use because it was stub-ended and was connected to both tracks southbound. Cars had to back out onto the outbound track before departing or back into the siding from the inbound track. In 1948, the MTA added a connection from the inbound track to the stub-end, making the siding more easily accessible.

A most unusual visitor to the subway was Eastern Massachusetts Street Railway lightweight car No. 7010, shown here on May 2, 1948, on the way to Everett Shops to be scrapped, just a day after the remaining trolley service of this company ended in Quincy.

Foster M. Palmer

PCC car 3224 on a trip to Lechmere transfers passengers at Scollay Square Station in 1948. *MTA*

Wartime ridership was very high. What could handle loads like this the best? Why, the "crowd swallower," otherwise known as the center-entrance car, shown here at Arlington Street Station in 1943 doing an admirable job with its double-wide doors.

Arthur Griffin, Daniel R. Cohen Collection

Arlington Heights-bound 5864 sweeps around the serpentine bend from the incline at the north portal of the Harvard Square Trolley Subway to Massachusetts Avenue. A Type 4 not far behind emerges from the subway incline, while another Type 5 is already running down the ramp on the way to the tunnel. Note the red LIMITED designation on the destination sign. This scene was repeated endlessly on this section of track, one of the two heaviest service segments on the system.

Foster M. Palmer

Chapter 6

Lines West of Boston

Transit ridership has always been heavy in the western suburbs of Boston, now and in the 1940s. This chapter covers car lines in the City of Cambridge and three towns: Arlington, Belmont and Watertown. The most significant destinations were Watertown Square, Waverley, Arlington Center, North Cambridge, Harvard Square, and Central Square, and the streetcar network tied them all together.

Cambridge is best known for the world-renowned institutions of Harvard College and the Massachusetts Institute of Technology (MIT), but the city has industrial and commercial roots as well, and considerable residential housing. Mt. Auburn Cemetery, the final resting place of the famous and powerful, was also an important streetcar destination (for the living) in this city.

Watertown, home to a United States Arsenal, was both a manufacturing center and a residential community. Belmont was and is largely a bedroom suburb with housing stock ranging from multi-family to expensive single homes. Arlington had considerable residential housing, which grew rapidly after World War II.

A number of railroad and rapid transit lines ran through this area. The Fitchburg Division of the B&M Railroad passed through North Cambridge and Belmont, and the Lexington Branch served Arlington. Harvard, Central, and Kendall Squares in Cambridge were served by the Cambridge–Dorchester rapid transit line of the Boston Elevated, with many surface lines connecting at these stations.

Service Overview

In 1940 five streetcar lines were based at the Bennett Street Carhouse in Cambridge, with substations at Arlington Heights and North Cambridge. These lines are shown on Map 6. Two more lines were based at Watertown Carhouse, and they are illustrated on Maps 5 and 6.

The Bennett Street lines are listed below:

Route No.	Route Description

71 **Watertown Carhouse–Harvard Station** *via Galen Street, Watertown Square, and Mt. Auburn Street*

73 **Waverley–Harvard Station** *via Trapelo Road, Belmont Street, and Mt. Auburn Street*
[cb] **Common Street, Belmont–Harvard**

76 **Harvard Square–Massachusetts Station** *via Massachusetts Avenue*

79 **Arlington Heights–Harvard Station** *via Massachusetts Avenue*
[cb] **Arlington Center–Harvard Station**

82 **North Cambridge–Harvard Station** *via Massachusetts Avenue*

The Waverley–Harvard and North Cambridge–Harvard lines were generally paired and through-routed, as were the Watertown–Harvard and Arlington Heights–Harvard lines. Cars from North Cambridge to Harvard were signed up "Waverley," since this was their ultimate destination. Similarly, cars from Waverley to Harvard Station were signed "North Cambridge."

While the cars from Arlington Heights to Harvard Square usually continued to Watertown, they were usually signed "Harvard" or less frequently, "Watertown." However, cars from Watertown to Harvard were usually signed "Arlington Heights." In December 1948, some trips began running between North Cambridge and Watertown, supplementing service between Arlington and Watertown. Also at some times during the decade, evening service operated between Arlington Heights and Waverley.

The Harvard Square–Massachusetts Station line had been abandoned by the end of the 1940s. Cars stopped running September 12, 1949, all the way to Massachusetts Station, although for a week longer they continued between Harvard Square and Memorial Drive.

In order of daily trips, the combined operation of Routes 71 and 79 was highest, followed by the Route 73 and 82 combination. Route 76 was next followed by Route 70 (see below), then by Route 79, operating by itself from Arlington Center to Bennett Street. Route 82 had the fewest daily trips when operated by itself in the evening only as far as Bennett Street. This information is covered more completely in Appendix 9.

As mentioned earlier, the heaviest service on the entire system was operated in two places: Massachusetts Avenue north

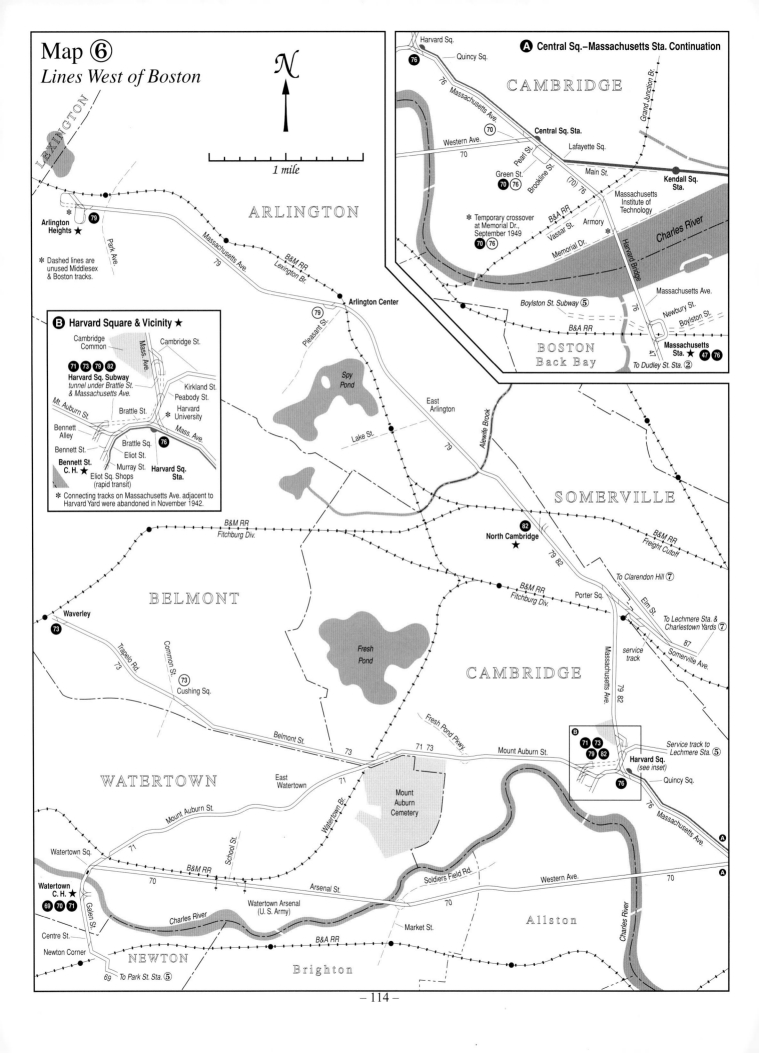

Map ⑥
Lines West of Boston

N

1 mile

LEXINGTON

ARLINGTON

* Dashed lines are
unused Middlesex
& Boston tracks.

79 Arlington Heights ★

* Arlington
Heights ★

Park Ave.

Massachusetts Ave.

B&M RR
Lexington Br.

79

79 Arlington Center

Pleasant St.

Spy
Pond

Lake St.

East
Arlington

79

Alewife Brook

SOMERVILLE

82 North Cambridge ★

79 82

B&M RR
Freight Cutoff

To Clarendon Hill ⑦

To Lechmere Sta. &
Charlestown Yards ⑦

87

Elm St.

Somerville Ave.

service track

B Harvard Square & Vicinity ★

Cambridge
Common

Cambridge St.

Mass. Ave.

71 73 79 82
Harvard Sq. Subway
*tunnel under Brattle St.
& Massachusetts Ave.*

Kirkland St.

Peabody St.

* Harvard University

Mt. Auburn St.

Brattle St.

Mass. Ave.

Bennett
Alley

Bennett St.

Brattle Sq.

76

Eliot St.

Murray St.

Harvard Sq.
Sta.

Bennett St.
C. H. ★

Eliot Sq. Shops
(rapid transit)

* Connecting tracks on Massachusetts Ave. adjacent to
Harvard Yard were abandoned in November 1942.

B&M RR
Fitchburg Div.

BELMONT

B&M RR
Fitchburg Div.

Porter Sq.

Massachusetts Ave.

79 82

CAMBRIDGE

Waverley

73

Trapelo Rd.

Common St.

73 Cushing Sq.

73

Fresh
Pond

Belmont St.

73

Fresh Pond Pkwy.

71 73

Mount Auburn St.

B 71 73
79 82
76

Harvard Sq.
(see inset)

Service track to
Lechmere Sta. ⑤

Quincy Sq.

76

Massachusetts Ave.

A

WATERTOWN

East
Watertown

71

Watertown Br.

Mount
Auburn
Cemetery

Mount Auburn St.

71

School St.

Watertown Sq.

70

B&M RR

Arsenal St.

70

Soldiers Field Rd.

Western Ave.

70

A

Watertown
C. H. ★

69 70 71

Galen St.

Charles River

Watertown Arsenal
(U. S. Army)

Market St.

Allston

Charles River

Centre St.

Newton Corner

NEWTON

69 To Park St. Sta. ⑤

B&A RR

Brighton

A Central Sq.–Massachusetts Sta. Continuation

Harvard Sq.

76

Quincy Sq.

CAMBRIDGE

Massachusetts Ave.

76

Grand Junction Br.

70 Central Sq. Sta.

Western Ave.

70

Lafayette Sq.

Pearl St.

Main St.

Kendall Sq.
Sta.

Green St.

70 76

Brookline St.

(70) 76

70 76

Massachusetts Institute of
Technology

Armory

Harvard Bridge

Charles River

* Temporary crossover
at Memorial Dr.,
September 1949

70 76

B&A RR

Vassar St.

Memorial Dr.

Boylston St. Subway ⑤

76

Massachusetts Ave.

Newbury St.

Boylston St.

B&A RR

**BOSTON
Back Bay**

Massachusetts
Sta. ★ 47 76

To Dudley St. Sta. ②

of Harvard Square as far as North Cambridge Yard, and on Warren Street in Roxbury between Dudley Street and Walnut Avenue. In Cambridge the combined service from Harvard Square to North Cambridge and Arlington totaled 605 trips per day, with a 1.0 minute morning headway and a 0.9 minute headway in the evening! Routes 19, 22, 23, and 44 on Warren Street in Roxbury had the same weekday daily trip total and identical service frequencies but reversed in the morning and evening rush hours from those in Cambridge.

Initially, the Lechmere Station–Lake Street line via Subway and Commonwealth Avenue was operated from Bennett Street Carhouse as mentioned in Chapter 5. Cars used service tracks on Cambridge Street from Harvard Square to Lechmere as a pull-in, pull-out route.[a] This deadheading ended on May 6, 1940, when the line was transferred to Reservoir Carhouse and the Cambridge Street tracks were abandoned. This operation was discussed in detail in Chapter 5.

The Watertown lines were:

69 **Watertown Carhouse–Park Street Station** *via Galen Street, Centre Street, Washington Street, Park Street, Tremont Street, Washington Street, Cambridge Street, Brighton Avenue, Commonwealth Avenue, and Subway*
[cb] **Oak Square–Park Street Station**
70 **Watertown Carhouse–Central Square, Cambridge** *via Galen Street, Watertown Square, Arsenal Street, and Western Avenue*

The service frequency of Route 69 was discussed in Chapter 5. Route 70 was quite busy and had a similar frequency to Route 76. See Appendix 9 for additional details.

The Watertown–Park Street Station line was discussed in Chapter 5 because it is more closely associated with the Central Subway than with the other lines in this chapter, surviving long after they were abandoned.

Bennett Street Carhouse

Bennett Street Carhouse, located off Mt. Auburn Street near Harvard Square, had three large adjoining carbarns, a lobby building, a garage building housing overhead line department vehicles and equipment, and an adjacent caryard with two full loops and passing sidings used for storage. Running around the entire perimeter of the facility was yet another track loop with parallel passing sidings. This outer perimeter loop passed through the carhouse adjacent to University Road and had parallel storage tracks within it as well.

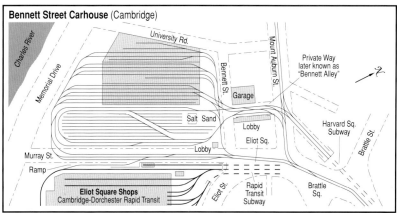

An aerial view of Bennett Street taken about 1947 shows the three carhouse buildings on the left, then moving right we see the car storage yard and the adjoining Eliot Square Rapid Transit Shops and yard *MTA*

An unusual track connection ran from the perimeter loop down a ramp to the Eliot Square Shops of the Cambridge–Dorchester rapid transit line. This track allowed the interchange of surface and rapid transit rail vehicles, primarily trash and work cars, and it had been used in earlier years for the delivery of the original Cambridge–Dorchester Rapid transit cars.[b]

Some of the yard tracks had been paved in 1936 and 1938 for use by the Lechmere and Huron Avenue trackless trolleys. Despite these changes, in 1940, this yard was still a very large streetcar facility. Some carhouse tracks were converted to trackless trolley lanes in 1942 and 1949.[168]

Bennett Street regularly housed many Type 5s and somewhat fewer Type 4 and center-entrance cars. The loop tracks allowed PCCs to use this yard, but in the 1940s, they were almost never seen here.[169]

Bennett Street Equipment Assignments

At the start of the 1940s, 99 streetcars including spares were stationed at Bennett Street and its satellites, North Cam-

---

[a] As previously mentioned, not all the Lake Street cars were stored at Bennett Street; some were stored at Lechmere and at Lake Street.

[b] These cars were towed from a railhead over surface car trackage to Bennett Street and the ramp.

While the Bennett Street Carhouse primarily maintained passenger streetcars, it also handled work cars, such as the snowplow in the center of this lineup. Center-entrance cars and a trailer are also stored in the yard, where we are looking north toward Mt. Auburn Street in this shot taken in May 1945.　　*Charles A. Duncan*

The main yards at Bennett Street Carhouse were adjacent to the Eliot Square Shops of the Cambridge–Dorchester rapid transit line, and we see a Differential dump car in the foreground climbing the ramp from the rapid transit yard to Bennett Street. To the left of the ramp are trackless trolleys in day storage for the Lechmere–Harvard and the Huron Avenue–Harvard lines and a large assortment of Type 4 and 5 cars, a few work cars, and, if we look closely enough, we can even see the roofline of a PCC, a rare visitor to Bennett Street. Left of the streetcars in this comprehensive view from about 1946 is the most easterly of the three carhouse buildings.　　*BERy*

bridge and Arlington Heights. The May 6, 1940, rating showed 10 Type 4s and 89 Type 5s, with 24 cars at Arlington Heights, 19 at North Cambridge, and the balance of 56 at Bennett Street itself.

At the end of the decade, the Bennett Street car total had risen to 140 including spares. According to the November 28, 1949, car requirement sheets, the roster consisted of 131 Type 5s and nine spare center-entrance cars. Of these 140 cars, 26 were stored at North Cambridge, 34 at Arlington Heights, and the remaining 80 cars at Bennett Street.

Appendix 6 details rolling stock assignments. Type 5 cars were mainly used on the Bennett Street routes. From 1939 to 1941, a few Type 4s were also used on the North Cambridge–Waverley route, including the Cushing Square cutback. From 1944 through 1950, a small number of Type 4s were also regularly assigned to the Arlington and Watertown lines. Type 4s, Type 5s, and center-entrance cars were all available as spares at varying times during the 1940s, and center-entrance cars were regularly scheduled on the Arlington Center–Harvard cutback in 1943.

PCC cars would eventually be used on the Arlington Heights–Watertown route, but not until the early 1950s. Track changes to handle PCCs, however, were begun at Arlington Heights and Bennett Street in mid-1950. Starting in mid-December, 1946, however, PCC cars were assigned to Watertown–Central Square during Sundays and non-rush hours on weekdays.

Type 5 cars were used on the Harvard Square–Massachusetts Station Line for the entire decade with one exception: the very end of service in the fall of 1949 in conjunction with the reconstruction of the Harvard Bridge. The Watertown–Central line was extended from the Green Street Loop in Central Square to a temporary crossover at Memorial Drive and Massachusetts Avenue. In this instance, the Type 4s normally assigned to Watertown–Central were used on this part of Massachusetts Avenue, a rare sight indeed.

Arlington, North Cambridge, Waverley, and Watertown

The lines to Arlington, North Cambridge, Waverley, and Watertown were all based at Bennett Street Carhouse near Harvard Square. As previously mentioned, the basic route structure was Arlington–Watertown and North Cambridge–Waverley, with other combinations operated at various times.

These lines shared track between North Cambridge Yard and a point near Belmont and Mt. Auburn Streets. Here the lines separated. Watertown cars followed Mt. Auburn Street; Waverley cars ran onto Belmont Street. Shortly after separating, but before Belmont Street, both lines crossed a wide bridge over the Watertown Branch of the B&M Railroad.

The Arlington Heights North Carhouse

At one time, two carhouses were located at Arlington Heights on either side of Massachusetts Avenue from one another. In 1940 part of the North Carhouse, the larger of the two, and an adjoining streetcar storage yard were still situated on the north side of the street. The North Carhouse remained in use until 1946, but later that year, the remainder of the building was demolished. This work was completed on November 11, 1946, and after the building was torn down, the tracks that were formerly inside simply became a part of the existing outdoor storage yard.

In 1940 the carhouse trackage included six stub-end storage tracks that ended in the north side of the building. Six parallel passing sidings ran through the south side of the carhouse and were connected to a partial loop at the rear of the building. The loop continued around the northerly end of

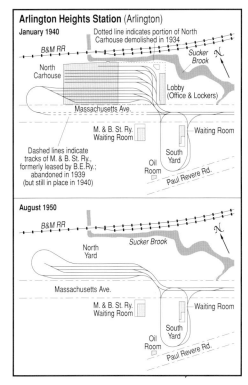

Arlington Heights Station (Arlington)

January 1940
Dotted line indicates portion of North Carhouse demolished in 1934

B&M RR

Sucker Brook

North Carhouse

Massachusetts Ave.

Lobby (Office & Lockers)

M. & B. St. Ry. Waiting Room

Waiting Room

South Yard

Dashed lines indicate tracks of M. & B. St. Ry., formerly leased by B.E.Ry.; abandoned in 1939 (but still in place in 1940)

Oil Room

Paul Revere Rd.

August 1950

B&M RR

Sucker Brook

North Yard

Massachusetts Ave.

M. & B. St. Ry. Waiting Room

Waiting Room

South Yard

Oil Room

Paul Revere Rd.

Viewed from the street, the front end of the North Carhouse at Arlington Heights shows a broad car shed completely filled with streetcars. Special work coming out of the yard connects with track on Massachusetts Avenue and the South Yard Loop. *Charles A. Duncan*

the yard and back onto Massachusetts Avenue. At this point the loop electrification ended, although the track was still connected to unused double tracks on Massachusetts Avenue. These tracks had been leased in earlier years from the Middlesex & Boston Street Railway (M&B), and in 1940 they were still connected to the loop and to the El's own Massachusetts Avenue tracks at the street entrance to the North Carhouse trackage.

The Boston Elevated made significant track changes at Arlington Heights in 1945. The former M&B trackage was disconnected at the main yard entrance from the Elevated's Massachusetts Avenue tracks between April 17 and April 30 as part of the reconstruction of the special work into the former South Carhouse loop and the leads to the North Carhouse. Also, about 2930 feet of unused yard track was removed between November 19 and November 30, 1945.

In anticipation of PCC car operation, in 1950, the loop was shifted north, completely off the street onto MTA property, and fully reconnected.[170]

The Arlington Heights South Yard Loop and Waiting Station

On the south side of Massachusetts Avenue, slightly east of the North Carhouse, was a yard with a loop around a waiting station. This was the site of the South Carhouse, torn down in 1932. A passing siding was located beside the waiting station lobby entrance for additional cars to lay over before starting their trips to Harvard Square. Streetcar passengers connected here with M&B buses to Lexington and beyond, as they had with M&B streetcars until 1924.

Type 4 No. 5331 has left the waiting station at Arlington Heights and is running south on Massachusetts Avenue for Harvard Square, despite the fact that the roll sign says otherwise. In the background, a Type 5 turns into the waiting station loop with the North Carhouse behind it.

Charles A. Duncan

This waiting station and operators' lobby was a remnant of the former South Carhouse at Arlington Heights. Type 5 No. 5800 is about to leave for Harvard Square on this lazy summer day, July 14, 1946. A Middlesex & Boston bus waits for riders on the opposite side of the building.

Norton D. Clark

79 Arlington Heights–Harvard Station

The Arlington Heights line and its cutback at Arlington Center ran entirely along the middle of broad Massachusetts Avenue in a generally southeasterly direction to Porter Square, Cambridge. From here the line ran due south all the way to Harvard Square. The cars crossed the Cambridge city line on the center of a bridge over Alewife Brook. Concrete pedestrian safety islands with flashing yellow traffic warning signals at stops on Massachusetts Avenue in Arlington Center, at Lake Street in East Arlington, and through most of Cambridge as far as Harvard Square, identified this line as a very busy route.

Service between Arlington Heights and Watertown was operated rush hours and midday, and covered a round-trip distance of 18.554 miles with an average running time of 87 minutes. Evening service between Arlington Heights and Waverley was even longer: 18.754 miles round-trip but the same running time of 87 minutes.

At Arlington Center, a passing siding west of Pleasant Street allowed inbound cars to bypass a section of the main line inbound rail. Arlington Center cars changing ends for the return trip to Harvard Square used this inbound rail segment, reaching it via a facing point crossover from the outbound rail.

Cars ran between Arlington Center and Bennett Street during the rush hours and midday, covering a round-trip distance of 8.036 miles and taking 42 minutes to complete. Evening service between Arlington Center and Watertown was 15.029 miles round-trip and with an average running time of 73 minutes.

Track work in 1941 forced a southbound Type 5 (top) for Watertown to use the northbound track just south of Park Avenue on busy Massachusetts Avenue in Arlington Heights. Compressed air to drive the jackhammers that broke up the paving blocks between the rails came from one of the system's four compressor cars, Type 2 No. 5071, seen at top left and above. These cars had a powerful air compressor mounted in the carbody that vibrated so strongly that the carbody noticeably shook when the compressor was in use. *Top, MTA; above, Charles A. Duncan*

This circa 1948 overview of Arlington Center from the Central Fire Station shows a Type 4 in the distance heading north to Arlington Heights, an ACF bus turning onto Medford Street for a trip to Lechmere, and a Ford bus waiting at the monument before leaving for Clarendon Hill Carhouse. *MTA*

At Arlington Center, a passing siding allowed cars heading for Harvard Square from Arlington Heights to bypass the Arlington Center cars laying over on the southbound main line. At left, northbound Type 4 No. 5364 has passed a Type 5 changing ends. At right, in February 1944, center-entrance extra 6007 has changed ends on the main line and will soon depart for Harvard Square. The red stone building behind the car is the Old Town Hall.

Both, Charles A. Duncan

The streetcars crossed the Lexington Branch of the B&M Railroad at grade in Arlington Center. This railroad line offered direct service from North Station to Bedford, with stations in Arlington at Lake Street, Arlington Center, Brattle Street, and Arlington Heights. The railroad roughly paralleled the car line, but ran on a comparatively limited schedule.

North Cambridge Yard

A little more than a third of a mile after entering Cambridge, inbound cars from Arlington crossed the Hill Crossing Freight Cutoff of the B&M Railroad at grade, then almost immediately crossed the yard lead switches from the North Cambridge caryard. The amount of special work at the entrance to the caryard was substantial. Arlington cars ran over the switches frequently and rapidly, producing a lot of noise as this author can attest.

North Cambridge Yard adjoined the site of a former carhouse, which had been torn down in 1937. The back of the yard abutted the right-of-way of the Hill Crossing Freight Cutoff. The yard trackage consisted of a loop with a passing siding and four stub-end storage tracks off to the east side, and six stub-end tracks in the center of the loop itself.

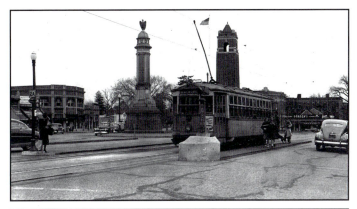

The passenger safety island in Arlington Center (top) was one of two in the town, the other being at Lake Street opposite the Capitol Theatre in East Arlington (above). At top, a Type 5 boards passengers for Harvard Square about 1949, while at bottom, rail grinder 724 performs its duty in 1950. *Top, MTA; above, Clarke Collection*

Type 4 No. 5300 has just crossed the B&M Railroad in North Cambridge on its way to Arlington. Note the trolley guard over the railroad crossing to protect against dewirements in this vulnerable location.

Charles A. Duncan

Type 5s dominate this view of North Cambridge Yard in October 1942. Differing paint schemes ranging from faded to fresh were common during the war years.   *Charles A. Duncan*

82 North Cambridge–Harvard Station

The Arlington Heights–Harvard and North Cambridge–Harvard lines shared the track on Massachusetts Avenue from North Cambridge Yard to the Harvard Square trolley subway station. Cars leaving North Cambridge Yard ran to Waverley throughout the 1940s, but starting in 1948, they also began running to Watertown on selected trips. After leaving Porter Square, inbound cars for Harvard Square crossed a bridge over the Fitchburg Division of the B&M Railroad and ran south down Massachusetts Avenue to Harvard Square. Between North Cambridge and Harvard, a round-trip was 4.422 miles and required 24 minutes to complete, and between North Cambridge and Waverley, the through route mentioned above, the round-trip distance was 11.597 miles and took 55 minutes. Service between North Cambridge and the Common Street cutback was 9.642 miles round-trip and had an average running time of 46 minutes.

The Porter-Square–Sullivan Square Service Track

A double-track service line on Somerville Avenue joined the Massachusetts Avenue tracks at Porter Square. The service line followed Somerville Avenue to Union Square, Somerville, then left Somerville Avenue, and followed Washington Street to Sullivan Square. Work cars going to and from the Charlestown Yards near Sullivan Square and passenger streetcars headed to the Everett Shops for repair or scrapping used the service track.

Near Porter Square, on the Cambridge side of the boundary line with Somerville, there were two crossovers between the service tracks. Lines that had ended here in earlier years had used this special work. On the Somerville side of the boundary there was another crossover. A long passing siding around the crossover in Somerville ran inbound from the Cambridge line to Mossland Street and Somerville Avenue.[171] In 1949, the MTA abandoned 7757 feet of the inbound service track from Porter Square to Union Square, leaving only the outbound track in use.

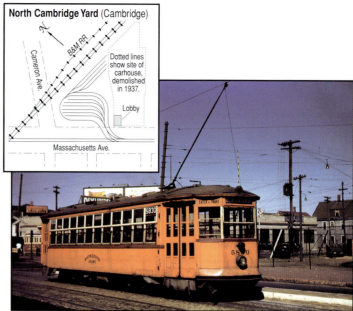

The end of the limited zone for northbound cars from Harvard Square was this traffic island stop right beside the North Cambridge Yard. At this point, passengers could freely get off the cars. No. 5830 is heading toward Arlington in this October 1942 scene.

Charles A. Duncan

Here we are looking north on Somerville Avenue at Porter Square along the service track connection that joins the regular revenue track on Massachusetts Avenue. The Type 4 is headed toward North Cambridge near the local Masonic Hall in this August 1944 photograph.   *Charles A. Duncan*

Service cars often used service tracks. Surprise! Here Type 3 sand car 5140 heads south on Somerville Avenue from Massachusetts Avenue for Union Square in 1944.   *Charles A. Duncan*

The Harvard Square Trolley Subway and Surface Bypass

The trackage in Harvard Square, both on the surface and in the trolley subway was complex. Map 6, Inset B used in conjunction with the diagram below will help clarify the description that follows.

On reaching Harvard Square, streetcars from Arlington and North Cambridge, Watertown and Waverley avoided traffic congestion by running through a special subway tunnel and underground trolley station. Riders enjoyed a direct connection to the Cambridge Subway through ramped underground foot passageways that connected the streetcar and rapid transit platforms.

Southbound streetcars from Arlington and North Cambridge and trackless trolleys from Huron Avenue veered left off Massachusetts Avenue beside Cambridge Common, descended a paved ramp to the north portal, and entered the two-bore Harvard Square Trolley Subway. Southbound cars deposited their riders at the start of a long platform on the left side of the track and then moved forward to a second set of berths where riders for Watertown or Waverley boarded. Streetcars and trackless trolleys used their left-hand doors in the southbound tunnel because of the unusual platform boarding and alighting arrangement.

For northbound cars the station platform was on the right, and right-hand doors were used. Watertown and Waverley cars dropped their passengers off, then moved ahead to a loading zone further along the platform for Arlington and North Cambridge riders. Huron Avenue trackless trolley passengers also had a berth at this platform.

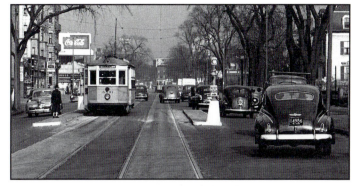

Type 5 No. 5801 stops in the spring of 1946 for a passenger pickup at the traffic safety island just south of Shepherd Street on Massachusetts Avenue in Cambridge. These safety islands extended from Harvard Square all the way to the Arlington town line and were also located at two major stops in Arlington. *MTA*

Rail grinder 724 heads north on Massachusetts Avenue behind another single-trucker in the same direction. A Type 5 emerges from the North Portal of the Harvard Square Subway, about to round the corner and change ends. *Charles A. Duncan*

It's February 15, 1948, and 5913 passes the Harvard campus as it makes its way to the trolley station under Harvard Square. *Foster M. Palmer*

Type 4 No. 5360 has left the northerly portal of the Harvard Square Trolley Tunnel and is on its way to Arlington Heights. This scene was taken about 1950. *Foster M. Palmer*

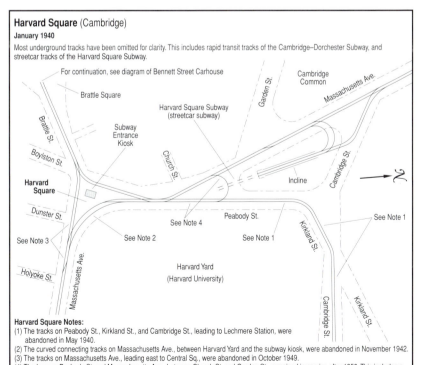

Harvard Square (Cambridge)

January 1940

Most underground tracks have been omitted for clarity. This includes rapid transit tracks of the Cambridge–Dorchester Subway, and streetcar tracks of the Harvard Square Subway.

For continuation, see diagram of Bennett Street Carhouse

Brattle Square

Cambridge Common

Garden St.

Massachusetts Ave.

Harvard Square Subway (streetcar subway)

Subway Entrance Kiosk

Church St.

Brattle St.

Boylston St.

Harvard Square

Dunster St.

See Note 4

Peabody St.

Incline

Cambridge St.

See Note 1

See Note 3

See Note 2

See Note 1

Kirkland St.

Massachusetts Ave.

Holyoke St.

Harvard Yard (Harvard University)

Cambridge St.

Kirkland St.

Harvard Square Notes:

(1) The tracks on Peabody St., Kirkland St., and Cambridge St., leading to Lechmere Station, were abandoned in May 1940.
(2) The curved connecting tracks on Massachusetts Ave., between Harvard Yard and the subway kiosk, were abandoned in November 1942.
(3) The tracks on Massachusetts Ave., leading east to Central Sq., were abandoned in October 1949.
(4) The loop on Peabody St. and Massachusetts Ave., between Church St. and Garden St., remained in service after 1950. This includes a short segment of the northbound track on Peabody St.

The tunnels in the Harvard Square Trolley Subway did not run horizontally parallel. The northbound tunnel, in fact, ran above the passenger platform of the southbound tunnel for a considerable distance.

In 1938, when Huron Avenue trackless trolleys began running through the subway, paving was installed around the rails, and the cars and trolley buses shared the positive overhead wire as well as the roadway. This installation was one of the few instances on the Boston system in which streetcars and trolley coaches shared the same wire, a practice usually frowned upon but required here because of the unusually tight space.

Cars leaving Harvard Square for Arlington Heights usually carried the **LIMITED** designation in red letters underneath the destination ARLINGTON HEIGHTS in white letters. "Limited" meant that while passengers bound for points beyond North Cambridge would be picked up, no one would be allowed to leave before North Cambridge. This measure speeded up service on this busy line. Local riders were carried on the North Cambridge cars.

A double-track street bypass of the trolley subway ran through Harvard Square. This track was kept for emergencies, for cutbacks to Bennett Street Carhouse, and for Owl Cars running to the surface level of Harvard Square from Arlington Heights. The bypass tracks followed Massachusetts Avenue onto Brattle Street and ran through Brattle Square before entering Bennett Street Carhouse at Mt. Auburn Street. These tracks connected on Massachusetts Avenue in Harvard Square with the Massachusetts Station–Harvard line, which will be discussed later.[c] The bypass tracks also connected with the service tracks on Cambridge Street, which were used until 1940 for Lake Street cars pulling in and out of Bennett Street Carhouse.

There was a trailing point crossover alongside the north portal on Massachusetts Avenue on the bypass tracks, which allowed cars coming through the subway from Watertown, Waverley, or Bennett Street Carhouse to reverse direction. Cars left the subway and turned 180 degrees south onto Massachusetts Avenue toward Harvard Square. The cars ran just beyond the crossover, changed ends, took the crossover, and ran back into the subway to board passengers or return to the carhouse empty. There was also a single-track loop on Peabody Street, adjacent to Harvard Yard, that allowed cars to go north through Harvard Square, reverse direction, and return on the inbound Massachusetts Avenue surface bypass track.

The south portal of the Harvard Square Subway was on Mt. Auburn Street, opposite the entrance to Bennett Street Carhouse. On leaving the subway, Bennett Street Carhouse-

[c] A double-track connection that allowed cars from Massachusetts Station arriving at Harvard to turn right onto Massachusetts Avenue toward North Cambridge and for movements in the opposite direction was in place until November of 1942. Its use had long since ended, and the Elevated wrote this track off its books by formally abandoning it in November 1942. This track ran beside the famous Harvard Square subway kiosk and had a crossover between the rails.

A three-car train of center-entrance cars makes its way down the incline to the Harvard Square Trolley Subway. Trains like this were stored at Bennett Street for use on the Lake Street–Lechmere line, and they deadheaded over Cambridge Street and through Harvard Square to get between these two points. This train has apparently come from North Cambridge, very likely having made the uncommon route over Somerville Avenue from Lechmere and then over the service track to Porter Square before changing ends to get to this point.
Charles A. Duncan

Center-entrance cars 6122 and 6162 enter Cambridge Street from Kirkland Street just north of Harvard Square for a non-revenue move to Lechmere. The line was retained for such moves after its conversion to trackless trolley operation on April 11, 1936.
Charles A. Duncan

Type 4 No. 5336 will soon change ends at the trailing point crossover just outside the Harvard Square trolley tunnel on May 31, 1949.
Charles A. Duncan

Type 5 No. 5816 hauls Type 4 No. 5296 through Brattle Square, adjacent to Harvard Square, on February 12, 1948. Type 4s like this one were worn out after the rigorous extension of their normal service lives forced by World War II, and this classic Boston streetcar type would only be around a few more years and in diminishing numbers.   *Foster M. Palmer*

Compressor car No. 40, a former passenger trolley from a much earlier time, is smack-dab in the middle of Harvard Square on April 18, 1950, supporting an on-going track job..   *Foster M. Palmer*

Type 5 No. 5933 is waiting to enter the Harvard Square subway on September 24, 1948, having changed ends at the crossover on Massachusetts Avenue.   *Foster M. Palmer*

bound cars ran up another paved ramp, crossed Mt. Auburn Street, and followed a paved private way past the Bennett Street Carhouse lobby building to the caryard.[d] Waverley and Watertown cars turned west at the top of the ramp onto Mt. Auburn Street.

71 Watertown Carhouse–Harvard Station

Watertown and Waverley cars traveled west from Harvard Square on Mt. Auburn Street. Enroute they ran through a short private reservation that passed through a traffic circle at Fresh Pond Parkway. Opposite Mount Auburn Cemetery, there was a long passing siding around a section of the westbound rail.[e] A trailing point crossover was located before the east end of the siding. This arrangement, functionally similar to that in Arlington Center and other parts of the system, was used by cemetery cutbacks.

Watertown-bound cars crossed into Watertown at the junction of Mt. Auburn and Belmont Streets. The cars followed Mt. Auburn Street generally southwest all the way to Watertown Square. Just before entering the square, the cars crossed the Watertown Branch of the B&M Railroad again, but in this instance over an unusual single-track grade crossing. Here the westbound rail to Watertown switched onto the eastbound

The southerly portal of the Harvard Square subway was always a busy place. Huron Avenue trackless trolleys and Watertown and Waverley streetcars regularly ran under the decorative arch to and from the subway. Constant pull-ins to Bennett Street Carhouse via Bennett Alley, from which this picture of center-entrance car 6232 was taken on March 22, 1946, added to the traffic.
Charles A. Duncan

Stately Type 4 No. 5364 heads east on Mt. Auburn Street beside the cemetary bound for Harvard Square in September 1945.
Charles A. Duncan

---

[d] This private way is used today by buses and trackless trolleys and has been dubbed "Bennett Alley" by the MBTA.

[e] On the north side of Mt. Auburn Street, also opposite the cemetery, stood one of the earliest carbarns in the Boston area. Originally built to serve horsecars in 1861, the Mount Auburn carhouse had been converted into a Big Bear Market in 1935. The building still stands, although greatly altered, as a Star Market in 2002.

It is Memorial Day, May 30, 1949, and Type 5 No. 5826 has changed ends on the passing siding on Mt. Auburn Street at Mount Auburn Cemetary. Type 4 No. 5313 is outbound to Watertown, passing the Big Bear supermarket, a local fixture for many years and formerly Mount Auburn Carhouse. The building stands today as Star Market.

Charles A. Duncan

Two trains of 6000-series center-entrance cars, a Type 4, and a Type 5 make up this busy scene on the bridge over the Charles River at Watertown Square. It is July 4, 1942, and the Boston El was undoubtedly inundated with heavy traffic. *Charles A. Duncan*

The Mt. Auburn Street trolley line was single-track over the B&M Railroad crossing at Watertown Square until 1949. Here, in September 1947, car 5845 heads across the railroad tracks for Watertown Square. *Robert A. Kennerly*

rail just east of the crossing. The actual crossing of the railroad then took place on the eastbound rail in both directions of travel. On the westerly side of the crossing, a switch ran back to the westbound rail and the cars resumed double-track operation.

In 1942, the Boston Elevated Maintenance Department began rebuilding this crossing, from Taylor Street, on the east side of the B&M Railroad, through the switch west of the crossing, including the crossing special work.[172] Later, in 1949, the MTA Maintenance Department double tracked the streetcar crossing by removing the switches and directly connecting the westbound main line from Taylor Street to a point on the westbound track approximately 120 feet west of the crossing.[173]

In Watertown Square, streetcars stopped at a special platform. Riders could transfer here to the Arsenal Street car line or to buses of the Middlesex & Boston Street Railway or the Lovell Bus Company. The Watertown–Harvard cars then crossed a stone arch bridge over the Charles River and turned east into Watertown Carhouse.

73 Waverley–Harvard Station

Continuing past Mt. Auburn Cemetery, Waverley cars ran to the right onto Belmont Street and crossed the Belmont boundary line near Bird Street.[f] The line followed Belmont Street northwest and bore right onto Trapelo Road, again in a generally northwesterly direction.

Shortly after entering Trapelo Road, Waverley–bound cars came to a set of crossovers that were used for rush hour cutbacks and located between Willow and Common Streets near Cushing Square. In 1944 the Boston Elevated Maintenance Department removed the facing point crossover just west of Willow Street.[174]

The line continued on Trapelo Road to Waverley, an important section of Belmont. Here there was another set of crossovers for cars to change ends, just short of the Fitchburg Division tracks of the B&M Railroad.[g]

---

[f] Bird Street is now known as Sullivan Road.

[g] During the 1940s, the B&M Railroad tracks crossed Trapelo Road at grade. The railroad tracks were depressed in 1952 in a grade separation project, and two years later, the MTA extended the Waverley line over a new loop that bridged this depression.

Two Type 5s on Belmont Street make their way outbound toward Waverley in April 1950.   *Clarke Collection*

Boston Elevated Railway cars never crossed the B&M Railroad grade crossing at Waverley. They would cross the railroad in later years, but on a loop built in 1954 over the railroad when it was depressed in a cut. Here a Type 5 has just changed ends while a smoky freight train rumbles over the crossing behind it.

Clarke Collection

Late afternoon shadows fall across the front of car 5827, which has just changed ends at the end of the Waverley line in 1949 to return to Harvard Square.   *O.R. Cummings*

76 Harvard Square–Massachusetts Station

The Harvard–Massachusetts Station line is shown in Map 6, Inset A. The line began at Bennett Street Carhouse, running over Mt. Auburn Street, Brattle Square, and Brattle Street to Harvard Square. Cars continued from Harvard Square southeast along Massachusetts Avenue, past Harvard University and through Central Square.

At Central Square, tracks on Western Avenue coming in from Watertown joined the Harvard–Massachusetts Station line. Harvard–Massachusetts Station cars crossed switches at Pearl Street and Brookline Street, which were parts of the Green Street Loop used by the cars from Watertown. Further on, just before MIT, the line crossed the four-track Grand Junction Branch of the B&A Railroad.

The cars then followed Massachusetts Avenue past MIT and across the Harvard Bridge over the Charles River. Cars entered the Back Bay at the Cambridge-Boston line in the middle of the draw span over the river, and continued on Massachusetts Avenue, crossing a bridge over the B&A Railroad main line before arriving at Boylston Street.

Turning northeast onto Boylston Street, the line turned again, immediately northwest into the easterly loop track at Massachusetts Station. The return trip to Harvard began by turning southwest onto Newbury Street, then immediately northwest onto Massachusetts Avenue. Connections were made at Massachusetts Station to the Boylston Street Subway, cars for Dudley Street Station, and buses to Queensberry Street and Bowdoin Square. The round-trip distance between Bennett Street and Massachusetts Station was 5.545 miles and had a running time of 36 minutes.

It was possible for cars to go straight through to Harvard Square or Dudley Street Station using Massachusetts Avenue on the block between Newbury and Boylston Streets. The Harvard–Dudley Owl Cars regularly used this track.[h]

The Harvard–Massachusetts Station line was very busy. Like the track through North Cambridge, Harvard–Massachusetts Station had concrete pedestrian safety islands at a number of important car stops.

The Harvard–Massachusetts Station line and its companion, Dudley–Massachusetts Station, were among the last surface lines to run close to downtown Boston. Both lines were subject to traffic delays. However, both lines were also heavy rush hour routes, so management decided to continue using streetcars, but to limit them to peak traffic periods. The tradeoff was a higher operating cost but greater passenger carrying capacity. In maintaining the schedule, buses and streetcars fared the same in heavy street traffic. Streetcars, however, could handle far more riders.

---

[h] The northbound track on Massachusetts Avenue between Boylston and Newbury streets and the connecting special work at these two cross streets was removed in 1949. The Dudley Street Station–Harvard Square Owl Cars had last used this rail, but the end of the Harvard–Massachusetts Station line in 1949 made it redundant. Removal began on October 24, 1949, and the work was finished November 24. Also at this time, the inner, or westerly loop track at Massachusetts Station was disconnected at Boylston Street and at Newbury Street, leaving only the outer loop in operation for the Dudley cars. Finally, the Boylston Street entrance to Massachusetts Station was changed to one opening centered in the existing station span, from the two openings that had been there. This wider opening was created to accommodate the wide turning radius of the soon-to-arrive trackless trolleys for the Harvard–Massachusetts Station line.

Cars for Massachusetts Station were usually lined up on the two tracks at Bennett Street adjacent to the Eliot Square rapid transit shops. The entrance to the ramp to Eliot Square can be seen between the second and third Type 5s in this lineup.

Charles A. Duncan

By the 1940s, the only regular streetcar service through Harvard Square was on the Massachusetts Station line. This view, taken in December 1939, shows a Type 5 on its way to Bennett Street Carhouse. To the right is the famous subway kiosk and behind it the signature Harvard Coop building still prominent in Harvard Square.

Charles A. Duncan

Taken in Harvard Square, this December 1939 view is looking toward Central Square, Cambridge, and Massachusetts Station, the destination of the car.

Charles A. Duncan

MTA 5529 passes Lamont Library as it enters Harvard Square on May 25, 1949.

Foster M. Palmer

A rider boards Massachusetts Station car 5881 at Massachusetts Avenue and Hancock Street on July 10, 1949.

Charles A. Duncan

Car tracks run prominently through this mid-1940s view of Central Square, Cambridge. To the right is the tower of Cambridge City Hall. The bus is stopped on Massachusetts Avenue just outside the Post Office.

Clarke Collection

Track jobs were a necessary fact of life wherever streetcars ran. Here we see a crew busy between a Type 2 compressor car and No. 40, a former 25-foot box passenger car, in May 1946 east of Central Square near Vassar Street.

Charles A. Duncan

Type 5 No. 5928 passes the New England Confectionary Company factory on Massachusetts Avenue at Albany Street on July 10, 1949.

Charles A. Duncan

A lone Type 5 crosses the Harvard Bridge from Cambridge into the Back Bay section of Boston on its way to Massachusetts Station. The 1949 reconstruction of this bridge ended streetcar service on this line.
Robert A. Kennerly

In the late 1930s, an underpass was built for Commonwealth Avenue traffic below the intersection with Massachusetts Avenue. Here we see it in action on February 16, 1938, with a Type 5 about to cross on its way to Massachusetts Station.
BERy

Car 5826 from Harvard Square is on Newbury Street, the last leg to Massachusetts Station, approaching the westerly loop track and a passenger exchange between inbound and outbound riders.
Charles A. Duncan

The date on the Boylston Street entrance to Massachusetts Station leaves nothing to the imagination as to when the station opened. The crowd inside will soon transfer to the subway or to connecting surface lines.
Charles A. Duncan

Starting on September 9, 1939, Harvard–Massachusetts Station became a weekday rush-hour-only streetcar line. Cars were assigned from the early morning start of service until 9 a.m. and from 3:45 p.m. to 6:52 p.m. During midday hours and evenings, streetcars ran between Green Street Loop and Massachusetts Station. On Saturdays, trolleys were used until 9 a.m. only.

During midday hours and after 7 p.m., buses were operated from Harvard Square to Lafayette Square, at Main Street and Massachusetts Avenue. On November 18, 1939, these buses were extended to MIT to supplement the Massachusetts Station–Green Street Loop streetcar service.

On February 10, 1940, the midday buses from Harvard Square to MIT were discontinued and through bus service from Harvard Square to Massachusetts Station was run during all but rush hours. The car service between Green Street Loop and Massachusetts Station was discontinued. Finally, on September 14, 1940, on Saturdays, Sundays, and holidays, the Boston Elevated began operating the line with buses the entire day.

In March 1942, in compliance with ODT directives to conserve rubber and gasoline for the war effort, the Boston Elevated made plans to discontinue all bus operation on this

Type 5 No. 5826 has left Massachusetts Station and is turning from Boylston Street onto Massachusetts Avenue for Harvard Square.
Charles A. Duncan

line. This change took place on May 2, 1942, and streetcars were restored to full-time operation. After the war, on March 30, 1946, the streetcar and bus combination service resumed.

On June 23, 1947, short turn service began between Harvard Square and a crossover located just beyond Vassar Street near the Armory beside the MIT campus. Three trips were usually run in the late afternoon. The round trip distance was 3.550 miles and the average running time was 24 minutes.

On September 12, 1949, the Harvard Bridge was closed to traffic for reconstruction. Type 4 cars from the Watertown–Central Square line were extended from Central Square to this crossover, and all service from Harvard Square came to an end. Car 5315 has changed ends and is facing wrong direction on the eastbound track near Memorial Drive in this view taken in the fall of 1949. The crossover is ahead of the car, and the Type 4 will use it to return to Central Square before heading for Watertown.

Leon Onofri

On September 12, 1949, the Harvard Bridge was closed for reconstruction and resurfacing, and the removal of its draw structure. The bridge closing permanently ended Harvard–Massachusetts Station and Harvard–Armory streetcar service.

The MTA decided to continue running streetcars to MIT for a brief period. For one week, until September 19, streetcars ran from Harvard Square to a temporary crossover at Massachusetts Avenue and Memorial Drive. After this date, the Watertown–Central Square car line was extended to the Memorial Drive crossover, continuing until November 19, 1949.

A shuttle bus began service on September 13, 1949, between Harvard and Lafayette Squares. It supplemented the temporary car service from Harvard Square, and later Watertown, to MIT. On the same day, a new Owl Bus route between Harvard and Scollay Squares via Massachusetts Avenue, Vassar, and Main Streets temporarily replaced the Harvard–Dudley Owl Bus in the section between Harvard and Massachusetts Station.

On September 16, 1949, the MTA Maintenance Department began removing the tracks from the Harvard Bridge. Between October 7 and November 4, 1949, the MTA tore out the special work at Harvard Square connecting Brattle Street to Massachusetts Avenue. At this time, the special work was also removed at Western Avenue in Central Square, connecting the Massachusetts Avenue track from Harvard to the track that still ran to MIT. Shortly thereafter, the city of Cambridge paved over the unused car tracks between Harvard and Central.

The Harvard Bridge reopened on November 11, 1949, and buses resumed the Harvard–Massachusetts Station route soon thereafter. The Harvard–Dudley Owl Bus was also reinstated at this time. The MTA also added a rush hour bus line between Quincy Square and Vassar Street as well. On April 22, 1950, trackless trolleys replaced all the regular buses and supplementary bus service on the Harvard–Massachusetts Station line.

Watertown Carhouse

Cars for Arlington, Central Square, Cambridge, and Park Street Station were all dispatched from Watertown. This large yard and carhouse complex was located off Galen Street beside the Charles River, across the bridge from Watertown Square.

There was a long, rambling carbarn on the river side of the property, with an adjoining car storage yard. The yard had two concentric loop tracks, one of which passed through the carhouse itself, and a number of stub-end storage tracks, mainly inside the loops. There were also four stub-end sidings near the entrance to the yard on Galen Street, and one stub-end siding in front of the carhouse on the river side of the property. An operators' lobby and a small passenger waiting station were located near the entrance from Galen Street.

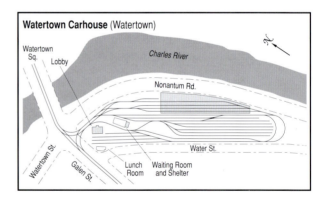

Watertown Carhouse housed a wide variety of equipment in this scene taken at the rear of the facility on March 23, 1941. PCC 3016 in the middle between Type 4 No. 5362 and center-entrance car 6019 is brand-new and probably the reason for the shot.

Charles A. Duncan

Before the Boston El's first PCCs were assigned to the Watertown–Park Street Station line, Type 4 cars mainly served this route. Three of them are on display in the afternoon sun in this 1941 photo.
Winthrop Greene, BSRA Collection

Factory fresh, PCC 3016 basks outside the entrance to the Watertown Carhouse in 1941. *Winthrop Greene, BSRA Collection*

Watertown Equipment Assignments

In 1940 this facility was assigned 76 streetcars including spares. The May 6, 1940 rating showed 45 Type 4s, 16 Type 5s, and 15 center-entrance cars. By the end of the decade, the number of cars stationed here had increased to 90 including spares. The November 28, 1949 rating showed 39 Type 4s and 51 PCCs.

Cars for Harvard Square and Arlington were normally based at Bennett Street, but a few Type 5s were stored at Watertown for Harvard Square and Arlington service from 1940 to 1944. From 1944 to 1950, a small number of Type 4s were used in this service, and again, they were stored at Watertown.

Watertown–Park Street cars were also based at Watertown. This assignment has been previously discussed in Chapter 5 and summarized in Appendices 5 and 6.

Type 4 cars were always assigned to Watertown–Central Square in the 1940s, but Type 5s joined them at various times between 1941 and 1944. As previously mentioned, in 1949, the line was extended to MIT, ending at a temporary crossover at Memorial Drive and Massachusetts Avenue. At this time, the lumbering Type 4s made a rare appearance on this section of Massachusetts Avenue.

In December 1946, the Elevated's management decided to operate PCC cars between Watertown and Central Squares on Sundays and during non-rush hours on weekdays. Doing so depended on the availability of PCC cars, and they were used sporadically. The February 1947 Boston Chapter NRHS newsletter, *The Turnout*, mentioned that the Elevated was also running PCC cars between Watertown and Central in the evening hours.[175]

70 Watertown–Central

The Watertown–Central line started at Watertown Carhouse and crossed the Charles River into Watertown Square. The line turned east onto Arsenal Street, and midway it crossed two freight spurs of the B&M Railroad.[i] Continuing on Arsenal Street, the line made a second crossing of the Charles River, but this time into the Brighton District of Boston. Immediately after this river crossing, the line ran through a short private right-of-way located in the center of the traffic circle at Soldiers Field Road and Western Avenue.

The line continued along Western Avenue and made a third crossing of the Charles, on this occasion into Cambridge, before continuing to Central Square. Here Watertown–Central joined the Harvard–Massachusetts Station line, turning to the right onto Massachusetts Avenue and then right again onto single track on Pearl Street. The cars then turned left onto Green Street, the layover point of the line. Leaving Green Street, the cars turned left onto Brookline Street and finally left onto Massachusetts Avenue for the return trip to Watertown, traversing entirely on single track what was then known as the Green Street Loop.[j] Route 70 had a round-trip distance of 9.141 miles. The average running time was 38 minutes.

From 1945, and possibly earlier, to the end of service in 1950 the line was short-turned at a crossover on Western Avenue at Green Street, just outside Central Square.[k] Cutbacks took place between 3:30 p.m. and 6 p.m. weekdays, and on

---

[i] These spurs served the Vose Piano Company and the Watertown Arsenal. The Elevated also installed a third steam railroad spur into the Watertown Arsenal west of School Street in 1944 using materials supplied by the U.S. Government. A double track streetcar grade crossing for the Arsenal Street cars over this last spur was included in the installation work.

[j] Both the Pearl and Brookline Street trackage had extended further southwest toward the Charles River in earlier years, joining tracks on Putnam Avenue that had run from River Street as far as Brookline Street. The Brookline Street tracks changed from single to double iron at Putnam Avenue and continued to the Charles River. The line then crossed the river over the Essex Street Bridge (later replaced by the Cottage Farm Bridge) and followed Essex Street in Boston until it joined the Commonwealth Avenue tracks in Boston.

[k] The cutback was not in effect during the period that the Watertown–Central line was extended to the Memorial Drive crossover at MIT.

Western Avenue in June 1950 was relatively undeveloped compared to the Brighton Mills shopping center near this location today. The radio tower behind the car to the left remains to this day. Later that month, the line would be converted to bus operation and later that year, from buses to trackless trolleys.
Foster M. Palmer

Saturdays between 11 a.m. and 9 p.m., and kept the Watertown cars off Massachusetts Avenue during the busy hours of the day. On April 7, 1947, some morning rush hour trips were extended on Massachusetts Avenue to the crossover at Vassar Street near the Armory. This service ran only during one rating, ending on June 20, 1947. As previously mentioned, cutbacks from Harvard Square also used this crossover. The mileage and running times of these cutbacks is given in Appendix 9.

The extension of this line in 1949 to the crossover at Massachusetts Avenue and Memorial drive has been previously discussed. The round-trip distance of the short-lived route to Memorial Drive was 10.263 miles, and the running time was 45 minutes.

Route 70 crossed the Charles River three times between Watertown and Central. Type 4 No. 5337 and a sister car cross from Brighton into Watertown in this scene near the end of service on June 16, 1950.
Foster M. Palmer

PCCs were often used in off-hours on the Watertown–Central line. This is a fan trip, however, and 3211 does the honors in the traffic circle at Soldiers Field Road, Market Street, and Western Avenue in Brighton.
Clarke Collection

Type 4 No. 5313 turns from Green Street onto Brookline Street at Central Square, Cambridge, in June 1944. It will soon be on its way back to Watertown.
Charles A. Duncan

Type 4 No. 5301 unloads at a traffic island on Massachusetts Avenue in Central Square, Cambridge, before turning onto Pearl Street and entering the Green Street Loop. This view was taken on June 16, 1950. *Foster M. Palmer*

PCC 3123 turns onto Western Avenue from Massachusetts Avenue in the heart of Central Square on its way back to Watertown on May 29, 1949. *Foster M. Palmer*

Watertown–Central barely made it through the 1940s as a streetcar operation. It was converted to buses on June 17, 1950. Later, on October 28, 1950, the buses gave way to trackless trolleys.

All-electric PCC 3211 takes a break on the Green Street loop during a fan trip as patrons scramble to capture one-of-a-kind photos such as this one. *Clarke Collection*

– 131 –

Those crazy railfans are at it again! Seriously, though, despite the improbable destination sign this is one of the few good pictures of the streetcar tracks in use on Cross Street, Somerville. Streetcars on the Davis Square–Sullivan Square Station line used this track until 1939. By July 13, 1941, when this picture was taken during a Boston Chapter NRHS fan trip, the iron on Cross Street had been relegated to a service track. Car 4373 has just crossed the bridge over the B&M Railroad in this extraordinary view. *Charles A. Duncan*

Chapter 7

Lines North of Boston

The Charlestown District of Boston, the cities of Everett, Medford, and Somerville, and the town of Stoneham comprise the area covered in this chapter. By 1940 the streetcar routes in this area were almost completely gone. The Fellsway line to Elm Street, Medford, in fact, was the only active revenue trolley line in 1950, but an interesting variety of non-revenue trackage remained active elsewhere in this area for work cars and equipment transfers.

Charlestown was annexed to Boston in 1874 and is home to the Bunker Hill Monument, the Charlestown Navy Yard, and USS *Constitution*.[176] In the 1940s, Charlestown was connected to Boston Proper by two bridges—the Charlestown Bridge and the Warren Bridge. The district was densely populated and was served by two streetcar lines to downtown Boston and three more from Somerville and Medford, all ending at Sullivan Square Station. The Main Line Elevated stopped at City Square, Thompson Square, and Sullivan Square Stations, all in Charlestown. Charlestown was known for light manufacturing, and for the B&M Railroad terminal facilities at Mystic and Hoosac Piers. The main engine servicing complex and freight yards of the railroad were located nearby, straddling the Charlestown-Somerville boundary.

The city of Everett lies across the Mystic River northeast of Charlestown. Everett was a busy manufacturing center. The city was densely populated, and the housing stock was largely multi-family.

By 1940, the only streetcars in revenue operation in Everett were the Owl Cars between Sullivan Square and Everett Station. Everett Shops, the principal repair facility of the Boston Elevated Railway, was located on Broadway. Service tracks also ran from Charlestown to Everett Shops and from there to Chelsea. The B&M Railroad Eastern Route and the B&M Saugus Branch both had stations in Everett. The B&A Railroad Grand Junction Branch shared the right-of-way with the B&M Eastern route, running freight on parallel track through Everett to Chelsea and to the East Boston docks.

Somerville, adjoining Charlestown on the northwest, had a strong industrial base, the largest part of which was a Ford Motor Company assembly plant. The housing stock was primarily multi-family, but there were many older single-family homes as well. The B&M Railroad New Hampshire Division furnished limited commuter service. Five streetcar lines, three operating from Clarendon Hill in Somerville and two from Salem Street in Medford, also served Somerville.

Medford, north of Somerville, was mainly residential. The city is known for Tufts University, and in the 1940s had a lot of light manufacturing. A popular destination in Medford was the Middlesex Fells, a park system in the north of the city, which extended into Stoneham and was served by streetcars jointly run by the Eastern Mass. and the Boston El. A car line from Salem Street and the B&M Railroad Medford Branch each served Medford Square. Trains on the New Hampshire Division and the Western Route of the B&M Railroad also stopped at several stations in the city.

Stoneham is north of Medford. It was both residential and light industrial in nature. The Middlesex Fells, mentioned above, took up a substantial part of the town, making Stoneham a prime recreational destination. The Stoneham Branch of the B&M Railroad and the Eastern Mass. trolley line through the Fells and Stoneham Center to the Farm Hill railroad crossing both provided public transportation in the town.

By the end of the decade, only the Fellsway car line running mainly in Somerville and Medford would still be in regular operation. Service tracks, however, would still be used from the Tremont Street Subway through Charlestown to Sullivan Square; from Porter Square, Cambridge, to Sullivan Square; from Sullivan Square to Everett Shops; and from Everett to Chelsea. The tracks in the Charlestown Yard, on Arlington Avenue and the ramp up to Sullivan Square Station, in the Charlestown Neck Carhouse, and the tracks in the Everett Shops were also active and would remain so with a life of their own for many more years.

Service Overview

The trolley lines in this area were based at Clarendon Hill Carhouse in Somerville and Salem Street Carhouse in Medford. At one point, the Elevated considered closing both Clarendon Hill and Salem Street as active trolley barns, and reopening the largely unused Charlestown Neck Carhouse beside Sullivan Square Station for trackless trolleys and any remaining streetcar operations.

Map ⑦
Lines North of Boston

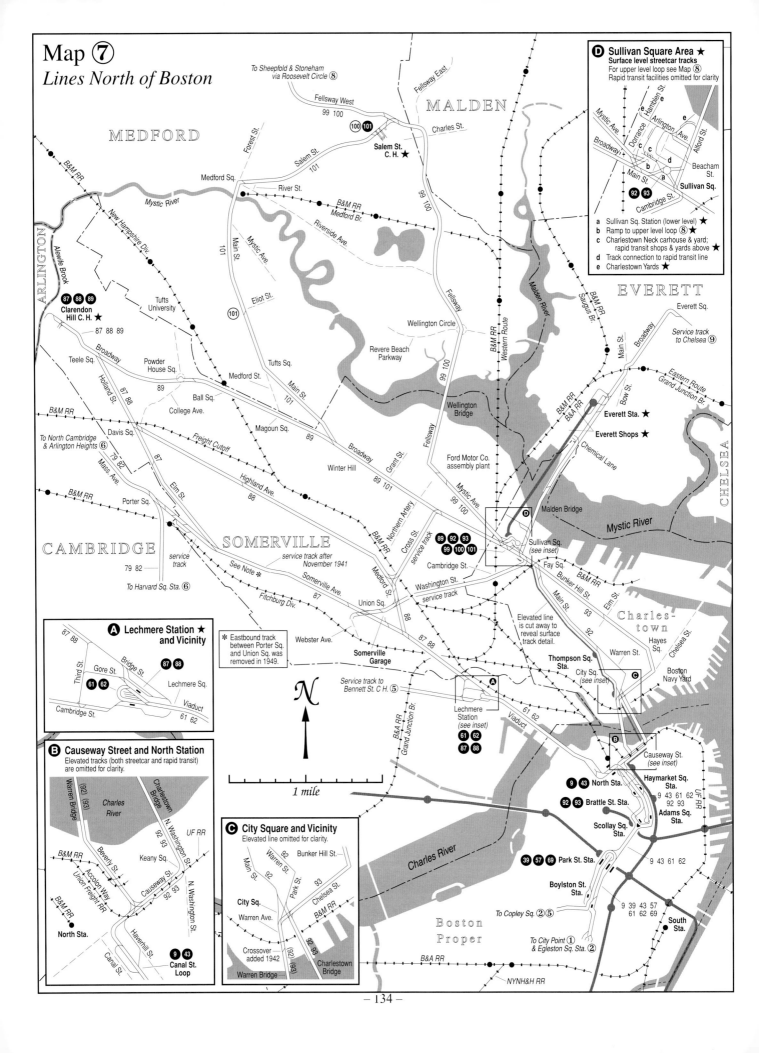

MEDFORD

MALDEN

To Sheepfold & Stoneham via Roosevelt Circle ⑧

Fellsway East

Fellsway West

99 100

Charles St.

Salem St.
C. H. ★

Medford Sq.

River St.

B&M RR

Forest St.

Salem St.
101

99 100

Mystic River

Riverside Ave.

B&M RR
Medford Br.

D Sullivan Square Area ★
Surface level streetcar tracks
For upper level loop see Map ⑧
Rapid transit facilities omitted for clarity

Mystic Ave.

Hamblen St.

Dorrance

Arlington Ave.

Broadway

Main St.

Alford St.

Beacham
St.

92 93

Sullivan
Sq.

Cambridge St.

a Sullivan Sq. Station (lower level) ★
b Ramp to upper level loop ⑧ ★
c Charlestown Neck carhouse & yard;
    rapid transit shops & yards above ★
d Track connection to rapid transit line
e Charlestown Yards ★

ARLINGTON

Alewife Brook

New Hampshire Div.

87 88 89
Clarendon
Hill C. H. ★

87 88 89

Main St.
101

Eliot St.

101

Tufts
University

Teele Sq.

Broadway

Powder
House Sq.

87 88

89

Medford St.

Tufts Sq.

Wellington Circle

Revere Beach
Parkway

Fellsway

99 100

EVERETT

Everett Sq.

Broadway

Main St.

Service track
to Chelsea ⑨

Eastern Route
Grand Junction Br.

Everett Sta. ★

Everett Shops ★

Holland St.

87 88

Ball Sq.

College Ave.

89

Magoun Sq.

Broadway

89 101

Grant St.

Wellington
Bridge

Ford Motor Co.
assembly plant

B&M RR
B&A RR

Chemical Lane

CHELSEA

B&M RR

To North Cambridge
& Arlington Heights ⑥

Davis Sq.

79 82

Freight Cutoff

Highland Ave.

Winter Hill

89 101

Mystic Ave.

99 100

Malden Bridge

Mystic River

Mass. Ave.

B&M RR

Porter Sq.

88

SOMERVILLE

Northern Artery

Cross St.
service track

89 92 93
99 100 101

Sullivan Sq.
(see inset)

Fay Sq.

Bunker Hill St.

93

Main St.

92

Charles-
town

CAMBRIDGE

Elm St.

service
track

79 82

See Note *

service track after
November 1941

Somerville Ave.

87

B&M RR

Medford St.

Washington St.
service track

Cambridge St.

Elevated line
is cut away to
reveal surface
track detail.

B&M RR

Thompson Sq.
Sta.

Warren St.

Hayes
Sq.

Chelsea St.

To Harvard Sq. Sta. ⑥

Fitchburg Div.

87

Union Sq.

88

City Sq.
(see inset)

C

Boston
Navy Yard

A Lechmere Station ★
and Vicinity

87 88

Third St.

Gore St.

Bridge St.

61 62

Cambridge St.

Lechmere Sq.

Viaduct

61 62

* Eastbound track
between Porter Sq.
and Union Sq. was
removed in 1949.

Webster Ave.

Somerville
Garage

87 88

Service track to
Bennett St. C H ⑤

Lechmere
Station
(see inset)

61 62

87 88

N

Viaduct

61 62

B Causeway Street and North Station
Elevated tracks (both streetcar and rapid transit)
are omitted for clarity.

(92) (93)

Warren
Bridge

Charles
River

Charlestown
Bridge

N Washington St.

92 93

UF RR

B&M RR

Beverly St.

Accolon Way

Union Freight RR

Keany Sq.

Causeway St.

92 93

N Washington St.

B&M RR

Haverhill St.

North Sta.

Canal St.

9 43
Canal St.
Loop

C City Square and Vicinity
Elevated line omitted for clarity.

Main St.

Warren St.

Bunker Hill St.

Park St.

93

Chelsea St.

City Sq.

92

Warren Ave.

B&M RR

Crossover
added 1942

(92) (93)

Warren Bridge

Charlestown
Bridge

Charles River

1 mile

9 43 North Sta.

Haymarket Sq.
Sta.

92 93 Brattle St. Sta.

9 43 61 62
92 93

Scollay Sq.
Sta.

Adams Sq.
Sta.

9 43 61 62

39 57 69 Park St. Sta.

Boylston St.
Sta.

To Copley Sq. ② ⑤

9 39 43 57
61 62 69

South
Sta.

Boston
Proper

To City Point ①
& Egleston Sq. Sta. ②

B&A RR

NYNH&H RR

– 134 –

Charlestown Neck never replaced Clarendon Hill or Salem Street, but Charlestown Neck was used as a substation for Salem Street to store cars for the two lines from Sullivan Square to Brattle Street Station. Work cars were also stored at Charlestown Neck well after all car lines in the area, including the Fellsway line and the service tracks, had been abandoned.

There were three streetcar lines based at Clarendon Hill Carhouse in 1940. They are illustrated on Map 7 and are listed below.

Route No.	Route Description
87	**Clarendon Hill–Lechmere Station** *via Broadway, Holland Street, Elm Street, Somerville Avenue, and Bridge Street*
88	**Clarendon Hill–Lechmere Station** *via Broadway, Holland Street, Highland Avenue, Medford Street, Somerville Avenue, and Bridge Street*
89	**Clarendon Hill Station–Sullivan Square Station** *via Broadway*

Appendix 9 shows the August 1941 rating for Routes 87 and 88. Route 87 was running 100 trips per day and Route 88 had 128. In the April 1945 rating, Route 89 was operating 179 trips each day.

The five Salem Street lines in 1940 are listed below and are shown on Map 7. The northerly extension of Routes 99 and 100, and the Eastern Mass. line from the end of the Elevated's Route 99 to Stoneham are shown on Map 8.

92	**Sullivan Square Station–Brattle Street Station (Scollay Square)** *via Main Street, Causeway Street, and Subway*
93	**Sullivan Square Station–Brattle Street Station (Scollay Square)** *via Main Street, Bunker Hill Street, Chelsea Street, Main Street, Causeway Street, and Subway*
	[cb] **Elm and Bunker Hill Streets–Brattle Street Station**
99	**Stoneham (Spot Pond)–Sullivan Square Station** *via Fellsway and Mystic Avenue*
100	**Elm Street–Sullivan Square Station** *via Fellsway and Mystic Avenue*
	[cb] **Salem Street Carhouse–Sullivan**
101	**Salem Street Carhouse–Sullivan Square Station** *via Salem Street, Main Street, Winter Hill, and Broadway*
	[cb] **Eliot and Main Streets–Sullivan**

In terms of daily trips, the heaviest of these lines was the combined service on Route 99 and Route 100 with its cutback at Salem Street, followed by the combined service on Route 101 and its cutback at Eliot Street, Route 93 and its cutbacks, and finally, Route 92. Appendix 9 presents this information in more detail.

Eastern Mass. streetcars ran between Stoneham and Sullivan Square Station, using ESMR rails in Stoneham to Spot Pond, located in the Middlesex Fells, and the Boston Elevated Route 99 tracks from Spot Pond to Sullivan Square. Eastern Mass. cars operating this service were housed at Salem Street.

The Clarendon Hill Lines

Clarendon Hill Carhouse

Clarendon Hill Carhouse was a large two-bay eight-track carbarn with two adjoining car storage yards, one on either side of the building. This property was located off Broadway in Somerville near the Arlington-Somerville boundary. In 1940, it was a relatively modern facility, the carhouse interior having been completely rebuilt after a disastrous fire in 1918. A long single stub-end siding ran along the rear of the carhouse building and was mainly used for supply and fuel deliveries.

The caryard on the front or Broadway side of the property had a loop track with several inside passing sidings for live storage. There were also several stub-end sidings off the live storage siding nearest Broadway. An operators' lobby was located near the passenger waiting area adjacent to Broadway.

Southwest of the carhouse building was a second yard with an inner loop that had inside passing sidings for storage. There was also an outer loop, at the outermost segment of which there were stub-end sidings. The trackage in this rear yard was primarily used to store mothballed streetcars.

The top view of Clarendon Hill from Broadway shows the two-bay carhouse, the operators' lobby to the right, the easterly ramp running to the rear storage yard, and the passenger boarding area, which was in front of the parked automobile and slightly inside the property line from the Broadway sidewalk. The rear yard, above, had ample storage room for cars too good for scrap, such as these mothballed center-entrance cars seen in late 1938 that were quickly brought back to life during World War II. *Both, Charles A. Duncan*

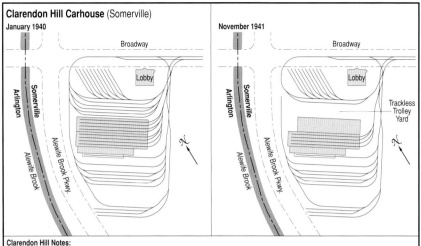

Clarendon Hill Carhouse (Somerville)

January 1940 — Broadway — Arlington — Somerville — Alewife Brook — Alewife Brook Pkwy. — Lobby

November 1941 — Broadway — Arlington — Somerville — Alewife Brook — Alewife Brook Pkwy. — Lobby — Trackless Trolley Yard

Clarendon Hill Notes:
(1) Trackless trolley operation began November 8, 1941. Revenue service trackless trolleys usually entered the yard just northwest of the lobby, or to the left of the lobby as shown here. (Four stub-end streetcar storage tracks had been removed from this area in 1937.) They then looped around the lobby, and departed via the streetcar exit on the southeast side of the lobby. Trackless trolleys going into storage entered the yard from Broadway near Alewife Brook Parkway; this entrance was also occasionally used by revenue service trackless.
(2) The carhouse was converted entirely to trackless trolley operations December 7, 1946. All remaining tracks were removed in 1947.
(3) The rear yard of the carhouse (at the bottom of the diagrams) was known as the "west" side of the property. This was the site of a large wooden carhouse, which burned in 1918. The land was sloped, and the rear yard was much lower than the newer carhouse building shown here.

When this shot was taken on November 18, 1941, trackless trolleys had replaced streetcars on the Somerville Avenue and Highland Avenue lines to Lechmere. Only the line to Sullivan Square remained and it would do so throughout World War II. To the extreme left of the picture, we can see one of the remaining streetcars at this facility. *BERy*

In 1941 the Elevated removed three yard storage tracks on the Broadway side of the carhouse and disconnected the switch to the rear yard near the entrance to the property on Broadway. This new space made way for a paved trackless trolley loop and storage lanes for the impending Highland and Somerville Avenue line conversions to trackless trolleys. Four track bays inside the Broadway side of the building were also remodeled for trackless trolley maintenance.[177] Later in the year, another yard track parallel to the ones taken out earlier was also removed and paved for trackless trolleys.[178]

Late in 1946, to prepare for the conversion of the Clarendon Hill–Sullivan line from streetcars to trackless trolleys, the Elevated began the complete changeover of the facility for trackless trolleys. Most of the remaining tracks were removed to prepare for paving and work in the carhouse.[a]

Equipment Assignments

As of April 1, 1940, 45 Type 5s, including 12 spares, were assigned to the Clarendon Hill lines. The last rating that showed streetcars was for September 16, 1946, at which time 18 Type 5s including 5 spares were assigned to the Clarendon Hill–Sullivan line. See Appendix 7 for detailed car assignments.

Type 5 cars ran on both the Highland and Somerville Avenue lines during the short period that these routes were oper-

ated with streetcars in the 1940s. Other than an occasional work car, Type 5s were the only streetcars used on these routes.

The Clarendon Hill–Sullivan line also used Type 5 cars, right up to its postwar conversion to trackless trolley operation on December 7, 1946.

87 Clarendon Hill–Lechmere *via Somerville Avenue*

Leaving Clarendon Hill, the Highland and Somerville Avenue lines followed Broadway to Teele Square, turned southeast onto Holland Street, and continued to Davis Square. Here they crossed the Hill Crossing Freight Cutoff of the B&M Railroad. Just after the railroad crossing, at Davis Square, the Highland and Somerville Avenue routes diverged.

The Somerville Avenue line left the Holland Street tracks and bore right onto Elm Street. It followed Elm Street southeasterly to Somerville Avenue, joining the double-track service line coming in from nearby Porter Square in Cambridge. The revenue cars followed Somerville Avenue southeast to Union Square. The service track turned northeast here onto Washington Street toward Charlestown. From Union Square, the line to Lechmere continued on Somerville Avenue, rejoining the Highland Avenue line at Medford Street.

The Highland and Somerville Avenue routes both continued on Somerville Avenue, crossing a bridge over the Fitchburg Division of the B&M Railroad, and then the Cambridge–Somerville boundary.[b] At this point Somerville Avenue became Bridge Street.[c] At Third Street, inbound cars turned south onto single track. After running two blocks on Third

---

[a] This work was done between October 21 and November 8, 1946. Construction, however, continued well after the actual conversion of the Broadway line on December 7, 1946. The last tracks in the carhouse and rear yard were removed between May 5 and May 23, 1947. The long stub-end siding along the rear of the building remained in place until the building was demolished in April 1967. *Co-operation* for September 1947 reported that conversion work on the westerly section at Clarendon Hill Carhouse had almost been done, so the project was still active at that late time. "Alterations Almost Complete at Clarendon Hill Carhouse," *Co-operation*, 26 (September 1947), 64.

[b] The section of Somerville Avenue between Medford Street and the Cambridge city line is now part of the Monsignor McGrath Highway.

[c] Bridge Street, Cambridge, is now known as the Monsignor O'Brien Highway.

Highland Avenue car 5749 returning to Clarendon Hill joins Holland Street near the B&M Railroad crossing at Davis Square, Somerville. Both the Somerville Avenue and Highland Avenue cars used the Holland Street tracks before diverging at Davis Square.
Charles A. Duncan

Route 87 ran through busy Union Square, Somerville. Car 5650 is heading northeast on Somerville Avenue and is crossing Washington Street in the center of the square. The section of Somerville Avenue trackage just ahead of the car was also part of the service line from Porter Square to Sullivan Square. To the left, the Washington Street tracks ran a short distance to a crossover, rounded the corner onto Webster Avenue, and ended. To the right, the Washington Street tracks ran to Sullivan Square. *Charles A. Duncan*

Medford Street and Somerville Avenue was the point at which the Highland Avenue and Somerville Avenue lines rejoined after separating at Davis Square. The Somerville Avenue line comes in from the left in this view, while the line on Medford Street runs straight ahead to Highland Avenue. *BERy*

Street, both lines turned east onto Cambridge Street and followed it for a block and a half before turning left into the unloading area at Lechmere Station. This route was 8.142 miles round-trip and the running time was 44 minutes.

For the return trip, both lines looped under the Lechmere Viaduct onto Bridge Street and entered the northbound station transfer area that was parallel to Bridge Street. Leaving Lechmere Station, outbound cars reentered Bridge Street and followed it to Third Street, returning to double-track territory. The trackage in and around Lechmere is detailed on Inset A of Map 7.

Starting on September 3, 1941, the Elevated reset the surface car tracks in Lechmere Station in paving for a trackless trolley coachway. This work was completed on October 4. A month later, on November 8, 1941, trackless trolleys replaced the streetcars on both lines.

At Union Square, spur tracks on Washington Street from the service line crossed Somerville Avenue and ran west to Webster Avenue, turning south onto Webster Avenue itself and abruptly ending. A crossover was located on Washington Street west of Somerville Avenue, just before the turn onto Webster Avenue. This spur trackage was formally abandoned and written off in 1940. At the Somerville Garage, the site of the former Union Square Carhouse, a short single-track spur for work cars ran into the south yard off the northbound Somerville Avenue track.

88 Clarendon Hill–Lechmere *via Highland Avenue*

At Davis Square, the Highland Avenue line diverged from the Somerville Avenue line on Elm Street, and turned left onto its namesake street. The line ran along Highland Avenue southeast for nearly two miles until it reached Medford Street, just after passing the Somerville City Hall. The line followed Medford Street, generally south, past Cross Street. Here there was a double-track connection in both directions from Medford Street to a service track on Cross Street that ran to Broadway and connected inbound in the direction of Sullivan Square Station.[d]

The line continued along Medford Street, crossing the double-track service line on Washington Street between Charlestown and Cambridge. A double-track connection ran between the Medford Street tracks and the service line, heading toward Union Square, Somerville. At Somerville Avenue and Medford Street, the Highland Avenue line turned southeast, sharing track from here to Lechmere Station with the Somerville Avenue line as previously described. This line was 8.178 miles round-trip, slightly longer than the Somerville Avenue route, but both routes had the same running time of 44 minutes.

On November 8, 1941, the Clarendon Hill–Lechmere via Highland Avenue and via Somerville Avenue lines were simultaneously converted from streetcar to trackless trolley opera-

[d] The section of Medford Street between Greenville Street and Somerville Avenue is also now part of the Monsignor McGrath Highway, as is the section of Somerville Avenue between Medford Street and the Cambridge city line.

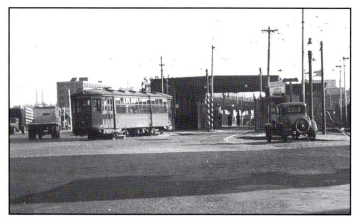

The Highland and Somerville Avenue lines ended at Lechmere. At left, Type 5 No. 5790 has discharged passengers on the inbound side on October 16, 1941, and will soon loop on the street under the viaduct and enter the covered outbound boarding area on the opposite side of the station. At right, a Type 5 leaves Lechmere on Bridge Street for Clarendon Hill Carhouse. Buses still serve the station this way today, and the scene has only changed by the presence of modern automobiles and street furniture.　　*Both, Charles A. Duncan*

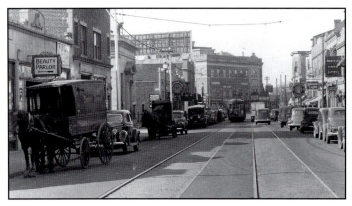

The Highland Avenue line ran along its namesake street immediately after leaving Davis Square, which shows up behind the Type 5 coming toward us headed for Lechmere. Note the two horse-drawn delivery wagons mixed in with the motor vehicles parked at the curb on the left.　　*BERy*

A Type 5 grinds up Highland Avenue near Willow Avenue in this late 1930s scene.　　*BERy*

tion. Twelve trackless trolley routes were now in operation, all north of Boston.

89 Clarendon Hill–Sullivan

The Clarendon Hill–Sullivan line survived World War II, having been reprieved by the ODT wartime restriction on bus substitutions. Starting at Clarendon Hill Carhouse, this line

followed Broadway in a southeasterly direction, crossing the double-track connection on Holland Street used by the Somerville and Highland Avenue cars. Sullivan-bound cars continued on Broadway to Powder House Square, where the outbound track ran in a private reservation through an island in a traffic circle. The inbound track stayed in the street, however, bypassing the center island completely.[179]

The line continued on Broadway through Ball Square, crossing a bridge over the New Hampshire Division of the B&M Railroad and entering Magoun Square. The cars then ran up and over Winter Hill, joining the Salem Street–Sullivan line at Main Street, and sharing the remaining track on Broadway and Main Street (Charlestown) into Sullivan Square. A private streetcar reservation protected the tracks from Grant Street to the Northern Artery, now the McGrath Highway. The remaining tracks were set in pavement.

The line had a double-track connection at Broadway and Cross Street with the service line on Cross Street and continued on Broadway to the Charlestown–Somerville line. Here Broadway became Main Street. The line crossed a bridge over the B&M Railroad, and shortly thereafter turned left,

The Boston Elevated maintained a lengthy service line between Sullivan Square, Charlestown, and Porter Square, Cambridge, via Washington Street and Somerville Avenue. Here a service car operates on Washington Street, Somerville, in November 1942.

Charles A. Duncan

Type 5 No. 5708 enters Teele Square, Somerville, the intersection of Broadway and Holland Street, on its way from Sullivan Square to Clarendon Hill. The Highland and Somerville Avenue cars both veered off to the left on Holland Street.   *Charles A. Duncan*

Type 5 No. 5634 crests Winter Hill on Broadway as it heads for Sullivan Square Station on April 7, 1946.   *Foster M. Palmer*

A traffic circle was installed in Powder House Square in 1939, and contrary to usual Boston Elevated practice of running *both* tracks through the circle, only the outbound track did so. The inbound rail shared the general traffic lane around the circle.   *BERy*

An April 28, 1946, Boston Chapter NRHS fan trip brought PCC 3022 to the traffic circle at Powder House Square.   *Leon Onofri*

crossing tracks on Mystic Avenue before proceeding up the ramp to the rapid transit level of Sullivan Square Station. The round-trip distance of Route 89 was 6.973 miles. The average running time was 38 minutes.

The Fellsway cars also used the ramp to Sullivan Square, accessing it from a separate set of track leads off Mystic Avenue. After discharging their riders, cars from both lines turned around on the elevated loop on the east side of the station and reentered to pick up outbound passengers. There were two tracks on the loading platform—the main line and a passing siding. Ramp details and related surface tracks are shown on Inset B of Map 8 and in the Sullivan Square and vicinity detail drawing.

Tracks also continued straight ahead on Main Street beyond the ramp, providing a connection to the lower level of Sullivan Square Station and the service tracks beyond the station to Porter Square.

Trackless Trolley Preparations at Sullivan Square

The Elevated began work at Sullivan Square on September 11, 1946, for the conversion of the Clarendon Hill–Sullivan line to trackless trolleys. The project included rebuilding the ramp track and the ramp from Main Street and Mystic Avenue, removing the 373-foot passing siding on the outbound streetcar loading platform, and replacing the upper level surface streetcar loop.

Beginning on October 13, 1946, the old trolley loop was torn down and a new loop was installed with a roadway for trackless trolleys and a track for the streetcars. The original loop built in 1912 was only wide enough for streetcars and could not handle the wide swing of the trolley coaches. All of this work was completed on November 30, 1946.

During construction the Clarendon Hill and Salem Street via Winter Hill cars were routed into the lower level of Sullivan Square Station. The Fellsway cars continued to the upper level, using a special temporary crossover installed in the station.

Buses normally assigned to the lower station level were operated from the street outside the station to make way for the additional streetcars now using the lower level. Between 1 a.m. and 5 a.m., Owl Cars to Boston, Everett, Medford, and Somerville also remained outside the station and reversed ends using a temporary crossover on Main Street.

The Boston Elevated wasted no time in completing the changeover from streetcar to trackless trolley operation. A trackless trolley test trip carrying Boston Elevated officials took place on November 29, 1946. Further testing began on December 2. Five days later, on December 7, trackless trolleys commenced operation between Clarendon Hill and Sullivan Square station; the streetcars were history.

Rebuilding The Sullivan Square Trolley Loop

In September 1946 the Boston Elevated began paving around the rails on the ramps leading to the upper level of Sullivan Square Station from Mystic Avenue and Main Street. This was done to allow buses and trackless trolleys to make an across-the-platform transfer to the Main Line Elevated. By October 9 (top left), the work was well underway, while by November 4 (above), the project is almost complete. Cars from the Fellsway continued to use the ramp during construction, changing ends at a special crossover in the station. Winter Hill and Salem Street cars were diverted to the lower level of the station. The streetcar loop on the upper level was completely removed in early October and a new loop, with a radius sufficient for trolley buses, installed. At left, as the demolition of the support steel takes place on the night of October 16, a night car to the Tremont Street Subway is partly concealed on Main Street behind the more distant construction crane and a line truck. By November 4 (below left), the new loop was in place, but the roadway decking had not yet been installed. Streetcars, however, could use it right away. Starting with a trial trip on November 29, trackless trolleys began using the completed loop, taking over the Clarendon Hill route on December 7. In the early days of trackless operation (below), Clarendon Hill-bound trolley coach 8177 leaves Sullivan Square.

All, BERy

The Salem Street Carhouse Lines

Salem Street Carhouse

Salem Street Carhouse was located on Salem Street, Medford, near Fellsway West. This complex included a large carhouse, an adjoining bus garage, a heating plant, and a lobby building.[180] On the west side of the carhouse there was an adjoining yard with two concentric loop tracks around the lobby. The outer lobby loop also had a passing siding for additional storage. A third much larger loop extended to the rear of the property and had parallel storage tracks connected to the lobby loops and an inner single-track spur called the "ash track."

In 1946 the Boston Elevated Maintenance Department removed the inner lobby loop and its connections and paved the area over for trackless trolleys. Considerable reconstruction work also took place on the outer loop tracks.[181]

Equipment Assignments

In 1940 most of the cars at Salem Street were Type 5s. In the April 1, 1940, rating, there were 67 cars based at Salem Street consisting of 52 type 5s, three Boston Elevated 4400s,[e] and 12 Eastern Mass. 4300s. At the end of the decade, the only car line based at Salem Street was the Fellsway line. The December 12, 1949, rating showed 24 Type 5 cars including 6 spares assigned to this route. Appendix 7 has detailed car assignments.

Salem Street was made a substation of City Point Carhouse in December 1949, after the Charlestown lines were converted to bus operation. The cars assigned to the Fellsway line remained at Salem Street Carhouse, but the rating station was now City Point.

The line to Stoneham along the Fellsway and through the Middlesex Fells was really comprised of four distinct routes using three types of equipment. The Eastern Mass. provided twelve of its own 4300s for Boston Elevated Route 99 running from Sullivan Square Station to Spot Pond, and for EMSR service from Spot Pond to Stoneham over EMSR tracks. The Elevated also supplied Type 5s for use as required as far as Spot Pond during the summer. The Boston Elevated ran Type 5 cars on Route 100, Elm Street–Sullivan Square and on the cutback of this line, Salem Street–Sullivan. The El also used three of its own 4400s as well between Salem Street and Sullivan until March 1941.

Type 5 cars were used exclusively on the Salem Street–Sullivan via Winter Hill line and on both lines from Sullivan to Brattle Street Station throughout the 1940s.

[e] The majority of the 4400s were assigned to Chelsea and Revere, but as of the March 15, 1937, rating, four were assigned to Salem Street Carhouse for use on the Salem Street–Sullivan via Fellsway cutback. After April 1, 1940, only three were assigned to the line, and by the March 17, 1941, rating, no 4400s remained at Salem Street.

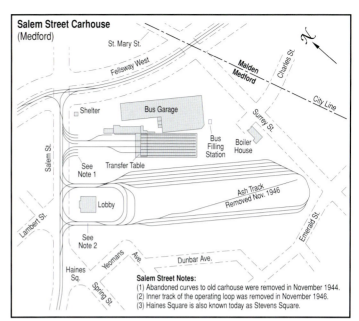

Salem Street Carhouse (Medford)

Salem Street Notes:
(1) Abandoned curves to old carhouse were removed in November 1944.
(2) Inner track of the operating loop was removed in November 1946.
(3) Haines Square is also known today as Stevens Square.

The Salem Street Carhouse housed trolleys of the Eastern Massachusetts Street Railway as well as those of the Boston Elevated, as these 1946 views of the front yard (top) and looking toward the lobby building (above) illustrate. *Both, Charles A. Duncan*

By the time this view of the car storage yard was taken about 1948, only Boston Elevated passenger and service cars remained. *Charles A. Duncan*

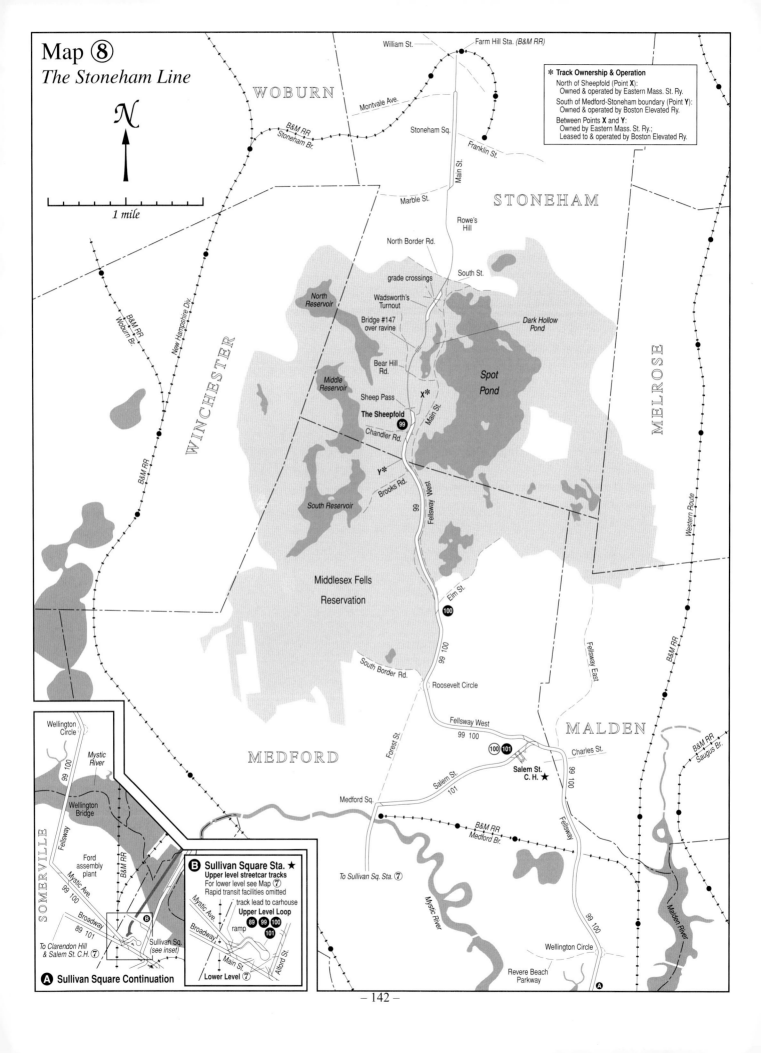

Map ⑧
The Stoneham Line

N

1 mile

WOBURN

WINCHESTER

STONEHAM

MELROSE

MEDFORD

MALDEN

SOMERVILLE

William St.

Farm Hill Sta. (B&M RR)

Montvale Ave.

B&M RR
Stoneham Br.

Stoneham Sq.

Franklin St.

Main St.

Marble St.

Rowe's Hill

North Border Rd.

South St.

grade crossings

Wadsworth's Turnout

Bridge #147 over ravine

Dark Hollow Pond

Bear Hill Rd.

Spot Pond

Middle Reservoir

North Reservoir

Sheep Pass

X*

The Sheepfold
99

Chandler Rd.

Y*

Brooks Rd.

South Reservoir

99

Fellsway West

Middlesex Fells
Reservation

Elm St.

100

99 100

South Border Rd.

Roosevelt Circle

Fellsway West

99 100

100 101

Charles St.

Salem St.
C. H. ★

Forest St.

Salem St.

101

Medford Sq.

Medford Br.

B&M RR

To Sullivan Sq. Sta. ⑦

Mystic River

Fellsway

99 100

Wellington Circle

Revere Beach Parkway

Western Route

Fellsway East

B&M RR

Saugus Br.

Malden River

B&M RR

New Hampshire Div.

B&M RR
Woburn Br.

* Track Ownership & Operation

North of Sheepfold (Point **X**):
  Owned & operated by Eastern Mass. St. Ry.
South of Medford-Stoneham boundary (Point **Y**):
  Owned & operated by Boston Elevated Ry.
Between Points **X** and **Y**:
  Owned by Eastern Mass. St. Ry.;
  Leased to & operated by Boston Elevated Ry.

Wellington Circle

Mystic River

Wellington Bridge

Ford assembly plant

Mystic Ave.

B&M RR

Fellsway

99 100

Broadway

89 101

To Clarendon Hill & Salem St. C.H. ⑦

Sullivan Sq. (see inset)

Ⓐ Sullivan Square Continuation

Ⓑ **Sullivan Square Sta.** ★
Upper level streetcar tracks
For lower level see Map ⑦
Rapid transit facilities omitted
track lead to carhouse
Upper Level Loop
ramp

89 99 100
101

Mystic Ave.

Broadway

Main St.

Alford St.

Lower Level ⑦

Ⓑ

The Fellsway Lines

Perhaps the best remembered line north of Boston ran from Sullivan Square Station via the Fellsway and the Middlesex Fells to Spot Pond.[f] From there the line continued to Stoneham over a section owned and operated by the Eastern Massachusetts Street Railway.[g]

The Eastern Mass. Stoneham Line

Starting in the Town of Stoneham, this line began as a stub-end single track on Main Street, at the Farm Hill railroad crossing of the B&M Railroad Stoneham Branch, just north of William Street. Between Union Street and Montvale Avenue, the line changed to double track and continued though Stoneham Square to Marble Street, changing back at this point to single track.

After passing Marble Street, the line ran along the west side of the road in a private right-of-way over Rowe's Hill. At North Border Road, the cars bore right, crossing North Border Road, and entering the Middlesex Fells Reservation. For the next 1.8 miles, the cars operated on a private right-of-way through the park. Much of this right-of-way remains a hiking trail today.

Shortly after entering the reservation, the cars stopped at Wadsworth's Turnout, a 940-foot passing siding.[h] The line returned to single track, and then crossed a ravine near Dark Hollow Pond on a spectacular concrete viaduct.[i] While the viaduct was wide enough for double track operation, only single track ever ran across it. This viaduct remains today, a lone and forgotten monument to the trolley riders it once served.[j]

The line crossed a short bridge over Bear Hill Road and then an underpass originally built for sheep. The bridge over the sheep pass was only ten feet long. Just after the sheep pass, the track went from single to double and cars arrived at the transition point of the line that was known originally as the Sheep Pasture, and later as the "Sheepfold."[k] The round-trip distance from the end of track on Main Street to the Sheepfold was 4.765 miles. To Sullivan Square Station from the Main Street railroad crossing, the round-trip distance was 16.345 miles and required a running time of 60 minutes. Appendix 9A presents this information and service frequencies.

99 Spot Pond–Sullivan Square Station *via Fellsway*

At the Sheepfold, the line became Boston Elevated territory for the final three-tenths of a mile in Stoneham and the starting point of Boston Elevated Route 99, Spot Pond–Sullivan Square Station. The Bay State Street Railway leased the track operated by the Elevated in Stoneham to the El on March 11, 1916. This lease expired with the end of service in 1946.

Cars from Stoneham stopped at the Sheepfold and Boston Elevated motormen took over for the run into Sullivan Square Station.[l] Fare box readings were taken for each company, and passengers continuing through paid an additional fare to the Elevated upon leaving the car.[m] This procedure was reversed in the outbound direction.

There was a trailing point crossover located just south of the Sheepfold. This allowed Boston El Route 99 cars to drop off and pick up riders at a boarding area north of the crossover, change ends, take the crossover onto the southbound track to return to Sullivan Square. Eastern Mass. cars dropped off riders here as well and boarded passengers for Stoneham.

Most of the service from Sullivan Square to the Sheepfold, however, was handled with Eastern Mass. cars running on Route 99 with Boston El motormen and continuing to Stoneham with Eastern Mass. operators. Boston El Type 5 cars, while they did run occasionally when needed in the summer months to the Sheepfold crossover, seldom ran beyond Elm Street the rest of the year. During evening weekday rush hours before World War II, the Stoneham cars ran limited from Sullivan Square Station to Charles Street. Passengers could not get off the car before Charles Street, but outbound riders beyond that point could board. Later, during the war, the limited service was operated to Salem Street.

---

[f] The Middlesex Fells Reservation was and is a large public park operated by the Metropolitan District Commission. The Park was opened in 1894, and the trolley line in 1910.

[g] The line to Stoneham continued on to Reading until 1918, and branched off to Wakefield until 1929. It connected with lines to Woburn and Melrose Highlands until 1931 and to Winchester until 1929.

[h] The turnout name comes from Wadsworth's Cafe, which was located near the point that the line entered the Middlesex Fells Reservation.

[i] This structure was simply referred to in the company's track maps as Bridge No. 147. It is a reinforced concrete structure 224 feet long with seven spans and a maximum elevation of 40 feet. It has the proportions of a viaduct and is abnormally large for a suburban trolley operation.

[j] The viaduct is partially visible in the winter from I-93 southbound, and is accessible by foot in the Middlesex Fells reservation.

[k] Before the streetcar line was built through the Middlesex Fells, the Metropolitan District Commission kept a flock of sheep in a large pasture area. The car line separated the grazing ground from the barn in which the sheep were housed for the night, and a tunnel or underpass was built under the car line to allow the sheep to safely return to their barn. Sheep keeping was discontinued eventually, and the sheep barn was converted to "Mary's Refreshment Stand," which catered to large crowds of visitors to the Fells in the pleasant months of the year. The stand was finally torn down in 1942, but the term "Sheepfold" is still used to the present day.

[l] While on Boston Elevated property, the Eastern Mass. cars were always operated by Boston Elevated motormen.

[m] At Neponset, the other Eastern Mass. and Boston Elevated joint operation dividing point, fareboxes from each company were physically exchanged.

The Eastern Mass. Stoneham Line

The Eastern Mass. line to Stoneham ended at the Farm Hill railroad crossing of the B&M. Cars changed ends and returned to Sullivan Square Station. Here a B&M switcher and caboose crosses Main Street as 4383 waits to return to Sullivan Square Station on July 27, 1946.
Lawson K. Hill, Stephen P. Carlson Collection

Car 4390 is seen on the side-of-the-road private right-of-way on Main Street, Stoneham, on March 21, 1946. *Charles A. Duncan*

After leaving Main Street, Eastern Mass. cars entered Wadsworth's Turnout, just inside the Middlesex Fells Reservation. This was the only turnout on the largely single-track line beyond the Sheepfold to the Farm Hill railroad crossing. Here, 4385 meets another 4300 in July 1944. *Charles A. Duncan*

Car 4387, now preserved at the Seashore Trolley Museum, crosses the multi-arched bridge over Chandler Road on March 21, 1946. *Charles A. Duncan*

Although the tracks were owned by the Eastern Mass. only as far as the Medford city line, the Boston Elevated usually operated the line with its own cars inbound from Elm Street. In this unusual August 1942 view, the operator of a Type 5 operating on Route 99, Spot Pond–Sullivan, changes ends, while motormen from the Boston Elevated and the Eastern Mass. swap off on the Stoneham car in the background. *Charles A. Duncan*

Eastern Mass. snow sweeper B-620 is seen at the Sheepfold in February 1945. To the right is the shelter for motormen waiting to pick up their cars. *Charles A. Duncan*

On February 22, 1940, 4396 made its way through the snow-covered Middlesex Fells to Sullivan Square Station.   *Charles A. Brown*

Eastern Mass cars arriving from Stoneham loaded and unloaded on the inbound side opposite the boarding area on the outbound track. Going south, cars from Stoneham and Route 99 crossed a bridge over Chandler Road. A facing point crossover installed during the construction of the line many years earlier was located south of this bridge.

The line continued across the Stoneham-Medford boundary into Medford, still on private right-of-way within the park. Beyond the city boundary, the Boston Elevated owned the line. There was a fifth and final bridge over Brooks Road, after which the line closely paralleled the Fellsway West on the west side of the roadway. About half a mile south of Brooks Road, the tracks crossed the southbound lanes of the Fellsway West at an oblique angle, leaving the Middlesex Fells Reservation and entering a private reservation in the center of the road.

At this point, the north and southbound roadways of the Fellsway West were separated by a very wide curving median in which the streetcar reservation was located.[n] At Elm Street, the median narrowed, and there was a crossover for Route 100, Elm Street–Sullivan Square. The Route 99 round-trip was 11.580 miles between the Sheepfold and Sullivan Square and required a running time of 48 minutes.

100 Elm Street–Sullivan Square Station *via Fellsway*

From the Elm Street crossover, Route 99 from Spot Pond and the Eastern Mass. line from Stoneham shared track with Route 100, Elm Street–Sullivan Square Station. Route 100 was a full service line, running from approximately 5 a.m. to 1:30 a.m. with its own weekday rush hour cutback at Salem Street.

The line ran from Elm Street along the Fellsway West reservation, crossing Roosevelt Circle at Forest Street in a stretch of private reservation through the circle. The track

---

[n] The landscaped median was known for its large trees, most of which were destroyed in the Hurricane of 1938. The topography of this area was completely changed by the construction of I-93 in the 1960s.

An Eastern Mass. semi-convertible and a Boston Elevated Type 5 are seen at Elm Street in August 1942. Although the Boston Elevated's trackage extended to just beyond the Stoneham line, Type 5s seldom ventured past Elm Street, most of the service being run by Eastern Mass. cars.   *Charles A. Duncan*

Type 5 No. 5635 crosses over at Elm Street for the trip back to Sullivan Square on April 2, 1949. The former streetcar right-of-way into the Middlesex Fells shows in the background, but the rails have been removed.   *Norton D. Clark*

The grass is beginning to show the first signs of spring as 5788 heads inbound through Roosevelt Circle for Sullivan Square on March 26, 1950.   *Foster M. Palmer*

followed the Fellsway West, again in a reservation to Salem Street, where a single-track connection inbound and a double-track connection outbound led to Salem Street and the carhouse. Crossovers on the Fellsway West on either side of Salem Street permitted cars to turn back in either direction but were primarily for the Salem Street cutback.

Cars continued in the Fellsway West reservation to St. Mary Street where they crossed into Malden. Fellsway East

At left, Eastern Mass. 4387 pauses at the Salem Street stop to take on passengers in October 1945. At right, Type 5 No. 5788 operates on the Fellsway around 1946. *Both, Charles A. Duncan*

then joined the Fellsway West and the combined street became known simply as the Fellsway. After just 2,000 feet in Malden, the line crossed back into Medford at Malden Street. At Revere Beach Parkway, the line crossed through Wellington Circle.[182]

After leaving Wellington Circle, the line reached the end of the private reservation at the Wellington Bridge over the Mystic River. Crossing the bridge in street pavement, the line entered Somerville at the boundary line in the middle of the river.

Reentering the reservation on the Somerville side of the bridge, the line continued on the Fellsway to Mystic Avenue. Here the tracks entered street paving. The line then followed Mystic Avenue past two crossovers near the Ford Assembly plant all the way to the ramp at Sullivan Square Station.[183] A round-trip on Route 100 between Elm Street and Sullivan Square was 9.138 miles and had an average running time of 40 minutes. The Salem Street–Sullivan cutback was 6.675 miles long, round-trip, and had an average running time of 28 minutes.

Cars crossed the Mystic River in street trackage on the Wellington Bridge, rejoining the reservation at both ends. Above, an Eastern Mass. car crosses the bridge on March 19, 1946. At right, PCC 3001, the "Queen Mary," crosses the bridge with a carload of railfans in a prewar outing on June 19, 1938. This single-end car would not run past Salem Street Carhouse, and returned via Medford Square and Winter Hill. *Above, Charles A. Duncan; right, Charles A. Brown*

Near the Charlestown-Somerville boundary on Mystic Avenue, the cars crossed a bridge over the B&M Railroad. Immediately after this bridge, the line turned left off the street onto Boston Elevated property, crossing a single track that led to the Charlestown Neck Carhouse. The Fellsway line then joined the Broadway line on the ramp to the rapid transit level of Sullivan Square Station as previously described. Tracks also continued straight on Mystic Avenue to its junction with Main Street. The trackage in this immediate area of Sullivan Square is detailed on Inset D of Map 7, on Map 8, Insets A and B, and on the Sullivan Square detail drawing.

The End of the Stoneham Line

After World War II, the end of streetcar service to Stoneham was just a matter of time. On Wednesday, June 12, 1946, just prior to the planned conversion of the line to buses, Eastern Mass. cars 4382 and 4396 collided head-on near Spot Pond about 5:30 p.m. Malfunctioning signals caused the crash. Twenty-three were injured, some seriously, including both operators, James Purtle, 70, of Stoneham, and Herbert Fitzpatrick, 24, of Melrose. Purtle later died.

Both cars were wrecked and were replaced with two Boston Elevated 4300s from Revere. The Eastern Mass. leased these cars, 4373 and 4395, from the Elevated and returned them after the abandonment of the Stoneham line. An almost

The car tracks on the reservation on the short stretch of the Fellsway on the Somerville side of the Wellington Bridge were a refuge from the local motor vehicle traffic. Here 5689 nears Mystic Avenue on April 25, 1948.

Foster M. Palmer

At Mystic Avenue the Fellsway and the streetcar reservation came to an end, the tracks transitioning from reservation to street running in this scene taken June 11, 1943. On this innermost section of the line, the very place that streetcar service could have used private right-of-way, the cars were forced to mix with street traffic. To the left, the view is straight up Mystic Avenue to Medford Square.

BERy

This lone Type 5 on Mystic Avenue is nearing the crossing over the B&M Railroad near the Charlestown boundary with Somerville. Right after the bridge, the car will turn onto the ramp at Sullivan Square Station.

BERy

Eastern Mass. 4388 is seen on Mystic Avenue at Sullivan Square in 1946. Tracks in the foreground are on Main Street, which becomes Broadway when they cross the Somerville line a short distance to the left of this location.

Charles A. Duncan

Above, Eastern Mass. car 4383 from Stoneham rounds the loop on the upper level of Sullivan Square Station to take on passengers for a return trip about 1946. At right, on October 1, 1946, roadway construction on the upper level is underway as this Type 5 starts around the loop.

Above, Arthur Ellis; right, BERy

identical head-on collision had occurred at the same place on July 17, 1921. After this tragedy, a local transportation committee that had been formed in Stoneham earlier pressed for conversion of the line to buses. The Eastern Mass. hastened to satisfy this request.

Saturday, July 27, 1946, was the last full day of service for the Eastern Mass. segment of the Stoneham–Sullivan Square Station line. The following day, the line was abandoned from the Sheepfold to the Farm Hill railroad crossing. Veteran operators George Barnes and Pete Dulong, wearing traditional blue uniforms of the Bay State Street Railway, and Howard Sproul, another veteran but in Eastern Mass. khaki, operated the cars all day. By this time, the cars were locally referred to as the "Yellow Peril" because of the Fells accident a month earlier.

The last regular revenue car arrived at the Sheepfold on its way to Stoneham on Sunday, July 28. "At 1:03 (a.m.) it thundered into the Sheepfold and stopped," according to the *Stoneham Independent* of August 2, 1946, and a crowd of rowdy well wishers clambered aboard.[184] With much singing and high jinks, the car, 4385, ran through the Fells onto Main Street, up over Rowe's Hill, and down to Central Square. Here, almost everyone debarked, danced around the car, whooped and cheered. As the car continued to Farm Hill, the crowd continued its antics.

On the return trip, most of the interior fittings and equipment, including light bulbs, hand straps, and seats were torn out for souvenirs. The trolley was also pulled off the wire several times. When the car arrived at the Sheepfold, most of the riders got off, but a few went on to Salem Street, ending a very wild night.

The Boston Elevated also abandoned its tracks in the Middlesex Fells from Elm Street to Spot Pond at this time. Streetcars now ran only from Elm Street to Sullivan Square Station, with the cutback at Salem Street. Starting on May 12, 1947, the Elevated removed the track from Elm Street to the Stoneham line, completing this project on June 9. The short stretch of track operated under lease just over the Stoneham line by the El was the property of the Eastern Mass, which removed this section as well as the track to the end of the line.

The Eastern Mass. was granted permission by the Boston Elevated to operate buses from Stoneham into the lower level of Sullivan Square Station. The buses ran on Main Street and the Fellsway West, just outside the Middlesex Fells reservation, since no replacement could be made for the route within the park itself. In Boston El territory, the Eastern Mass. buses operated "closed door," and a 10¢ cash fare at Sullivan Square Station was required from Eastern Mass. passengers to take the El or exit to the street. After numerous complaints, the Eastern Mass. was given permission to stop at Salem Street to allow riders to make a more convenient transfer to Medford or Malden.

Concurrent with the abandonment of the Eastern Mass. line to Stoneham, the Boston Elevated abandoned its service from Elm Street to the Sheepfold. Here in 1947, El forces are tearing up the multi-arched bridge across Chandler Road.
Roger F. Jenkins

Lester H. Stephenson, Sr., an Eastern Mass. motorman and one of the early Seashore Trolley Museum pioneers, ran the last trolley on a ceremonial trip to Stoneham on Sunday afternoon, July 28, 1946. The car was 4387, now at the Seashore Trolley Museum. It was operated to the Farm Hill railroad crossing, where hundreds of Stoneham residents had gathered to photograph the car and bid farewell to the line. Stephenson had also been the operator of the last revenue car in the wee hours of the morning that same day.

Officials and prominent local residents boarded 4387 at 2 p.m., and the car carried the party to Stoneham Square. Here the dignitaries boarded new ACF-Brill C-36 2200-series buses for a round-trip to Sullivan Square and back. The August 2, 1946, *Stoneham Independent* had an extensive article with photo coverage on the conversion of the line to buses, and Lester H. Stephenson, Sr. was prominently featured.

101 Salem Street–Sullivan *via Winter Hill*

The Salem Street–Sullivan via Winter Hill line ran almost entirely on street trackage from Salem Street Carhouse to Sullivan Square Station. Like the lines from Clarendon Hill, this route was also converted to trolley coach operation. However, the Winter Hill line would be the only trackless trolley operation ever based at Salem Street.

Leaving Salem Street Carhouse, the car line turned southwest onto Salem Street, and ran to Medford Square. The last block on Salem Street between River Street and Forest Street at Medford Square was one-way westbound for automobiles, but two-way for streetcars. Eastbound streetcar trips in this block were run with caution, particularly during the rush hours.

At Medford Square, the line turned south onto Main Street and crossed the Mystic River. A trailing point crossover at Main and Eliot Streets, a half-mile beyond the intersection of Main Street and Mystic Avenue, was the only cutback on the line. Cars continued on Main Street, crossing the Medford–Somerville boundary near Tremont Street. The line turned left onto Broadway, joining the Clarendon Hill–Sullivan line and continuing into Sullivan Square Station on Broadway and Main Street. A round-trip on Route 101 was 8.761 miles and had a

Route 101, Salem Street Carhouse–Sullivan Square Station via Winter Hill, was not as well known as the Fellsway operations. It nearly was converted to full-time bus operation before World War II, but survived because of ODT regulations. This view shows Type 5 No. 5700 on Main Street in March 1947; in April the line will be converted to trackless trolleys. *Charles A. Duncan*

Route 101 tracks ran right through Medford Square and included a short stretch of two-way car operation on the one-way section of Salem Street to the right. This view is circa 1945. *Arthur Griffin*

running time of 45 minutes. The Eliot Street cutback was 5.192 miles round-trip and took 27 minutes to complete.

This line was converted to part-time bus operation, starting on September 9, 1939.[185] Streetcars were used in weekday and Saturday rush hours, and buses were used at all other times. On May 9, 1942, ODT restrictions ended limited bus service, and trolleys were restored to full time operation. After the war, however, the line returned to the prewar streetcar and bus mix.

Starting on December 16, 1946, buses replaced streetcars during off-peak hours on the Winter Hill line and on December 28 began running to the newly rebuilt upper level at Sullivan Square Station. On April 19, 1947, trackless trolleys completely replaced streetcars and buses on this line. Twenty-five trolley coaches were assigned and the round-trip running time was cut by five minutes. The Eliot Street streetcar cutback was replaced by trackless trolley cutbacks at Tufts Square and Medford Square.

Medford Square receding in the background, Type 5 No. 5786 crosses Craddock Bridge on Main Street over the Mystic River and heads for Sullivan Square. *Charles A. Duncan*

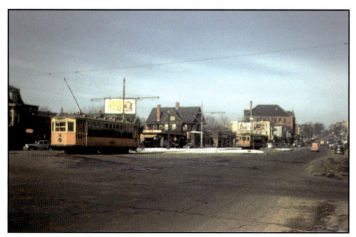

Broadway in Somerville was indeed broad, so much so that it sported a private streetcar reservation running from Grant Street to the Northern Artery, behind the photographer. The Clarendon Hill–Sullivan and Salem Street–Sullivan lines both used this trackage. Winter Hill looms in the distance in this scene taken in March 1946. *Charles A. Duncan*

A Type 5 from Salem Street bound for Sullivan is nearing Broadway on Main Street in Somerville on December 10, 1946. *Foster M. Palmer*

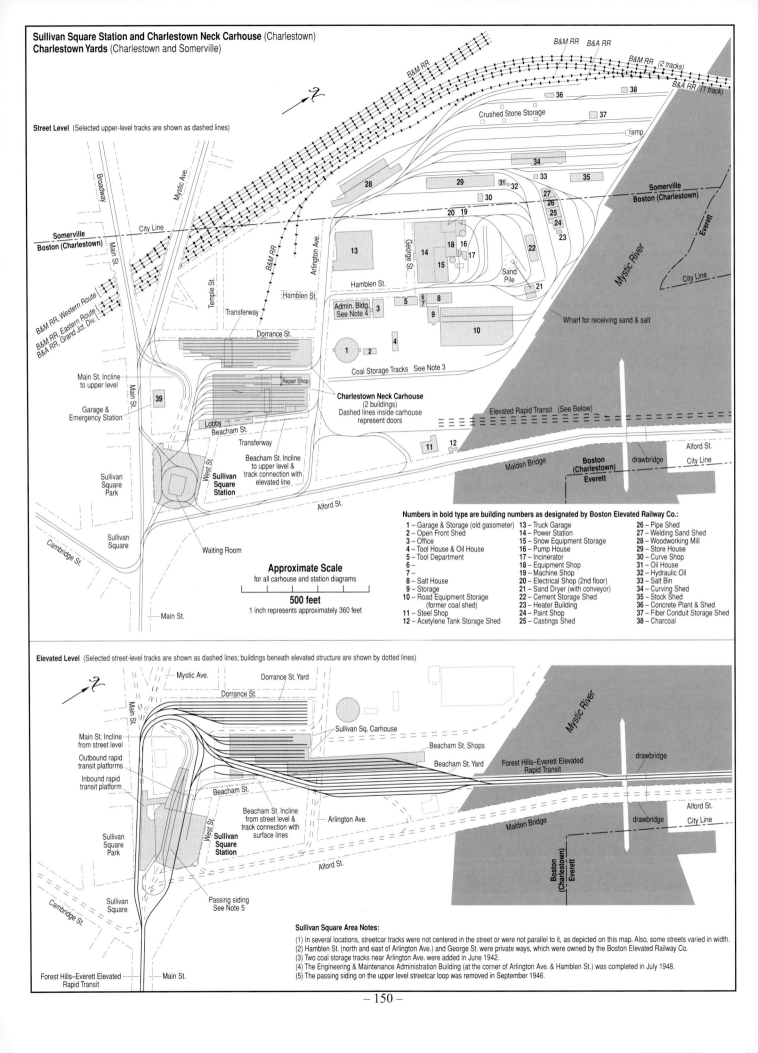

Sullivan Square Station and Charlestown Neck Carhouse (Charlestown)
Charlestown Yards (Charlestown and Somerville)

Street Level (Selected upper-level tracks are shown as dashed lines)

Broadway

Mystic Ave.

B&M RR

B&M RR

B&M RR

B&M RR (2 tracks)

B&A RR (1 track)

Somerville
Boston (Charlestown)

City Line

36

38

Crushed Stone Storage

37

ramp

34

28

29

33

35

31 32

30

27

26

20 19

25

24

13

George St.

14

18 16

23

22

Main St.

B&M RR, Western Route

B&M RR, Eastern Route

B&A RR, Grand Jct. Div.

Temple St.

Transferway

Arlington Ave.

15

17

Sand
Pile

21

Hamblen St.

Hamblen St.

Admin. Bldg.
See Note 4

3

5

6
7

8

Mystic River

Everett

City Line

Somerville
Boston (Charlestown)

Dorrance St.

9

Repair Shop

4

10

Wharf for receiving sand & salt

Main St. Incline
to upper level

1

2

Coal Storage Tracks   See Note 3

39

Garage &
Emergency Station

Main St.

Charlestown Neck Carhouse
(2 buildings)
Dashed lines inside carhouse
represent doors

Elevated Rapid Transit   (See Below)

Lobby

Beacham St.

Transferway

11

12

Alford St.

West St.

Beacham St. Incline
to upper level &
track connection with
elevated line

**Sullivan
Square
Station**

Malden Bridge

**Boston
(Charlestown)**

drawbridge

City Line

Everett

Sullivan
Square
Park

Alford St.

Waiting Room

Sullivan
Square

Numbers in bold type are building numbers as designated by Boston Elevated Railway Co.:

1 – Garage & Storage (old gasometer)	13 – Truck Garage	26 – Pipe Shed
2 – Open Front Shed	14 – Power Station	27 – Welding Sand Shed
3 – Office	15 – Snow Equipment Storage	28 – Woodworking Mill
4 – Tool House & Oil House	16 – Pump House	29 – Store House
5 – Tool Department	17 – Incinerator	30 – Curve Shop
6 –	18 – Equipment Shop	31 – Oil House
7 –	19 – Machine Shop	32 – Hydraulic Oil
8 – Salt House	20 – Electrical Shop (2nd floor)	33 – Salt Bin
9 – Storage	21 – Sand Dryer (with conveyor)	34 – Curving Shed
10 – Road Equipment Storage (former coal shed)	22 – Cement Storage Shed	35 – Stock Shed
11 – Steel Shop	23 – Heater Building	36 – Concrete Plant & Shed
12 – Acetylene Tank Storage Shed	24 – Paint Shop	37 – Fiber Conduit Storage Shed
	25 – Castings Shed	38 – Charcoal

Cambridge St.

Main St.

Approximate Scale
for all carhouse and station diagrams

500 feet

1 inch represents approximately 360 feet

Elevated Level (Selected street-level tracks are shown as dashed lines; buildings beneath elevated structure are shown by dotted lines)

Mystic Ave.

Dorrance St. Yard

Dorrance St.

Main St.

Main St. Incline
from street level

Sullivan Sq. Carhouse

Beacham St. Shops

Mystic River

drawbridge

Outbound rapid
transit platforms

Beacham St. Yard

Inbound rapid
transit platform

Forest Hills–Everett Elevated
Rapid Transit

West St.

Beacham St.

Beacham St. Incline
from street level &
track connection with
surface lines

Arlington Ave.

**Sullivan
Square
Station**

Alford St.

Malden Bridge

drawbridge

Alford St.

City Line

**Boston
(Charlestown)**

Everett

Sullivan
Square
Park

Sullivan
Square

Cambridge St.

Passing siding
See Note 5

Forest Hills–Everett Elevated
Rapid Transit

Main St.

Sullivan Square Area Notes:

(1) In several locations, streetcar tracks were not centered in the street or were not parallel to it, as depicted on this map. Also, some streets varied in width.
(2) Hamblen St. (north and east of Arlington Ave.) and George St. were private ways, which were owned by the Boston Elevated Railway Co.
(3) Two coal storage tracks near Arlington Ave. were added in June 1942.
(4) The Engineering & Maintenance Administration Building (at the corner of Arlington Ave. & Hamblen St.) was completed in July 1948.
(5) The passing siding on the upper level streetcar loop was removed in September 1946.

The Charlestown Lines

Two car lines ran through Charlestown to the Tremont Street Subway at Canal Street, and from there into the Brattle Street platform adjoining Scollay Square Station. One line ran via Main Street, and the second ran via Bunker Hill Street on roughly parallel routes. Both lines started at the lower level of Sullivan Square Station and used Type 5s exclusively.

Charlestown Neck Carhouse

The Charlestown cars were serviced at Salem Street but were stored at Charlestown Neck Carhouse, which was located under the rapid transit yard and shops complex adjoining Sullivan Square Station. Charlestown Neck consisted of two large carhouse buildings separated by an alley. Storing the cars for the Charlestown lines at Charlestown Neck avoided excessive deadhead mileage between Salem Street Carhouse and Sullivan Square.

Dorrance Street, Arlington Avenue, Beacham Street, and the ramp leading from Main Street and Mystic Avenue to the upper level of Sullivan Square Station bordered the Charlestown Neck complex. The building on Beacham Street was still in active use in the 1940s, but the second structure along Dorrance Street had long since fallen into disuse. Two tracks from the loop on the lower level of Sullivan Square crossed Beacham Street and fanned out into twelve storage tracks that ran into the carhouse. Main Street and Bunker Hill cars were stored both in and outside of the building.

92 Sullivan Square Station–Brattle Street Station *via Main Street*

Both the Main Street and Bunker Hill cars shared a full loop on the street level of Sullivan Square Station. Both routes turned southeast from the station onto Main Street, and crossed the B&M Railroad Mystic Branch at grade.[°] The Main Street line diverged from the Bunker Hill line at Fay Square (Main and Bunker Hill Streets) and continued southeast on Main Street.

At Thompson Square, the inbound rail ran on Main Street, which was one-way, into City Square. The outbound rail returned from City Square to Thompson Square via Park and Warren Streets. Map 7, Inset C shows the tracks in and around City Square in detail.

Until 1942, the Bunker Hill and Main Street car lines followed North Washington and Causeway Streets under the Main Line Elevated from City Square to the Canal Street Loop. North Washington Street crossed the Charlestown Bridge over the Charles River from Charlestown into Boston proper. The Charlestown Bridge with the Main Line Elevated and the street-

[°] This railroad branch served the Charlestown waterfront.

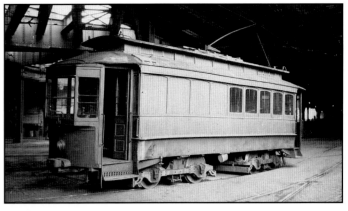

Charlestown Neck Carhouse was obscured by its location underneath the elevated structure adjacent to Sullivan Square Station. While primarily used in later years for the storage of work equipment such as car 40 pictured here on April 28, 1946, the tracks into the building were also used for day storage of cars running to the Tremont Street Subway via Bunker Hill or via Main Street.
Stanley M. Hauck

cars running underneath the elevated were an impressive display of massive transit infrastructure and investment.

Once across the bridge, the car lines and the elevated turned southwest onto Causeway Street. After passing Haverhill Street, the streetcars turned southeast and entered the Canal Street Loop. From Canal Street, the cars followed the center tracks of the Tremont Street Subway to the Brattle Street Station platform. Details of the subway operation of these lines have been given in Chapter 5. A round-trip on Route 92 was 4.360 miles and required a running time of 29 minutes.

On Causeway Street, the car tracks shared the roadway with the Union Freight Railroad. Both the surface car tracks and the Union Freight track were located beneath the Main Line Elevated. For the block between North Washington Street and Medford Street, the single-track freight line was in the middle, with one streetcar track to either side. A facing point

Main Street and Bunker Hill Street cars for Brattle Street Station loaded on the lower level of Sullivan Square Station. Here we see Type 5 No. 5545 taking on passengers about 1947. *BERy*

A car bound for Brattle Street via either Main or Bunker Hill Street emerges from the lower level of Sullivan Square Station in September 1945. Note the Fellsway car on the upper loop and the elevated train on the storage track opposite the inbound platform. The foreground tracks were part of the service line to Porter Square.
Charles A. Duncan

crossover between the car tracks added to the trackage complexity in this block.

At Medford Street, the freight line moved to the south side of the street, avoiding the Boston Elevated's special work leading to Beverly Street. The freight track then turned northwest onto Accolon Way, a private way running beside the North Station building. At Accolon Way, the freight line crossed over both car tracks just before they turned southeast into the Canal Street Loop and the Central Subway. Inset B on Map 7 details this complicated track arrangement.

The Main Street line had much lower ridership than the line over Bunker Hill. Because the Main Street line ran under the Main Line Elevated along most of its route, it was useful only to local riders between elevated stations. To a great extent it was redundant to the Bunker Hill line and to the rapid transit line above.

Warren Avenue

At City Square, the Main Street and Bunker Hill Street car lines both connected to a double-track line on Warren Avenue, as well as to the tracks across the Charlestown Bridge. The Warren Avenue tracks ran over the Warren Bridge across the Charles River to Beverly Street in Boston Proper. The line continued on Beverly Street to Causeway Street, where the tracks connected in both directions on Causeway Street.[p] Insets B and C on Map 7 show this trackage.

The Warren Avenue tracks were an alternate route to the Charlestown Bridge between City Square and the Tremont Street Subway. Their last regular use had been on June 9, 1936, by Eastern Mass. shuttle cars running between Mystic

---

[p] The streetcar tracks crossed two B&M Railroad freight spurs on Beverly Street and one on Warren Avenue near City Square.

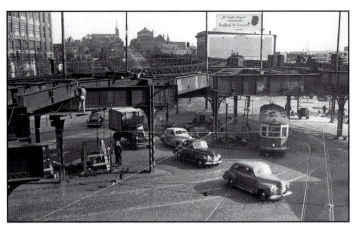

Both Charlestown routes used this section of Main Street. This Type 5 is returning from Brattle Street amid the reconstruction of the streetcar loop on October 15, 1946.
BERy

The Main Street line ran under the Main Line Elevated for most of its route. Here, automobile traffic is light as Type 5 No. 5529 approaches Thompson Square in April 1948.
Charles A. Duncan

From Thompson Square to City Square, the Main Street line split, with inbound cars following Main Street while outbound cars operated on the parallel Warren Street. This scene shows the Victorian Thompson Square Elevated station with Type 5 No. 5529 on Warren Street heading for Sullivan Square.
Charles A. Duncan

Wharf and Brattle Loop. Heavy Boston Navy Yard traffic during World War II would bring these tracks back to life.

In 1942, the Elevated rebuilt the Beverly Street and Warren Avenue tracks from Causeway Street to a B&M Railroad grade crossing located just south of City Square. A new crossover was also installed on Warren Avenue near the grade crossing.[186]

Center-entrance car 6156 brings up the rear of a two-car train rounding the bend at Park and Warren Streets, Charlestown, in April 1945. These cars are on their way to Everett Shops for repairs. The Main Street line continued to be used for equipment transfers such as this until 1962, long after regular car service ended.
Charles A. Duncan

The crossover would be used for Route 93 cars shuttling between this point and another crossover at Elm and Bunker Hill Streets and for a cutback from Sullivan Square. The shuttle service was operated for only one rating starting on April 3, 1944, because of a streetcar shortage and a change in working hours at the Navy Yard. When the shuttle operated, it was independent of both the Warren Avenue and Charlestown drawbridges yet it offered a direct connection to downtown Boston via the Main Line Elevated at City Square Station. See Appendix 9 for operating details of the shuttle.

From 1942 to 1947, Charlestown streetcars followed Warren Avenue inbound and the North Washington Street tracks over the Charlestown Bridge outbound. In the winter of 1946, both tracks on Warren Avenue and Beverly Street were used during an emergency that will be covered later. As mentioned in Chapter 1, for a time during World War II in the early morning hours, the Beverly Street tracks were used as a staging area for newspaper cars.

On April 17, 1947, the Massachusetts Department of Public Utilities (DPU) prohibited the operation of outbound streetcars on the Warren Bridge and buses in either direction. This ban was later lifted.

93 Sullivan Square Station–Brattle Street Station *via Bunker Hill Street*

Sullivan Square–Brattle Street Station via Bunker Hill was by far the heavier of the two Charlestown streetcar lines. The Bunker Hill line diverged from the Main Street line at Fay Square onto Bunker Hill Street. The cars then ran up and over Bunker Hill.

The line continued to Chelsea Street, where it turned southwest, passed the Navy Yard and ran into City Square, rejoining the Main Street route. From City Square to the subway and onto Brattle Street Station, the line shared the same track with the Main Street cars. The round-trip distance of this route was 5.173 miles. The average round-trip running time was 35 minutes.

Pictures of cars on the Warren Avenue Bridge are scarce. At top, Type 4 No. 5191 stands on the draw of the Warren Avenue Bridge in this fan trip photo stop on January 15, 1939. Since Type 5s normally ran here, this shot of a Type 4 here is rare despite the fact that it was staged. Above, thirteen months later, on February 16, 1940, Type 5 No. 5554 copes with the aftermath of the 1940 blizzard. The Charlestown Bridge is off to the right, and in the background is the B&M Railroad grain elevator at Hoosac Pier.
Both, Charles A. Duncan

This line had a morning rush hour cutback at a crossover at Elm and Bunker Hill Streets. Cars from Brattle Street Station could turn back here, and did so intermittently during the 1940s. The round-trip distance of this route was 3.164 miles and cars operating on the line had a running time of 26 minutes.

No. 5522 turns the corner from Bunker Hill Street onto Chelsea Street in April 1948. Workers from the Boston Naval Shipyard right ahead of the car were heavy users of the line, which might have continued for many more years if it had not been displaced by construction of the Mystic River (Tobin) Bridge above the tracks on Chelsea Street.
Charles A. Duncan

Streetcar Route 93 was famous for its speed traps along Bunker Hill Street. Clearly marked, they nevertheless did ensnare many an unwary motorist, and for those in the know, they were an effective deterrent. This one is at Elm Street, looking down Bunker Hill toward the Navy Yard. The crossover for the Elm Street turnback was behind the company photographer.   *BERy*

This view of lower Bunker Hill Street was taken about 1945. Oh, the joys of winter commuting!   *BERy*

Cars from Sullivan Square used the crossover on Warren Avenue mentioned above as an evening cutback point, also on an intermittent basis. This short turn route was 3.417 miles round-trip and took 23 minutes to complete.

Speed traps consisting of unpaved track located between pedestrian traffic safety islands at hazardous locations along the street were an interesting feature of this line. Automobiles were forced to the right of the islands rather than being able to speed between them. A safety lamp atop a beacon and a sign at the end of the islands that read, " SLOW KEEP RIGHT RESERVATION FOR ELECTRIC CARS ONLY," made the intent of these areas very clear.

Bob FitzGerald remembers…

During the summer of 1941, my family moved to Charlestown. We lived two blocks from Chelsea Street and the Boston Navy Yard. We used the Bunker Hill-Brattle Street Station trolley line, and our stop was at Vine Street, near St. Catherine's Church and Bond Bread Bakeries.

During the summer of 1943, at age seven and unknown by my parents, I took my first fan trip on the Boston Elevated Railway. I had a little money and decided to go to the Woolworth 5 & 10 at Dudley Street, an area I knew. I boarded the trolley at Vine Street and changed at City Square for the Main Line Elevated. After buying a toy, I returned home. I made these trips a few more times. To this day, I do not believe my parents ever knew.

I also recall traveling by trolley to Brattle Street Station with my father, going on occasion to Eric Fuchs' hobby store to see the model trains. We traveled from City Square inbound via Warren Avenue (over the low bridge) and outbound via North Washington Street under the elevated (over the high bridge). I also remember the inbound Charlestown streetcars "racing" the cars bound for Park Street on
the outside track, and likewise, outbound through Adams Square Station.*

In June 1944, we moved to West Medford. My family often rode to Revere Beach via Everett, taking the Revere Carhouse via Park Avenue trackless to Revere Carhouse and changing there for either Revere Beach trolley.

Usually we walked across Broadway and waited on Central Avenue for the Beach Street car. Often the car would so be packed that no one could get on. After several trackless trolleys had unloaded, sometimes there would be so many people waiting that the El would pull an "extra" trolley out of Revere Carhouse. Always, when waiting for the Revere Beach car, I hoped for a 4400 rather than a Type 5. I did not know the model names or trolley numbers, but I did know the differences. The two wide front windows, the destination signs, the leather seats, and the linoleum floors of the 4400s were distinctive features.

I often went to ballgames and rode 3-car center-entrance trains to both Fenway Park and Braves Field. At Braves Field Loop, the cars loaded behind the stands near the first base side of the field. The turnstiles were right at the ballpark exit, and the double-track siding held four 3-car trains. With luck, I might also see a 3-car train of PCC cars!

Robert W. FitzGerald is Entertainment Chairman of the BSRA. By the late 1940s, at age 13, he was making personal fan trips and building a lifetime of memories.

The Charlestown Bridge Accident

The track rebuilding on Beverly Street and Warren Avenue in 1942 was a fortunate move, for an unusual accident took place later. On Monday, December 17, 1945, about 10:30 a.m., the "Liberty" ship cargo vessel SS *John Hathorn* rammed the Charlestown Bridge while backing out of Hoosac Pier in a high wind. The collision seriously damaged the bridge and the Main Line Elevated structure. The Boston Transit Commission at the turn of the century had built a section of the elevated railway into the superstructure of the bridge.

Main Line Elevated service was immediately suspended. The B&M Railroad hurriedly loaned the Boston Elevated a turntable to support the elevated structure and make a temporary fix. Repairs began at once, continuing nonstop through a blinding snowstorm on December 19.

Many elevated trains had been put up at Sullivan Square Station after the morning rush hour, leaving only a few trains to serve the southern part of the line. The Forest Hills Shop was reopened in record time after a 12-year hiatus to handle running repairs and routine maintenance for the remaining but now stranded rapid transit cars running between Forest Hills and North Station. On December 20, after three days of frantic work, Main Line Elevated service was partially restored. Full service, however, could not resume until March 6, 1946, when all repairs had finally been completed.

In the interim about 50 streetcars provided service between Sullivan Square Station and Brattle Street, running over the Warren Bridge in both directions. Bi-directional streetcar service continued on Warren Avenue and Beverly Street until March 7, 1946.

On December 17, 1945, an improbable direct collision between a ship and an elevated structure occurred when SS *John Hathorn* rammed the Charlestown Bridge, seriously damaging the bridge and the Main Line Elevated which ran across it. This view shows the missing section of the bridge and the bend in the elevated structure.

Using a spare turntable borrowed from the B&M Railroad, the elevated structure was propped up and trains were running again by December 20. Streetcar service across the bridge, however, was impossible and all car traffic was diverted to the nearby Warren Bridge.
BERy

Repairs to the bridge were far enough along to allow cars bound for Charlestown and Everett Shops to begin using the span by March 1946. Somewhat later, Eastern Mass. cars used it on their final trip—to the scrap track at Everett in 1948.
Charles A. Duncan

The End of Charlestown Streetcar Service

The Main Street car line was abandoned on April 3, 1948, when a bus line between Sullivan Square Station and City Square replaced the cars. Inbound or outbound bus riders could transfer at City Square to or from the Main Line Elevated or the Bunker Hill car line.

The Main Street tracks remained active for Owl Cars between Sullivan Square and Brattle Street Stations until December 1949, when an Owl Bus between Sullivan and Haymarket Squares replaced them. The previously discussed Brattle Station shuttle car also used these tracks to get from Sullivan Square to the subway and regular riders also took advantage of this operation, possibly on the half-trip run in the early morning, but definitely in the evening trip around 6:55 p.m. Some trackage of the Main Street line, in fact, continued in use until 1962 for repair and work cars being moved between the subway and the Charlestown Yard or Everett Shops.

Buses replaced streetcars on the Bunker Hill line on July 2, 1949. The September 1949 edition of *Co-operation* stated that the car line was no longer operable because of construction for the new Mystic River Bridge,[q] which was expected to open early in 1950.[187] Some of the footings for the new bridge on Chelsea Street near Chestnut Street had been placed in the area occupied by the car tracks.[r]

The new Bunker Hill bus line ran from Sullivan Square to North Station via Haymarket Square. It followed a complicated route along Main, Bunker Hill, Chelsea, Adams, Common, Park, Henley, and Main Streets. It then passed through City Square onto Warren Avenue, ran over the Warren Bridge and then on Beverly, Causeway, and North Washington Streets to Haymarket Square. From here, the buses returned to North Station via Haverhill Street.

The new bus line had several transfer points. Passengers could change at City Square to the Main Line Elevated; at the corner of Beverly and Causeway Streets to North Station; at Haymarket Square to the Central Subway or the Main Line Elevated; and at Haverhill and Causeway Streets to North Station. Inbound passengers could ride all the way to Haverhill and Causeway Streets; outbound riders could also board at Haymarket Square.

As mentioned in Chapter 5 and earlier in this chapter, to replace the subway service that was lost because of the abandonment of the Charlestown lines, the MTA began running a shuttle between North Station and Brattle Street Station on October 15, 1949. The shuttle car ran on a 15-minute headway, and the bus fare from Charlestown included a free transfer to the shuttle. The MTA used a single Type 5 on this route, which finally ended in September 1952.

[q] The Mystic River Bridge opened on February 27, 1950, and eliminated the need for the north and south drawbridges to Chelsea, both of which closed the same day.

[r] Sections of Chelsea Street were closed permanently for the new bridge, and the street was split into two disconnected segments.

The Charlestown Yard located near Sullivan Square Station was a major supply depot for the Boston Elevated. Here we see a side dump car in the foreground beside a pile of ballast, the work train that accessed the elevated along the connection on Arlington Avenue, and one of the larger storage buildings.   *BERy*

The Charlestown Yard

The Charlestown Yard ran along the northeast side of Arlington Avenue near the Sullivan Square Station complex. Track and maintenance of way material storage facilities, a steel fabrication shop, and interchanges with the B&M and B&A Railroads were all located in this sprawling yard.

A single track ran from the northwest end of Arlington Avenue to a point east of Beacham Street. Here the line changed to double track. Six spur tracks ran off the Arlington Avenue single track to various points in the yard, Charlestown Neck Carhouse, and Sullivan Square Station.

Moving along Arlington Avenue toward Alford Street, there were four single-track yard connections on the northeast side of the street. The first two connections were roughly parallel and ran into the sections of the yard used for bulk materials, track fabrication, and millwork. Next a yard track on Hamblen Street ran to the machine shop, sand dryer, cement shed and paint shop. The third connection ran to the steel shop and looped back onto Alford Street.

The presence of passenger car 5678 in the Charlestown Yard in September 1947 makes it clear that this is another of the many fan trips of that era.   *Charles A. Duncan*

A July 14, 1940, fan trip found a variety of work equipment at the Charlestown Yard. Clockwise, from top, steeple cab locomotive No. 0527 has coupled onto a Pittsburgh & Lake Erie Railroad box-car. Another of the versatile steeple cabs brings up the rear. Flat car 2005, carrying wheelsets, is in front of fan trip car 5745. Side dump car 3626 is stacked with ties. Its mate, 3623, is behind it.
Right, Stanley M. Hauck; others, Charles A. Duncan

On the southwest side of Arlington Avenue there were two more connections. The first ran down the alley between the two Charlestown Neck carhouse buildings and into the lower level of Sullivan Square Station. The second ran up a ramp from Arlington Avenue to the rapid transit level of Sullivan Square Station. Work cars bringing materials to and from the Main Line Elevated used this ramp. Surface cars from Everett and Malden to Sullivan Square Station had formerly used the ramp before the extension to Everett Station was built.

At the east end of Arlington Avenue, a double-track connection joined the tracks on Alford Street in the direction of Sullivan Square Station. A single-track spur also connected the double track section on Arlington Avenue to the steel shop track mentioned above.

There were few changes at the Charlestown Yard during the 1940s. In 1942, the Elevated installed 1470 feet of coal storage tracks.[188] On July 31, 1948, the MTA opened its new Charlestown Administration Building at 21 Arlington Avenue. This facility housed the MTA Engineering Department. A building addition was later opened on December 9, 1949.

Everett Shops

The Everett Shops complex was the most important maintenance facility of the Boston Elevated. It was opened in 1923 and expanded in 1939. Almost any repair could be made here to the streetcars, rapid transit cars, trackless trolleys, buses, and utility vehicles that the company owned.

Everett Shops was connected to most of the surface rail system by a double-track line that ran on Alford Street and Broadway from Sullivan Square Station. A double track spur ran off Broadway onto Chemical Lane and into the Everett Shops. A service track connection on Broadway continued from Chemical Lane past Everett Station to Chelsea. This

A charming relic of the early electric trolley era resided at Everett Shops. This was No. 1412, a 16-foot horsecar built in 1888 and motorized in 1889 and used that year on the Bowdoin Square–Harvard Square–Arlington electric line. It is shown here as a shop locomotive, a role it played until 1942. *Pitt Holland*

Everett Shops, the principal repair facility on the system, boasted two transfer tables, one of which is seen behind 5653, obviously in need of repair and a likely candidate for a ride on the transfer table in this mid-1940s scene. The transfer tables themselves operated like trolley cars, rolling on tracks, using a trolley pole power pickup, and controlled with a streetcar controller and air brakes.
Daniel R. Cohen Collection

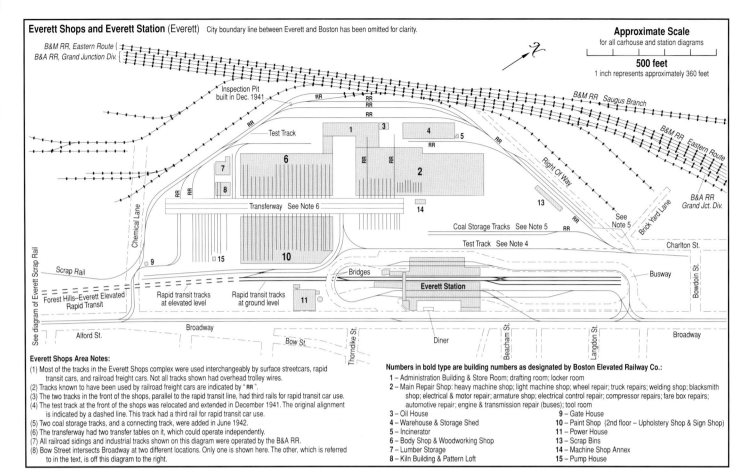

Everett Shops and Everett Station (Everett) City boundary line between Everett and Boston has been omitted for clarity.

B&M RR, Eastern Route
B&A RR, Grand Junction Div.

B&M RR Saugus Branch

B&M RR Eastern Route

B&A RR Grand Jct. Div.

Inspection Pit built in Dec. 1941

Test Track

Right Of Way

See Note 5

Brick Yard Lane

Charlton St.

Chemical Lane

Transferway See Note 6

Coal Storage Tracks See Note 5

Test Track See Note 4

Scrap Rail

Bridges

Busway

Bowdoin St.

Everett Station

Forest Hills–Everett Elevated Rapid Transit

See diagram of Everett Scrap Rail

Rapid transit tracks at elevated level

Rapid transit tracks at ground level

Alford St.

Broadway

Bow St.

Thorndike St.

Diner

Beacham St.

Langdon St.

Broadway

Approximate Scale
for all carhouse and station diagrams
500 feet
1 inch represents approximately 360 feet

Everett Shops Area Notes:
(1) Most of the tracks in the Everett Shops complex were used interchangeably by surface streetcars, rapid transit cars, and railroad freight cars. Not all tracks shown had overhead trolley wires.
(2) Tracks known to have been used by railroad freight cars are indicated by " RR ".
(3) The two tracks in the front of the shops, parallel to the rapid transit line, had third rails for rapid transit car use.
(4) The test track at the front of the shops was relocated and extended in December 1941. The original alignment is indicated by a dashed line. This track had a third rail for rapid transit car use.
(5) Two coal storage tracks, and a connecting track, were added in June 1942.
(6) The transferway had two transfer tables on it, which could operate independently.
(7) All railroad sidings and industrial tracks shown on this diagram were operated by the B&A RR.
(8) Bow Street intersects Broadway at two different locations. Only one is shown here. The other, which is referred to in the text, is off this diagram to the right.

Numbers in bold type are building numbers as designated by Boston Elevated Railway Co.:
1 – Administration Building & Store Room; drafting room; locker room
2 – Main Repair Shop: heavy machine shop; light machine shop; wheel repair; truck repairs; welding shop; blacksmith shop; electrical & motor repair; armature shop; electrical control repair; compressor repairs; fare box repairs; automotive repair; engine & transmission repair (buses); tool room
3 – Oil House
4 – Warehouse & Storage Shed
5 – Incinerator
6 – Body Shop & Woodworking Shop
7 – Lumber Storage
8 – Kiln Building & Pattern Loft
9 – Gate House
10 – Paint Shop (2nd floor – Upholstery Shop & Sign Shop)
11 – Power House
13 – Scrap Bins
14 – Machine Shop Annex
15 – Pump House

track connected with the remaining car lines in East Boston, Chelsea, and Revere.

There was a large storage yard at Everett Shops equipped with two transfer tables and transfer tracks to the adjoining shop buildings. Test tracks ran to the south and to the north of the shop-building complex. In 1941 the Elevated rebuilt and extended the northerly test track and installed an inspection pit.[189] A scrap rail where the Elevated burned and cut up obsolete vehicles ran parallel to Alford Street almost all the way to the Mystic River through a junkyard filled with the skeletons of scrapped rolling stock.

As at Charlestown, coal storage tracks were installed at Everett during World War II. This installation of two parallel spur tracks, with a combined length of 1445 feet, was completed June 23, 1942, shortly after the coal tracks had been installed at Charlestown.

The Sullivan Square Station–Everett Station Connector Track

A double-track line ran on Alford Street, Charlestown, and Broadway, Everett, from Sullivan Square to Everett Station.[s] Work cars, revenue cars that required heavy maintenance, cars destined to be junked on the scrap rail, and Owl Cars used this

[s] Alford Street upon entering Everett became Broadway. The city line is about 2100 feet north of the Mystic River, near the intersection of Chemical Lane and Broadway.

The service track between Sullivan Square Station and Everett Shops saw a lot of traffic between work cars such as side dump car 3623, shown here on November 6, 1946, on Alford Street at Arlington Avenue, and passenger trolley cars for repair or to be scrapped.
Lorris J. Bass

Chemical Lane was the entrance to Everett Shops. Here, in 1946, Type 4 tow car No. 5465 pulls center-entrance car 6264 onto Chemical Lane from Broadway on the way to the scrap track.
Richard L. Wonson

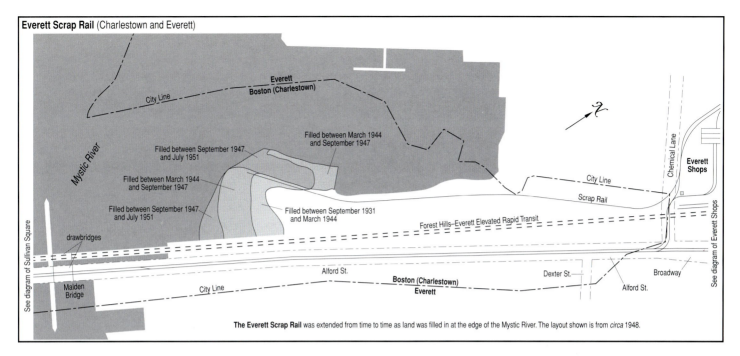

Everett Scrap Rail (Charlestown and Everett)

Mystic River

City Line

Everett
Boston (Charlestown)

Filled between March 1944
and September 1947

Filled between September 1947
and July 1951

Filled between March 1944
and September 1947

Filled between September 1947
and July 1951

Filled between September 1931
and March 1944

Forest Hills–Everett Elevated Rapid Transit

Chemical Lane

**Everett
Shops**

City Line

Scrap Rail

See diagram of Sullivan Square

drawbridges

Malden
Bridge

City Line

Alford St.

Boston (Charlestown)
Everett

Dexter St.

Alford St.

Broadway

See diagram of Everett Shops

The Everett Scrap Rail was extended from time to time as land was filled in at the edge of the Mystic River. The layout shown is from *circa* 1948.

On May 2, 1948, following the end of Eastern Mass. rail service in Quincy, the 7000s assigned to that operation moved under their own power to Everett Shops to be scrapped. Charlie Duncan caught the parade on Alford Street (left) while Foster M. Palmer snapped the shot of the cars turning into Chemical Lane (below).

Left, Charles A. Duncan; below, Foster M. Palmer

After useful equipment had been removed from a car to be scrapped, the next step was to burn the body to get rid of the wooden parts, leaving the scrap metal behind for salvage. Here, three 6200s meet their fate on the Everett Shops scrap track in March 1946.

Charles A. Duncan

track. The track remained in use as far as Everett Shops until 1962, when its connection with the Central Subway via Main Street, Charlestown, was finally severed.

At Sullivan Square the line connected to service tracks from Porter Square, Cambridge, and to the revenue tracks from Charlestown, Medford, and Somerville. The line left Sullivan Square and crossed the Malden Bridge, a drawbridge over the Mystic River. A double-track branch off the Broadway track onto Chemical Lane mentioned earlier led directly into the Everett Shops storage yard and transfer table area.

The track on Broadway continued to Everett Station, where it entered and looped for Owl Cars to return to Sullivan Square. Beyond Everett Station, the track continued on Broadway to Chelsea as discussed later.

As mentioned in Chapter 1, Owl Cars from Salem Street via the Fellsway and Sullivan Square to Everett Station used this track until April 19, 1947. Owl Cars between Sullivan and Everett were discontinued at this time, and replaced by Owl Trackless Trolleys from Linden Street and from Lebanon Street to Sullivan Square Station.

A lengthy service track connected Everett Station with Bellingham Square in Chelsea. On January 14, 1940, Boston Elevated 4400, formerly Eastern Mass. 7005, stops at the B&M Railroad crossing on Everett Avenue, Chelsea, as it traverses this route during a railfan charter. Car 4400 would be sold to the Seashore Trolley Museum in 1950. *Charles A. Duncan*

The Everett–Chelsea Service Track

The entire streetcar network in Everett had been abandoned by 1940, with two exceptions: the service track running from Sullivan Square to Everett Station, which has been discussed above, and another non-revenue line that ran from Everett to Chelsea. The second service line was used for equipment transfers and was cobbled together from several abandoned car lines. The Everett-Chelsea service line is partially shown as of 1940, on Map 7 and completely shown on Map 9.

From Everett Station, the line followed Broadway as double track to Everett Square. This section was a remnant of the car lines from Everett Station to Malden Square via Ferry Street, to Woodlawn Cemetery, and to Linden.

The line turned right at Everett Square onto Chelsea Street. Here the track was a leftover of the Everett Station–Woodlawn Cemetery and Everett Square–Chelsea Square car lines. On turning the corner, the line immediately went to single track, running in both directions on the former inbound rail to Everett.

Near Mead Street, the line switched to the outbound rail for a distance of 317 feet before resuming double-track operation at Ferry and Chelsea Streets. From Ferry Street east, the Chelsea Street track had been part of the former Malden Square–Chelsea Square and Everett Square–Chelsea Square car lines.

The tracks followed Chelsea Street to Everett Avenue, then Everett Avenue to the Everett–Chelsea boundary at Locust Street. The tracks continued to a grade crossing of the B&M Railroad followed immediately by a parallel grade crossing of the B&A Railroad. Here the double streetcar tracks jogged to single iron on the inbound side of the roadway to Everett and crossed the railroad tracks.

On the other side of the railroad crossing, the line resumed double-track operation and turned left onto Broadway, Chelsea. The track continued on Broadway, connecting at Bellingham Square with the active car lines from Chelsea, East Boston, and Revere.[t]

Like the other service tracks, this line was useful. From a financial point of view, however, it was pure overhead, since it carried no revenue passengers. The Elevated did everything it could to maintain this connection, but at minimal cost. As the track and special work wore out, the company would simply cut out the bad segments and reconnect the good ones.

In 1946, the Boston El installed a switch west of Irving Street, Everett, to eliminate the Chelsea Street outbound rail between this point and the Chelsea–Everett boundary line.[190] In 1947, a second switch was installed at the Everett–Chelsea boundary, at which time the outbound rail was abandoned.[191]

The MTA Maintenance Department performed track work on Broadway, Everett in 1947. This project encompassed the section from the Boston-Everett boundary line to the B&M Railroad crossing, near Main Street and Broadway. The inbound, or southbound, track was resurfaced and regraded. A new switch was installed near Bow Street and Broadway, near

---

[t] Bellingham Square is the intersection of Bellingham Street, Washington Avenue, Broadway, and Hawthorne Street.

the B&M Railroad crossing. Unused special work leading into Everett Station was removed, and the northbound, or outbound, track was paved over by the city of Everett in conjunction with resurfacing of the street.[192]

Work continued in 1948, when the outbound track from the B&M Railroad crossing on Broadway to Chelsea Street was abandoned and paved with asphalt. The inbound track was resurfaced and regraded, and unused special work at Main Street was removed.[193] By now what was left of this line was mainly single track, with a few double track sections in places. Where there was single track only, the remaining rail shifted from one side of the street to the other, depending on which direction had been good enough to keep in service!

Delivered in 1895 as a 20-foot closed passenger car, No. 1059 became a fare box repair car in 1915 and a rail grinder twenty years later. Seen here at Everett Springs on the Everett–Chelsea service track in December 1942, it would ultimately be preserved at the Seashore Trolley Museum. *Charles A. Duncan*

A Type 5 turns from Everett Avenue onto Chelsea Street over the service track around 1948. The presence of passengers on the car indicates that it was on a railfan excursion. *Charles A. Duncan*

Ancient electric car No. 396 has just turned onto Everett Avenue from Broadway in Chelsea Square in August 1938 and is headed for Everett. The car was built in 1900 and exists today at the Seashore Trolley Museum. Originally a passenger car, it was converted to an electrical test car in 1923. The museum acquired the car in 1954, and since then 396 has enjoyed an improbable movie career, appearing the *The Cardinal* (1963) and the public television series *The Best of Families* (1977). *Charles A. Duncan*

Many Bostonians experienced a trip to Revere Beach by streetcar. Revere Beach Loop was behind the beach, off Ocean Avenue. Doubtless, few were swimming the day this shot was taken about 1949. The Revere Beach Bath House is prominent in this scene, one reason that the Elevated often used the term "Bath House Loop." *Clarke Collection*

Chapter 8

Lines In East Boston, Chelsea, & Revere

Three compact and similar communities constitute the East Boston District of Boston and the cities of Chelsea and Revere. All three municipalities are tightly linked economically and geographically, and all three have similar residential and industrial characteristics.

In 1940, the Sumner Tunnel, used for motor vehicle traffic, connected East Boston to Boston Proper. There were also several local public transportation connections. A Boston El bus line ran from Haymarket Square in downtown Boston to Porter Street in East Boston via the Sumner Tunnel. The East Boston rapid transit tunnel, used by today's Blue Line, connected Bowdoin Square near the West End of Boston with Maverick Square in East Boston. Finally, two ferries, one run by the City of Boston and one by the Boston, Revere Beach & Lynn Railroad (BRB&L Railroad) connected the docks along Atlantic Avenue with the East Boston waterfront.

The housing stock in East Boston was primarily multi-family, a perfect setting for a heavy public transit infrastructure. Local transportation was provided by the Elevated's streetcars, which connected the community with the rapid transit line at Maverick Station, and by the BRB&L Railroad, which stopped at five stations in East Boston including the ferry terminal.

Boston Municipal Airport was located in East Boston. Renamed Logan Airport in 1943, it became increasingly important in the 1940s.[a] The principal business of East Boston, however, was the commercial activity along the large number of harbor freight and shipbuilding docks.

The city of Chelsea is located directly north of East Boston across Chelsea Creek. It was connected to East Boston by two drawbridges, one on Meridian Street and the other on Chelsea Street. Both bridges required constant maintenance, disrupting street traffic and the shipping that depended on their reliable operation. This situation was a major problem, particularly in the case of the Meridian Street Bridge.

In the 1940s, Chelsea was known for manufacturing clocks, furniture, paints, shoes, and wallpaper. The city had much residential housing, most of it multi-family. In addition to the Boston Elevated's streetcar service, Chelsea also had two sta-

tions on the Eastern Route of the B&M Railroad. B&A Railroad freight tracks paralleled the B&M Railroad through much of the city.

The city of Revere adjoins Chelsea and East Boston to the north. Revere was primarily residential, but over the years Revere Beach and its adjoining amusement park complex drew generations of Bostonians. Suffolk Downs Racetrack, which straddled the East Boston-Revere city line, and the Wonderland Dog Track, located beside the Revere Beach Loop, both opened in 1935 and rapidly became popular attractions.

The beach and the two racetracks were important destinations for area streetcar lines and for the BRB&L Railroad. No less than three car lines ran to Revere Beach. The BRB&L stopped at six stations in Revere, four of which were along Revere Beach! The B&M Railroad Eastern Route also ran through Revere, making a single regular stop and running racetrack specials over a separate branch to Suffolk Downs and on a short spur to Wonderland.

The streetcar lines in this area were always busy and the Boston El and MTA made extraordinary efforts to avoid service disruptions. Streetcars operated on very tight schedules, even during track construction, route diversions, and other major projects.

Abandonment of the Narrow Guage
(Boston, Revere Beach & Lynn Railroad)

The 1940s began on a sour note locally: the abandonment of the three-foot gauge Boston, Revere Beach & Lynn Railroad on January 27, 1940. Affectionately known to the public as the *Narrow Gauge*, it was hardly the backwoods operation that this name connotes.

The railroad carried large numbers of riders to Revere Beach during the summer months and many year-round commuters between Lynn and downtown Boston. The BRB&L also operated a short but busy loop line from Orient Heights that served the town of Winthrop.

The BRB&L Railroad harbor ferry was a vital link. The ferry ran from the railroad's East Boston terminal across the harbor to the company ferry slip and terminal building, located on Atlantic Avenue along the downtown Boston waterfront between Fosters Wharf and Rowes Wharf.

---

[a] The airport was named after Gen. Edward Lawrence Logan, a distinguished Boston judge, World War I colonel, and former general in the Massachusetts National Guard.

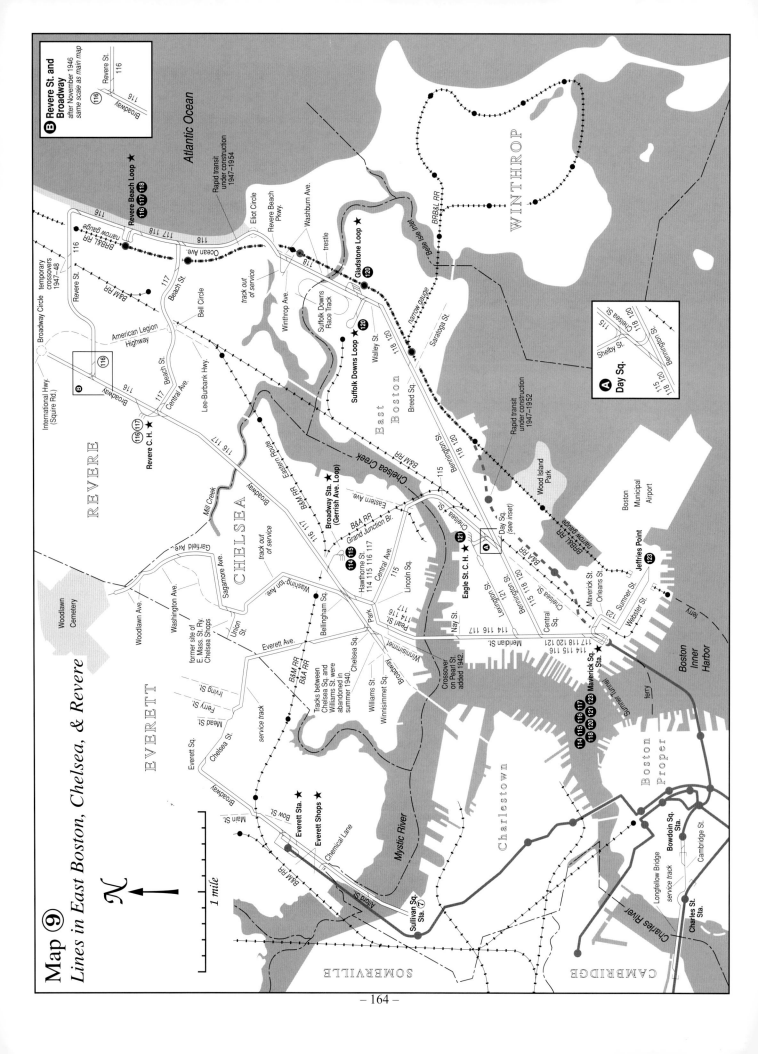

Map ⑨
Lines in East Boston, Chelsea, & Revere

N

1 mile

Ⓑ Revere St. and Broadway
after November 1946
same scale as main map

Revere St.

116

Broadway

116

Revere St.

116

Atlantic Ocean

Rapid transit under construction 1947–1954

Revere Beach Loop ★

116 117 118

BRB&L RR narrow gauge

116

117 118

Broadway Circle temporary crossovers 1947–48

116

117

118

Ocean Ave.

track out of service

Eliot Circle

Revere Beach Pkwy.

Washburn Ave.

trestle

Gladstone Loop ★

120

Revere St.

Beach St.

Bell Circle

International Hwy. (Squire Rd.)

American Legion Highway

116

Ⓑ

Broadway

116

117

Beach St.

Central Ave.

Lee-Burbank Hwy.

Suffolk Downs Race Track

Suffolk Downs Loop ★

120

Walley St.

120

118 120

Saratoga St.

narrow gauge

Breed Sq.

Bennington St.

118 120

R E V E R E

Revere C. H. ★

116 117

116 117

Winthrop Ave.

118

E a s t   B o s t o n

W I N T H R O P

BRB&L RR

Belle Isle Inlet

Garfield Ave.

Mill Creek

Woodlawn Cemetery

Woodlawn Ave.

Sagamore Ave.

Washington Ave.

Broadway

Eastern Route

B&M RR

116 117

track out of service

Broadway Sta. (Gerrish Ave. Loop) ★

B&A RR

Grand Junction Br.

Chelsea Creek

Eastern Ave.

Central Ave.

115

Hawthorne St.

114 115 116 117

114 115

Lincoln Sq.

B&A RR

B&M RR

Rapid transit under construction 1947–1952

Day Sq. (see inset)

Wood Island Park

Boston Municipal Airport

Eagle St. C. H. ★

121

Ⓐ

Lexington St.

Bennington St.

Central Sq.

115 118 120

121

BRB&L RR narrow gauge

Jeffries Point

123

Ⓐ Day Sq.

Shelby St.

115

118 120

Chelsea St.

115

118 120

Bennington St.

C H E L S E A

Union St.

former site of E. Mass. St. Ry. Chelsea Shops

Everett Ave.

Washington Ave.

Bellingham Sq.

Park St.

Chelsea Sq.

Williams St.

Winnisimmet Sq.

Broadway

Winnisimmet

Nay St.

Pearl St.

114 116

114 116 117

Crossover on Pearl St. added 1942

Meridian St.

114 115 116

117 118 120 121

Maverick Sq. Sta. ★

Maverick St.

Orleans St.

123

Webster St.

Sumner St.

123

E V E R E T T

B&M RR

B&M RR

Irving St.

Ferry St.

service track

Mead St.

Chelsea St.

Tracks between Chelsea Sq. and Williams St. were abandoned in summer 1940.

Everett Sq.

Broadway

Main St.

Bow St.

Everett Sta. ★

Everett Shops ★

Chemical Lane

Alford St.

B&M RR

Sullivan Sq. Sta. Ⓣ

Mystic River

C h a r l e s t o w n

Summer Tunnel

114 115 116 117

118 120 121 123

ferry

ferry

Boston Inner Harbor

B o s t o n   P r o p e r

Longfellow Bridge

Bowdoin Sq. Sta.

Cambridge St.

service track

Charles St. Sta.

Charles River

C A M B R I D G E

S O M E R V I L L E

– 164 –

The loss of the Boston, Revere Beach & Lynn Railroad in 1940 was a heavy blow to North Shore commuters all the way to Lynn. This narrow-gauge short line had been electrified from steam railroad operation only twelve years earlier, and the Great Depression had prevented it from realizing its full potential. The East Boston ferry slip (left) was the departure point for commuters going to and from downtown Boston and North Shore communities. The ferry *Newtown* is closest in this view, with *Ashburnham* off to the right. At right, one of the former steam railroad coaches, now electrified, crosses the Saugus River from Lynn into Revere in January 1940. The General Edwards Bridge can be seen in the background. *Left, Seashore Trolley Museum Collection; right, Charles A. Brown*

This railroad was originally steam-operated, but in 1928 it was electrified in anticipation of lower operating costs, a continuation of high ridership, and the potential for future growth. Little did its owners know what lay ahead. The railroad struggled through the Great Depression with the debt service created by the electrification. Faced with declining ridership, the railroad was forced to end service, despite the pleas of local residents and their legislators.

This abandonment was a major loss to mass transit in the Boston area. One positive result, however, was that the demise of the *Narrow Gauge* had helped to increase Boston Elevated ridership over that of 1939, a fact that was noted in the Boston Elevated 1940 annual report.[194]

The day following the closure of the *Narrow Gauge*, to help ease the loss of service, the Boston El began running buses from the Point of Pines section of Revere to Revere Beach Loop.[b] Also at this time, the Saugus Transit Co. started a bus line between Winthrop and Maverick Square, East Boston.[c]

First Trackless Trolley to Revere

The first of many lines to come, a trackless trolley route was established on September 7, 1940, between Revere Carhouse and Everett Station via Park Avenue, Elm, Ferry, and Chelsea Streets, and Broadway. This trolley coach line was extended to Revere Beach Loop on September 9, 1950, via Beach Street and Ocean Avenue, running beside the Beach Street streetcars. By early 1952, the streetcars in East Boston, Chelsea, and Revere would be gone, mainly replaced by trackless trolleys.

---

[b] The El bus had lighter ridership than expected, and it was discontinued March 27, 1940. The official reason given was that the temporary license under which the bus operated had expired and no permanent license had been granted.

[c] Shortly after starting this route, Saugus Transit changed its name to Rapid Transit, Inc. A new surface level shelter was opened at Maverick Station on September 11, 1941, to handle this traffic.

Service Overview

In 1940, eight streetcar lines served this area, and all of them had a common destination: Maverick Station, at the East Boston end of the East Boston Tunnel rapid transit line. The lines operated from three facilities: Broadway Station, also known as Gerrish Avenue Loop, in Chelsea; Revere Carhouse; and Eagle Street Carhouse in East Boston.

The eight lines are listed below and are shown on Map 9.

Route No.	Route Description
114	**Broadway Station (Gerrish Avenue Loop)–Maverick Station** *via Broadway, Hawthorne Street, Park Street, Pearl Street, and Meridian Street*
115	**Broadway Station (Gerrish Avenue Loop)–Maverick Station** *via Broadway, Hawthorne Street, Central Avenue, Chelsea Street, Bennington Street, and Meridian Street*
116	**Revere Beach Loop–Maverick Station** *via Ocean Avenue, Revere Street, Broadway, Hawthorne Street, Park Street, Pearl Street, and Meridian Street*
117	**Revere Beach Loop–Maverick Station** *via Ocean Avenue, Beach Street, Central Avenue, Broadway, Hawthorne Street, Park Street, Pearl Street, and Meridian Street* [cb] **Revere Carhouse–Maverick Station**
118	**Revere Beach Loop–Maverick Station** *via Ocean Avenue, Washburn Avenue, Walley Street, Bennington Street, and Meridian Street*
120	**Gladstone Loop–Maverick Station** *via Washburn Avenue, Walley Street, Bennington Street, and Meridian Street*

121   Eagle Street Carhouse–Maverick Station
via Eagle Street, Lexington Street, and Meridian Street

123   Jeffries Point–Maverick Station *via Sumner Street, Orleans Street, Maverick Street; return via Maverick Street, Orleans Street, and Webster Street*

Daily trips were greatest on Route 120. Next in frequency was Route 118, then the combination of Route 117 and its cutback at Revere Carhouse, the combination of Route 116 and its cutback at the Revere Street crossover, Route 123, Route 115, Route 114, and Route 121, in that order. See Appendix 9 for more detailed information regarding operations.

The Gerrish Avenue Lines

Broadway Station (Gerrish Avenue Loop)

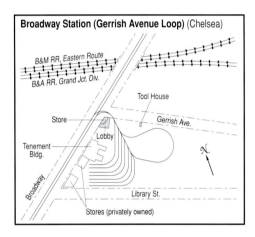

Broadway Station, as it was officially called, consisted of a caryard with a single loop, seven storage tracks, a small tool house, and a lobby building. Broadway Station was located on the south side of Broadway, Chelsea, at Gerrish Avenue, near the B&A Railroad. Also called Gerrish Avenue Loop, Broadway Station was the site of the former Chelsea Carhouse.

Gerrish Avenue Loop was located off Broadway, Chelsea, on the site of the former Chelsea Carhouse. It was the terminal point of Routes 114 and 115 to Maverick Square via Meridian Street and Central Avenue, respectively. Here, a lone Type 5 is seen in this view of the yard taken around 1950.   *Clarke Collection*

Broadway Station was a terminal for two major car lines, both running to Maverick, Route 114 via Meridian Street and Route 115 via Central Avenue. In 1940 it was a substation of Eagle Street Carhouse. After March 1941, Broadway Station became a substation of Revere Carhouse.

The intersection of Gerrish Avenue and Broadway was the limit of Type 4 car operation on Broadway. Beyond this point, the former Eastern Mass. tracks to Revere were too closely spaced to allow two Type 4 cars to pass without side-swiping one another.

Equipment Assignments

As of March 18, 1940, ten Type 5s were stored at Broadway Station for the Meridian Street line. The three 4400s required for Central Avenue were stored at Eagle Street. A decade later, the April 24, 1950, rating showed 14 Type 5s stored at Broadway Station, eleven for Meridian Street, and three for Central Avenue.

Type 5s were used on the Maverick via Meridian Street line until March 1941. They were taken off and assigned again from November 1946 through September 1947. Type 5s were reassigned again, from June 1949 through 1950. After March 1941, 4400s and some 4300s were assigned to this route. The 4400 cars lasted until June 1949, but the 4300s were completely withdrawn in 1947. Type 4s from Eagle Street Carhouse were also used briefly between April and November 1946. See Appendix 8 for more detailed information on car assignments on this line.

While cars for the Meridian Street line were physically stored at Broadway Station, they were assigned to Eagle Street Carhouse until March 1941, and thereafter, to Revere Carhouse

Approximately fifteen years earlier, Type 4 No. 5368 turns onto Gerrish Avenue from Broadway, but it won't be on Gerrish Avenue for long. As you can see, the track off Broadway turned right into the yard! Behind 5368, a 4300 waits on Broadway for the Type 4 to clear the switch. St. Rose Catholic Church is in the background.   *BERy*

through April 1946. From April 1946 to September 1947, cars from both carhouses were used on this line. Finally, after September 13, 1947, the Meridian Street cars for were assigned to Revere Carhouse for the remainder of the decade and beyond.

Equipment used on the Broadway Station–Maverick via Central Avenue line included 4400s and 4300s until December 1944. Type 5s ran here from December 1944 through the end of the decade. Between April and September 1946, a few Type 4 cars joined the Type 5s.

Until March 1941, the Central Avenue cars were based and stored at Eagle Street Carhouse. After this date, they were assigned to Revere Carhouse.

114 Broadway Station–Maverick *via Meridian Street*

Leaving Gerrish Avenue, cars on Route 114 ran southwest along Broadway through the Chelsea business district. At Bellingham Square, the line turned left onto Hawthorne Street.[d] A double-track connection to Everett Avenue also ran straight ahead on Broadway, connecting with the service track to Everett Shops as discussed in Chapter 7.

In earlier years, revenue cars of the Eastern Massachusetts Street Railway continued straight on Broadway running over the Chelsea Bridge and through Charlestown to the Tremont Street Subway.[e] An inactive double-track line with overhead wire that ran from Chelsea Square to Woodlawn Cemetery also connected with the Broadway tracks at Bellingham Square. The Boston Elevated formally abandoned this line in March 1941.[f]

The Meridian Street line ran south on Hawthorne Street to Lincoln Square, at Central Avenue and Park Street.[195] Here

[d] The city of Chelsea uses the spelling "Hawthorn." The Boston Elevated spelled it "Hawthorne"; this is the spelling that will be used in this book.

[e] From Everett Avenue to Williams Street, 1645 feet east of the Chelsea Bridge, the track on Broadway, Chelsea was still intact. It was formally abandoned in the summer of 1940, along with track connections from Everett Avenue going west on Broadway and a segment of single track on Winnisimmet and Park Streets between Winnisimmet Square and Chelsea Square.

[f] The line connected in the westerly direction with Broadway and followed Washington Avenue past the Chelsea Shops of the Eastern Massachusetts Street Railway. A direct connection ran from the inbound rail on Washington Avenue to the shop building, and an 872-foot spur track ran from the inbound rail onto Union Street beside the shop building as far as the Chelsea–Everett city line. The Woodlawn line continued on Washington Avenue, turned right onto Sagamore Avenue, then left onto Garfield Avenue, and returned to Washington Avenue. The line then ran into Woodlawn Avenue, crossed the Chelsea–Everett boundary line, and ended in a Y stub-end at the Woodlawn Cemetery just short of the Elevated's other line to Woodlawn from Everett on Elm Street. The one-way track length of this former Eastern Mass. line was approximately 2.21 miles. The El operated this line after the acquisition of the Chelsea Division on June 9, 1936, to May 8, 1937, when the company replaced the streetcars with buses. Eastern Mass. cars continued to be maintained and prepared for resale at the Chelsea Shops until 1937 under a special provision of the Chelsea Division purchase. This provision also included access by Eastern Mass. cars over Boston El tracks to the shops with Boston Elevated motormen operating them.

Boston Elevated Railway car 4404 operates on Broadway in Chelsea in 1946. The former Eastern Mass. 7024 was one of ten lightweights purchased by the El in August 1936 to replace 4200-class semi-convertibles that had been acquired with the Chelsea Division two months before. *Charles A. Duncan*

Hawthorne Street left Broadway just after Bellingham Square, and here an inbound 4300 heads for Maverick Station. The tower of the Chelsea City Hall can be seen in the background of this 1941 view. *BERy*

The line from Chelsea Square to Woodlawn Cemetary was acquired by the Boston Elevated with the purchase of the Chelsea Division from the Eastern Mass. in 1936. For slightly less than a year, the El operated this line with streetcars. This view on April 25, 1937, shows 4406 running past the Eastern Mass. Chelsea Shops. Still in active use at this time, they remained standing years later. *Charles A. Duncan*

– 167 –

Type 5 No. 5649 has just turned the corner from Park Street onto Pearl Street bound for Maverick in 1950.   *Foster M. Palmer*

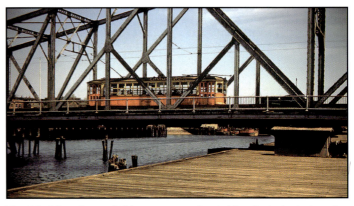

The Meridian Street Bridge was a swing bridge that pivoted on the pier from which this shot of an MTA Type 5 speeding across the span was taken on May 7, 1950.   *Foster M. Palmer*

Car 4404 has just crossed the Meridian Street Bridge on its way to Maverick Station.   *Charles A. Duncan*

The crossover at Nay and Meridian Streets was where cars from Maverick cut back during Meridian Street Bridge repairs, reconstruction, or whenever the bridge simply got stuck in the wrong position. MTA 5560 lays over during a reconstruction period on August 12, 1950.   *Stanley M. Hauck*

the Meridian Street cars turned right onto Park Street then left on Pearl Street.[196] The line then ran south across the Meridian Street Bridge over Chelsea Creek, crossing the Boston-Chelsea boundary line on the middle of the bridge.

In East Boston, the line continued along Meridian Street. The cars crossed a double-track connection with the Lexington Street line, and soon after, a second double-track crossing with the tracks from Bennington Street at Central Square.

The cars then ran to Maverick Square where they descended an incline into Maverick Station and unloaded. Here riders made an across-the-platform transfer to rapid transit trains for downtown Boston. The streetcars then rounded a tight loop above the two rapid transit tracks at west end of the platform. The round-trip distance on this line was 4.364 miles and required an average running time of 28 minutes.

Returning to the outbound platform area, the cars collected their riders for the return trip. Above ground in Maverick Square, there was a surface bypass loop around the incline and headhouse.

The Meridian Street Bridge

Three car lines, Routes 114, 116, 117, and the Revere Carhouse and Revere Street cutbacks used the Meridian Street Bridge to get to Maverick Station. This steel swing bridge pivoted in the Chelsea Creek channel when shipping traffic required it to open. Starting on June 12, 1950, the bridge was closed, demolished, and rebuilt.

The bridge needed frequent repairs that interrupted streetcar and automotive travel. When the bridge was being repaired, Meridian Street service operated from Maverick to a crossover just beyond Nay Street, the last stop in East Boston before the bridge. Streetcar service from Revere and Chelsea was routed around the bridge onto Central Avenue. Distances and running times of these temporary routes are presented in Appendix 9.

From February to mid-March 1942, the Meridian Street Bridge closed for repairs. On the East Boston side of the bridge, 4300 and 4400 cars from Revere Carhouse ran between the Nay Street crossover and Maverick. Chelsea and Revere cars bound for Maverick were diverted over Central Avenue.

The Elevated also installed a crossover on Pearl Street, Chelsea, near Park Street during the work on the bridge.[197] The company planned to run service north of the bridge down Park and Pearl Streets to the new crossover much like the operation to Nay Street. The bridge repairs had been completed by the time the crossover was installed, however, and the plan did not materialize.

Type 4 No. 5388 heads for Maverick Station on Meridian Street at Lexington Street in 1946.
Charles A. Duncan

Central Square, East Boston, was the point at which the Meridian Street and Bennington Street lines met. From here to Maverick Station, the procession of cars was endless during rush hours and almost as heavy throughout much of the day. At left, a 4300 and two Type 4s are seen on Meridian Street around 1942, while above, Type 5 No. 5680 runs through the square in 1949.
Left, BERy; above, Paul M. Paulsen

115 Broadway Station–Maverick *via Central Avenue*

This line was a circuitous alternative route to the Meridian Street line. In terms of ridership, it was definitely the lighter of the two lines between Broadway Station and Maverick. The Central Avenue line followed the same route as the Meridian Street line to Lincoln Square. Here it turned southeast onto Central Avenue. Just before Eastern Avenue, the line crossed a B&A Railroad freight spur at grade. The line then crossed Eastern Avenue and immediately ran onto the Chelsea Street Bridge.[g]

The line crossed from Chelsea into East Boston at the center of the bridge and curved southwest on Chelsea Street, crossing another B&A Railroad freight spur at grade. One block after Eagle Square, there was an inbound and outbound double-track connection from Chelsea Street to Shelby Street and Eagle Street Carhouse.

At Day Square the line turned southwest onto Bennington Street. Here it joined the lines coming from the Gladstone

Route 115, Broadway Station–Maverick Station via Central Avenue, was an excellent bypass around the Meridian Street Bridge. It was the lighter of the two lines based at Gerrish Avenue but had its own periodic obstructions: a freight railroad crossing shown here with Chelsea-bound 4395 approaching in November 1940, and the Chelsea Street Bridge, almost as trouble prone and subject to delay as its relative on Meridian Street.
Charles A. Duncan

Semi-convertible 4373 crosses the Chelsea Street Bridge on October 12, 1941. This bridge had replaced an older span five years earlier.
Charles A. Duncan

---

[g] Prior to 1936, streetcars turned right off Central Avenue and ran a short distance on Eastern Avenue. They then turned left onto the old Chelsea Street Bridge. A new bridge opened in 1936, and it eliminated the jog onto Eastern Avenue. For many years afterwards, however, Boston Elevated and MTA system route maps indicated, incorrectly, that the route still ran over a short stretch of Eastern Avenue. It is interesting to note that the rails leading to the Chelsea side of the old bridge (pre-1936) are still visible, now on privately-owned land.

Maverick Square Station

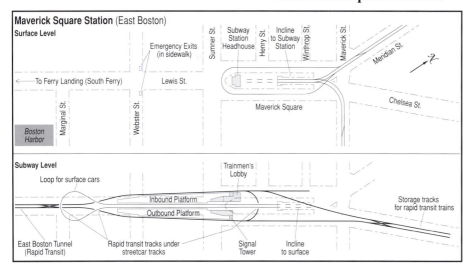

The top of the portal was a favorite spot for railfans. Here, No. 5381 descends the ramp into the station. *Paul M. Paulsen*

Maverick Station was the focal point of all the car lines from Chelsea, East Boston, and Revere. Type 4 No. 5279 approaches the incline from Meridian Street in 1948. *Paul M. Paulsen*

A Type 5 enters the Maverick Square incline in this September 1947 view. *Charles A. Duncan*

In this view taken on October 3, 1947, Type 4 No. 5408 is already signed for its outbound trip to the Gladstone Loop. *Robert A. Kennerly*

Type 5 No. 5960 is seen outbound at Maverick Station in 1948. Large overhead signs denoting berths for different destinations were a feature of surface car subway platforms. *Paul M. Paulsen*

An MTA bus heads for the surface station in Maverick Square as No. 5210 emerges from the tunnel for its run to Suffolk Downs around 1948. *Paul M. Paulsen*

A bypass loop ran around the Maverick Station trolley incline and was used for emergencies. Buses, however, normally stopped at this surface station for passengers to Logan Airport and Winthrop. The station had opened on September 11, 1941, a little over three months before this shot was taken.   *BERy*

Snow sweeper 3613 is seen operating around the Maverick surface loop at midnight on an inclement evening around 1949.
Paul M. Paulsen

Loop and Revere Beach. Also at Day Square, there was a double-track curve connection from Chelsea Street inbound to Bennington Street outbound. This trackage allowed cars from Eagle Street Carhouse to go to directly east on Bennington Street or westbound Bennington cars to return directly to the carhouse. Map 9, Inset A details the track arrangement in and around Day Square.

Beyond Day Square inbound, concrete safety islands were located at a number of important stops on Bennington Street, especially where the roadway was wide. The tracks on Bennington Street joined those on Meridian Street at Central Square, East Boston. From here to Maverick Square the route was identical to that of Route 114 described above. A round-trip on Route 115 consumed 6.402 miles and had a running time of 34 minutes.

The Revere Carhouse Lines

Revere Carhouse

Revere Carhouse was acquired in 1936 from the Eastern Massachusetts Street Railway with the purchase of the Chelsea Division. It was located on the west side of Broadway, Revere, between Fernwood and Park Avenues. The property was diagonally offset across the street from the intersection of Central Avenue and Broadway.

Cars accessed Revere Carhouse by a single connection in either direction on Broadway. There was also a cross connection from Central Avenue. All three connections joined an off-street yard lead track parallel to Broadway. Stub end storage tracks ran from this lead into the single carhouse building and to a small storage yard area on the Park Avenue side of the building.[h]

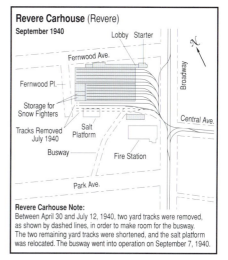

Revere Carhouse Note:
Between April 30 and July 12, 1940, two yard tracks were removed, as shown by dashed lines, in order to make room for the busway. The two remaining yard tracks were shortened, and the salt platform was relocated. The busway went into operation on September 7, 1940.

Revere Carhouse was typical in appearance to other Eastern Mass. carbarns. After the acquisition of the Chelsea Division in 1936, Type 5s of the Boston Elevated Railway were based here along with ex-7000 series cars renumbered by the El as 4400s as seen in this October 21, 1941, view.   *Charles A. Duncan*

In addition to passenger cars which came with the Chelsea Division, the El acquired Eastern Mass. service cars including Russell sweeper P-603, seen at Revere Carhouse in September 1945.

Charles A. Duncan

---

[h] Two of the yard tracks were taken up starting on April 4, 1940, to make room for a trackless trolley way for the new line from Everett. This work was completed July 12. Later, between January 24 and July 31, 1945, the entire group of eleven track leads into the carhouse building were rebuilt as well as the lead to the yard track nearest the building.

Type 5 No. 5848 moves onto the yard lead to Broadway inbound at Revere Carhouse about 1948. Ahead of the car is the Revere fire station that adjoined the property and remains to this day.   *MTA*

Equipment Assignments

At the start of the decade, 41 cars including spares were based at Revere Carhouse, and all were of the 4300 and 4400 types according to the March 18, 1940, rating. By 1949 the September 12 rating showed fifteen 4400s and 49 Type 5s, a total of 64 streetcars including spares. Detailed car assignments are presented in Appendix 8.

The Revere Beach Loop–Maverick via Revere Street line used 4300s until 1947 and 4400s until June 1949. From this time on, Type 5s served the line almost exclusively, although they had begun running on this route in July 1948. Equipment assignments for both of the two cutbacks on this line, one on Revere Street, and later, one at Broadway and Revere Street were virtually the same as for the main line.

The equipment assigned to the Beach Street line was similar to that on Revere Street, former Eastern Mass. cars and Type 5s also seeing use on Beach Street. Revere Street was the heavier of the two routes, however, and fewer cars were needed to run the Beach Street service. Both the 4300 and 4400-series were used on the Beach Street line through April 1947 with 4400s continuing to June 1949. Type 5s began running here in September 1946 and continued to do so through the end of the decade and into the 1950s. As with the Revere Street line, the equipment assignments for the Beach Street cutback at Revere Carhouse were essentially the same as those for the main line.

Revere Beach Loop

The Revere Beach Loop[i] was located on Ocean Avenue, parallel to the site of Wonderland station on the present day

---

[i] Revere Beach Loop was sometimes referred to as "Bath House Loop." It was located directly across Ocean Avenue from a large public bath house operated by the Metropolitan District Commission.

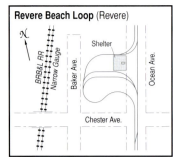

Revere Beach Loop featured this distinctive waiting shelter, seen here in 1936 shortly after the El acquired it.   *Richard L. Wonson*

A pair of Type 4s are seen at Revere Beach Loop in September 1941.   *Charles A. Duncan*

Blue Line.[198] This facility had a loop and a parallel storage track connected to the Ocean Avenue tracks to and from the south toward Beach Street. Another track connected the loop with the tracks going north on Ocean Avenue toward Revere Street. Cars from Revere Street reversed ends here to make their return trips because the track arrangement did not allow the cars to loop for turning.

On Ocean Avenue, beside the loop, there was a northbound track, but no southbound track. For a car to go from a point north of the loop to a point south of the loop on Ocean Avenue, it had to run through the loop trackage first. There were also two nearby crossovers on Ocean Avenue. One was just south of the southerly leads to the loop, and the second was located near the corner of Revere Street and Ocean Avenue.

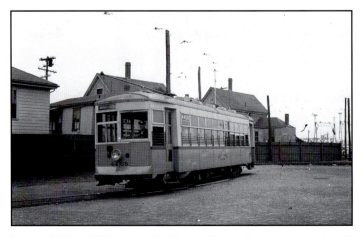

Boston El No. 4408 rounds the Revere Beach Loop track on July 5, 1941, for its trip to Maverick Station via Beach Street.

Stanley M. Hauck

116 Revere Beach Loop–Maverick Station *via* *Revere Street*

This line turned north from Revere Beach Loop onto Ocean Avenue. At Revere Street the line took a very sharp super elevated left turn west onto Revere Street, and immediately crossed a bridge over the former BRB&L Railroad. A quarter mile further, the line crossed another bridge over the B&M Railroad Eastern Route. The line continued from the bridge to Broadway. A crossover on Revere Street near Broadway was the first of the two Broadway and Revere Street cutbacks in the 1940s.

The track switches and an 1800-foot remnant of the Eastern Mass. line to Lynn were still in the street on Broadway at Revere Street. This trackage was also a part of a temporary short line that the El itself had operated in 1936 between Chelsea Square and the International Highway (later Squire Road) for a brief period following the acquisition of the Chelsea Division.[j] This trackage was formally abandoned in 1941, although it had been dormant for a long time.

Between November 6 and November 20, 1946, the Elevated restored 226 feet of the southbound track on Broadway, Revere, beyond Revere Street toward Lynn to active service and installed a crossover from the northbound rail to this track. This short stub-end *Y* spur was the second cutback to Broadway and Revere Street used in the 1940s. Inset B on Map 9 details the track arrangement here.

The Revere Street line turned southwest onto Broadway. The tracks continued past Revere Carhouse, and joined the Beach Street line coming onto Broadway at Central Avenue. The Revere Street and Beach Street lines continued together on Broadway, crossing into Chelsea from Revere at Mill Creek.

After approximately three quarters of a mile, the cars crossed a bridge over the B&M Railroad Eastern Route and the B&A Railroad Grand Junction Branch. Shortly thereafter, the cars also crossed the leads of the Gerrish Avenue Loop. From here into Maverick, the route details were essentially the same as those for the Broadway Station–Maverick via Meridian Street line, Route 114, described earlier. A round-trip on Route 116 was 11.201 miles long and had an average running time of 62 minutes.

Also mentioned earlier was the diversion of this route via Central Avenue, East Boston in 1942. See Appendix 9 for round-trip distances and running times for this temporary route and its cutback at Revere Street.

The bridge over the B&M Railroad on Revere Street was rebuilt in 1947. Streetcars could not use the bridge during construction, and the MTA extended the Beach Street line to a temporary crossover on Revere Street east of the bridge. Northbound cars on Ocean Avenue continued past the Revere Beach

---

[j] This line was part of a joint operation between the Eastern Mass. and the El to provide through streetcar service between Chelsea Square and Lynn.

– 173 –

A Type 5 is silhouetted as it crosses the Revere Street bridge over the B&M Eastern Division line around 1949.   *Paul M. Paulsen*

Former Eastern Mass. car 4357 rounds the bend between Stowers and Bryant Streets heading east on Revere Street towards Broadway, Revere, in 1940. Revere Street was the most easterly of Boston Elevated streetcar lines.   *MTA*

Car 4409 is seen on Broadway, Revere, at Pleasant Street in the summer of 1947.   *Robert A. Kennerly*

Several cars, including 4402, closest to the camera, operate on Broadway, Revere, in 1942.   *Charles A. Duncan*

Type 5 No. 5650 speeds southwest along Broadway, Revere, inbound to Maverick Station in May 1950. *Foster M. Palmer*

Ex-Eastern Mass. 4402 heads along Broadway for Revere Beach Loop in the summer of 1947, having just passed under the Revere Beach Parkway. *Robert A. Kennerly*

Loop, turned west onto Revere Street, and followed Revere Street to the crossover. Here they changed ends and returned to Ocean Avenue.

There was no southbound rail on Ocean Avenue beside the loop as mentioned earlier. Maverick via Beach Street cars had to use the loop trackage before they could continue on Ocean Avenue to Beach Street. This extended operation started on August 9, 1947, and continued until July 10, 1948. Concurrently, the Revere Street line ran only as far as a second temporary crossover on the west side of the railroad bridge. See Appendix 9 for round-trip distances and running times of these temporary routes.

117 Revere Beach Loop–Maverick Station *via* *Beach Street*

Leaving Revere Beach Loop, this line turned south onto Ocean Avenue, sharing the track with the Maverick via Ocean Avenue line. It followed Ocean Avenue about one-third of a mile and turned west onto Beach Street, where it immediately crossed a bridge over the former BRB&L Railroad. The line continued on Beach Street, crossing a bridge over the B&M Railroad Eastern Route, and running through a traffic circle (Bell Circle) at the junction of Lee-Burbank Highway and American Legion Highway.[k]

The line resumed on Beach Street and turned northwest onto Central Avenue (Revere), which it followed for one long block. The line then turned southwest onto Broadway, joining the Revere Street line. From this point, the Beach Street line followed the same route into Maverick as the Revere Street line discussed above. The round-trip distance on the Beach Street line was 10.203 miles and had an average running time of 58 minutes. At Broadway, there was a switch in the inbound direction from Central Avenue to the Revere Carhouse.

[k] The traffic circle is officially named Timothy J. Mahoney Circle. However, it is commonly known as Bell Circle.

This route was diverted via Central Avenue, East Boston, in 1942 because of work on the Meridian Street Bridge. See Appendix 9 for round-trip distances and running times for this temporary route and its cutback at Revere Carhouse.

As mentioned above, this route was extended in 1947-1948 to the temporary crossover at the B&M Railroad Bridge on Revere Street and mileage and running time details are in Appendix 9.

Route 117, Revere Beach–Maverick Station via Beach Street, ran through Bell Circle, Revere, right through the center, as was common Boston El practice. The circle, officially Timothy J. Mahoney Circle, took its common name from an automobile dealership, Bell Oldsmobile, located there. *Charles A. Duncan*

Passengers alight from 4405 on Beach Street at the corner of Central Avenue in Revere. *Charles A. Duncan*

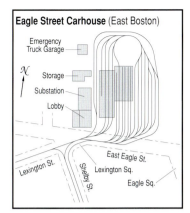

Eagle Street Carhouse (East Boston)

Emergency Truck Garage

Storage

Substation

Lobby

East Eagle St.

Lexington St.

Shelby St.

Lexington Sq.

Eagle Sq.

Eagle Street Carhouse was a large facility that typically stored and serviced sixty to seventy cars during the 1940s. Type 4 and Type 5 cars were predominant here, with an occasional trailer. The view above from around 1950 was taken looking down Lexington Street into a yard full of Type 5s. At left, only a couple of years earlier, Type 4s were much in evidence.

Above, Paul M. Paulsen; left, Leon Onofri

Also based at Eagle Street were work cars such as Type 3 snow plow 5173, seen here on October 31, 1947. *Robert A. Kennerly*

The Eagle Street Carhouse Lines

Eagle Street Carhouse

Eagle Street was a large carhouse and yard complex located in East Boston at the intersection of Lexington, Shelby, and East Eagle Streets. Prior to March 1941, former Eastern Mass. cars were stored here, but after this date only Type 4 and Type 5 cars were based at this carhouse.

This facility consisted of two adjacent carhouse buildings and an adjoining yard with concentric loops. All outside storage tracks were passing sidings. In the westerly carhouse, there were also three passing sidings running through the building and one stub-end spur. The easterly carhouse had five stub-ends and one through track running completely through the building.

Equipment Assignments

The March 18, 1940, rating showed 64 cars including spares assigned to Eagle Street, 10 of which were 4300 and 4400s, 32 were Type 4s, and 22 were Type 5s. Ten of the Type 5s were stored overnight at Gerrish Avenue Loop.

By the end of the decade, in the September 12, 1949, rating, the 4300s and 4400s were gone. Eleven Type 4 cars remained as spares, and there were 55 Type 5s including 25 spares, leaving a total of 66 cars assigned to Eagle Street.

Detailed equipment assignments by line are shown in Appendix 8. The discussion of car assignments below is a summary of this information.

The Revere Beach Loop–Maverick via Ocean Avenue line was assigned Type 4 cars almost exclusively until June 1949. At this time, Type 5s took over for the balance of the decade. From March 1940 to March 1941, Type 5 cars were also used briefly in addition to the Type 4s.

The Gladstone–Maverick line was regularly assigned Type 4 cars until 1950. Type 5s were in service intermittently from 1941 through 1943 and in 1949 and 1950. The last regularly scheduled use of trailer cars on the system occurred on this line during two periods in the 1940s: September 1942 to June 1943 and September 1943 to May 1944.

Cars used on the Suffolk Downs–Maverick via Bennington Street service included Type 4s from April 19 through June 7, 1948, and from July 12, 1948, through June 13, 1949.

The Eagle Street Carhouse–Maverick via Lexington Street line saw former Eastern Mass. cars between December 1939 and March 1941. Type 5s were used on this line from March 1941 to January 1947 and from June 1949 into the 1950s. Type 4s were also used here from March through November 1945, and January 1947 to June 1949.

Until March 1941, 4300s and 4400s were assigned to the Jeffries Point line. Type 5 cars were used from March 1941 through September 1946, and generally from January 1947 through April 1949, when the line was converted to bus operation. Type 4s were regularly operated on this line from September 1946 through September 1947, and sporadically thereafter in off-peak hours.

118 Revere Beach Loop–Maverick Station *via* *Ocean Avenue*

One could go directly to Revere Beach from Maverick using the Beach Street or Revere Street lines. However, the Ocean Avenue line, with its fast reservation running and much more direct route, was the streetcar line of choice for riders destined for Revere Beach from other parts of Boston. For this reason, the Ocean Avenue line is the best remembered of the three car lines from Maverick to Revere Beach.

Leaving Revere Beach loop, the cars turned south onto Ocean Avenue, soon crossed the switches to the Beach Street line, and continued on Ocean Avenue to Eliot Circle. The streetcar line passed through a short private reservation in the center of the traffic circle, turned to the right, and entered a reservation in the Revere Beach Parkway. The line then crossed a bridge over the former BRB&L Railroad. Just beyond this point the line turned southwest onto a private right-of way which ran as far as Winthrop Avenue, parallel to Washburn Avenue and the BRB&L right-of-way.

Just before entering the right-of-way, the Maverick line crossed an outbound track switch to an unused track still in Revere Beach Parkway. This track joined an abandoned single-track line on Winthrop Avenue that had been used by the Beachmont line.

At Winthrop Avenue, Washburn Avenue jogged west a short distance, directly into the alignment of the trolley tracks. The Maverick line then crossed the former Beachmont line on Winthrop Avenue at grade and entered and followed Washburn Avenue in pavement to the Belle Isle Inlet, the boundary of East Boston and Revere. Here the tracks crossed Belle Isle Inlet into East Boston on a small wooden trestle.

On the other side of the Belle Isle Inlet, continuing southbound, Washburn Avenue became an unpaved way with open rail and exposed ties and ran to Walley Street through a marsh.[1] Just before Waldemar Avenue, the line crossed the yard leads of first the Gladstone Loop and then the Suffolk Downs Loop. Entering Walley Street, cars climbed a steep grade, descended, and bore right onto Bennington Street at Orient Heights.

From Breed Square (Saratoga Street) to Day Square, the Bennington Street tracks ran in a private reservation. Just before Day Square, the line crossed a bridge over the B&A Railroad freight line to the East Boston docks. From Day Square to Maverick Station, the line shared the same route as the Broadway Station–Maverick via Central Avenue line described earlier. This line was the shortest of the three Maverick–Revere Beach routes, a round-trip requiring only 9.426 miles and a running time of 44 minutes.

Unlike the two other lines to Revere Beach Loop, this line could handle Type 4 cars because the track spacing between the two inner rails was sufficient to allow their use. Service on this route was always heavy, and a substantial number of cars were constantly required.

Cars on this line ran express to Orient Heights between 4:30 p.m. and 6:30 p.m. on weekdays, starting late in 1945 and through the end of the 1940s. Initially, these express cars displayed a NO STOPS sign. The Elevated felt that this signage was improper, and installed new signs that read REVERE BEACH, and underneath in red letters, LIMITED TO ORIENT HEIGHTS. All roll signs had this change added by March 1947.

A special pull-in, pull-out route from Eagle Street Carhouse to Maverick Station via Bennington Street was used supplement or reduce service on Route 118 as needed in the weekday morning and evening rush hours. The round-trip distance of this route was 3.032 miles with a running time of 20 minutes.

Streetcars operated on Ocean Avenue, one block west of and parallel to Revere Beach Boulevard, which fronted the beach itself. The intervening block contained various amusements and rides such as the ferris wheel seen in the background of this view of Type 5 No. 5565 and a sister car operating on Ocean Avenue as part of an NHRS Convention special trip. *Richard L. Wonson*

An ex-Eastern Mass. 4300 is about to turn from Beach Street onto Ocean Avenue to complete its run from Maverick Station to Revere Beach Loop. It is February 1947, and these cars will be retired shortly. *Charles A. Duncan*

---

[1] It is doubtful that anything but streetcars used this section of the roadway on a regular basis. This Washburn Avenue should not be confused with another street of the same name located a few blocks away on the southeast side of Bennington Street. The other "Washburn Avenue" was apparently laid out, but never built. However, it appears on many maps of the area.

At the south end of Ocean Avenue, the tracks crossed the junction of Revere Beach Boulevard and Revere Beach Parkway and entered Eliot Circle. Here, Type 4s and center-entrance trailers provide service on a warm August day in 1942. *Charles A. Duncan*

The right-of-way leading from Winthrop Avenue to Eliot Circle was exclusively for the use of streetcars, as the sign makes clear. Heading for Revere Beach Loop, Type 4 No. 5451 is about to cross and enter the Revere Beach Parkway on March 13, 1948.

Foster M. Palmer

At the eastern edge of Belle Isle Inlet, Washburn Avenue turned more or less into an unpaved right-of-way over which only streetcars could pass. This shot is of Type 4 No. 5443 crossing the inlet on a trestle, still part of Washburn Avenue, on October 4, 1947.

Robert A. Kennerly

Outbound Type 5 No. 5611 in the background is in Eliot Circle while inbound Type 4 No. 5465 is entering a reservation in the Revere Beach Parkway.   The Spanish Gables dance hall can be seen in the background. *Paul M. Paulsen*

The northeastern end of Washburn Avenue on the other side of Winthrop Avenue was paved, and 5868 makes its way toward Revere Beach in this scene shot around 1949. *Paul M. Paulsen*

Inbound car 5271 crosses Saratoga Street at Orient Heights in 1949.
Paul M. Paulsen

Cresting Walley Street, 5209 will head down to Orient Heights and Bennington Street on a trip to Maverick Station. It's May 31, 1949, and Type 4 cars will soon disappear from this area.

Charles A. Duncan

Between Saratoga Street and Day Square, cars on Bennington Street ran in a private reservation. Type 4 No. 5212 is seen here in August 1942.
Charles A. Duncan

At Day Square, East Boston, two Type 4 cars pull off Bennington Street onto Chelsea Street running "NO STOPS" and deadheading to Eagle Street Carhouse on August 9, 1940.
Charles A. Duncan

Type 4 No. 5383 and a trailer is entering service on July 10, 1940, turning onto Chelsea Street from Shelby Street, one of the streets adjacent to Eagle Street Carhouse. Since Chelsea Street connected with Bennington Street in both directions, this train could go either way, but the roll sign makes the destination clear.
Charles A. Duncan

Type 5 No. 5874 heads for Revere as a Rapid Transit bus from Winthrop heads for Maverick. The tracks in the foreground connected to Chelsea Street to allow access to Eagle Street Carhouse.
Paul M. Paulsen

Type 5 No. 5584 passes the Central Theater in 1949. Closer to Central Square, East Boston, Bennington Street took on the air of a more traditional streetcar line. Riders boarded and got off the cars directly in the street. No private reservation operation or safety islands here!
Paul M. Paulsen

A handful of heavy Boston Elevated street-running lines had pedestrian safety islands at key stops for considerable distances. Bennington Street, East Boston, was one of these locations, as in this scene at Bennington and Swift Streets on May 14, 1950. By now Type 5s were handling most of the Route 118 and 120 work on Bennington Street.
Foster M. Palmer

The Bennington Street line joined the Meridian Street line at Central Square for the final leg of its run to Maverick. Here, Type 5 No. 5550 is making the turn outbound from Meridian onto Bennington in 1949.
Paul M. Paulsen

Tony Tieuli remembers…

A Summer's Ride to Revere Beach

A journey to Revere Beach was to be savored in the stifling hot days of July and August. And a journey it was! Early in the morning my mother would consult with her neighbors and a decision would be made whether or not to go to the "beach." Revere Beach was glorious for children! Amusement games, Cyclone roller coaster, Virginia Reel, cotton candy, Tilt-A-Whirl, Bluebeard's Castle, the "clock" at the Bath House, and the carousel at the Hippodrome. If all adults agreed, three women and nine children would begin the trek by 10 a.m. Usually the mothers would carry several paper shopping bags filled with towels, suntan lotion, sandwiches, tonic in thermos bottles, dry underwear, goggles, snorkels, webbed rubber feet, and some kind of liniment for sunburn.

Jamaica Plain could be two hours from Revere Beach on a hot day. We took the elevated train from Green Street to State Street Station and then negotiated a scary escalator up to the "East Boston Tunnel" trains. The escalators were wood cleat affairs that had to be "jumped" on in a certain way or you risked failing down. RUMBA RUMBA RUMBA RUMBA RUMBA RUMBA they would drone on–almost defying your attempts to climb aboard. Once at Devonshire Station upstairs, we waited impatiently for the train to Maverick Station.

Soon a packed four-car train would roar into the station. We jockeyed for position at the doors, mothers making sure we were together. The quick, but sometimes suffocating trip to Maverick completed our rapid transit ride.

At Maverick, the train would unload 400 or more passengers. They swarmed to board a convoy of shiny Type 5 streetcars waiting on the track across the platform. Each streetcar air compressor was singing a different song at a different pitch. We thought they were the motors revving up, impatient to leave for the beach.

Once everyone was on the car, the starter blew his whistle, the doors closed and we were off! Up the hill and out of the dark tunnel we chugged, and then burst into the hot sun of East Boston streets. All the windows were open of course, allowing whatever cool breezes there were to enter the car. Breezes were more internal, however. The scents of perspiration, bologna, egg salad sandwiches, popcorn, cheddar cheese, and suntan lotion were usually our lot. Yet, a festive mood always managed to accompany us to the beach. Everyone was happy and it seemed that they all were talking at once. Yes, there were parents telling children, "Sit, hold on, get out of the bag, stop pushing, leave her alone, it's only a few more minutes

before we are there …" Resigned to their fate, standing passengers swayed on leather straps hung from the ceiling. We could not wait to get there!

All the way, there were the noises of motion: the steady acceleration and deceleration of the car as the gears sung our progress. The motorman stomped on the bell button continuously to warn motorists out of the way. All the windows rattled in their frames and every few minutes the air compressor thumped away telling us all was well.

Not soon enough, the car carefully climbed up the hill near Orient Heights and down to the private tracks in the marshes. As if to prove that it was not his fault that there was so much traffic, the motorman turned the controller to its highest point. The car raced across a trestle swaying and lurching like an amusement ride much to the delight of all on board. The car was alive with motion—unused hand straps swayed back and forth, people shouted, laughed, squealed, and talked, the motors and gears screamed with energy, and the wheels whirred their tattoo on the rail joints.

We slowed quickly, crossed a road, and then climbed more private tracks to the crest of a hill. Suddenly, strong ocean breezes filled the car with the tang of salt air and we knew we were "here." We saw a panorama of the whole beach from the car windows and the mood of the car changed. Excitement built as we swept onto a reservation in the middle of the road, then down through the rotary and onto Ocean Avenue. How glorious all of the sights were to young eyes. Thousands of people, roller coasters, Ferris wheels, smells of pepper steaks, Turkish taffy, clams, fish and chips!

Soon the crowd began to melt away as the car stopped to let people off. We always traveled to the end of the line at the Bath House. Here we would go up the hill near Mary O'Neill's Stand to the pavilion. The giant clock was a landmark. Again, all of us were counted. We scouted for a place on the sand to stake our claim to space for the blanket and our belongings. The clock, incidentally, was everyone's beacon; if you got lost, instructions were to wait at the foot of the clock until an adult found you.

At the end of the day, our friendly Type 5 cars were basking in the sun on Revere Beach Loop. We knew they were waiting just for us and would take us home safely.

The Ocean Avenue line had it all: a fast run to the beach, an ocean view in places, and some private right-of-way like this in Eliot Circle.
Charles A. Duncan

– 179 –

Gladstone Loop

The Gladstone Loop had parallel passing sidings for storage within the loop area. It was a relatively recent addition to the system, having been opened by the Elevated in 1930. The loop was located on the east side of Washburn Avenue, just north of its intersection with Walley Street and Waldemar Avenue. The loop site is very close to the present Blue Line Suffolk Downs Station.

Suffolk Downs Race Track Loop

Leading from the west side of Washburn Avenue, just south of the track leads to the Gladstone Loop, was a half-mile double-track line to the Suffolk Downs Race Track property. This line was entirely in private right-of-way and ended in a loop. It was also a recent addition, having been installed by the Elevated in 1935, just before the race track opened to the public.

120 Gladstone Loop (Suffolk Downs)– Maverick Station *via Bennington Street*

This extremely heavy line began at Gladstone Loop near Orient Heights. On entering Washburn Avenue, cars followed exactly the same route to Maverick Station as the Revere Beach Loop–Maverick Station via Ocean Avenue line discussed above. The round-trip between Gladstone Loop and Maverick was 6.177 miles. The average round-trip running time was 32 minutes.

Regular Suffolk Downs–Maverick service partially replaced the Gladstone–Maverick service April through June 1948 and from July 1948 through June 1949. Whereas previously Suffolk Downs cars ran only as needed, they now ran from 9 a.m. to 6 p.m. seven days a week during these periods.

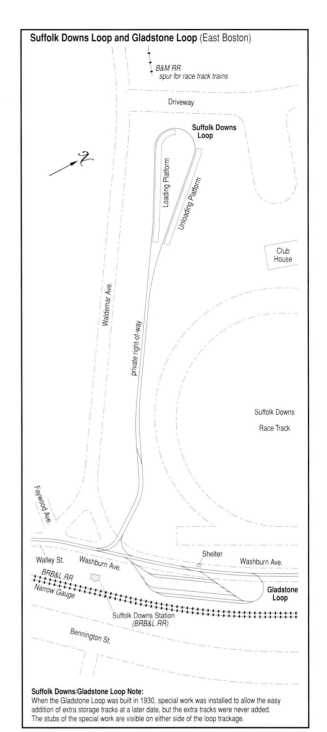

Suffolk Downs Loop and Gladstone Loop (East Boston)

Suffolk Downs/Gladstone Loop Note:
When the Gladstone Loop was built in 1930, special work was installed to allow the easy addition of extra storage tracks at a later date, but the extra tracks were never added. The stubs of the special work are visible on either side of the loop trackage.

Route 120, serving the racetrack at Suffolk Downs, was the last line to regularly use Type 4 and trailer trains. Here, semi-convertible 4322 passes a Type 4 and a trailer waiting in Gladstone Loop in July 1943 as it proceeds towards Revere on Route 118 along the unpaved Washburn Avenue. *Charles A. Duncan*

By street railway standards, Gladstone Loop was relatively new, having been constructed by the Boston Elevated in 1930. This scene, taken from Bennington Street on June 17, 1940, shows the catenary towers of the recently abandoned BRB&L running right beside the Gladstone Loop where a number of Type 4 cars and trailers are stored. Behind the loop we see the distant grandstands of the Suffolk Downs Racetack. *Charles A. Duncan*

Suffolk Downs Loop was virtually adjacent to Gladstone Loop. It was built in 1935, only five years after Gladstone, to serve the new Suffolk Downs Race Track, which opened the same year. At left, a Type 4 turns into Suffolk Downs from Washburn Avenue about 1948, while at left another Type 4 is running wrong direction on the Loop in late May 1949. *Left, Stanley M. Hauck; right, Charles A. Duncan*

Suffolk Downs Loop provided an alternative to Gladstone Loop during the racing season. Race track patrons stream from ex-Eastern Mass. cars operating on the Suffolk Downs–Maverick line in July 1943. *Charles A. Duncan*

Swan Song For Center-Entrance Trailers

The Maverick–Gladstone/Suffolk Downs service was the last to use trains of Type 4s and center-entrance trailers. In June 1943, trailer 7174 is seen at Suffolk Downs Loop. *Charles A. Duncan*

There is no question as to where this train is headed as it crests Walley Street around 1942. *Charles A. Duncan*

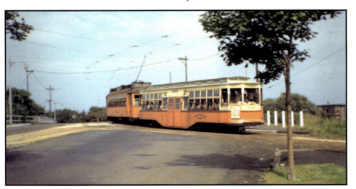

Revere Beach was one of the most popular Boston El destinations on hot summer days. To handle the crowds, trailer trains would be used, such as this one with trailer 7115 seen at Beachmont. *Charles A. Duncan*

A Type 4 and center-entrance trailer combination is seen near Day Square on May 19, 1942. *Charles A. Duncan*

121 Maverick Station–Eagle Street *via*
Lexington Street

This extremely short line featured single-track operation on Lexington Street and a 270-foot long turnout at the Prescott Street intersection. Leaving Maverick Station, cars on this line followed Meridian Street through Central Square to Lexington Street.

The line turned right onto Lexington Street and went from double to single track, continuing northeast to the turnout. Just before intersecting with Shelby Street, the line again became single track and ran to the caryard entrance at Eagle Street.

During the rush hours, streetcars ran one-way on Lexington Street, using Bennington Street in the opposite direction. Cars ran inbound on Lexington Street in the morning rush hours, returning via Bennington Street, Chelsea Street, and Shelby Street to Eagle Street Carhouse.

In the evening rush hours, cars ran outbound on Lexington Street and inbound via Bennington Street. Regardless of the street used for rush-hour return trips to Eagle Street, the cars were signed "Lexington." The round-trip distance using either rush hour routing was 2.775 miles, with a running time of twenty minutes. This special operating procedure is well documented for the period from 1942 to the end of the 1940s and may well have been in effect prior to 1942.

In the off-peak hours, the single car assigned to the line ran in both directions on Lexington Street. Using Lexington Street alone, the running time was also twenty minutes, but the round-trip mileage was 2.758 miles, slightly less than the Lexington-Bennington routings.

Apart from the Mount Auburn Street grade crossing in Watertown, the only regularly scheduled bi-directional single-track operation the Boston Elevated ran in the 1940s was on Lexington Street in East Boston. The line was single-track once it left Meridian Street and continued all the way to Eagle Street Carhouse with one turnout located near the Shelby Street end of Lexington Street. At left, 5542 turns from Meridian onto Lexington Street in 1949, while at right, Type 4 No. 5415 operates outbound on Lexington Street on October 3, 1947. Note the laundry hanging from the lines between the houses on the left. *Left, Paul M. Paulsen; right, Robert A. Kennerly*

Type 5 No. 5918 is seen at Shelby Street as it approaches the lead into Eagle Street Carhouse around 1948. The car has just crossed the switch from Lexington onto Shelby used for rush-hour loop operation via Bennington Street. *Charles A. Duncan*

Car 5783 has just climbed the Lexington Street hill from Eagle Street Carhouse, navigated the only turnout on the line, and stopped to pick up a lone passenger at the end of the turnout at the stop at Lexington and Prescott Streets. The car in inbound to Maverick on a sunny July 18, 1945. *Foster M. Palmer*

123 Jeffries Point–Maverick Station *via Sumner Street*

This curious little East Boston loop line traveled a short distance from Maverick Square in the general direction of the Logan Airport. Leaving Maverick Station, it turned southeast at the head of the incline onto Maverick Street. It crossed a bridge over the B&A Railroad and turned right onto Orleans Street for three blocks. At Webster Street, the line turned southeast into a single-track loop and climbed the hill to Jeffries Point.

Just beyond Lamson Street, the car line passed over the BRB&L Railroad, which ran in two parallel tunnels under the Jeffries Point section. From here the line ran down the hill to the intersection of Sumner and Webster Streets, the end of the neighborhood and the layover point of the line.

Returning cars then turned almost 135 degrees to the left onto Sumner Street, and ran northwest up and over the hill and the BRB&L tunnels to Orleans Street. Here the cars turned right onto Orleans Street and reentered double-track territory. Streetcars then turned left onto Maverick Street, again crossing the bridge over the B&A Railroad, and ran back to Maverick Square for the trip down into the station. This was truly the shortest streetcar line on the system, with only 1.754 miles required for a round-trip. The average running time was short as well—only 12 minutes!

A local observer, Paul Paulsen, remembers Type 4 cars on the line the last day of operation. This line was converted to buses on Saturday, April 30, 1949, amid protests to the MTA from local representatives.[199]

Paul Paulsen remembers…

The Jeffries Point Loop

I fondly recall riding over the very short, partially "single tracked" loop line from Maverick Station to the nearby Jeffries Point section of East Boston. On the last evening of service, April 30, 1949, I rode in Type 4 car 5281, which, along with car 5383, provided all service for the last few runs. I made a few photos of these two Type 4a cars during that last night of streetcar operation.

I watched for the logo, "JEFFRIES POINT" to appear on the large Hunter destination sign of a Type 4 car, as it descended the steep trolley grade at Maverick Station to pick up passengers from the Maverick Subway rapid transit line.

Soon we would be traveling up that same grade into daylight, in our favorite streetcar, the huge Type 4. Car 5281, with its noisy traction motors, really "growled" as it ran slowly up the grade from the underground Maverick Station.

The cars would come up into daylight, then hit the switch to make a right turn onto Maverick Street for a few hundred yards, crossing over the Boston and Albany Railroad "Grand Junction Railroad," as it was called. The B&A Railroad still operated a few old 0-6-0 steam shifters at this time; loco 144 was working late this evening below us, as we headed toward Jeffries Point.

Our route was double tracked along Maverick Street. It turned a sharp 90 degrees onto Orleans Street, for a couple of blocks. We passed the Maverick bound track, which suddenly turned onto Sumner Street from Orleans Street, so now we were riding over a classic "single track" line!

The single track turned another 90 degrees up Webster Street toward the end of the Loop. It soon passed by the Samuel Adams School (which is still in use in 2003). We saw the many two and three decker houses along the route. Soon, a park, Belmont Square, appeared on Webster Street, where British troops were once encamped in Colonial times, long before this section of East Boston was named for Dr. Jeffries.

The Loop curved broadly where Webster and Sumner Streets join, at the end of the line. The single track portion continued back toward Maverick Square along Sumner Street, passing an attractive red brick church, Our Lady of the Assumption. At the junction of Sumner and Orleans streets the line met the outbound track. Here the line again became double-track to Maverick Station.

This trip was like many others I had made to Jeffries Point. The difference, however, was the sobering realization that I was doing so for the very last time. I hoped that the few photos I had made that day would be good remembrances of this lovely old streetcar line. This was one of two remaining "single tracked" routes (along with the Lexington Street line, also in East Boston) on the MTA.

I acquired an MTA "Notice of Discontinuance of Service," posted at Maverick subway station. It indicated that all Jeffries Point streetcar runs would be abandoned on April 30, 1949. The next day a new autobus service would begin, routed up Sumner Street and continuing on to the Logan Airport civil airline terminals of the day. I never did have an occasion to ride that bus line!

Paul M. Paulsen grew up in East Boston and closely observed and photographed the local trolleys.

Paul Paulsen took this view of 5281 on Sumner Street in front of Belmont Square Park in March 1949.
Paul M. Paulsen

Type 4 No. 5417 enters the incline at Maverick Square Station after its short run on the Jeffries Point line in May 1947.

Charles A. Duncan

Emerging from Maverick, the Jeffries Point line turned right across Chelsea Street onto Maverick Street. *Paul M. Paulsen*

Headed for Maverick, 5361 approaches the Maverick Street bridge over the B&A Railroad's Grand Junction Branch in March 1949.

Paul M. Paulsen

Orleans Street was one of three double-track sections of the Jeffries Point car line, the other two being the Maverick Station streetcar incline and Maverick Street. This shot of 5379 was taken on January 18, 1947.

Stanley M. Hauck

The classic shot was at the end of the Jeffries Point line, where Webster Street curved into Sumner Street. Car 5387 is shown at this location on October 3, 1947. *Robert A. Kennerly*

From Jeffries Point, the loop followed Sumner Street back to Orleans Street. Two women wait in the middle of Sumner Street at Seaver Street for the Type 4 to reach them in this view from around 1946. *Charles A. Duncan*

Rush Hour Cutbacks

Several cutbacks were operated from Revere to Maverick Station at various times during the 1940s. These cutbacks are listed below.

> Route 116 Cutback: **Revere Street Crossover–Maverick** *via Broadway & Meridian Street*, 8.311 miles round-trip, with a running time of 46 minutes.
>
> Route 116 Cutback: **Broadway & Revere Street Crossover–Maverick** *via Broadway & Meridian Street*, 8.251 miles round trip with a running time of 46 minutes.
>
> Route 117 Cutback: **Revere Carhouse–Maverick** *via Broadway & Meridian Street*, 7.26 miles round-trip with a running time of 42 minutes.
>
> Routes 116 and 117 Cutback Bypass Routing around Meridian Street Bridge in 1942: **Revere Carhouse or Revere Street Crossover–Maverick** *via Broadway & Central Avenue*. See Appendix 9 for round-trip distances and running times.

From 1941 to 1946, some trips were operated to the Revere Street crossover on Revere Street, near Broadway.[m] In 1946, the cutback point, still called Revere Street Crossover, was relocated to Broadway and Revere Street, where a segment of stub-end track was reinstated from the former line to Lynn, as previously discussed.

Revere Carhouse was the principal cutback on the Beach Street line from Maverick to Revere Beach Loop. Extra service between Revere Carhouse and Maverick was regularly operated through most of the 1940s, running into Maverick via Broadway and Meridian Street.

Orient Heights Rapid Transit Extension

The abandonment of the BRB&L Railroad had left a gaping hole in the local transit network, and there was a strong need for replacement service. The Coolidge Commission in 1945 had recommended an extension of the Bowdoin–Maverick rapid transit line from Maverick Square to Day Square in East Boston.

The Massachusetts Legislature authorized the extension to Day Square in 1945 and a further extension to Orient Heights in 1946. In May 1947, the Boston Transit Department began construction on the 2-1/2-mile extension, and by October 1, 1948, work was well underway.

In 1947 the Metropolitan Transit Authority made new plans to continue the Orient Heights extension to a point near the

---

[m] The crossover on Revere Street was removed between August 11 and August 15, 1947.

The second of the Revere Street cutbacks actually ended on Broadway rather than Revere Street itself. In 1946, this trackage, still in the street at the corner of Broadway and Revere Street, was restored to operation. No. 4409 has changed ends and is about to return to Maverick Station in this scene taken on March 13, 1948.
Foster M. Palmer

This view of the cutback at Broadway and Revere Streets on September 12, 1948, was taken looking west toward Revere Carhouse. Both poles are up on Type 5 No. 5684 shown here changing ends on the spur. The car is on Broadway, and the street coming in from the left by the drug store is Revere Street. *Charles A. Duncan*

Revere Beach Loop. This future extension would include stations at Suffolk Downs, Beachmont, Crescent Beach, and Bath House. The last two stations would ultimately open renamed Revere Beach and Wonderland, respectively. The rapid transit extension opened to Orient Heights and Suffolk Downs in 1952, and to Wonderland in 1954.

MTA dump cars 1024 and 3619 are seen working on the extension of the Bowdoin–Maverick rapid transit line to Revere. This shot was taken near Day Square on December 30, 1950. The new line followed the old Boston, Revere Beach & Lynn right-of-way.
Foster M. Palmer

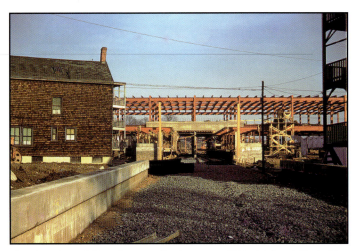

The framing of Day Square Station, now Wood Island Park Station, is seen in this December 30, 1950, view taken along the right-of-way, which has received ballast but not yet had track laid. The upper level of the station would accommodate a loop for the trackless trolleys that would replace streetcars upon the completion of the new rapid transit route to Orient Heights in 1952.

Foster M. Palmer

Converted Type 2 compressor car 5071 was actively involved in the construction project. Here it is seen on an isolated section of track near Orient Heights in April 1950. *Foster M. Palmer*

A new storage yard and shop facility would be built at Orient Heights as well. Until this shop was completed in 1952, the existing maintenance facilities, which were odd to say the least, continued in use. For minor running repairs, the rapid transit cars on this line were maintained in a small two–story shop in a short tunnel at the Maverick end of the East Boston Tunnel. This tunnel extended under Chelsea Street, East Boston, just north of Maverick Station. Heavier repairs, however, required a trip over surface and subway tracks to Eliot Square at the end of the Cambridge–Dorchester Subway.

The East Boston Tunnel Surface Maintenance Track

A single-track service line ran on sections of former surface car lines through Boston's West End and over the Longfellow Bridge, where it finally joined the Cambridge–Dorchester line.[n] This was the access track from the East Boston Tunnel to the Eliot Square Rapid Transit Shops, located just south of Harvard Square. East Boston Tunnel rapid transit cars were sent to Eliot Square for work that was more extensive than the Chelsea Street maintenance facility could handle.

Rapid transit cars were usually moved in the early hours of the morning (and occasionally in broad daylight) to Eliot Square. The trip began when a train left the subway on an incline located in the middle of Cambridge Street near its intersection with North Russell Street.[o]

A trolley-pole-equipped work train regularly assigned to the East Boston Tunnel was often used to tow East Boston Tunnel rapid transit cars up the incline and out onto Cambridge Street. Some observers report having seen the rapid transit cars running under their own power on this line, using portable trolley poles.

From the incline a typical procession would trundle down Cambridge Street on a short stretch of double track that quickly changed to single iron, and would round the north side of Charles Circle. From here the train continued across the Longfellow Bridge and joined the Cambridge–Dorchester line through a switch that connected the westbound rapid transit track and Longfellow bridge surface track just before the incline into Kendall Square Station.

A special electrically powered rolling gate allowed the trains through the fence from the street track to the rapid transit track. The gate was installed in 1924 when rapid transit cars replaced trolleys in the East Boston Tunnel. Pieces of the gate are still in place as of this writing.

A matching gate and switch on the south side of the incline was installed at the same time, but the second gate and the eastbound track on the street surface of the bridge were abandoned in the 1930s. The westbound track, however, remained in use for bi-directional travel until 1952, when the opening of the Orient Heights Shop ended the need for this unusual connection. On this note, we also end this book.

---

[n] The bridge was officially renamed the Longfellow Bridge in 1927, but Boston Elevated records still called it the West Boston Bridge.

[o] This incline, known as the North Russell Street Incline, dated from the opening of the East Boston Tunnel in 1904 and was originally used by streetcars running from East Boston to Cambridge over the Longfellow Bridge.

The service track emerging onto Cambridge Street from the former East Boston Tunnel trolley incline was regularly used until the opening of the Orient Heights rapid transit shop in 1952. Here we see a locomotive crane stored behind the fence in the incline. The buildings in the background gave way in the 1960s to the Government Center renewal project, while most of those closest on the left fell victim to the West End redevelopment scheme.

BERy

Peering deeply into the incline and beyond the wooden doors to the tunnel itself, a motor flat and a standard East Boston Tunnel rapid transit car are revealed in this shot circa 1949. The rapid transit car has already been equipped with a headlight for use on the Orient Heights–Revere extension. *Kevin T. Farrell Collection*

The other end of the East Boston Tunnel Surface Maintenance Track joined the Cambridge–Dorchester Subway line on the Cambridge end of the Longfellow Bridge at the switch shown in the center of this photograph.

BERy

Bound for Jamaica Plain Loop, car 5705 has just crested the hill on the single-track section of Roxbury Street into John Eliot Square. The Eliot Congregational Church in the background could be in any New England country town, but this building is just two miles or so from downtown Boston. This great shot was taken April 24, 1948.

Foster M. Palmer

Appendix 1

End Notes

Notes to Foreword

[1] Boston Elevated Railway Co., *Twenty-Second Annual Report of the Board of Public Trustees for the Year Ended December 31, 1940* (Boston: Boston Elevated Railway Co., 1941), p. 43. All mileage figures are rounded off.

Notes to Chapter 1

[2] An eighth route, Faulkner–Everett Station, was converted on June 17, 1939 from bus to trackless trolley. On December 11, 1943, the Faulkner–Malden Square bus line via Cross and Main streets was also converted from bus to trackless trolley operation. The outer end of the Linden–Everett Station line, from Everett Carhouse to Linden, was converted from bus to trackless trolley November 28, 1936.

[3] Boston Elevated Railway Company, *Annual Return of the Boston Elevated Railway Company to the (Massachusetts) Department of Public Utilities for the Year Ended December 31, 1939*, p. 401.

[4] Ibid.

[5] Boston Elevated Railway Co., *First Report of the Trustees of the Boston Elevated Railway Company for the Year Ended December 31, 1918* (Boston: Boston Elevated Railway Co., 1919), p. 34.

[6] Boston Elevated Railway Co., *Twenty-Second Annual Report of the Board of Public Trustees for the Year Ended December 31, 1940* (Boston: Boston Elevated Railway Co., 1941), p. 43.

[7] Ibid., p. 7.

[8] Ibid.

[9] Boston Elevated Railway Co., *Twenty-Eighth Annual Report of the Board of Public Trustees for the Year Ended December 31, 1946* (Boston: Boston Elevated Railway Co., 1947), p. 36.

[10] Metropolitan Transit Authority, *Fourth Annual Report of the Board of Public Trustees of the Metropolitan Transit Authority Year Ended December 31, 1950* (Boston: Metropolitan Transit Authority, 1951), p. 30.

[11] Metropolitan Transit Authority, *Third Annual Report of the Board of Public Trustees of the Metropolitan Transit Authority Year Ended December 31, 1949* (Boston: Metropolitan Transit Authority, 1950), p. 45.

[12] A good example is found in the Boston Chapter National Railway Historical Society (NRHS) newsletter for August 1940, *The Shrieking Journal*, which commented that someone in the Boston Elevated apparently had read an earlier issue, which mentioned unused trolley wire on the West Boston Bridge. The wire was still in place but had not been used for years. The wire was promptly removed after this was mentioned in the publication. The writer suggested in this article that the El consider removing the unused trolley brackets over the abandoned Dorchester Avenue ramp to Broadway Station. Just two years later, they were removed along with the entire ramp. *The Shrieking Journal*, 1 (Aug.1940), 6.

[13] The Boston Chapter NRHS operated extensive fan trips in the 1940s. There were many noteworthy trips: July 14, 1940, Type 4 and trailer system-wide; March 23, 1941, 3 car PCC tour highlighted by a trip to the Quincy Shipyard; April 28, 1946, Type 4 car in the morning, MU PCC car in the afternoon; May 18, 1947 all-electric PCC car on the Quincy Division of the Eastern Mass. and various Boston Elevated lines; October 17, 1948, 4400 series car on a system-wide trip; December 5, 1948, Type 4 on the soon-to-be abandoned Dorchester and Roxbury lines; and June 19, 1949, Type 5 in the morning, PCC car in the afternoon.

[14] Boston Elevated 4400 has been preserved at the Seashore Trolley Museum in Kennebunkport, Maine.

[15] Boston Elevated Railway Co., *Twenty-Second Annual Report of the Board of Public Trustees for the Year Ended December 31, 1940* (Boston: Boston Elevated Railway Co., 1941), p. 47.

[16] Metropolitan Transit Authority, *Third Annual Report of the Board of Public Trustees of the Metropolitan Transit Authority Year Ended December 31, 1949* (Boston: Metropolitan Transit Authority, 1950), p. 44.

[17] *The Shrieking Journal* for June 1941 mentioned that the Queen Mary had received a new paint job to match the newly arrived PCC fleet for the Watertown line. *The Shrieking Journal*, 2 (June 1941) 3.

[18] This group of 4400s was part of a 50-car order, built in two lots by Osgood Bradley and Wason for the Eastern Mass. Street Railway. The Eastern Mass. numbered them in the 7000-series, and the ones purchased by the Boston Elevated were renumbered in the 4400-series.

[19] O. R. Cummings, *Street Cars of Boston, Vol. 6* (Forty Fort, Pa.: Harold E. Cox, 1980), p. 65.

[20] Ibid., p. 33, 34, where Cummings notes that sixteen Type 5 cars were equipped with 300-volt motors and self-lapping brake valves in 1934, 1936 and 1937. These cars were capable of higher speeds than the rest of the Type 5 fleet and were primarily used on the Salem Street Station–Sullivan Square Station via Fellsway and Salem Street–Sullivan via Winter Hill lines.

[21] O. R. Cummings, *Street Cars of Boston, Vol. 5* (Forty Fort, Pa.: Harold E. Cox, 1977), p. 27.

[22] Ibid., p. 45.

[23] The final tally for wartime reconditioning programs was given in the Boston Elevated 1945 annual report. The company stated that it had reconditioned 44 Main Line Elevated cars, eight Cambridge-Dorchester subway cars, six East Boston Tunnel rapid transit cars, 73 surface cars, and had used and kept in safe operating condition as many as 151 over-age buses.

[24] O. R. Cummings, *Street Cars of Boston, Vol. 5* (Forty Fort, Pa.: Harold E. Cox, 1977), p. 46.

[25] O. R. Cummings, *Street Cars of Boston, Vol. 4* (Forty Fort, Pa.: Harold E. Cox, 1977), p. 59. The Elevated did not sequentially renumber this fleet, hence the obvious difference between the fleet total and the car numbers.

[26] Ibid., p. 62.

[27] Ibid., p. 19.

[28] Ibid., p. 20.

[29] Ibid., p. 7.

[30] Ibid., p. 52.

[31] Ibid., p. 24.

[32] Ibid., p. 26.

[33] Boston Elevated Railway Co., *Twenty-Fifth Annual Report of the Board of Public Trustees for the Year Ended December 31, 1943* (Boston: Boston Elevated Railway Co., 1944), p. 13.

[34] Boston Elevated Railway Co., *Twenty-Sixth Annual Report of the Board of Public Trustees for the Year Ended December 31, 1944* (Boston: Boston Elevated Railway Co., 1945), p. 24.

[35] Boston Elevated Railway Co., *Twenty-Seventh Annual Report of the Board of Public Trustees for the Year Ended December 31, 1945* (Boston: Boston Elevated Railway Co., 1946), p. 31.

[36] "Ventilating and Riding Qualities of PCC Cars Being Studied – Changes In Sight," *Co-operation*, 24 (Oct. 1945), 67-70, 74.

[37] "Calling All Streetcars!," *Co-operation*, 24 (Oct. 1945), 72, 73.

[38] Included in this roster were two former parlor cars, 924 and 925, which were on the property until 1954. Car 925 was acquired by the Seashore Trolley Museum and 924 was scrapped. School instruction cars were converted back to passenger operation for service during World War II, and stayed in revenue operation until retirement.

[39] *The Shrieking Journal* for January 1941 mentioned that the Boston Chapter NRHS was interested in acquiring 12-bench open car, 2858, originally used at Albany Street, then put in storage at Everett Shops. The September 1941 issue noted that the Boston El Trustees were undecided on the proposal, and that ultimately the Public Trustees rejected this acquisition. *The Shrieking Journal*, 2 (Jan. 1941), 12.

[40] O. R. Cummings, "The Eastern Massachusetts Street Railway 6000 and 7000 Class Cars," *Transportation Bulletin*, 71 (Jan. 1965), 34.

[41] Discussion with George Zieba of Quincy, Massachusetts on August 30, 2002.

[42] See Robert C. Stanley, *Narrow Gauge: The Story of the Boston, Revere Beach & Lynn Railroad,* (Boston: Boston Street Railway Association, 1980).

[43] Metropolitan Transit Authority, *First Annual Report of the Board of Public Trustees of the Metropolitan Transit Authority Year Ended December 31, 1947* (Boston: Metropolitan Transit Authority, 1948), p. 21.

[44] "St. Valentine's Blizzard in Retrospect," *Co-operation*, 19 (Apr. 1940), 19, 20.

[45] The Works Progress Administration was renamed the Work Projects Administration in 1939.

[46] Boston Elevated Railway Co., *Twenty-Third Annual Report of the Board of Public Trustees for the Year Ended December 31, 1941* (Boston: Boston Elevated Railway Co., 1942), p. 5-7.

[47] Ibid.

[48] Boston Elevated Railway Co., *Twenty-Fourth Annual Report of the Board of Public Trustees for the Year Ended December 31, 1942* (Boston: Boston Elevated Railway Co., 1943), p. 13.

[49] Boston Elevated Railway Co., *Twenty-Fifth Annual Report of the Board of Public Trustees for the Year Ended December 31, 1943* (Boston: Boston Elevated Railway Co., 1944), p. 5.

[50] Boston Elevated Railway Co., *Twenty-Sixth Annual Report of the Board of Public Trustees for the Year Ended December 31, 1944* (Boston: Boston Elevated Railway Co., 1945), p. 5.

[51] Boston Elevated Railway Co., *Twenty-Seventh Annual Report of the Board of Public Trustees for the Year Ended December 31, 1945* (Boston: Boston Elevated Railway Co., 1946), p. 21.

[52] Boston Elevated Railway Co., *Twenty-Eighth Annual Report of the Board of Public Trustees for the Year Ended December 31, 1946* (Boston: Boston Elevated Railway Co., 1947), p. 5.

[53] "Test Blackouts Successful," *Co-operation*, 21 (Apr. 1942), 24.

[54] Ibid.

[55] Boston Elevated Railway Company, Employee Directive Pamphlet Regarding Air Raids and Blackouts dated August 1, 1942, pp. 1, 2.

[56] Commonwealth of Massachusetts, Department of Public Works, Registry of Motor Vehicles, Regulations Designating Areas Within Which Are Prescribed Reduced Light Intensity and Speed Regulation of Motor Vehicles, August 10, 1942.

[57] Memorandum from D. D. Hall, Boston Elevated Superintendent of Transportation, to Superintendents of Divisions 1 & 2 dated August 14, 1942.

[58] "How the Transportation Department is Meeting the War Demand for Riding," *Co-operation*, 22 (Apr. 1943), 27-31.

[59] Office of Defense Transportation, General Order ODT No. 2, Substitution of Motor Vehicle for Rail Passenger Service, March 25, 1942.

[60] Office of Defense Transportation announcement dated August 25, 1945.

[61] Office of Defense Transportation, Letter to Field Representatives, Special Projects Salvage Section from J. Widman Birch, Subject: Street Car Rail Removal, April 6, 1942.

[62] In another instance, the lightly patronized Riverside Avenue bus line in Medford was slated for elimination. However, this would have caused hardship for some riders, and the El worked out a compromise. The section of the Medford Square–Malden Square bus line between Medford Square and Salem Street Station was dropped because streetcars running on the Sullivan–Winter Hill–Salem Street line served this section as well. The Riverside Avenue line was dropped as a separate route, but part of the Quincy–Linden bus service was extended via Fellsway and Riverside Avenue to Medford Square, replacing the Riverside Avenue line in its entirety. Thus, one bus line was partly replaced, another was eliminated, and a third bus line was extended, maintaining essential service but greatly reducing the combined mileage of the three routes.

[63] Boston Elevated Railway Co., *Twenty-Fifth Annual Report of the Board of Public Trustees for the Year Ended December 31, 1943* (Boston: Boston Elevated Railway Co., 1944), p. 11.

[64] Boston Elevated Railway Co., *Twenty-Sixth Annual Report of the Board of Public Trustees for the Year Ended December 31, 1944* (Boston: Boston Elevated Railway Co., 1945), p. 14.

[65] Ibid., p. 15.

[66] The first line converted from conventional trolley wheels to carbon insert shoes was the route jointly-operated by the Boston El and the Eastern Mass. between Stoneham and Sullivan Square Station. The changeover took place in late 1942. Also that year two more Boston Elevated routes based at Salem Street Carhouse in Medford were converted. Fifty-four cars were given carbon insert shoes in this first round. During the spring of 1943, streetcars on the Clarendon Hill–Sullivan line were changed over. Somewhat later that year, cars at the Revere and Eagle Street Carhouses were equipped with carbon insert shoes. *Ohio Brass Traction News*, 14 (June 1943), 3.

[67] Boston Elevated Railway Co., *Twenty-Fifth Annual Report of the Board of Public Trustees for the Year Ended December 31, 1943* (Boston: Boston Elevated Railway Co., 1944), p. 18.

[68] Boston Elevated Railway Co., *Twenty-Fifth Annual Report of the Board of Public Trustees for the Year Ended December 31, 1943* (Boston: Boston Elevated Railway Co., 1944), p. 27.

[69] O. R. Cummings, *Street Cars of Boston, Vol. 4* (Forty Fort, Pa.: Harold E. Cox, 1977), pp. 48, 50.

[70] Boston Elevated Railway Co., *Twenty-Seventh Annual Report of the Board of Public Trustees for the Year Ended December 31, 1945* (Boston: Boston Elevated Railway Co., 1946), p. 21.

[71] Boston Elevated Railway Co., *Twenty-Fifth Annual Report of the Board of Public Trustees for the Year Ended December 31, 1943* (Boston: Boston Elevated Railway Co., 1944), p. 10.

[72] Boston Elevated Railway Co., *Twenty-Sixth Annual Report of the Board of Public Trustees for the Year Ended December 31, 1944* (Boston: Boston Elevated Railway Co., 1945), p. 19.

[73] Twenty-four were killed in action. Boston Elevated Railway Co., *Twenty-Seventh Annual Report of the Board of Public Trustees for the Year Ended December 31, 1945* (Boston: Boston Elevated Railway Co., 1946), pp. 17, 18.

[74] Boston Elevated Railway Co., *Twenty-Fifth Annual Report of the Board of Public Trustees for the Year Ended December 31, 1943* (Boston: Boston Elevated Railway Co., 1944), p. 12.

[75] Ibid.

[76] "Anticipating Conductorettes," *Co-operation, 22* (Mar. 1943), 7.

[77] Boston Elevated Railway Co., *Twenty-Seventh Annual Report of the Board of Public Trustees for the Year Ended December 31, 1945* (Boston: Boston Elevated Railway Co., 1946), pp. 18, 20.

[78] Ibid., p. 20.

[79] "Two-Way Radios Help Greatly," *Co-operation*, 25 (Aug. 1946), 55.

[80] "To Maintain Tops in Service, The MTA Takes to the Air," *Co-operation, 28* (Dec. 1949), 84, 85.

[81] Boston Elevated Railway Co., *Twenty-Sixth Annual Report of the Board of Public Trustees for the Year Ended December 31, 1944* (Boston: Boston Elevated Railway Co., 1945), p. 20, 24.

[82] The Washburn Avenue referred to here is parallel to and west of the former Narrow Gauge right-of-way. See Chapter 8 for additional information.

[83] Boston Elevated Railway Co., *Twenty-Sixth Annual Report of the Board of Public Trustees for the Year Ended December 31, 1944* (Boston: Boston Elevated Railway Co., 1945), p. 26.

[84] Boston Elevated Railway Co., *Twenty-Seventh Annual Report of the Board of Public Trustees for the Year Ended December 31, 1945* (Boston: Boston Elevated Railway Co., 1946), p. 34.

[85] Ibid.

[86] Ibid.

[87] Ibid., p. 35.

[88] Commonwealth of Massachusetts, *Report of the Legislative Commission on Rapid Transit–1945* (Boston: Commonwealth of Massachusetts, 1945), p. 16.

[89] The Boston Metropolitan Transit District was established by Chapter 383 of the Acts of 1929 to fund transit improvements in the area served by the Boston Elevated Railway.

[90] On July 15, 1948, four remodeled Cambridge Tunnel cars (0706, 0719, 0720, and 0724) were placed in revenue service. The cars were painted in the basic surface lines orange. Cross-seats could be reversed by swiveling them. The cars were ventilated with overhead fans and had fluorescent lighting. Taking a cue from the Coolidge Commission, these Cambridge Tunnel cars were called "Braintree Cars" in anticipation of an extension that would not be started until the 1970s and not completed through to Braintree until March 22, 1980. By the time the extension to Braintree was opened, the four "Braintree Cars" had long been out of service. One car, 0719, has been preserved at the Seashore Trolley Museum.

[91] Commonwealth of Massachusetts, *Report of the Legislative Commission on Rapid Transit–1947* (Boston: Commonwealth of Massachusetts, 1947).

[92] "Bradford Signs El Bill, to Pick Trustees Today", *Boston Globe*, 151 (June 20, 1947), pp. 1, 4.

[93] Metropolitan Transit Authority, *First Annual Report of the Board of Public Trustees of the Metropolitan Transit Authority Year Ended December 31, 1947* (Boston: Metropolitan Transit Authority, 1948), p. 9.

[94] Ibid., p. 9, 10.

[95] Ibid., p. 10.

[96] Metropolitan Transit Authority, *Third Annual Report of the Board of Public Trustees of the Metropolitan Transit Authority Year Ended December 31, 1949* (Boston: Metropolitan Transit Authority, 1950), p. 22.

[97] Boston Elevated Railway Co, Schedules of Night Service, No. 4, January 1940, p. 3.

[98] O. R. Cummings, *Street Cars of Boston, Vol. 6* (Forty Fort, Pa.: Harold E. Cox, 1980), p. 56.

[99] "Surface Lines Service Changes", *Co-operation*, 21 (Nov. 1942), 74.

[100] Ibid.

[101] Boston Elevated Railway Co., *Twenty-Seventh Annual Report of the Board of Public Trustees for the Year Ended December 31, 1945* (Boston: Boston Elevated Railway Co., 1946), p. 31, 32.

[102] "Early Morning Service," *Co-operation*, 26 (July 1947), 33.

[103] "Dudley to Massachusetts Station," *Co-operation*, 27 (Aug. 1948), 32.

[104] "Changes in 'Owl' Service in Prospect," *Co-operation*, 27 (Oct. 1948), 65, 66.

[105] "Change in Service Due to Closing of Harvard Bridge," *Co-operation*, 28 (Sept. 1949), 63.

[106] Metropolitan Transit Authority, Schedules of Owl Service, 2nd MTA edition, December 1949, p. 3.

Notes to Chapter 2

[107] This work was done between May 15 and 21, 1942.

[108] This work was done between January 28 and March 1, 1944.

[109] This work was done between May 14 and May 17, 1945.

[110] This work was done between October 30 and December 31, 1945.

[111] This work was done between January 3 and March 15, 1946.

[112] This work was done between October 7 and October 31, 1946.

[113] This work was done between August 25 and October 15, 1947.

[114] This work was done between March 13 and April 29, 1944.

[115] This work was done between May 3 and May 13, 1949.

[116] During this period, on March 11, 1942, the Boston Elevated Maintenance Department also began removal of unused tracks from the nearby West Fourth Street Bridge as part of bridge repair work by the City of Boston and the New Haven Railroad. The track removal was completed September 19, 1942.

[117] This work was done between December 8, 1941, and May 15, 1942.

[118] This trailing point crossover had been installed a few years earlier, between July 29 and August 8, 1942.

[119] This work was done between September 17 and October 28, 1947.

[120] This crossover was installed between October 5 and October 8, 1943.

[121] Canal Street Loop was abandoned in 1997.

[122] A crossover was built in 1940 between the two tracks to Warren Street from the lower level.

Notes to Chapter 3

[123] Boston Chapter NRHS meetings were held in the second floor of the Park Street Carhouse lobby in the early 1940s.

[124] O. R. Cummings, *Street Cars of Boston, Vol. 6* (Forty Fort, Pa.: Harold E. Cox, 1977), p. 62.

[125] The loop onto Geneva Avenue was completely rebuilt between June 16 and June 30, 1945.

[126] After the line was abandoned on June 19, 1948, track was removed on Gibson Street from Dorchester Avenue to Adams Street between September 27 and October 6, 1948, as part of a City of Boston repaving project.

[127] After the line was abandoned on January 8, 1949, removal of rail and special work in the Blue Hill Avenue reservation from a point south of Washington Street to Seaver Street began on July 15, 1949, and was completed on July 29.

[128] This project started on September 29, 1941, and was completed November 24.

[129] This work began on August 23, 1950 and ended on October 11.

[130] This work took place between November 8 and December 14, 1950.

[131] The stub end track on Depot Street was removed in 1941.

[132] "The Eastern Mass Quincy-Weymouth District," *Motor Coach Age*, 35 (Feb. 1983), pp. 17-19.

[133] Ibid.

[134] Eastern Massachusetts Street Railway Co., *Twenty-Fourth Annual Report of the Board of Public Trustees for the Year Ended December 31, 1943* (Boston: Eastern Massachusetts Street Railway Co., 1944), p. 9.

[135] The Eastern Mass. cars were operated by Boston Elevated motormen while on Boston Elevated property.

[136] "How the Transportation Department is Meeting the War Demand for Riding," *Co-operation*, 22 (Apr. 1943), 30.

[137] "The Eastern Mass Quincy-Weymouth District," *Motor Coach Age*, 35 (Feb. 1983), p. 20.

[138] Eastern Massachusetts Street Railway Co., *Twenty-Seventh Annual Report of the Board of Public Trustees for the Year Ended December 31, 1946* (Boston: Eastern Massachusetts Street Railway Co., 1947), p. 15.

[139] *The Turnout*, 7 (May 1948), 69.

[140] This work was begun on September 22, 1941, and was completed November 15.

[141] "Converting to Trackless Trolley Calls for Many Construction Changes," *Co-operation*, 27 (Aug. 1948), pp. 19-22.

[142] This work occurred between April 21 and May 14, 1948,

[143] "The Seventieth Coach Arrives," *Co-operation*, 28 (Feb. 1949), 14.

Notes to Chapter 4

[144] In earlier years, the Elevated's Arborway facility had been known as Lotus Place Carhouse. The site remains today with most of the structures demolished, and it will eventually be the location of a new garage for compressed-natural gas buses and possibly a small carhouse facility to service equipment on the Arborway car line, should service be restored from Heath Street to Forest Hills.

[145] The Eastern Massachusetts Street Railway was the successor to the Old Colony Street Railway, which had leased these lines to the Boston Elevated on February 16, 1903. The Boston & Northern Street Railway succeeded the Old Colony on July 1, 1911. The Boston & Northern became the Bay State on August 8, 1911, and the Eastern Massachusetts Street Railway succeeded the Bay State on June 1, 1919.

[146] The imminent conversion of the Charles River line to trackless trolley operation forced the MTA to buy the line from the Eastern Mass. in 1951 for $229,205. The conversions in 1952 and 1953 of the Dedham Line and Cleary Square lines to trackless trolleys, and the Roslindale Square and the Mattapan lines to buses saw the MTA purchase these routes as well. The price paid in 1952 for these four routes was $484,251.

[147] After the lease of February 16, 1903, the Old Colony Street Railway and its successors, including the Eastern Mass, continued to operate through service from Hyde Park to Forest Hills over the section of the Hyde Park Avenue line from the Hyde Park-Boston boundary to Forest Hills. Hyde Park became part of Boston on January 1, 1912, and pressure mounted for a single fare in the city limits. The Transit Department of the City of Boston purchased

the section from Cleary Square to the Hyde Park–Boston boundary for $317,000 under provisions of Acts of 1923, Chapter 405 on August 31, 1923. In anticipation of the purchase, the Boston El signed a lease for the line with the Transit Department on August 23, 1923, and began through service from Cleary Square to Forest Hills on September 1, 1923, the day after the purchase of the line by the City.

[148] An additional parallel yard storage track was added between November 4 and December 15, 1944.

[149] In 1940 the Boston El built a 273-foot track from the loop trackage to salt and sand storage bins.

[150] This work took place between August 26 and December 22, 1948.

[151] This project started June 9 and was completed September 4, 1947.

Notes to Chapter 5

[152] See Bradley H. Clarke and O. R. Cummings, *Tremont Street Subway, A Century of Public Service,* (Boston, Mass: Boston Street Railway Association, 1997).

[153] Boston Elevated Railway Co., *Twenty-Eighth Annual Report of the Board of Public Trustees for the Year Ended December 31, 1946* (Boston: Boston Elevated Railway Co., 1947), p. 12, 13.

[154] September 1, 1997 was the centennial of the subway opening. Observances on this day and later, and a book, *Tremont Street Subway, A Century of Public Service,* by Bradley H. Clarke and O. R. Cummings, published by the Boston Street Railway Association marked this event. There was substantial local press coverage of the official observance by the Massachusetts Bay Transportation Authority, held on October 20, 1997, at South Station and on October 21 on Boston Common, adjacent to Boylston Street Station. The Authority also held a ceremonial ride between Park Street and Boylston Street Stations with Type 5 No. 5734 from the Seashore Trolley Museum and the MBTA's own PCC 3295 leading the procession. On board were Paul A. Cellucci, Governor of Massachusetts, and Mayor of Boston, Thomas M. Menino, with a large number of other local dignitaries.

[155] "How the Transportation Department is Meeting the War Demand for Riding," *Co-operation,* 22 (Apr. 1943), 30.

[156] "Huntington Avenue Subway," *Co-operation,* 20 (Apr. 1941), 24.

[157] O. R. Cummings, *Street Cars of Boston, Vol. 4* (Forty Fort, Pa.: Harold E. Cox, 1977), p. 52.

[158] "New PCC Cars to be Operated in Train Service on Subway Lines. Track and Yard Changes Necessary," *Co-operation,* 23 (Mar. 1944), 14.

[159] "New PCC Cars to be Operated in Train Service on Subway Lines. Track and Yard Changes Necessary," *Co-operation,* 23 (Mar. 1944), 14.

[160] The May 1944 NRHS newsletter, *The Shrieking Journal,* noted that PCC cars 3022-3039 were assigned to the Reservoir. Cars 3098-3105 and 3141-3153 plus 3114 and 3120 were assigned to Watertown.

[161] Between July 22 and July 29, 1949, a crossover was removed from the Beacon Street line just west of the St. Mary's Street platform.

[162] During the 1940s, few track changes of significance occurred here. A major change occurred in March 1942, when a crossover was installed between the inbound and outbound yard tracks to and from the street just before the loop area.

[163] A facing point crossover just east of Lake Street on Commonwealth Avenue was removed by the Elevated between October 30 and November 3, 1944.

[164] This project ran from September 11, 1946, to September 21.

[165] This work took place between April 5 and April 24, 1945,

[166] This project ran from October 14 to October 20, 1946.

[167] "M.T.A. Schedules Extra Cars, Buses for World Series", *Boston Globe,* 154 (Oct. 5, 1948), p. 13.

Notes to Chapter 6

[168] Removal of the rails over one carhouse pit and an extension of the pit itself took place took place on March 17 and 18, 1942, to provide additional trackless trolley maintenance space. Between August 3 and September 30, 1949, two tracks were removed from the central carhouse shed to provide more space for trackless trolleys for the future Harvard–Massachusetts Station line.

[169] The May 1944 NRHS newsletter, *The Shrieking Journal,* mentioned that two PCCs had been seen at Bennett Street, but it was believed they were there awaiting repair because Everett Shops had no room to store them. *The Shrieking Journal,* 4 (May 1944), 5.

[170] The work began on May 31, 1950, and was completed August 7, 1950.

[171] The passing siding was abandoned in 1940.

[172] This project ran from September 21 to October 8, 1942.

[173] This work began on October 7, 1949, and ended on October 28,

[174] The work started on October 30, 1944, and was completed on November 30.

[175] *The Turnout,* 5 (Feb. 1947), 12.

Notes to Chapter 7

[176] The Charlestown Navy Yard was originally named the Boston Navy Yard. The Boston Navy Yard was renamed the Boston Naval Shipyard on November 30, 1945, and the Charlestown Navy Yard in 1974.

[177] This work started on May 24, 1941, and was done by June 15.

[178] This project ran between November 17 and November 27, 1941.

[179] The track in the traffic circle was removed on June 4 and 5, 1947.

[180] Starting on November 9, 1944, and finishing on December 31, the Elevated removed six unused track switches and leads off the southerly track on Salem Street to the carhouse.

[181] This work began on October 28, 1946. It was finished November 30.

[182] Starting on April 13, 1942, and continuing until September 15, the Elevated rebuilt the trackage in this circle.

[183] The facing point crossover was removed between January 1 and 7, 1946. The trailing point crossover remained.

[184] "Townspeople Bid Farewell to Streetcars, Welcome Buses Over Weekend," *Stoneham Independent,* 76 (Aug. 2, 1946), 4.

[185] The same day, streetcars between Davis Square, Somerville, and Sullivan Square Station via Highland Avenue and Cross Street were replaced by buses. On September 13, 1947, this bus line was converted to trackless trolleys.

[186] This project was completed rapidly, beginning on August 12 and ending on September 5, 1942.

[187] "Bus Replaces Car Line," *Co-operation,* 28 (Sept. 1949), 69.

[188] This project ran between May 14 and June 8, 1942,

[189] This work was done between November 18 and December 15, 1941. A bumper was installed at the end of the test track from March 23-26, 1942.

[190] This work started on September 9, 1946, and was completed on November 30.

[191] The switch was installed beginning on February 25, 1947, and ending on March 5.

[192] The work took place from September 10 to November 1, 1947.

[193] This activity occurred between July 21 and September 13, 1948.

Notes to Chapter 8

[194] Boston Elevated Railway Co., *Twenty-Second Annual Report of the Board of Public Trustees for the Year Ended December 31, 1940* (Boston: Boston Elevated Railway Co., 1941), p. 5.

[195] Lincoln Square is the intersection of Central Avenue, Park Street, and Hawthorne Street in Chelsea.

[196] Six-hundred sixty-seven feet of abandoned track on Pearl Street from Park Street northeast to Hawthorne Street was removed in 1940.

[197] The crossover was installed between March 10 and March 16, 1942.

[198] Some of the loop trackage was visible until the mid-1980s through the pavement of a parking lot that had been built at the loop site.

[199] "Jeffries Pt. Cars Replaced By Bus After 50 Yrs. Here," *East Boston Times,* 10 (May 5, 1949), 1, 10.

Appendices 2–9

Boston Streetcar Assignments & Service Levels

Appendices 2–8 are keyed to chapters of the same number and cover rush hour equipment assignments for the lines discussed in that chapter. For Example, Appendix 2, South Boston Lines, is keyed to Chapter 2, The South Boston Lines. Appendix 9 covers the entire Boston Elevated Railway system.

The route numbers in the appendices are from Boston Elevated Railway System Route Map No. 5, which represents the system as it was in early December 1941. Between 1940 and 1941, the route numbers used in the maps handed out to the public underwent the last of a series of changes. The route numbers in the 1941 map, however, were used in subsequent maps for years and are the numbers that many readers remember.

Route numbers were generally assigned in an ascending spiral pattern. Starting in South Boston, and moving clockwise around the Boston hub, the route numbers steadily increased, with the highest numbers generally ending up in Revere.

The route numbers shown on the public maps had four-digit equivalents used by the company internally, and these four-digit numbers are shown beside the public map numbers that they match. The four-digit numbers were used to describe route variants such as cutbacks and substitute routings as well as the main line itself. The four-digit system captured differences in mileage, running times, and labor man-hours, and helped tally fares. This information determined operating costs and revenues and was used for service planning and other purposes.

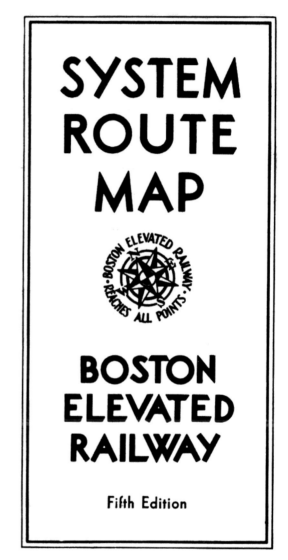

Equipment Assignments

The equipment information in Appendices 2–8 is intended to give the reader an idea of the types of streetcars that were running at various times and where. It is not a comprehensive analysis. Newer equipment than that used during rush hours was often run in off-peak service. For example, PCC cars were not normally used on the Charles River and Watertown–Central lines at peak times, but they were often run middays, evenings, and on weekends and holidays. Where off-peak car use information is available, it has been included in the body of this book but not in these appendices. Similarly, older equipment often filled in as spares. For example, a Type 4 might fill in for a disabled Type 5.

For these reasons, Appendices 2–8 show only official car assignments during peak ridership periods, and these guidelines were always subject to the discretion of officials responsible for proper system operation. Sometimes the pictures shown in a given chapter were taken during off-peak hours or emphasized the unusual such as the assignment of an older spare car. While colorful, this situation could mislead the reader about the types of equipment in *regular* use and should be borne in mind when using these appendices.

Park Street Station was generally considered to be the central point of the Boston Elevated subway-surface streetcar system. Here, Type 4 No. 5343, placed in service in January 1912, is running out its last miles on the Oak Square–Park Street Station cutback of the Watertown line in 1950. *Paul M. Paulsen*

Each year in the 1940s the Boston Elevated and the MTA made four system-wide service adjustments, usually in March or April, June, September, and December, called *rating changes*. At the time the rating changes were made, the rush hour equipment requirements and operating personnel for each line were set to cover the planned service levels for the next three months. Supplemental rating changes were made when needed. Using Boston Elevated and MTA rush hour car requirement listings by lines, which were prepared for each rating change, the streetcar types assigned to each line and their periods of use have been summarized in Appendices 2–8 and discussed in each chapter.

Rating changes directly affected the personnel assigned to a given line as well as equipment. Rating changes were posted in the rating stations, usually in the operators' lobbies at the carhouses. The available work was based on the expected service requirements for the coming season. Operating employees picked their working hours based on their seniority, or *rating*, in strict succession of their employment date. Thus the longest-term employees, who had the best ratings, could pick first and pick the best work.

Service Levels and Line Statistics

The service levels on Boston Elevated streetcar lines varied widely during the 1940s. Appendix 9: *Boston Elevated*

Railway Weekday Streetcar Line Service Levels and Statistics, Selected Rating Dates, presents a snapshot of the levels of weekday service and line statistics of most Boston Elevated streetcar lines for the Spring 1945 rating, a time of very high ridership. The reader can quickly grasp from this information the comparitive activity of the lines and judge their relative importance at that time. Appendix 9A has similar information for the car lines of the Eastern Massachusetts Street Railway.

In a few cases, however, information has been included for lines that were not running in the Spring of 1945, so the rating dates are different and documented accordingly. For the few routes that are not covered in the 1945 rating, but for which the data are given for other years, the reader should take this distinction into account before making any comparisons between the routes.

For example, the Somerville and Highland Avenue lines based at Clarendon Hill were converted to trackless trolley operation in 1941, but the Broadway Line to Sullivan Square, also based at Clarendon Hill, remained a streetcar line until 1946. Operating information for Highland and Somerville Avenue are shown in Appendix 9 for 1941, but for Broadway, this information is for 1945, along with most other car lines. For this reason, data for 1941, a time of much lower ridership systemwide than that in 1945, would make a comparison between the Somerville and Highland Avenue lines and the Broadway line misleading.

Two MTA streetcars bask in the sun in the private reservation alongside Seaver Street at Maple Street in Roxbury alongside the Franklin Park Zoo. Type 4 No. 5266 entered service in 1911, yet Type 5 No. 5795, built slightly more than a decade later, in 1923, looks disproportionately newer. This was the line from Mattapan to Egleston, and the shot was taken July 29, 1948. *Robert A. Kennerly*

Appendix 2

Rush Hour Car Assignments – South Boston Lines

Public Map No.	Internal Route No.	Streetcar Line	Carhouse	Type 4	Type 5	Center Entrance	PCC	Remarks
7	1005	City Point–South Station via Summer Street	City Point	-	9/5/39–5/17/43 9/3/43– 3/20/50	-	-	Cutback to Army Base added 5/17/43. See Route 1011. No service 5/43–9/43 due to Reserved Channel bridge repairs.
None	1011	Army Base–South Station via Summer Street	City Point	-	5/17/43 – 12/12/49	-	-	Cutback of Route 1005 effective 5/17/43.
8	1066	City Point–South Station (Dewey Square) via Broadway and Dorchester Avenue	City Point	-	9/5/39 – 2/15/47	-	-	Line ended as two separated cutbacks. See Routes 1065 and 1068.
None	1065	City Point–Dorchester Avenue Bridge via Broadway and Dorchester Avenue	City Point	-	12/2/46 – 4/4/47	-	-	One of two separated and final cutbacks of Route 1066 effective 12/2/46.
None	1068	Dorchester Avenue Bridge – South Station (Dewey Square) via Dorchester Avenue	City Point	-	12/2/46 – 4/4/47	-	-	One of two separated and final cutbacks of Route 1066 effective 12/2/46.
9	1046	City Point–North Station via Broadway and Subway	City Point	9/5/39 – 5/17/43 9/3/43 - 9/3/46	-	-	10/22/45 – 6/20/49 9/6/49 – 3/20/50	Summer variant was Marine Park - North Station. See Route 1047. Line temporarily cut back to Broadway Bridge during bridge repair in 1943. See Route 1070 for 1943. Permanent cutback line was City Point - Broadway Station after 3/17/47. See Route 1070 for 1947.
None	1047	Marine Park – North Station via Broadway and Subway	City Point	-	-	-	6/20/49 – 9/6/49	Route 1046 terminal variant for summer operation.
None	1069	Marine Park–Broadway Station via Broadway	City Point					Summer supplement to Route 1046.
None	1070	City Point – Broadway Bridge via Broadway	City Point	5/17/43 – 9/3/43	-	-	-	Temporary Route 1046 cutback during Broadway Bridge repairs.
None	1070	City Point – Broadway Station via Broadway	City Point	-	3/17/47 – 3/20/50	-	-	Regular cutback of Route 1046 effective 4/15/47.
10	1020	City Point–Dudley Street Station via Dorchester, Southampton, and Washington Streets	City Point	9/5/39 – 6/20/49	11/24/41 – 3/2/42 9/6/49 – 3/20/50	-	-	Summer variant was Marine Park - Dudley Street. See Route 1024.
None	1024	Marine Park–Dudley Street Station via Dorchester, Southampton, and Washington Streets	City Point	-	6/20/49 – 9/6/49	-	-	Route 1020 terminal variant for summer operation.
16	1200	Franklin Park – Andrew Station via Columbia Road	City Point	-	9/5/39 – 12/10/49	-	-	Dorchester – South Boston route. Covered in Chapter 3.
47	1262	Dudley Street Station – Mass. Station via Massachusetts Avenue	City Point	-	9/5/39 – 3/20/50	-	-	Back Bay – Roxbury route. Covered in Chapter 6.
100	4081	Elm Street–Sullivan Square Station via Fellsway	City Point	-	12/12/49 – 3/20/50	-	-	Former Salem Street line transferred to City Point rating station 12/49. Cars remained at Salem Street. Cutback was Salem Street – Sullivan Square Station. See Route 4082.
None	4082	Salem Street–Sullivan Square Station via Fellsway	City Point	-	12/12/49 – 3/20/50	-	-	Route 4081 cutback. Former Salem Street line transferred to City Point rating station 12/49. Cars remained at Salem Street.
None	4015	North Station – Brattle Street Station Shuttle	Salem Street City Point	-	10/12/49 – 3/20/50	-	-	Shuttle established 10/15/49; discontinued 9/52. Line transferred to City Point rating station 12/49.

Appendix 3

Rush Hour Car Assignments – Dorchester/Roxbury Lines

Public Map No.	Internal Route No.	Streetcar Line	Carhouse	Eastern Mass Cars	Type 4	Type 5	Center Entrance	PCC	Remarks
15	1182	Uphams Corner to Dudley Street Station via Dudley Street	Park Street	-	-	9/11/39 – 12/25/48	-	-	Line converted to trackless trolley and extended to Kane Square 12/25/48.
16	1200	Franklin Park – Andrew Station via Columbia Road	City Point	-	-	9/11/39 – 12/10/49	-	-	-
17	1150	Fields Corner Station – Andrew Station via Meeting House Hill	Park Street	-	-	9/11/39 – 2/12/49	-	-	-
19	1191	Fields Corner Station – Dudley Street Station via Geneva Avenue	Park Street	-	-	9/11/39 – 1/8/49	-	-	-
20	1122	Fields Corner Station – Neponset Loop	Park Street	9/11/39 – 5/1/48	-	9/11/39 – 6/19/48	-	-	Eastern Mass cars were 4200 and 7000-series.
22	1093	Ashmont Station – Dudley Street Station via Talbot Avenue	Park Street	-	-	9/11/39 – 1/8/49	-	-	-
23	1241	Ashmont Station – Dudley Street Station via Washington Street	Park Street	-	-	9/11/39 – 1/8/49	-	-	-
28	1147	Mattapan Station – Ashmont Station High-Speed Trolley Line	Park Street, Arborway	-	9/11/39 – 4/5/49	4/5/49 – 3/20/50	-	-	Cars stored at Mattapan Station Yard. Line transferred to Arborway 4/19/48.
29	1231	Mattapan Station–Egleston Station via Blue Hill Avenue and Seaver Street	Park Street, Arborway	-	9/11/39 – 6/20/49	4/5/49 – 3/20/50	-	-	Cars stored at Mattapan Station Yard. Cutback line was Morton Street crossover to Egleston Station. See Route 1234. Line transferred to Arborway 4/19/48.
None	1234	Morton Street Crossover – Egleston Station via via Blue Hill Avenue and Seaver Street	Park Street, Arborway	-	9/11/39 – 6/20/49	4/5/49 – 3/20/50	-	-	Cars stored at Mattapan Station Yard. Line transferred to Arborway 4/19/48. Route 1231 cutback.
41	2110	Jamaica Plain Loop – Dudley Street Station via Centre Street	Arborway	-	-	12/4/39 – 6/8/49	-	-	Cutback line was Route 2111.
None	2111	Hyde Square Loop – Dudley Street Station via Centre Street	Arborway	-	-	4/12/48–6/21/48 9/13/48–6/8/49	-	-	Route 2110 cutback.
42	2293	Egleston Station – Dudley Street Station via Washington Street	Arborway	-	-	12/4/39 – 9/17/49	-	-	-
44	2338	Seaver Street Loop – Dudley Street Station via Humboldt Avenue	Arborway	-	-	12/4/39 – 1/29/49	-	4/2/45 – 9/15/47	One PCC was used, usually No. 3001.
None	2339	Egleston Station – Dudley Street Station via Humboldt Avenue	Arborway						Experimental route for one rating only to test outbound riding.
45	1210	Grove Hall – Dudley Street Station via Blue Hill Avenue	Park Street	-	-	9/11/39 – 12/25/48	-	-	-
47	1262	Dudley Street Station – Mass. Station via Massachusetts Avenue	City Point	-	-	9/11/39 – 3/20/50	-	-	-
None	ESMR Line	Fields Corner Station – Quincy Shipyard	Park Street Quincy Carhouse	9/11/39 – 4/4/48	-	-	-	-	Eastern Mass cars were 4200 and 7000-series cars. Line cut back to Quincy Square 4/4/48.
None	ESMR Line	Fields Corner Station – Quincy Square	Quincy Carhouse	9/11/39 – 5/1/48	-	-	-	-	Eastern Mass cars were 4200 and 7000-series cars.
None	ESMR Line	Hough's Neck – Quincy Square	Quincy Carhouse	1940 – 6/30/46	-	-	-	-	Eastern Mass cars were 4200 and 7000-series cars.

Appendix 4

Rush Hour Car Assignments – Arborway Lines

Public Map No.	Internal Route No.	Streetcar Line	Carhouse	Type 4	Type 5	Center Entrance	PCC	Remarks
28	1147	Mattapan Station – Ashmont Station High-Speed Trolley Line	Park Street, Arborway	4/19/48 – 4/5/49	4/5/49 – 3/20/50	–	–	Cars stored at Mattapan Station Yard. Line transferred to Arborway 4/19/48.
29	1231	Mattapan Station–Egleston Station via Blue Hill Avenue and Seaver Street	Park Street, Arborway	4/19/48 – 6/20/49	6/20/49 – 3/20/50	–	–	Cars stored at Mattapan Station Yard. Cutback line was Morton Street crossover to Egleston Station. See Route 1234. Line transferred to Arborway 4/19/48.
None	1234	Morton Street Crossover – Egleston Station via Blue Hill Avenue and Seaver Street	Park Street, Arborway	4/19/48 – 6/20/49	6/20/49 – 3/20/50	–	–	Cars stored at Mattapan Station Yard. Line transferred to Arborway 4/19/48. Route 1231 cutback.
30	2278	Mattapan Station – Arborway via Cummins Highway	Arborway	–	12/4/39 – 3/20/50	–	–	–
32	2270	Cleary Square – Arborway via Hyde Park Avenue	Arborway	–	12/4/39 – 3/20/50	–	–	–
33	2275	Cummins Highway and Washington Street (Roslindale Square) – Arborway	Arborway	–	12/4/39 – 3/20/50	–	–	–
34	2280	Dedham Line – Arborway via Washington Street	Arborway	–	12/4/39 – 3/20/50	–	–	Cutback line was Washington & LaGrange Street crossover to Arborway. See Route 2283.
None	2283	Washington & LaGrange Street Crossover – Arborway via Washington Street	Arborway	–	12/4/39 – 3/20/50	–	–	Route 2280 cutback.
36	2251	Charles River Loop – Arborway via Centre Street	Arborway	12/21/42 – 6/43 9/3/43–6/23/47 9/15/47 – 12/20/48	12/4/39 –9/15/47 12/20/48 –3/20/50	–	12/4/39 – 3/23/42	Cutback line was Centre & LaGrange Street crossover to Arborway. See Route 2254. The PCC assigned to this line was 3001.
None	2254	Centre & LaGrange Street Crossover – Arborway via Centre Street	Arborway	12/21/42 – 6/43 9/3/43–6/23/47 9/15/47 – 12/20/48	12/4/39 –9/15/47 12/20/48 –3/20/50	–	–	Route 2251 cutback.
39	2075	Arborway – Park Street Station, Subway via Huntington Avenue	Arborway	12/4/39 – 6/24/40 9/16/40 –3/23/42 9/13/48 – 6/20/49	–	12/4/39 – 6/23/41 3/23/42 – 6/24/46 12/2/46 –6/23/47 9/15/47 –6/21/48 9/13/48 –6/20/49 9/12/49 –3/20/50	12/17/45 – 3/20/50	Cutback lines were Northeastern University to Park Street Station, and for all practical purposes, both variants of Route 57, since they shared the same track. See Routes 2071, 2066, and 2067.
None	2071	Northeastern University – Park Street Station, Subway	Arborway	6/23/47 – 6/20/49	–	–	–	Route 2075 cutback.
40	2295	Arborway–Egleston Station via Washington Street	Arborway	–	12/4/39 – 3/20/50	–	–	–
43	2016	Egleston Station –North Station via Tremont Street	Arborway	12/4/39 – 7/2/45 9/10/45 – 6/24/46 12/2/46 –6/23/47 12/20/48–6/20/49 9/12/48 - 3/20/50	–	9/16/40 – 3/31/41	12/11/44 – 3/20/50	Cutback line was Lenox Street Yard – North Station. See Route 2001.
None	2001	Lenox Street Yard –North Station via Subway	Arborway	4/12/48 – 9/13/48	–	–	–	Route 2016 cutback.
57	2067	Francis Street and Huntington Avenue – Park Street, Subway	Arborway	12/4/39 – 12/17/45	–	4/5/43–6/43 3/20/44 – 6/19/44 9/11/44 – 12/11/44	–	Route 2075 cutback. Replaced by Heath Street – Park Street on 12/15/45.
57	2066	Heath Street and South Huntington Avenue – Park Street, Subway	Arborway	12/17/45 – 6/24/46 9/16/46 – 6/23/47 9/15/47 – 6/20/49 9/12/49–3/20/50	–	–	3/18/46 – 3/20/50	Route 2075 cutback. Replaced Francis Street-Park Street on 12/15/45.

Appendix 5

Rush Hour Car Assignments – Central Subway Lines

Public Map No.	Internal Route No.	Streetcar Line	Carhouse	Type 4	Type 5	Center Entrance	PCC	Remarks
9	1046	City Point–North Station via Broadway and Subway	City Point	9/5/39 – 5/17/43 9/3/43 - 9/3/46	–	–	10/22/45 – 6/20/49 9/6/49 – 3/20/50	Summer variant was Marine Park - North Station. See Route 1047. Line temporarily cut back to Broadway Bridge during bridge repair in 1943. See Route 1070 for 1943. Permanent cutback line was City Point - Broadway Station after 3/17/47. See Route 1070 for 1947. See Appendix 2 for data referenced but not shown on this table.
39	2075	Arborway – Park Street Station, Subway via Huntington Avenue	Arborway	12/4/39 – 6/24/40 9/16/40 –3/23/42 9/13/48 – 6/20/49	–	12/4/39 – 6/23/41 3/23/42 – 6/24/46 12/2/46 –6/23/47 9/15/47 –6/21/48 9/13/48 –6/20/49 9/12/49 –3/20/50	12/17/45 – 3/20/50	Cutback lines were Northeastern University to Park Street Station, and for all practical purposes, both variants of Route 57, since they shared the same track. See Routes 2071, 2066, and 2067.
None	2071	Northeastern University – Park Street Station, Subway	Arborway	6/23/47 – 6/20/49	–	–	–	Route 2075 cutback.
57	2067	Francis Street and Huntington Avenue – Park Street, Subway	Arborway	12/4/39 – 12/17/45	–	4/5/43–6/43 3/20/44 – 6/19/44 9/11/44 – 12/11/44	–	Route 2075 cutback. Replaced by Heath Street – Park Street on 12/15/45.
57	2066	Heath Street and South Huntington Avenue – Park Street, Subway	Arborway	12/17/45 – 6/24/46 9/16/46 – 6/23/47 9/15/47 – 6/20/49 9/12/49–3/20/50	–	–	3/18/46 – 3/20/50	Route 2075 cutback. Replaced Francis Street-Park Street on 12/15/45.
43	2016	Egleston Station –North Station via Tremont Street	Arborway	12/4/39 – 7/2/45 9/10/45 – 6/24/46 12/2/46 – 6/23/47 12/20/48–6/20/49 9/12/49 - 3/20/50	–	9/16/40 – 3/31/41	12/11/44 – 3/20/50	Cutback line was Lenox Street Yard – North Station. See Route 2001.
None	2001	Lenox Street Yard –North Station via Subway	Arborway	4/12/48 – 9/13/48	–	–	–	Route 2016 cutback.
61	2131	Reservoir Carhouse – Lechmere Station via Beacon Street	Reservoir	–	–	12/4/39 – 4/16/45 9/16/46 - 6/26/50	4/16/45 – 6/26/50	–
62	2145	Lake Street–Lechmere Station via Subway and Commonwealth Avenue	Reservoir	–	–	5/6/40 – 12/10/45	6/18/45 - 6/26/50	–
62	3077	Lake Street–Lechmere Station via Subway and Commonwealth Avenue	Bennett Street	–	–	12/4/39 – 5/6/40	–	Route transferred to Reservoir 4/1/40.
69	3200	Watertown Carhouse – Park Street Station, Subway	Watertown	12/4/39 – 9/11/44 6/19/45 – 4/1/46	–	–	6/23/41* – 4/24/50	*PCCs actually entered service 3/3/41. Cutback lines were Oak Square–Park Street, Route 3203; Braves Field - Park Street, Route 3202; Braves Field - North Station, Route 3207; Blandford Street - Park Street, Route 3205, and Blandford Street - North Station, Route 3210.
None	3203	Oak Square – Park Street Station, Subway	Watertown	12/4/39 – 9/11/44 6/19/45 – 4/1/46	–	–	6/23/41* – 4/24/50	*PCCs actually entered service 3/3/41.
None	3202	Braves Field Loop – Park Street Station	Watertown	11/19/45–4/1/46 12/9/46 – 6/23/47 9/13/47 – 6/19/50	–	–	11/19/45 – 12/9/46 6/23/47 – 9/13/47	Route 3200 cutback.
None	3207	Braves Field Loop – North Station	Watertown	11/19/45–4/1/46 12/9/46 – 6/23/47 9/13/47 – 6/19/50	–	–	11/19/45 – 12/9/46 6/23/47 – 9/13/47	Route 3200 cutback.
None	3205	Blandford Street Crossover – Park Street Station	Watertown Carhouse	9/20/43 – 11/19/45	–	–	–	Route 3200 cutback.
None	3210	Blandford Street Crossover – North Station	Watertown Carhouse	9/20/43 – 11/19/45	–	–	–	Route 3200 cutback.
92	4012	Sullivan Square Station–Brattle Street Station via Main Street and Subway	Salem Street	–	12/4/39 – 4/3/48	–	–	–
93	4021	Sullivan Station–Brattle Street Station via Bunker Hill Street and Subway	Salem Street	–	12/4/39 – 7/2/49	–	–	Cutback lines were Elm Street - Brattle Street Station, Route 4022; Elm Street - Warren Avenue Crossover, Route 4023; and Sullivan Square Station - Warren Avenue Crossover, Route 4024. See Appendix 7 for data referenced but not listed on this table.
124	2143	Braves Field Loop – North Station	Reservoir	–	–	2/14/49 – 6/26/50	–	–
None	2122	Blandford Street Crossover – Park Street Station	Reservoir Carhouse	12/4/39 – 6/1/43	–	11/1/48 – 2/14/49	–	June 1, 1943 date is approximate. Line tranferred to Watertown Carhouse 9/20/43; reinstated to Reservoir 1948.
None	2123	Blandford Street Crossover – North Station	Reservoir Carhouse	6/1/43 – 9/20/43	–	11/1/48 – 2/14/49	–	June 1, 1943 date is approximate. Line tranferred to Watertown Carhouse 9/20/43; reinstated to Reservoir 1948.
None	4015*	North Station – Brattle Street Station Shuttle	Salem Street City Point	–	10/15/49 – 3/20/50	–	–	*Route number 4015 is City Point Rating Station number. Shuttle established 10/15/49; discontinued 9/52. Line transferred to City Point rating station 12/49.

Appendix 6

Rush Hour Car Assignments – Lines West of Boston

Public Map No.	Internal Route No.	Streetcar Line	Carhouse	Type 4	Type 5	Center Entrance	PCC	Remarks
62	3077	Lake Street–Lechmere Station via Subway and Commonwealth Avenue	Bennett Street	–	–	12/4/39 – 5/6/40	–	Route transferred to Reservoir 4/1/40. Assignments after this date covered in Chapter 5.
69	3200	Watertown Carhouse – Park Street Station, Subway	Watertown	12/4/39 – 9/11/44 6/19/45 – 4/1/46	–	–	6/23/41* – 4/24/50	*PCCs actually entered service 3/3/41. Cutback lines were Oak Square–Park Street, Route 3203; Braves Field - Park Street, Route 3202; Braves Field - North Station, Route 3207; Blandford Street - Park Street, Route 3205, and Blandford Street - North Station, Route 3210. This route discussed in Chapter 5.
None	3203	Oak Square – Park Street Station, Subway	Watertown	12/4/39 – 9/11/44 6/19/45 – 4/1/46	–	–	6/23/41* – 4/24/50	*PCCs actually entered service 3/3/41. This route discussed in Chapter 5.
70	3220	Watertown Carhouse – Central Square, Cambridge via Western Avenue	Watertown	12/4/39 – 6/17/50	6/23/41 – 4/6/42 9/20/43 – 3/27/44	–	–	One Type 5 from Bennett Street assigned 9/20/43 – 3/27/44. Extension to Vassar Street and Massachusetts Avenue added 1947 only, Route 3222. Line extended from Central Square to Memorial Drive Crossover on 9/12/49, Route 3224.
None	–	Watertown Carhouse – Green Street & Western Avenue crossover	Watertown	1945 - 1950	–	–	–	Evening weekday rush hour and midday Saturday route.
None	3222	Watertown Carhouse – Vassar Street & Massachusetts Avenue crossover	Watertown	1947	–	–	–	Route 3220 extension. Only ran in 1947.
None	3224	Watertown Carhouse – Memorial Drive Crossover and Massachusetts Avenue	Watertown	9/19/49 – 11/28/49	–	–	–	Route 3220 extension. Line replaced Harvard–Memorial Drive 9/19/49. Discontinued and cut back to Green Street Loop in Central Square 11/28/49.
71	3003	Watertown Carhouse – Harvard Station via Mt. Auburn Street	Bennett Street	12/11/44-4/24/50	12/4/39-4/24/50	–	–	–
73	3005	Waverley – Harvard Station via Trapelo Road and Mount Auburn Street	Bennett Street	12/4/39 – 6/23/41	12/4/39-4/24/50	–	–	Cutback line was Cushing Square – Harvard Station. See Route 3018.
None	3018	Cushing Square – Harvard Station via Trapelo Road and Mount Auburn Street	Bennett Street	12/4/39 – 6/23/41	12/4/39-4/24/50	–	–	Route 3005 cutback.
76	3061	Harvard Square – Mass Station via Massachusetts Avenue	Bennett Street	–	12/4/39 – 9/12/49	–	–	Line abandoned 9/12/49. Temporary service Harvard Square–Memorial Drive crossover 9/12/49-9/19/49. Cutback was Harvard Square - Cambridge Armory, Route 3062.
None	3062	Harvard Square – Cambridge Armory Crossover	Bennett Street	–	12/4/39 – 9/12/49	–	–	Cutback Route 3061.
None	–	Harvard Square – Memorial Drive Crossover and Massachusetts Avenue	Bennett Street	–	9/12/49-9/19/49	–	–	Temporary line. Replaced by extension of Watertown–Central line to Memorial Drive 9/19/49. See Route 3224.
79	3003	Arlington Heights – Harvard Station via Massachusetts Avenue	Bennett Street	12/11/44-4/24/50	12/4/39 – 4/24/50	–	–	Cutback line was Arlington Center – Harvard Station. See Route 3004.
None	3004	Arlington Center – Harvard Station via Massachusetts Avenue	Bennett Street	12/11/44-4/24/50	12/4/39 – 4/24/50	1943*	–	Route 3003 cutback. *Only regularly assigned use of center-entrance cars on this line was in 1943. Used these cars as spares through most of 1940s, however.
82	3000	North Cambridge – Harvard Station via Massachusetts Avenue	Bennett Street	12/4/39 – 6/23/41	12/4/39 – 4/24/50	–	–	–
None	3202	Braves Field Loop – Park Street Station	Watertown	11/19/45-4/1/46 12/9/46 – 6/23/47 9/13/47 – 6/19/50	–	–	11/19/45 – 12/9/46 6/23/47 – 9/13/47	Route 3200 cutback.
None	3207	Braves Field Loop – North Station	Watertown	11/19/45-4/1/46 12/9/46 – 6/23/47 9/13/47 – 6/19/50	–	–	11/19/45 – 12/9/46 6/23/47 – 9/13/47	Route 3200 cutback.
None	3205	Blandford Street Crossover – Park Street Station	Watertown Carhouse	9/20/43 – 11/19/45	–	–	–	Route 3200 cutback.
None	3210	Blandford Street Crossover – North Station	Watertown Carhouse	9/20/43 – 11/19/45	–	–	–	Route 3200 cutback.

Appendix 7

Rush Hour Car Assignments – Lines North of Boston

Public Map No.	Internal Route No.	Streetcar Line	Carhouse	Eastern Mass Cars	Bery 4400	Type 5	Remarks
87	4124	Clarendon Hill Carhouse – Lechmere Station via Somerville Avenue	Clarendon Hill Carhouse	–	–	12/4/39 – 11/8/41	-
88	4140	Clarendon Hill Carhouse – Lechmere Station via Highland Avenue	Clarendon Hill Carhouse	–	–	12/4/39 – 11/8/41	-
89	4112	Clarendon Hill Carhouse – Sullivan Square Station via Broadway	Clarendon Hill Carhouse	–	–	12/4/39 – 12/7/46	-
92	4012	Sullivan Square Station–Brattle Street Station via Main Street and Subway	Salem Street Carhouse	–	–	12/4/39 – 4/3/48	-
93	4021	Sullivan Square Station–Brattle Street Station via Bunker Hill Street and Subway	Salem Street Carhouse	–	–	12/4/39 – 7/2/49	Cutback lines were Elm Street - Brattle Street Station, Route 4022; Elm Street - Warren Avenue Crossover, Route 4023; and Sullivan Square Station - Warren Avenue Crossover, Route 4024.
None	4022	Elm Street Crossover - Brattle Street Station via Bunker Hill Street and Subway	Salem Street Carhouse	–	–	*	Cutback of Route 4021. Used intermittently. *Car data not available, but likely to be Type 5s, the equipment used on Route 4021.
None	4023	Elm Street Crossover – Warren Avenue Crossover (City Square)	Salem Street Carhouse	–	–	4/3/44–6/19/44	Shuttle operation central part of Route 4021. Run April 3, 1944 rating only.
None	4024	Sulivan Station – City Square (Warren Avenue Crossover)	Salem Street Carhouse	–	–	*	Cutback of Route 4021. Used intermittently. *Car data not available, but likely to be Type 5s, the equipment used on Route 4021.
99	4080	Stoneham (Spot Pond) – Sullivan Square Station via Fellsway	Salem Street Carhouse	9/11/1939 – 7/28/46	–	*	Line abandoned 7/28/46 from Stoneham to Sheepfold by Eastern Mass. Boston Elevated concurrently abandoned from Sheepfold to Elm Street. Eastern Mass cars were 4300s. * Type 5 cars were used as required on this line during the 1940s if they were available, but they were not the primary rush hour cars assigned to this route.
100	4081	Elm Street–Sullivan Square Station via Fellsway	Salem Street Carhouse	–	–	12/4/39 – 12/12/49	Line transferred to City Point rating station 12/49. Cars based at Salem Street. Cutback was Salem Street – Sullivan Square Station, Route 4082.
None	4082	Salem Street–Sullivan Square Station via Fellsway	Salem Street Carhouse	12/4/39 – 3/17/41	12/4/39 – 12/12/49	Route 4081 cutback. Line transferred to City Point rating station 12/49. Cars based at Salem Street.
101	4042	Salem Street Carhouse or Eliot Street–Sullivan Square Station via Winter Hill	Salem Street Carhouse	–	–	12/4/39 – 4/19/47	Line converted to trackless trolley 4/19/47. Cutback was Eliot & Main Streets – Sullivan Square, Route 4049.
None	4049	Eliot & Main Streets Crossover – Sullivan Square Station via Winter Hill	Salem Street Carhouse	–	–	12/4/39 – 4/19/47	Route 4042 cutback. Line converted to trackless trolley 4/19/47. Trackless cutbacks at Medford Square and at Tufts Square replaced the streetcar cutback at Eliot & Main Streets.
None	4015*	North Station – Brattle Street Station Shuttle	Salem Street City Point	–	–	10/15/49 – 3/20/50	*Route number 4015 is City Point Rating Station number. Shuttle established 10/15/49; discontinued 9/52. Line transferred to City Point rating station 12/49.
Eastern Mass. Line	N/A	Sullivan Square Station – Farm Hill, Stoneham	Salem Street Carhouse	9/11/39 – 7/28/46	–	–	Eastern Mass cars were 4300-series cars. This line shared track with Boston Elevated Route 99 listed above. Line abandoned 7/28/46 from Stoneham to Sheepfold by Eastern Mass. Boston Elevated concurrently abandoned line from Sheepfold to Elm Street.

Appendix 8

Rush Hour Car Assignments – East Boston/Chelsea/Revere Lines

Public Map No.	Internal Route No.	Streetcar Line	Station	Bery 4300/4400	Type 4	Type 5	Trailer	Remarks
114	4170	Broadway Station (Gerrish Avenue Loop)–Maverick Station via Meridian Street	Eagle Street Carhouse Revere Carhouse	3/31/41 – 2/2/42 3/42 – 6/13/49	4/8/46 – 11/18/46	12/4/39 – 3/31/41 11/18/46 – 9/13/47 6/13/49 – 4/24/50	–	Cars stored at Broadway Station (Gerish Avenue Loop). Eagle Street line until 3/31/41; then Revere thru 4/46. Line divided between both Revere and Eagle Street 4/46 – 9/13/47. After 9/13/47, the line was exclusively assigned to Revere. Cutback was Nay Street–Maverick. See Route 4172.
None	4172	Nay Street Crossover – Maverick Station via Meridian Street	Eagle Street Carhouse Revere Carhouse	2/2/42 – 3/42	–	–	–	Temporary cutback of Route 4170 during closure of Meridian Street Bridge for repairs.
115	4171	Broadway Station (Gerrish Avenue Loop)–Maverick Station via Central Avenue	Eagle Street Carhouse Revere Carhouse	12/4/39 – 12/11/44	4/8/46 - 9/16/46	12/11/44 – 4/24/50	–	Cars were stored at Broadway Station (Gerish Avenue Loop). Line based at Eagle Street station until 3/31/41; thereafter at Revere rating station.
116	4174	Revere Beach Loop – Maverick Station via Revere & Meridian Streets	Revere Carhouse	12/4/39 – 2/2/42 3/42 – 6/13/49	–	7/10/48 – 4/24/50	–	Cutback was Route 4173, Revere Street Crossover-Maverick, and later, Revere Street and Broadway Crossover-Maverick.
None	4173	Revere Street Crossover – Maverick Station via Broadway & Meridian Street.	Revere Carhouse	9/8/41 – 2/2/42 3/42–11/46	–	–	–	Original cutback of Route 4174 at crossover on Revere Street near Broadway. Cutback location replaced by crossover on Broadway at Revere Street in 12/46.
None	4173	Broadway & Revere Street Crossover – Maverick Station via Broadway & Meridian Street.	Revere Carhouse	11/46-6/13/49	–	7/10/48 – 4/24/50	–	Crossover on Broadway near Revere Street. Replaced cutback of Route 4174 on Revere Street near Broadway in 12/46.
116	4174	Revere Beach Loop – Maverick Station via Revere Street & Central Avenue	Revere Carhouse	2/2/42 – 3/42	–	–	–	Substitute routing for regular Route 4174 during closure of Meridian Street Bridge.
None	4173	Revere Street Crossover – Maverick Station via Broadway & Central Avenue	Revere Carhouse	2/2/42 – 3/42	–	–	–	Route 4174 cutback. Substitute routing for regular Route 4173 cutback during closure of Meridian Street Bridge for repairs.
116	4223	Revere Street Bridge Crossover – Maverick Station via Revere Street	Revere Carhouse	8/9/47–7/10/48	–	8/9/47–7/10/48	–	Route 4174 shortened from 8/9/47 - 7/10/48 during closure of Revere Street Bridge over B & M Railroad for repairs. Assigned new temporary route number, 4223.
117	4176	Revere Beach Loop – Maverick Station via Beach Street	Revere Carhouse	12/4/39 – 2/2/42 3/42 – 6/13/49	–	9/16/46 – 4/24/50	–	Cutback was Revere Carhouse - Maverick. See Route 4177.
None	4177	Revere Carhouse – Maverick Station via Broadway & Meridian Street	Revere Carhouse	12/4/39 – 2/2/42 3/42 – 6/13/49	–	9/16/46 – 4/24/50	–	Route 4176 cutback.
117	4176	Revere Loop – Maverick Station via Beach Street & Central Avenue	Revere Carhouse	2/2/42 – 3/42	–	–	–	Substitute routing for regular Route 4176 during closure of Meridian Street Bridge for repairs.
None	4175	Revere Carhouse – Maverick Station via Central Avenue	Revere Carhouse	2/2/42 – 3/42	–	–	–	Route 4176 cutback. Substitute routing for regular Route 4175 cutback during closure of Meridian Street Bridge for repairs.
117	4224	Revere Street Bridge Crossover – Maverick Station via Beach Street	Revere Carhouse	8/9/47–7/10/48	–	8/9/47–7/10/48	–	Route 4176 extended from Revere Beach Loop to Revere Street Bridge from 8/9/47 - 7/10/48 during closure of Revere Street Bridge over B & M Railroad to provide service on this segment of the Revere Street line. Assigned new temporary route number, 4224.
118	4183	Revere Beach Loop – Maverick Station via Ocean Avenue	Eagle Street Carhouse	–	12/4/39 – 6/13/49	3/18/40 – 3/31/41 6/13/49 – 4/24/50	–	–
120	4181	Gladstone Loop – Maverick Station via Bennington Street	Eagle Street Carhouse	–	12/4/39 – 4/19/48 6/7/48 – 7/12/48 6/13/49–7/11/49 9/12/49–4/24/50	3/31/41–6/23/41 9/8/41–9/43 6/13/49–7/11/49 9/12/49–4/24/50	9/20/42 – 6/14/43 9/43 – 5/15/44	–
120	4186	Suffolk Downs – Maverick Station via Bennington Street	Eagle Street Carhouse	–	4/19/48 – 6/7/48 7/12/48 – 6/13/49	–	–	Alternative destination to Gladstone Street. Pull-in line was Eagle Street Carhouse - Maverick Station. See Route 4182.
None	4182	Eagle Street Carhouse – Maverick Station via Bennington Street	Eagle Street Carhouse	–	–	–	–	Pull-in line for Route 4186 to feed cars during rush hours.
121	4191	Eagle Street Carhouse – Maverick Station via Meridian & Lexington Streets	Eagle Street Carhouse	12/4/39 – 3/31/41	3/6/45 – 11/19/45 1/20/47 – 6/13/49	3/31/41 – 1/20/47 6/13/49 – 4/24/50	–	Morning rush hour service on the single track Route 4191 operated inbound on Lexington Street to Maverick Station, and outbound via Meridian and Bennington Sts. In the evening rush hour, the route reversed and outbound cars used Lexington Street.
121	4192	Eagle Street Carhouse – Lexington Street inbound and outbound	Eagle Street Carhouse	12/4/39 – 3/31/41	3/6/45 – 11/19/45 1/20/47 – 6/13/49	3/31/41 – 1/20/47 6/13/49 – 4/24/50	–	During off peak hours when a thirty minute service with one car was operated, the line ran both ways on Lexington Street as Route 4192.
123	4196	Jeffries Point – Maverick Station via Sumner Street	Eagle Street Carhouse	12/4/39 – 3/31/41	9/16/46 –9/13/47	3/31/41 – 9/16/46 1/20/47 – 4/30/49	–	–

Appendix 9

Weekday Streetcar Line Service Levels & Statistics, Selected Rating Dates

Boston Elevated Railway/Metropolitan Transit Authority

Public Map Number	Internal Route Number	Route Name	Round Trip Mileage	Round Trip Running Time (Minutes)	Headway AM (Minutes)	Headway Base (Minutes)	Headway PM (Minutes)	Headway Eve (Minutes)	Daily Round Trips	No. of Cars AM Rush Hour	No. of Cars PM Rush Hour	Car Requirement Information (Rating Date)	Comments
		CITY POINT CARHOUSE											
7	1005	City Point – South Station (Dewey Square) via Summer Street	5.006	28	4.5	9.0	3.5	10.0	173	7	9	March 26, 1945	
None	1011	Army Base (D Street Crossover) – South Station (Dewey Square) via Summer Street	2.227	10	2.0	N/S	1.4	3.5	282	11	17	March 26, 1945	Route 7 cutback for Army Base
8	1066	City Point – South Station (Dewey Square) via Dorchester Avenue	5.844	37	12.0	30.0	12.0	N/S	41	4	4	March 26, 1945	
None	1065	City Point – Dorchester Avenue Bridge via Broadway	4.746	28	7.5	15.0	7.5	N/S	68	6	6	December 2, 1946	Drawbridge repairs
None	1068	Dorchester Avenue Bridge – South Station (Dewey Square)	0.890	5	7.5	15.0	7.5	N/S	69	2	2	December 2, 1946	Drawbridge repairs
9	1046	City Point – North Station via Subway	8.157	54	4.0	10.0	3.7	10.0	179	16	19	March 26, 1945	
None	1047	Marine Park – North Station via Subway	8.141	55	N/S	9.0	6.0	10.0	92	N/S	19	June 19, 1945	Summer service. See Note 1
None	1069	Marine Park – Broadway Station	4.361	27	N/S	8.0	5.5	10.0	102	N/S	8	July 19, 1943	Summer service. See Note 1
None	1070	City Point – Broadway Station	4.377	27	4.0	8.0	3.0	10.0	195	11	14	May 17, 1943	Broadway Bridge repairs
10	1070	City Point – Broadway Station	4.377	27	10.0	N/S	12.0	N/S	23	4	4	March 17, 1947	Cutback for Route 9
10	1020	City Point – Dudley Station	7.880	49	4.0	15.0	4.5	15.0	148	14	12	March 26, 1945	
None	1024	Marine Park – Dudley Station	7.864	49	N/S	9.0	6.0	10.0	95	N/S	12	June 19, 1945	Summer service. See Note 1
16	1200	Franklin Park – Andrew via Columbia Road	4.995	27	3.7	9.5	3.5	15.0	164	11	12	March 26, 1945	
47	1262	Dudley Station – Mass. Station	3.393	28	2.6	9.0	4.0	15.0	207	13	9	March 26, 1945	
		PARK STREET											
15	1182	Uphams Corner – Dudley via Dudley Street	3.200	19	3.0	9.0	3.0	8.0	218	10	11	April 16, 1945	
17	1150	Fields Corner – Andrew via Meeting House Hill	5.981	36	4.0	10.0	4.0	15.0	155	11	11	April 16, 1945	
19	1191	Fields Corner – Dudley via Geneva Avenue	5.892	35	5.5	N/S	12.0	N/S	41	9	7	April 16, 1945	
20	1122	Neponset – Fields Corner	4.024	21	3.0	7.0	2.8	3.7	304	11	11	April 16, 1945	Part of route to Quincy Shipyard. See Note 2
22	1093	Ashmont – Dudley via Talbot Avenue	8.552	47	5.0	10.0	5.5	12.0	139	12	13	April 16, 1945	
23	1241	Ashmont – Dudley via Washington Street	7.545	43	2.5	7.0	2.8	8.0	240	21	22	April 16, 1945	
28	1147	Mattapan – Ashmont via High Speed Line	5.393	19	2.2	7.5	1.8	7.5	259	14	14	April 16, 1945	
29	1231	Mattapan – Egleston via Blue Hill Avenue	7.752	40	1.5	5.0	2.2	6.0	361	38	28	April 16, 1945	
None	1234	Morton Street Crossover – Egleston via Blue Hill Avenue	4.987	25	10.0	N/S	5.0	N/S	31	Incl Above	Incl Above	April 16, 1945	Route 29 Cutback
		Routes 1231 / 1234 Combined			1.3	5.0	1.6	6.0	392	38	28	April 16, 1945	
45	1210	Grove Hall – Dudley via Blue Hill Avenue	3.987	22	3.0	10.0	2.7	8.0	212	10	13	April 16, 1945	
		ARBORWAY											
30	2278	Mattapan – Arborway via Cummins Highway	6.911	34	10.0	15.0	10.0	15.0	87	4	5	April 2, 1945	
32	2270	Cleary Square – Arborway via Hyde Park Avenue	6.654	32	4.0	8.0	2.8	8.0	197	11	17	April 2, 1945	
33	2275	Roslindale Square – Arborway via Cummins Hwy	4.598	23	10.0	30.0	10.0	30.0	57	3	3	April 2, 1945	
34	2280	Dedham Line – Arborway via Washington Street	8.221	36	6.0	8.0	4.5	8.0	184	14	19	April 2, 1945	
None	2283	LaGrange Street Crossover – Arborway via Washington Street	5.470	25	5.0	N/S	4.5	N/S	32	Incl Above	Incl Above	April 2, 1945	Route 34 Cutback
		Routes 2280 / 2283 Combined			2.7	8.0	2.2	8.0	216	14	19	April 2, 1945	
36	2251	Charles River – Arborway via Centre Street	8.878	40	3.7	8.0	3.0	8.0	227	24	28	April 2, 1945	
None	2254	LaGrange Street Crossover – Arborway via Centre Street	6.595	32	3.7	N/S	5.0	N/S	45	Incl Above	Incl Above	April 2, 1945	Route 36 Cutback
		Routes 2251 / 2254 Combined			1.8	8.0	1.8	8.0	272	24	28	April 2, 1945	
39	2075	Arborway – Park Street Station via Huntington Avenue (Pre Huntington Avenue Subway)	11.208	68	4.0	8.0	4.0	10.0	177	35	23	December 2, 1940	Pre Huntington Avenue Subway
	2075T	Trailer	11.208	68	7.5	N/A	N/A	N/A	34	Incl Above	N/A	December 2, 1940	Pre Huntington Avenue Subway
		Routes 2075 / 2075T Total			4.0	8.0	4.0	10.0	211	35	23	December 2, 1940	Pre Huntington Avenue Subway
39	2075	Arborway – Park Street Station via Huntington Avenue Subway	11.383	57	4.0	8.0	4.0	5.0	218	18	18	April 2, 1945	
	2075T	Trailer	11.383	57	4.0	8.0	4.0	5.0	137	18	18	April 2, 1945	
		Routes 2075 / 2075T Total			4	8	4	5	355	36	36	April 2, 1945	
57	2067	Francis Street – Park Street Station via Subway	5.657	25	8.0	15.0	6.0	10.0	126	5	6	April 2, 1945	Route 39 cutback
57	2066	Heath Street Loop – Park Street Station via Subway	7.884	36	7.5	7.5	6.5	12.0	125	6	7	December 17, 1945	Route 39 Cutback
None	2071	Northeastern University – Park Street Station via Subway	4.027	20	15.0	N/S	15.0	N/S	17	2	2	June 23, 1947	Route 39 Cutback
40	2295	Arborway – Egleston	2.506	14	12.0	20.0	12.0	20.0	67	2	2	April 2, 1945	
41	2110	Jamaica Plain – Dudley	6.134	36	5.0	12.0	5.0	12.0	139	9	9	April 2, 1945	
None	2111	Hyde Square – Dudley	3.588	22	20.0	N/S	15.0	N/S	13	2	2	April 12, 1948	Route 41 Cutback
42	2293	Egleston – Dudley	2.613	16	7.5	8.0	7.5	8.0	143	3	4	April 2, 1945	
43	2016	Egleston – North Station via Tremont Street and Subway	8.934	55	3.0	7.5	3.0	7.5	237	23	21	April 2, 1945	
None	2001	Lenox Street – North Station via Tremont Street and Subway	5.127	35	12.0	N/S	12.0	N/S	28	4	4	April 12, 1948	Route 43 Cutback
44	2338	Seaver Loop – Dudley via Humboldt Avenue	3.245	20	3.0	10.0	3.0	10.0	185	9	10	April 2, 1945	
None	2339	Egleston – Dudley via Humboldt Avenue	–	27	4.0	12.0	4.0	12.0	157	–	–	Jan 25, 1943	Temporary extension of Route 44 to Egleston Station
		RESERVOIR											
61	2131	Reservoir – Lechmere via Subway	13.600	63	2.8	6.0	2.7	5.0	250	28	28	April 16, 1945	
	2131T	Trailer	13.600	63	2.8	6.0	2.7	N/A	173	28	28	April 16, 1945	
		Routes 2131 / 2131T Total			2.8	6.0	2.7	5.0	423	56	56	April 16, 1945	
62	2145	Lake Street – Lechmere via Subway	16.101	74	5.0	6.0	4.5	5.0	218	21	23	April 16, 1945	
	2145T	First Trailer	16.101	74	5.0	6.0	4.5	N/A	142	21	23	April 16, 1945	
	2145T	Second Trailer	16.101	74	5.0	N/A	4.5	N/A	62	21	23	April 16, 1945	
		Routes 2145 / 2145T Total			5.0	6.0	4.5	5.0	422	63	69	April 16, 1945	
None	2123	Blandford Street Crossover to North Station via Subway	6.236	32	20.0	N/S	12.0	N/S	18	4	4	Nov 1, 1948	
	2123T	Trailer	6.236	32	20.0	N/S	12.0	N/S	18	4	4	Nov 1, 1948	
		Routes 2123 / 2123T Total			20.0	N/S	12.0	N/S	36	8	8	Nov 1, 1948	
None	2143	Braves Field to North Station via Subway	8.245	43	N/S	10.0	N/S	N/S	40	N/A	N/A	Nov 1, 1948	
–	2143T	Trailer	8.245	43	N/S	10.0	N/S	N/S	40	N/A	N/A	Nov 1, 1948	
–	–	Routes 2143 / 2143T Total			N/S	10.0	N/S	N/S	80	N/A	N/A	Nov 1, 1948	

Public Map Number	Internal Route Number	Route Name	Round Trip Mileage	Round Trip Running Time (Minutes)	Headway AM (Minutes)	Headway Base (Minutes)	Headway PM (Minutes)	Headway Eve (Minutes)	Daily Round Trips	No. of Cars AM Rush Hour	No. of Cars PM Rush Hour	Car Requirement Information (Rating Date)	Comments
		BENNETT STREET AND WATERTOWN											
69	3200	Watertown – Park Street via Subway	14.859	66	3.0	7.0	2.7	4.6	251	38	39	April 30, 1945	
None	3203	Oak Square – Park Street Station	11.688	52	7.5	7.0	7.5	N/S	85	Incl Above	Incl Above	April 30, 1945	Route 69 Cutback
		Routes 3200 / 3203 Combined			2.3	3.5	2.0	4.6	336	38	39	April 30, 1945	
70	3220	Watertown – Central Square via Arsenal Street	9.141	38	3.5	15.0	N/A	15.0	107	16	N/A	April 30, 1945	See Note 3
None	-	Watertown – Western Avenue Crossover via Arsenal Street	8.618	–	N/A	N/A	4.0	N/A	34	N/A	18	April 30, 1945	See Note 3
None	3222	Watertown – Cambridge Armory Crossover via Arsenal Street	9.863	43	N/S	N/S	*	N/S	3	N/S	Incl Above	April 30, 1945	See Note 3
		Routes 3220 / 3222 combined			*3.5*	*15.0*	*4.0*	*15.0*	*144*	*16*	*18*	*April 30, 1945*	
None	3224	Watertown – Memorial Drive Crossover	10.263	45	4.0	10.0	5.0	10.0	147	15	12	September 12, 1949	
76	3061	Bennett Street– Massachusetts Station	5.545	36	3.5	9.0	4.0	10.0	164	11	11	April 30, 1945	See Note 4
None	3062	Bennett Street – Cambridge Armory Crossover	3.550	24	N/A	N/A	*	N/A	3	N/A	Incl Above	April 30, 1945	Route 76 cutback. See Note 4
	-	*Routes 3061 / 3062 combined*			3.5	9.0	4.0	10.0	*167*	*11*	*11*	*April 30,1945*	
71/79	3003	Arlington Hts – Watertown via Harvard Square Subway	18.554	87	4.0	7.0	3.7	N/A	170	36	40	April 30, 1945	See Note 5
None	3004	Arlington Ctr – Watertown via Harvard Square Subway	15.029	73	N/A	N/A	*	8.0	34	N/A	Incl Above	April 30, 1945	See Note 5
73/79	3005	Arlinton Heights – Waverley via Harvard Square Subway	18.754	87	N/A	N/A	N/A	8.0	33	N/A	N/A	April 30, 1945	
None	3002	Arlington Ctr. – Bennett via Harvard Square Subway	8.036	42	4.0	7.0	3.3	N/A	126	16	10	April 30, 1945	
82/73	3017	No. Cambridge – Waverly via Harvard Square Subway	11.597	55	4.0	7.0	3.7	N/A	163	33	35	April 30, 1945	
None	3018	No. Cambridge – Common Street crossover via Harvard Square Subway	9.642	46	4.0	N/A	4.5	N/A	38	Incl Above	Incl Above	April 30, 1945	Route 73 cutback
82	3000	No. Cambridge – Bennett via Harvard Square Subway	4.422	24	N/A	N/A	N/A	8.0	41	N/A	N/A	April 30, 1945	
		Combined service on Massachusetts Avenue between Harvard Station & North Cambridge			1.0	2.4	0.9	2.6	605			*April 30,1945*	See Service Overview, chapters 3 and 6
None	3202	Braves Field – Park Street Station via Subway	6.849	33	10.0	10.0	7.5	N/S	72	6	7	November 19, 1945	
None	3207	Braves Field – North Station via Subway	8.466	43	N/S	N/S	N/S	12.0	16	N/S	N/A	November 19, 1945	
None	3205	Blandford – Park Street Station via Subway	4.619	22	*	8.0	*	N/S	63	8	10	April 30, 1945	
None	3210	Blandford Street – North Station via Subway	6.236	32	N/S	N/S	8.5	8.5	26	N/A	Incl Above	April 30,1945	
		SALEM STREET AND CLARENDON HILL											
87	4124	Clarendon Hill – Lechmere via Somerville Avenue	8.142	44	8.0	–	7.0	–	100	7	8	August 18, 1941	Rush Hour headways estimated
88	4140	Clarendon Hill – Lechmere via Highland Avenue	8.178	44	3.7	–	5.0	–	128	15	11	August 18, 1941	Rush Hour headways estimated
89	4112	Clarendon Hill – Sullivan via Broadway	6.973	38	3.5	10.0	3.5	12.0	179	13	15	April 2, 1945	
92	4012	Sullivan – Brattle Street Station via Main Street	4.360	29	20.0	20.0	12.0	30.0	66	2	2	April 2, 1945	
93	4021	Sullivan – Brattle Street Station via Bunker Hill Street	5.173	35	2.6	12.0	3.3	9.0	189	21	21	April 2, 1945	Route 93 cutback. See Note 6
None	4022	Elm Street Crossover (Charlestown) – Brattle Street Station via Bunker Hill Street	3.164	26	*	N/S	N/S	N/S	4	Incl above	N/A	April 2,1945	Route 93 cutback. See Note 6
None	4024	Sullivan – City Square (Warren Avenue Crossover)	3.417	23	N/S	N/S	N/S	*	4	N/A	N/A	April 2, 1945	See Note 6
		Routes 4021 / 4022 / 4024 Combined			2.6	12.0	3.3	9.0	*197*	*21*	*21*	*April 2, 1945*	
None	4023	Elm & Bunker Hill Streets Crossover – Warren Avenue Crossover (City Square)	1.975	14	*	N/S	N/S	N/S	4	–	N/A	April 3, 1944	Route 93 shuttle operation run one rating only
99	4080	Sheepfold – Sullivan via Fellsway	11.580	48	12.0	20.0	10.0	30.0	61	7	8	April 2, 1945	See Note 7
100	4081	Elm St – Sullivan via Fellsway	9.138	40	5.0	10.0	6.0	12.0	130	9	9	April 2, 1945	
None	4082	Salem Street – Sullivan via Fellsway	6.675	28	5.0	N/S	6.0	N/S	48	7	7	April 2, 1945	
		Routes 4080 / 4081 / 4082 Combined			*2.0*	*6.5*	*2.3*	*8.5*	*239*	*23*	*24*	*April 2, 1945*	
101	4042	Salem Street CH – Sullivan via Winter Hill and Broadway	8.761	45	4.5	8.0	4.5	8.0	182	15	18	April 2, 1945	
None	4049	Eliot and Main Sts. – Sullivan via Broadway	5.192	27	6.0	N/S	6.0	N/S	30	Incl above	Incl Above	April 2, 1945	
		Routes 4042 / 4049 Combined			*2.8*	*8.0*	*2.8*	*8.0*	*212*	*15*	*18*	*April 2, 1945*	
None	4015	North Station - Brattle Loop via Subway	1.160	6	10.0	15.0	10.0	15.0	83	1	1	December 12, 1949	Route 93 subway replacement
		EAGLE STREET AND REVERE											
114	4170	Broadway Station (Gerrish Avenue Loop) – Maverick Station via Meridian Street	4.364	28	6.0	N/S	10.0	N/S	31	9	10	March 26, 1945	
115	4171	Broadway Station (Gerrish Avenue Loop) – Maverick Station via Central Avenue	6.402	34	10.0	20.0	8.5	20.0	67	4	4	March 26, 1945	
None	4172	Nay Street Crossover–Maverick Station via Meridian Street	2.506	16	–	–	–	–	122	4	4	February 2, 1942	Cutback due to Meridian Street Bridge closing for repairs
116	4174	Revere Beach Loop – Maverick Station via Revere Street	11.201	62	6.0	10.0	6.5	9.0	134	15	16	March 26, 1945	
None	4173	Revere Street Crossover–Maverick Station via Meridian Street	8.311	46	12.0	N/S	12.0	N/S	21	Incl Above	Incl Above	March 26, 1945	Route 116 Cutback *on* Revere Street *near* Broadway
		Routes 4174 / 4173 Combined			*4.0*	*10.0*	*4.5*	*9.0*	*155*	*15*	*16*	*March 26, 1945*	
None	4173	Broadway & Revere Street – Maverick Station via Meridian	8.251	46	12.0	N/S	10.0	N/S	31	N/A	N/A	February 20, 1947	See Note 8
116	4174	Revere Loop – Maverick Station via Revere Street, Central Avenue	12.818	68	–	–	–	–	108	15	13	February 2, 1942	Alternative routing due to Meridian Street Bridge closing for repairs
None	4173	Revere Street Crossover–Maverick Station via Central Avenue	9.924	52	N/S	N/S	–	N/S	71	–	8	February 2, 1942	Alternative routing due to Meridian Street Bridge closing for repairs
		Routes 4174 / 4173 Combined			–	–	–	–	*179*	*15*	*21*	*February 2, 1942*	
116	4223	Revere Street Bridge Crossover – Maverick Station via Revere Street	10.301	58	7.0	10.0	6.0	15.0	123	13	13	September 13, 1947	Line shortened during Revere Street Bridge closing for repairs
117	4176	Rever Beach Loop – Maverick Station via Beach Street	10.203	58	8.5	10.0	8.5	9.0	125	10	13	March 26, 1945	
None	4177	Revere Carhouse – Maverick Station via Meridian Street	7.260	42	7.5	N/S	7.5	N/S	39	Incl Above	Incl Above	March 26, 1945	Route 117 Cutback
		Routes 4176 / 4177 Combined			*4.0*	*10.0*	*4.0*	*9.0*	*164*	*10*	*13*	*March 26, 1945*	
117	4176	Revere Beach Loop – Maverick Station via Beach Street, Central Avenue	11.794	64	–	–	–	–	102	11	11	February 2, 1942	Alternative routing due to Meridian Street Bridge closing for repairs
None	4175	Revere Carhouse – Maverick Station, via Central Avenue	8.864	48	–	N/S	–	N/S	53	Incl Above	Incl Above	February 2, 1942	Alternative routing due to Meridian Street Bridge closing for repairs
		Routes 4176 / 4175 Combined			–	–	–	–	*155*	*11*	*11*	*February 2, 1942*	*Meridian Street Bridge Closed*
117	4224	Revere Street Bridge Crossover – Maverick Station via Beach Street	10.810	62	10.0	10.0	10.0	15.0	106	7	16	September 13, 1947	Line extended during Revere Street Bridge closing for repairs
118	4183	Revere Beach Loop – Maverick Station via Bennington Street	9.426	44	4.5	10.0	3.5	9.0	177	15	15	March 26, 1945	
None	4182	Eagle Street Carhouse – Maverick Station via Bennington Street	3.032	20	5.0	N/S	8.0	N/S	49	3	3	March 26, 1945	Supplemental pull-in, pull-out service on Route 118
120	4181	Gladstone Loop – Maverick Station via Bennington Street	6.177	32	3.0	10.0	3.3	9.0	178	12	15	March 26, 1945	
120	4186	Suffolk Downs – Maverick Station via Bennington Street	6.605	36	N/S	4.0	1.7	N/S	199	10	25	April 19, 1948	Seasonal service to Suffolk Downs Racetrack. See Note 9
121	4191	Eagle Street – Maverick Station via Meridian, Lexington Sts.	2.775	20	15.0	N/A	15.0	N/A	14	3	3	March 26, 1945	See Note 10
121	4192	Eagle Street – Maverick Station via Lexington Street inbound and outbound	2.758	20	N/A	30.0	N/A	30.0	26	N/A	N/A	March 26, 1945	See Note 10
		Route 4191 / 4192 Total			*15.0*	*30.0*	*15.0*	*30.0*	*40*	*3*	*3*	*March 26, 1945*	
123	4196	Jeffries Pt. – Maverick Station	1.754	12	3.5	20.0	5.0	20.0	115	9	8	March 26, 1945	

Notes

A. Asterisk (*) means service was irregular or run as directed by supervisory personnel. Hyphen (–) means data not available. N/A means not applicable. N/S means no service.
B Note that headways are averages based on the number of trips per hour. Headways are expressed in minutes and tenths of a minute.

1 During summer ratings on fine weather days, service on Routes 9 and 10 was extended to Marine Park on Farragut Road in South Boston to serve beach traffic. Cars looped via P Street, East Sixth Street and Farragut Road and returned on East Fourth Street to the normal route. Service ran from 10 AM to 11 PM, seven days a week.
2 Route 20. Route 1122 from Neponset to Fields Corner Station was operated as part of the Eastern Massachusetts Street Railway route from the Quincy Shipyard to Fields Corner via Quincy Square using EMSR cars and Elevated motormen and fareboxes. The Elevated supplemented service during peak hours with their own cars.
3 Route 70. From 3.30 PM to 6.30 PM, Route 70 cars ended at the Western Avenue and Green Street crossover to avoid traffic congestion in Central Square. During the PM rush hour, three trips were extended to the Cambridge Armory crossover at Massachusetts Avenue and Vassar Street operating as Route 3222, Watertown to Cambridge Armory.
4 Route 76. During afternoon rush hour, some cars on Route 3061 operated as short turns and used the Cambridge Armory crossover at Massachusetts Avenue and Vassar Street This was Route 3062, Bennett Street to Cambridge Armory.
5 Cars assigned to Routes 3003 and 3004 were divided between the carhouses at Watertown and Arlington Heights.
6 Route 93. Four trips in the morning rush hour operated as a short turn and used the crossover at Bunker Hill and Elm Sts. operating as Route 4022, Elm Street to Brattle Street Station. Also, four evening trips used the crossover on Warren Avenue near City Square and operated as Route 4024, Sullivan Square to City Square.
7 Route 99. Route 99 was part of the Eastern Mass. line between Stoneham and Sullivan Square Station using mostly EMSR streetcars. Between Sheepfold and Sullivan Square, the line was operated by Elevated motormen. Rather than change fareboxes as they did at Neponset, both companies took their own farebox readings at Sheepfold.
8 The crossover on Revere Street near Broadway in Revere was relocated to a new crossover on Broadway just north of Revere Street in November 1946, resulting in a slight change in mileage on Route 4173.
9 Regular service was operated to Suffolk Downs Racetrack during racing season in April and July from 1947 to 1951. Cars ran to Suffolk Downs Loop from 9 AM to 6 PM, seven days per week and used Gladstone Loop at other times.
10 Route 121. Morning rush hour service on Route 4191 operated inbound on Lexington Street to Maverick Station, and outbound via Meridian and Bennington Sts. The route reversed in the evening rush hour and outbound cars used Lexington Street. Off-peak service with one car was operated both ways on Lexington Street as Route 4192 .

Appendix 9A

Weekday Streetcar Line Service Levels & Statistics, Selected Rating Dates

Eastern Massachusetts Street Railway

Public Map Number	Internal Route Number	Route Name	Round Trip Mileage	Round Trip Running Time (Minutes)	Headway AM (Minutes)	Headway Base (Minutes)	Headway PM (Minutes)	Headway Eve (Minutes)	Number of Trips	No. of Cars A.M Rush Hr	No. of Cars P.M Rush Hr	Car Requirement Information (Rating Date)	Comments
		SALEM STREET CARHOUSE											
None	None	Main Street Stoneham - Sullivan Square Station	16.345	60	12	20	10	30	61	7	8	July 1, 1945	
		QUINCY CARHOUSE											
None	None	Fields Corner Station - Quincy Square	10.461	54	*	*	*	*				July 1, 1945	Irregular service to supplement line to Fields Corner Station
None	None	Fields Corner Station - Quincy Shipyard	13.752	78	6	7	6	7.5	-	17	17	July 1, 1945	Wartime service supplemented with Boston Elevated cars during peak shipyard traffic.
None	None	Houghs Neck - Quincy Square	6.868	36	10	15	10	30	-	4	4	July 1, 1945	

An Eastern Mass. semi-convertible car approaches Elm Street on the Fellsway in December 1942. Charlie Duncan outdid himself in this shot, panning the camera to match the speed of the car and creating a blurred background and the illusion of motion in an otherwise still photo. The Fellsway was part of the route to Stoneham, the only Eastern Mass. line north of Boston to operate into the 1940s.
Charles A. Duncan

Appendix 10

Reference List & Recommended Reading

Anderson, Edward A. *PCC Cars of Boston*. Boston: Boston Street Railway Association, 1968.

Boston Chapter, National Railway Historical Society. *The Shrieking Journal*, 1-4 (1940-44).

Boston Chapter, National Railway Historical Society. *The Turnout*, vol. 1-9 (1942-50).
> The original name of this publication was *The Shrieking Journal*, published from 1940-1944. Apparently the early issues of the latter publication were intermingled with the latter issues of the earlier publication, and the volume numbering appears to confirm this situation.

Boston Elevated Railway Company. *Annual Report of the Board of Public Trustees*, 1918-1947. Boston: Boston Elevated Railway, 1919-47.

Boston Elevated Railway Company. *Annual Return of the Boston Elevated Railway Company to the (Massachusetts) Department of Public Utilities for the Year Ended December 31, 1939*. Boston: Boston Elevated Railway, 1940.

Boston Elevated Railway Company. *Co-operation*, 20-29 (1940-50).

Boston Elevated Railway Company. *Fifty Years of Unified Transportation in Metropolitan Boston*. Boston: Boston Elevated Railway Company, 1938.

Boston Transit Commission. *Annual Report*. Boston: Boston Transit Commission, 1895-1918.

Carlson, Stephen P., and Fred W. Schneider, III. *PCC—The Car That Fought Back*. Glendale, Calif.: Interurban Press, 1980.

Carlson, Stephen P., with Thomas W. Harding. *From Boston to the Berkshires: A Pictorial Review of Electric Transportation in Massachusetts*. Boston: Boston Street Railway Association, 1990.

Cheape, Charles W. *Moving the Masses: Urban Public Transit in New York, Boston and Philadelphia, 1880-1912*. Cambridge: Harvard University Press, 1980.

Chiasson, George, Jr. *Boston's Main Line El: The Formative Years, 1879-1908*. New York: Electric Railroaders' Association, 1995.

Clarke, Bradley H. *The Boston Transit Album*. Boston: Boston Street Railway Association, 1977.

Clarke, Bradley H. *The Boston Rapid Transit Album*. Boston: Boston Street Railway Association, 1982.

Clarke, Bradley H. *The Trackless Trolleys of Boston*. Boston: Boston Street Railway Association, 1970.

Clarke, Bradley H., and O.R. Cummings. *Tremont Street Subway, A Century of Public Service*. Boston: Boston Street Railway Association, 1997.

Commonwealth of Massachusetts. *Report of the Legislative Commission on Rapid Transit–1945* (Boston: Commonwealth of Massachusetts, 1945).

Commonwealth of Massachusetts. *Report of the Legislative Commission on Rapid Transit–1947* (Boston: Commonwealth of Massachusetts, 1947).

Cudahy, Brian J. *Change at Park Street Under: The Story of Boston's Subways*. Brattleboro, Vt.: The Stephen Green Press, 1972.

Cummings, O.R. *Street Cars of Boston, Vol. 1-6*. Forty-Fort, Pa.: Harold E. Cox, 1973-1980.

Eastern Massachusetts Street Railway Company. *Annual Report*. 1943, 1946. Boston: Eastern Massachusetts Street Railway Company, 1943, 1946.

Metropolitan Transit Authority. *Annual Report of the Board of Public Trustees of the Metropolitan Transit Authority*, 1947-1950. Boston: Metropolitan Transit Authority, 1948-1951.

Miller, John Anderson. *Fares, Please! A Popular History of Trolleys, Horsecars, Streetcars, Buses, Elevateds and Subways*. 2nd ed.. New York: Dover Publications, 1960.

Rowesome, Frank, Jr. *Trolley Car Treasury: A Century of American Streetcars—Horsecars, Cable Cars, Interurbans and Trolleys*. New York: McGraw-Hill, 1956.

Schantz, James D., ed. *Budapest's Földalatti Subway and the Seashore Trolley Museum*. Kennebunkport, Me.: New England Electric Railway Historical Society, 1992.

Schneider, Fred W., III, and Stephen P. Carlson. *PCC—From Coast to Coast*. Glendale, Calif.: Interurban Press, 1983.

Stanley, Robert C. *Narrow Gauge: The Story of the Boston, Revere Beach & Lynn Railroad*. Boston: Boston Street Railway Association, 1980.

Werner, William. Chronological Listings of Boston Area Transit Events [Typescript].

Type 5 No. 5815 heads for Harvard Square as it rumbles through Central Square, Cambridge, in this late 1940s scene. The car has just passed over the track switch to Western Avenue and the line to Watertown Square. The F.W. Woolworth sign was once ubiquitous and now is ancient history.
Leon Onofri